Impact of
Uncertainty on
Location

Other Volumes in the Regional Science Studies Series
edited by Walter Isard

Impact of Uncertainty on Location

Michael J. Webber

THE M.I.T. PRESS
Cambridge, Massachusetts and London, England

Foreword

The subject of location theory has been among the
handful or so of fastest developing areas of the social
sciences during the last fifteen years. Whereas in 1956
it could have been said that location theory was of
interest to economists alone (and at that was considered
by them to be definitely among the least interesting and
significant areas), it now stands in the forefront of at
least four disciplines: geography, economics, planning,
and regional science. The reasons for this change of
status are clear. First, in 1956, the fields of both
geography and planning were remiss in the inadequate
attention they gave to theory and formal analysis.
To a significant extent, this shortcoming has been
recognised, and at least partly overcome.

Second, the dramatic social problems associated
with the city and metropolitan region have reared
their ugly heads so uncomfortably that traditional
economics has been forced to assign top priority to
the further development of location and other urban-
regional theory to attack these urgent problems. These
problems have also stimulated geographers to explore
new analytical directions—partly as a competitive
response—because in large part topics dealing with
space, region, location and place have long been the
province of geographers. Moreover, these problems
have compelled planners to go beyond the attempt to
find *ad hoc*, day-to-day solutions; together with
systems analysts, operation researchers, and many
others, planners seek those more comprehensive
frameworks and models for problem-solving which in
turn require further development of location and other
theory. These problems have also spurred on the rapid
development of the Regional Science Association, an
interdisciplinary scholarly arena from which have
come some of the most important developments in
location theory.

Nowadays, there are leading geographers boldly
claiming location theory as a core area of geography.

v

Urban and regional economists lay claim to it as economics, for has not most of location theory been the product of economists? Planners and system engineers also lay claim to it because of the central role it plays in their comprehensive models. And finally a new breed of social scientists, the regional scientists, who now set forth regional science as a social science discipline in its own right, lay claim to location theory as theirs, because of their seminal contributions in the last fifteen years.

Regardless of the viewpoint to which the reader is sympathetic, he will find the Webber book to be an important contribution to location theory. It does a fine job of surveying and critically evaluating, in a consistent analytical manner, many of the advances during the last fifteen years of rapid growth of location theory; consequently, location students can now obtain a better view of the field as a whole. More important, this book goes beyond a critical analytical survey. It focuses attention on an area seriously neglected by location theorists, namely, the impact of uncertainty upon location decisions and spatial patterns. Webber states the case for studying this impact. We do not need to repeat it here. It is a sound case. Further, Webber is not misled about his contribution. He modestly views his book as 'a preliminary account of one direction in which new location theory may profitably evolve'.

Webber's book, with its proper attention to uncertainty, does not imply that 'deterministic-type' location theory of the sort in my *Location and Space-Economy* is to be discarded. Rather, together with 'deterministic-type' theory and other location theory for uncertain situations (see, for example, my *General Theory: Social, Political, Economic and Regional*, chapters 4-9) this book makes possible a better understanding of the spatial dimensions of our society, and hopefully more effective planning—wherein the

vi

individual analyst and policy-formulator is left free to choose what he considers to be the best and most relevant mix of deterministic and non-deterministic analysis.

Webber's book constitutes an important addition to the Regional Science Study Series. It not only makes available an up-to-date survey of location analysis, and ploughs new ground in a neglected area likely to be of increasing significance in the future. It also brings effectively to bear upon location theory the views and approaches of one who is trained as a geographer. With a firm grounding in and abundant reference to the world of reality, Webber's location analysis effectively complements *Location and Space-Economy* and the *General Theory* written from the standpoint of one steeply immersed in the abstract traditions of economic theory. It thus lends considerable balance to the series, and represents a 'must' for all those concerned with location problems and analysis.

WALTER ISARD

Preface

Research into location patterns has occupied many geographers and economists. The mid-1950s witnessed the publication in English of several significant theoretical departures from traditional Weberian locational analysis: Lösch's work on central place theory was translated, Hagerstrand's ideas about innovation diffusion became known outside Sweden, and Isard and Greenhut published reviews and syntheses of location theory. At the same time, and partly in response to these new ideas, novel and exciting techniques were introduced, techniques which have revolutionised both the concepts and methods of geography. Haggett's 'report from an active battle-front' summarises and organises these developments and the new knowledge which they have yielded.

But geographers are once again becoming dissatisfied with the currently available body of theory. Two avenues of innovation are being explored. Firstly, probability models are being used to describe town patterns and other mass human interactions; secondly, locational analysis is shifting away from the traditional link with economics and is beginning to analyse the psychological bases of decision taking.

I have set out in this book to supply a preliminary account of one direction in which new location theory may profitably evolve. An attempt is made to define some of the ways in which uncertainty about the effects of decisions modifies location patterns. Theories of the location of economic activity under certainty and uncertainty are compared: the first chapter sets up the problems which have to be explained, Chapters 2 to 4 discuss location patterns under conditions of certainty, Chapter 5 examines decision making under uncertainty, and Chapters 6 to 9 use these decision-making models to analyse aspects of location patterns when entrepreneurs are uncertain. Chapter 10 concludes the discussion by comparing location patterns under certainty and under uncertainty, and by attempting to define the role of planning in terms of the models.

Individual aspects of uncertain decision taking and of

diffusion processes are analysed; the results seem sufficiently valuable to suggest that the combination of these two elements might form a useful basis for a general dynamic model of location. But before such a general dynamic model can be constructed, comparable in elegance to central place theory, additional analysis needs be performed: in particular, the properties of these two base models must be more fully elucidated.

It is in this sense that this book is a preliminary account. Individual models have been analysed and determined to be more or less useful. Now they must be combined, their inter-relationships analysed, and their predictions fully tested against data. Publication at this stage ensures that the final results do not suffer overmuch from inbreeding.

Initial work on these models formed part of my Ph.D. thesis, written while I was a Research Scholar at the Institute of Advanced Studies, Australian National University. Dr G. J. R. Linge and Dr G. M. Neutze acted as supervisors of my thesis, and by their supervision improved it. Mrs E. Parr has typed successive drafts of this book, and Mrs P. Millwood drew the maps and diagrams. Any errors in the book are mine.

M. J. WEBBER
CANBERRA 1970

Contents

Tables

Figures

B

1   The Location Problem

Economic activity is unevenly distributed over space. Population, income, and productive assets are largely concentrated in a few nations; within a nation, one or a few regions usually predominate; and a few cities and towns normally contain much of the productive assets and activity of a region. The immediate and most important task of location theory is therefore to provide reasons why activity is spatially concentrated. The causes adduced to explain the existence of areas of intense activity are then used as frameworks within which theory analyses the location of these concentrations, their size, and the activities present within them.

It is useful to define the problem more explicitly. This is done in two ways. First the meaning of the terms 'region' and 'town' is clarified and made unambiguous. And secondly the extent and the nature of the problem are gauged by means of examples: these examples illustrate the extent of concentration, the location of concentrations, their size, and the activities present within them. The validity of existing location theories can later be judged against these statements.

Definitions

An important distinction is that concentrations of activity are of two kinds. On the one hand, activity may be concentrated into nations or regions, and these concentrations have areal extent. Whatever the forces inducing concentration are, activities influenced by these forces can locate in the same region and yet be hundreds of miles apart. Thus the forces causing regional and national concentration may be expected to show broad variations over space. On the other hand, activity is also concentrated into towns and industrial or shopping districts: these appear essentially as points in space. Such points, to which the general term 'places' will be applied, reflect punctiform variation in the forces leading to concentration.

The term 'regions of relatively intense activity' has several justifiable meanings. It is assumed here that regions are classificatory units—that the units (points) within each region all have at least one characteristic in common and at least one characteristic distinguishing them in some way from all other points in space which are not within the region. In this case the distinguishing characteristic is intensity of activity, as measured by some variable, such as output per unit area or population density. Thus the problems are that when places are classified with respect to the intensity of activity within them, a few areas contain most of the activity, these areas may exhibit some regular spacing relationships, they vary in size, and there are empirical laws governing the activities present within them.

Point concentrations—places—may be defined in terms comparable to this. A town may be regarded as being simply another type of region. This is perfectly valid in some situations, but when evaluating theories of town formation, a functional definition of places is preferable. From the point of view of the formation of places, no theoretical difference is made between hamlets, villages, towns, cities, metropolitan areas, and shopping and industrial areas within cities. The term 'place' is assumed to encompass all these other terms: that is, it is supposed that all places have a common cause or causes, and that cities are differentiated from, say, hamlets on other grounds, such as size or complexity. 'Like pool, pond, and lake, the terms hamlet, village, and town are convenient modes of expression, but they do not refer to structurally distinct natural entities.' (Vining, 1955: 169. But for a different view, see Friedmann, 1961.) A theory of the growth of places is therefore not necessarily a theory of the formation of places.

There may be three types of place, or three types of function within a place. The first type is an agglomeration of people who work outside the place: for example the farmers in an area may wish to work outside but to live within a village, for defence or to use localised water supplies. A second type of place consists of one firm which sells goods beyond the place and of sellers which service the workers and the firm. Place formation and the size of the place depend on economies of scale of production within the firm and on the local multiplier effect. Thirdly, places may contain several firms which sell some goods outside the place, firms which may be in the same industry or in different industries.

The first two types are largely trivial, for the factors determining the formation and the size of these places are readily identified. Nor are such places very common in advanced economies. Their main importance to theory probably arises when they act as a locus upon which later activities may be grafted. Consequently most interest has been focused in location theory on the third type of place. This is in marked contrast to the older European tradition of settlement analysis, which was largely interested in the first type of settlement, the rural town (see Brunhes, 1925). Such a place has two essential characteristics: it is an agglomeration of two or more activities which perform functions for persons or firms, some of which are not within the place; and some of the firms are competing to locate at exactly the same point in space.

This characterisation contains several implications about the nature of these places. The characteristic activities of a place do not use land as an important factor of production, for otherwise the activities could not locate together: a place's activities are normally secondary or tertiary. The place may be formed initially by the location at the same spot of persons selling identical goods or of persons selling different goods. Theories of town formation have analysed both

2

these aspects. Competition to locate at the same point implies that rental payments are made for the privilege of locating in a place.

Scope of the Problem

Activity is unevenly distributed at all scales of inquiry, and the analysis of this phenomenon represents a primary task of location theory. Some examples are provided at four scales—the international, the inter-regional, the inter-urban, and the intra-urban—to illustrate the degree of heterogeneity which characterises the distribution of economic activity.

The Sydney Metropolitan Area in 1961 contained 2,197,022 people and covered an area of 1385 square miles. However, six Local Government Areas—Bankstown, Canterbury, Fairfield, Parramatta, Randwick, and the City of Sydney—which make up 8·20 per cent of the total area, contained 34·43 per cent of the population of the Metropolitan Area: one-third of the population of Sydney lives in one-twelfth of its area. Furthermore, one-half of the population of the city lives within one-fifth of its area (Commonwealth Bureau of Census and Statistics, 1961).

Similarly, a few large cities contain much of the population of many countries, especially the relatively rich countries. In 1956, one-third of the population of the United States lived in cities with more than one million inhabitants; Mexico City contained 11 per cent of the population of Mexico in 1955; one-third of the population of the Argentine lived in Buenos Aires in 1955; in 1954 Paris contained one-sixth of the population of France; in Sydney and Melbourne live more than one-third of all Australians; 22 million people lived in metropolitan areas of more than one million inhabitants in the United Kingdom in 1956 (International Monetary Fund [IMF], 1954, 1955, 1956; International Urban Research, 1959). The large city is a predominant feature of economic spatial organisation.

Activity is also unevenly distributed among regions. In 1961, Australia had a manufacturing labour force of slightly over one million workers, of whom three-quarters worked in New South Wales and Victoria, two States which account for less than one-fifth of the area of the Commonwealth (Commonwealth Bureau of Census and Statistics, 1961). A map of population densities in the British Isles reveals that marked differences exist between the various regions: extremely high densities occur in the London region, the Midlands and in parts of Lancashire and Yorkshire, while the Southwest, North Wales, Scotland, and Ireland generally exhibit low densities.

Similar patterns are apparent on the international scale. The density of income varies greatly among the different countries within Europe. The densities of gross domestic product in Belgium, West Germany, the United Kingdom and the Netherlands (over $200 per square kilometre) were more than five times the income densities in Austria, Finland, Norway, Portugal, Spain, Sweden, and eastern Europe in 1960 (United Nations Department of Economic and Social Affairs [UNDESA], 1965).

If the mere existence of concentrations is the first problem confronting loca-

3

tion theory, the location of these concentrations is the second problem. The question of the location of places and regions of intense activity may be approached in two ways (Neutze, 1967). On the one hand, one may ask why a place was established at a particular point: why is there a major metropolitan area on the site of London? Answers to such questions have tended to be unsatisfactory because they refer to one example only, rather than to general location factors. A more useful predictive theory may be derived by examining the second approach: in what way are places of various sizes spaced?

Lösch (1959: 389-94) has analysed the spacing of cities in Iowa. He divided cities into three size classes: those with 300 to 1000, those with 1000 to 4000, and those with 4000 to 20,000 inhabitants. Lösch then measured the distance between each city and its nearest neighbour of the same or greater size, and concluded that large cities are generally further apart than small cities. Although there is some overlap of distributions, large cities are more widely spaced than small cities: the modal distance apart of the smallest cities is 7·65-8·50 km, of the medium group is 16·15-17·00 km, while for the largest cities the modal distance to nearest neighbours is 34·00-38·25 km. Location theory must explain such spacing phenomena.

The third problem is that of the size distribution of concentrations of activity. Location analysis has discovered that there may be some empirical regularities which govern the sizes of concentrations. A common expression of one such regularity is the rank-size rule for cities, which may be expressed as

(1–1) $r.P^q = K,$

where q and K are constants for a given group of cities, r is the rank of a city and P its population (Lotka, 1925: 306-7; Singer, 1936: 254-63). An alternative form of (1–1) is

(1–2) $\log r = C - q.\log P,$

where $C = log\ K$.

Figure 1–1 represents some findings of Zipf (1949) about the empirical validity of the rank-size rule in the United States. There is clearly a tendency for a graph of the rank of cities against their size to yield a straight line when plotted on logarithmic axes. Other evidence (e.g. Stewart, 1958) is less close to the predicted relationship. Even so, Isard (1956: 57) has concluded that 'to a limited extent at least, there is some basis for the formulation of hypotheses and additional exploration'. Similarly, Haggett (1965: 101) summarises the evidence by suggesting that the rank-size rule provides a useful framework within which to generalise about the population distribution of a region. Empirical regularities of size and spacing, and deviations from them, must be analysed by location theory.

The fourth question which location theory must treat is that of the activities present within regions. Several relationships have been noticed. For example, larger settlements generally contain more functions and more establishments per

Figure 1–1: **Relationship between size of cities and their rank, U.S.A.**
Source: Zipf (1949).

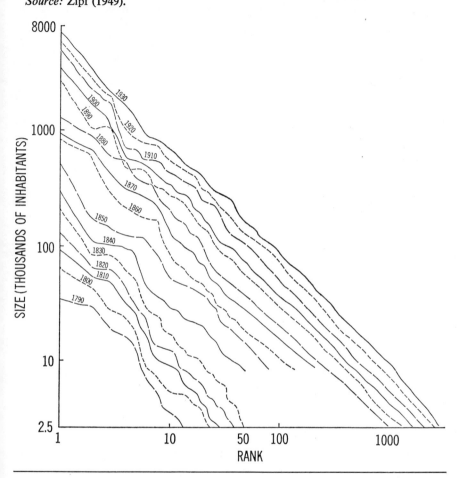

Table 1–1: **Characteristics of shopping centres, Chicago**

Type of centre	Peak land value $ per front ft	No. of functions	No. of establish-ments	Trade areas Shopping goods sq. m.	Convenience goods
Major regional	4625	60	205	12·2	2·0
Other shopping	1976	44	115	6·0	2·5
Community	1268	37	76	—	1·9
Neighbourhood	1036	24	43	—	1·9

Source: Berry, 1963: 36-43.

5

Table 1–2: **Factors associated with size of industrial sectors in nations**

Manufacturing sector $U.S. millions	Constant term	Income per head $U.S. (1953)	Population millions
All manufacturing	−1·64	1·37	1·12
Food, drink, and tobacco	−1·03	0·98	0·86
Textiles	−2·55	1·21	1·33
Clothing and footwear	−2·71	1·36	0·96
Wood products	−3·29	1·53	1·03
Paper and paper products	−5·01	2·04	1·12
Printing and publishing	−3·93	1·72	1·04
Leather products	−2·16	0·89	0·86
Rubber products	−4·18	1·58	1·20
Chemicals	−3·48	1·55	1·40
Non-metallic mineral goods	−2·26	1·16	1·01
Basic metals	−5·27	1·99	1·65
Metal products	−4·18	1·98	1·31

Regression equation: $\text{Log (Value Added)} = c + d \log y + e \log p$

Source: UNDESA, 1963: 7.

function than do smaller places. Table 1–1 presents typical results for suburban shopping centres in the Chicago Metropolitan Area. Whereas major regional centres display peak land values of more than $4500 per front foot and consist of sixty functions serving a shopping goods trade area of 12 square miles and a convenience goods trade area of 2 square miles, the neighbourhood centres exhibit peak land values of only about $1000 per front foot and contain only twenty-four functions serving a convenience goods trade area of 2 square miles.

Data pertaining to the types of industries located in countries have been presented by the United Nations Department of Economic and Social Affairs (1963). This study made cross-section analyses of the value added by manufacturing sectors in 1953 and 1958, excluding only the United States and the centrally-planned economies. Regression equations were developed to demonstrate the relationship between the value added in each industrial sector and *per capita* income (y) and population (p) of each country. Table 1–2 contains the parameters of these equations. Industries behave dissimilarly: some grow rapidly as *per capita* income rises (wood products, paper and paper products, printing and publishing, rubber products, chemicals, basic metals, and metal products); some grow rapidly as population rises (textiles, rubber products, chemicals, basic metals, and metal products). Thus as the degree of concentration of income

6

(population and *per capita* income) in a country rises, so the composition of that country's manufacturing output changes: rubber products, chemicals, basic metals, and metal products become more important relative to other sectors. Location theory must explain such variations in the activities present within both point and regional concentrations.

This evidence has been relatively brief: it merely illustrates some of the regularities associated with concentrations. More detailed discussions of these and other regularities may be found in Haggett (1965) and Isard (1956: 55-76). These studies describe a wider range of examples and discuss more fully the limitations upon the observations. Generally, the size, the spacing, and the activities present within concentrations appear to be subject to empirical rules; the theory of location attempts to interpret and explain these rules.

Methods
The existence of concentrations and of regularities in their size and spacing represent the real problems which location theory must solve. In creating theory about these relationships, location analysis has followed two distinct methods. The older method has used the theory of the firm to explain location patterns. The behaviour of individual firms is analysed under given assumptions in order to answer the two questions: what to produce? and where to locate? From these analyses of location and production decisions, theory constructs parallels to empirical regularities. Since the location patterns of firms are interdependent, it has usually been found desirable to analyse the behaviour of several firms together rather than to analyse the behaviour of one firm in isolation (the other firms being given).

A more recent method of analysis is concerned primarily with total patterns in reality and pays less attention to individual behaviour. Instead of building up location patterns from individual, determined actions, more recent models have made simple (and often probabilistic) assumptions about the behaviour of aggregates and from these have constructed location patterns. Whereas classical models analyse the behaviour of firms, the larger scale models make assumptions about the forces which operate to constrain the location of (say) towns. As an example, central place theory (a classical model) analyses the behaviour of individual firms to predict the size and spacing of towns; one simple larger scale model inquires into the probable distribution of towns if any place is equally likely to be the location of a town and if the location of one town has no influence upon the location of other towns.

The two methods of analysis face different problems. The classical models are unable to proceed from individual actions to social location patterns, except under very simplified circumstances. They are consequently difficult to test in reality. The full import of this difficulty will become apparent in Chapter 2. On the other hand, the more recent models can be readily tested against reality, but they make no assumptions about the behaviour of individuals: a variety of forms of individual action may be consistent with such large-scale models. There exists

7

a gap, which neither type of model can adequately fill, between individual behaviour and location patterns in society. Perhaps the main development required by location theory is a model which can link individual acts and social patterns under circumstances which reflect reality.

Most classical location analysis comprises theories of the patterns of location in a simplified society. Location theory has attempted to explain the spatial patterns of industry, agricultural land use types, and other economic activities. The theory applies to patterns which exist after two forces have modified them: these forces are the location decisions of firms and the economic pressures of society which mould location survival rates. Location theory is a theory of where firms survive, and as such makes assumptions about the behaviour of society as a whole, rather than merely about the entrepreneur who is making a decision. Even though theories of location are couched in terms of individual decision making and assume profit maximisation, these theories do not have to suppose that locators actually behave in this profit maximisation manner, but rather that society's economic pressures create location patterns which appear as if firms located to maximise profits (Alchian, 1950; Tiebout, 1957).

This point goes far to justify the postulate of certainty in location theory. Society is maximising *ex post*, and this is often equivalent to maximising under certainty. Consequently, much criticism of location theory as static and not concerned with uncertainty is in these terms spurious, for the theory is a theory of location patterns, not of individual decision taking.

Nevertheless, it seems worthwhile to explore location decisions made in the state of uncertainty, for several reasons. Firstly, it is interesting to try to understand how firms may or ought to behave in the face of uncertainty. Secondly, knowing about firms' behaviour, we may try to improve that behaviour, and thus reduce the social and private costs of firms' errors. Thirdly, it is possible that if several firms each make the same non-optimal decisions in uncertainty, those decisions may modify location patterns in the long run as well as in the short run. But perhaps most importantly, the analysis of uncertainty yields models which, although small scale, can be used to derive large-scale location patterns.

In order to understand this impact of uncertainty upon location patterns, the study has been divided into two portions. In the first part, location decisions are analysed under the assumption of certainty. The method followed will be to outline the main classical theories, to discuss the criticisms of, additions to, and revisions of these theories, and to indicate the degree to which the theories correspond to reality. From this review, a set of conclusions which predict location patterns under certainty are derived. The second portion of the book is devoted to an investigation of location decisions and patterns under uncertainty. Some of the models are well-established, some are new. They are all directed at different segments of the location problem in uncertainty. The two types of analysis are compared and conclusions drawn about the impact of uncertainty on location.

From empirical evidence about the factors which determine the behaviour of firms, most students have divided location theory into three main sectors. First, theory is classified according to scale and factor differences into regional analysis and the analysis of points. Point theory is further subdivided into the analysis of firms whose production occurs at points, but whose consumers are areally distributed (market areas) and of firms whose production occurs over space but whose consumers are located at points (supply areas). Differences between the analyses of supply and market area derive from the use of land as a factor of production in supply areas: units cannot be located in point concentrations, and the price of land is an important factor qualifying the location and production decisions of these units. Different behaviour in the three circumstances, regional analysis, point production, and areal production, merits the separation of the discussion into these three components.

2   Analysis of Point Agglomerations

In this chapter theories of the location of point concentrations are examined. There are three main classes of theory in this field. The first, Weberian theory, analyses the location of the individual firm under conditions of perfect competition. It explores the relative attractions of labour, raw material, and market locations when the location of all other firms is given. The second class is central place theory, which studies location at an industry level under conditions of imperfect competition and of zero raw material costs. Interdependence models, the third class, also abstract from costs and assume imperfect competition, but because these models analyse only a few firms they are more concerned with individual decision taking than central place theory. Whereas Weberian theory analyses location decisions when both markets and materials are concentrated at points, central place theory and the interdependence models assume areal markets and a homogeneous pattern of raw materials. The three groups of theory are reviewed in order to draw from them predictions about the reasons for the formation, the size, the spacing and the constituent activities of points under conditions of certainty.

Weberian Analysis

Weber (Friedrich, 1929) provided one of the earliest formulations of a theory to explain the location of manufacturing industry. The fundamental principle of his theory was borrowed from Launhardt (1885) and it has been employed in location theory ever since. The idea that firms locate to minimise transport and labour costs has been used in empirical analyses such as those of Hoover (1937) and McLaughlin and Robock (1949). Probst (1963: 1-2) suggests that a general theory of the location of communist industry is based on the principle that mining and production activities should be located to minimise the total costs of mining, production, and transport, subject to the general constraints of harmonic and proportionate development of each region and its resources. Weber's classification of industries into materials oriented, market oriented, and labour oriented has been used in studies of location trends through economic development (Friedmann, 1955) and in more general studies of patterns of location (Estall and Buchanan, 1961). These ideas have been one of the continuing mainstreams of location analysis.

Weber wished to construct a pure theory of location, one which could be applied to all industries at all times. He therefore analysed only the general factors that influence the location of all industries (Friedrich, 1929: 23-5), and these factors he divided into those influencing inter-regional location and those influencing intra-regional location (agglomerating factors). He found three elements which vary regionally—raw material costs, transport costs, and labour costs—but for analysis, raw material cost fluctuations are included within transport costs (Friedrich, 1929: 25-34). The plan was to locate firms in order to minimise transport costs, to introduce labour costs as distortions of this pattern, and finally to include the effect of agglomeration economies. The basic organising principle is that industry locates to minimise costs.

Three main simplifying conditions are introduced (Friedrich, 1929: 37-9). Weber supposed that the location of raw materials is given, an assumption which seems quite accurate for minerals but less accurate for agricultural raw materials. The location and the size of consuming centres is assumed given. Labour is supposed to be immobile, wages to be fixed, and the supply of labour at each location to be unlimited.

The first stage of the model comprises a discussion of transport orientation. Industry is attracted to locations where costs of transport are lowest—that is, to locations where the number of ton-miles of raw materials and finished product to be moved per ton of product is minimised. Weber realises that other elements besides weight and distance affect transport costs, and to allow for these he assigns 'ideal' weights to the goods moved rather than actual weights: for example, fragile goods whose cost of transport is $1.00 per ton-mile would be assigned an ideal weight four times as high as that assigned to a bulky good which costs only $0.25 per ton-mile to transport.

The materials which enter into the production process are classified in two ways (Friedrich, 1929: 50-3). First, materials may be either ubiquitous or localised—some materials occur more or less everywhere but the distribution of others is more circumscribed. This classification varies between regions and times: for example, cotton may be ubiquitous in the American Cotton Belt but it is not ubiquitous in Germany. The classification also varies according to the scale of the analysis. To a firm deciding whether to locate an aluminium processing plant in Australia or Japan, power and water may be considered ubiquitous; but within Australia, water is certainly not ubiquitous. Secondly, Weber divides materials into those which lose weight in processing ('gross' materials) and those whose weight enters entirely into the final product ('pure' materials).

Location is determined by the material index (MI) of the industry. This material index is defined as

11

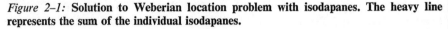

Figure 2–1: Solution to Weberian location problem with isodapanes. The heavy line represents the sum of the individual isodapanes.

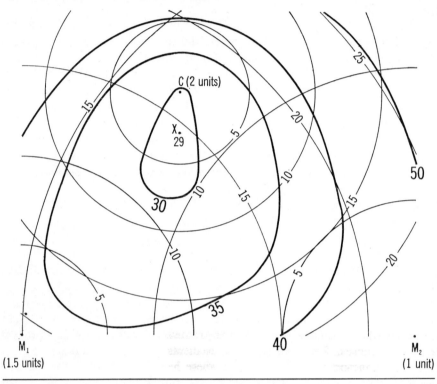

$$MI = \frac{\text{weight of localised materials}}{\text{weight of finished product}}.$$

Weber concludes that industries displaying a high material index are attracted towards the sources of raw materials, whereas those characterised by a material index of less than 1·0 locate at the place of consumption. Pure materials can never attract production to their deposits because they have no locational weight; a weight-losing material may attract production to its deposit, but only if its weight is greater than the combined weight of all the other materials and of the product (Friedrich, 1929: 59-61).

The actual solution of one of Weber's location figures may be illustrated (see Fig. 2–1). Two material sources, M_1 and M_2, are used in the ratio of 1·5:1·0 in manufacturing a product which weighs 0·80 of the material inputs. Lines of equal transport cost (isodapanes) are constructed around M_1 and M_2 and the consumption centre, C. The costs of moving M_1, M_2, and the final product are summed for each location to derive lines of equal total transport cost from which the minimum cost location, X, may be found.

Until recently the only means of solving location problems of this kind were analogue or graphical methods. But this simple case is amenable to a linear programming solution. Assume m raw materials, available at sites $j = 1$ to $j = m$; an ideal weight of w_j is required of each material. A consumption site, c, exists, needing w_c output. There exist n possible production sites ($n \geqslant m$), at the points $i = 1$ to $i = n$. The distance between each potential production site and raw material source, d_{ij}, is given, as is the distance, d_{ic}, between each production site and the consumption centre. Weber's model is: choose i in order to minimise Z, where

$$(2\text{–}1) \qquad Z = \sum_{j=1}^{m} (w_j \, d_{ij}) + w_c \, d_{ic},$$

subject to all distances being positive. Kuhn and Kuenne (1962) and Cooper (1963) have developed iterative methods, based on programming techniques, for the solution of general location polygons, while Cooper (1968) has extended his solution to cover the case of non-linear transport costs.

Having solved the location polygon in this manner for an industry, Weber has then to find which polygons among the available ones will be used by that industry. This discussion is less satisfactory than the previous one, but two conclusions do emerge. Firstly, if the location figure has only two points, a material source and a market, then the industry will use that raw material deposit which is nearest the market. Secondly, if the polygon has three or more sides, the raw material deposits are chosen to minimise total transport costs: for example, if the location has to be near a raw material, 'X', then 'X' is chosen to be the nearest deposit to the market; but the other raw material sources are chosen so as to be near the predominant material, 'X', not so as to be near the market (Friedrich, 1929: 67-71).

An important prediction derives from this analysis. The location chosen depends on the material index, which in turn depends on the weight loss of localised materials in comparison with the weight of ubiquitous materials contained in the final product. It follows that, although spatial variations in the structure of transport rates may modify location choices, the general level of transport costs has no influence on the pattern of location of industry in a society (Friedrich, 1929: 72-3). The increasing attraction of industry to markets is not to be explained in this model by the general lowering of transport costs.

The second stage of the model is the analysis of labour orientation. When examining spatial differences in labour costs, Weber does not consider differences which arise from organisational and technical efficiency, for these are not tied by location. He is interested only in those differences which are fixed. Furthermore, he neglects the facts that labour is in limited supply and that the location choice of the firm influences wage levels, because he wishes to explore the effects of cost variations on the location of industry (Friedrich, 1929: 95-101).

Data reveal that wages vary from point to point rather than gradually over areas. Therefore industry must actually locate at a low wage location and not

13

merely towards it if a labour cost saving is to be realised. An industry will choose a cheap labour site if the labour cost savings are greater than the increment in transport costs at this site above the minimum possible transport costs. If d_1 and d_2 are the number of ton-miles which must be moved per ton of product at the minimum transport cost location (1) and the cheap labour location (2), respectively; if w_1 and w_2 are the hourly wages at these locations; if h is the number of hours of labour required to produce a ton of product; and if c is the cost of transport per ton-mile; then a firm locates at the cheap labour location if

$$w_1 h + d_1 c > w_2 h + d_2 c,$$

that is, if

(2–2) $(w_1 - w_2)h > (d_2 - d_1)c.$

The analytical solution is obtained by drawing isodapanes around the minimum transport cost location; of these isodapanes, one connects points at which transfer costs exceed the minimum by an amount equal to the production cost economies at an alternative production point. This is the critical isodapane for that site. If the alternative site is inside the critical isodapane the firm moves to that point; if the alternative lies outside the critical isodapane the economy in production costs is less than the additional transport costs incurred there (Friedrich, 1929: 102-4).

Industries vary in the extent to which they are attracted to cheap labour sites. If an industry is characterised by high labour costs per ton of product, it is possible for that industry to effect large economies at a cheap labour location, and such industries are potentially attracted to labour locations. If an industry has a low material index, a small mass of material has to be moved per ton of product, and therefore the isodapanes for this industry are widely spaced: there is a high probability that the industry will be attracted to points of low labour cost. These two ideas are combined in Weber's coefficient of labour, which measures the labour cost per ton of location weight (location weight equals material index plus unity). A high coefficient of labour implies a strong attraction to cheap labour locations (Friedrich, 1929: 105-12).

The third portion of the analysis examines agglomeration. Weber defines an agglomerative factor as a cheapening of production when that production is concentrated at one place. Agglomerative factors include (i) economies of scale within a plant and (ii) economies from the association of several plants. Economies of association derive from the specialised division of labour between plants, better repair facilities, a specialised labour organisation, the development of markets for the materials and products of an industry, and the lowering of social overhead costs. The only deglomerative element is rent, which is related to the size of the city. Weber excludes from his definition of an agglomerative force the attraction of several plants to the same point in order to use cheap labour or raw materials (Friedrich, 1929: 126-35).

A plant locates in an agglomeration if the savings at this location offset the

14

concomitant increase in transport costs. The agglomeration is located in order to minimise the sum of the additional costs incurred by all the firms located there. If the agglomeration comprises n firms and if the jth firm requires d_{2j} ton-miles at the agglomeration and d_{1j} ton-miles at its minimum transport cost site, then the agglomeration is located in order to minimise

$$(2\text{-}3) \qquad C = \sum_{j=1}^{n} (d_{2j} - d_{1j}).$$

The tendency to agglomerate is strengthened if firms in an agglomeration can use local raw materials to replace their original material choices. The extent of agglomeration depends on the economies available, the spacing of isodapanes (that is, on the material index of the industry and on transport rates) and on the density of industry (the average distance separating production units). Weber points out, though, that the force of agglomeration is unlikely to cause independent concentrations to develop: since labour locations will almost always be points of accidental agglomeration, the firms' choice is between the economies of agglomeration available at agglomeration locations and the economies of labour plus accidental agglomeration economies available at labour locations. Only firms characterised by low labour orientation and extensive economies of agglomeration can be attracted to agglomeration locations which are independent of labour locations (Friedrich, 1929: 135-53).

Weberian analysis has been used as the framework of Isard's theoretical and empirical analyses of location. First, transport costs are examined, as a basic location factor; next, labour, power, and other production cost differentials are injected as elements distorting the optimal transport pattern; and finally, scale, localisation, and urbanisation economies are introduced as additional distorting elements (Isard, 1956). In empirical analyses, Isard has extended this approach to industrial complexes, defined as sets of activities occurring together at a given location and subject to important inter-relations (e.g. Isard, 1960: 375-412; Isard and Vietorisz, 1955; Isard and Schooler, 1959; and Isard, Schooler, and Vietorisz, 1959). Instead of analysing merely one industry at a time, whole inter-related complexes of activities are subject to comparative cost studies to determine optimal combinations of activities and least-cost locations: Isard, Schooler, and Vietorisz (1959) examined by such methods the potential of Puerto Rico as a site for a petro-chemical complex.

Several criticisms have been made of the postulates which Weber employs to construct his theory. By far the most important of these criticisms is that Weber assumes that firms are in a perfectly competitive situation. From this condition follows his treatment of the location decision as the search for a least cost site, for price and demand are then given. However, it can readily be shown that the assumption of perfect competition is incompatible with the postulate of a spatial framework for society: there cannot be perfect competition over space, for distance presents firms with monopoly advantages in proximate areas. Locational specialisation is but one aspect of the product differentiation which

15

C

Figure 2-2: **Market area of firm at *B* as a function of its selling price**

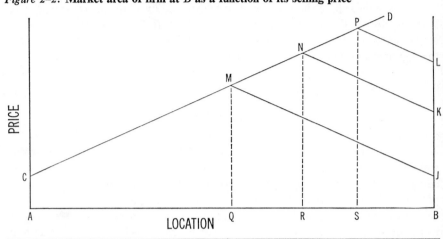

characterises monopolistic competition (Chamberlin, 1950; Greenhut, 1963: 55-76).

In reality, then, firms seek maximum profit locations, not least cost locations. Not only must firms analyse the location of raw materials and the costs of production, but they must also investigate the location of other firms. The location policies of all firms are interdependent because of the element of monopolistic competition conferred on markets by space. Demand varies with price and with the location chosen. The greatest total demand will be realised with a different location of the plant at each factory price. It is then meaningless to find the point of lowest cost (Lösch, 1959: 27-31). Weber's assumptions of space and of perfect competition are inconsistent and permit only a partial analysis of location decisions.

The point can be illustrated geometrically, as in Fig. 2–2. Assume a linear market, *AB*. There are many firms at *A*, selling goods at a mill price *AC*; because of distance costs, the delivered price rises with distance from *A*, in the form of the line *CD*. For any one of these firms, a price greater than *AC* results in its selling nothing. The sole firm at *B*, however, has some latitude in its choice of a selling price. If it sells at price *BJ* (= *AC*) the delivered price line takes the form *JM*, and the boundary of the sales areas of firm *B* and of the firms at *A* is *Q*, where *AQ* = *QB*. Alternatively, *B* may sell at mill price *BK*, when its sales area extends only as far as *BR*. Similarly at mill price *BL*, its sales area is *BS*. The firm at *B* does not lose all its sales if it charges a price greater than *BJ* (= *AC*). If we assume a linear demand curve for the products of the industry, then, whereas the demand curve for the product of any one firm at *A* is horizontal, the demand curve for the product of *B* is negatively sloping. Although firms at the same point may be perfectly competitive, distance offers *B* the advantages of

16

Figure 2-3: **Known parameters in a location triangle.**
Source: Moses (1958).

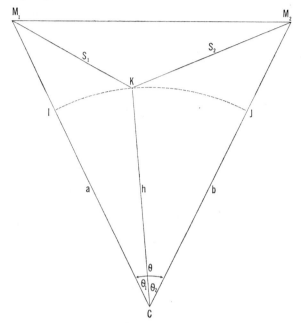

monopolistic competition, and such advantages are available to any firm in a spatial market.

Weber also assumes that the scale of production of the plant has no effect on costs and that the firm uses the same input mix at all locations. These assumptions have been criticised by Hoover (1937: 13-21 and 75-9), while Moses (1958) has shown that the optimum location depends upon production levels (which Weber assumed to be given). The criticism can be illustrated from Moses's treatment.

Consider a location triangle (Fig. 2-3) which contains two material sources (M_1 and M_2) and a single fixed consumption point (C). Let P be the price of an input at its source, r be the transport rate on an input, and P' be the delivered price of an input at the production point. Suppose that the distance of shipment of the final product is fixed—that production takes place somewhere along the arc *IJ*. This assumption is introduced merely to simplify the discussion: it has no effect on the conclusions.

The movement of the production point along this arc from *J* towards *I* reduces the distance that M_1 must be moved and increases the distance over which M_2 must be transported. If production takes place at *K*, s_1 and s_2 can be determined:

Figure 2–4: **A pair of iso-outlay curves**

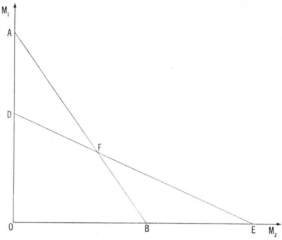

(2–4) $s_1 = \sqrt{a^2+h^2+2ahcos\theta_1}$

(2–5) $s_2 = \sqrt{b^2+h^2+2bhcos(\theta-\theta_1)}$.

Hence we know

$$P'_1 = P_1+r_1s_1 \text{ and } P'_2 = P_2+r_2s_2.$$

Therefore

(2–6) $P'_1/P'_2 = (P_1+r_1s_1)/(P_2+r_2s_2)$.

Each point along *IJ* is associated with a definite ratio, P'_1/P'_2, of the delivered prices of the two inputs. This ratio of delivered prices is the constant slope of the system of iso-outlay lines for production at *K*. These iso-outlay lines define how much of M_1 and how much of M_2 can be bought for a given outlay.

Two such iso-outlay lines are shown in Fig. 2–4. They represent the same total amount of spending on the two material inputs: *AB* is associated with production at *I* and *DE* with production at *J*. To the right of *F*, location at *J* permits the same quantity of M_1 to be purchased as at *I* but allows the firm to buy more of M_2, for a given expenditure. To the left of *F*, location at *I* permits the same quantity of M_2 to be bought as at *J*, but allows the firm to buy more M_1.

But each of the infinite number of points along *IJ* can be treated as a potential location. The discontinuous line *AFE* becomes a smooth iso-outlay curve defining a unique ratio of delivered prices at each site. Each point on this curve represents one location on the arc *IJ* and demonstrates the best combination of factors at that point for a given expenditure, transport rate, and base prices of inputs. Figure 2–5 illustrates a series of such iso-outlay curves, each of which represents a given level of spending on inputs. The solid lines are isoquants—

18

Figure 2–5: **Tangency of iso-outlay curves and isoquants yields expansion path (GBH) of the firm.**

Source: Moses (1958).

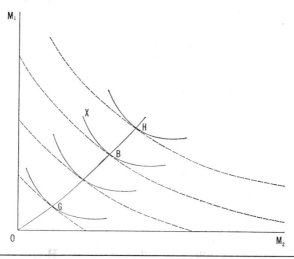

they show the physically feasible ways of combining the inputs to produce a given volume of outputs. Suppose the firm wishes to produce the output represented by isoquant X. Optimality is characterised by tangency—i.e. by point B, which represents not only a combination of inputs but also a location. This optimum location is that at which (for a given level of output) total expenditure is minimised: it is only by chance that this site might also be the point of minimum transport costs. Thus if factor substitution is possible, the optimum location is not defined by the point of minimum transport costs. The formulations of Weber (Friedrich, 1929), Hoover (1937), and Isard (1956) are not general in this respect.

The relation between output and location is suggested by the expansion path GBH in Fig. 2–5. This path connects the points of tangency between the iso-outlay curves and the sequence of isoquant lines. Product substitution is possible, and so the optimum location, as defined by the slope of the iso-outlay curve at the point of tangency, changes as does the level of output. Thus, Moses suggests, to introduce scale into the discussion after the location is chosen, as Weber, Hoover, and Isard do, is to omit an important variable which controls the optimum location.

Several other problems in Weberian analysis have been examined. Weber suggests that the different costs of mining ores and fuels be brought within the scope of the theory by supposing that high cost mineral sources are further away from the production site than low cost sources. Hoover (1937: 37-41) points out that this is no solution: since Weber had not yet found the production site,

19

from what point should the high cost sources be considered more distant? Weber's statement has no meaning.

Hoover (1937: 55-9) has also criticised Weber for assuming that freight rates are proportional to distance, and quotes evidence to the contrary. For example, Pirath (1934: 215) found that terminal costs as a proportion of total costs for a haul of average length were on natural waterways 45 per cent, on railroads (freight, less than carload lots) 47 per cent, on motorbus 30 per cent, on letter post 90 per cent, and on electric power 8 per cent. Freight rates, then, normally taper off with distance, and this encourages a small number of long hauls rather than a larger number of short hauls. The likelihood of production at a point which is neither a material source nor a consumption centre is correspondingly reduced. Isard (1956: 109) points out that Weber's model is unable to encompass freight rates which are less than proportional to distance. Weber suggests that fictitious distances be used to overcome this difficulty, but Isard indicates that we cannot calculate the amount by which to shorten the distance of any corner of a locational polygon from the site of production until that site of production has been determined.

Weber's assumptions of immobile, unlimited amounts of labour have also been criticised. One of the more serious deficiencies is that he does not analyse the causes of labour cost differentials. Hoover (1937: 60-74) classifies these causes as being due to (i) variations in the cost of living and (ii) labour immobilities. It may be profitable for the theory of location to use such a classification, for Hoover proposes that costs of living vary most in response to cheapness of food supplies. Therefore labour oriented industries seek locations to which food can be sent cheaply: Hartshorne (1926: 53) argues that location near agricultural areas is advantageous to firms which use unskilled labour, while Jewkes (1930: 102-3) has discussed the value of nearby agricultural areas for the growth of Preston, Lancashire. Weber's assumption that labour cost variations are given caused him to pass over some conclusions of locational significance.

Weber's treatment of agglomeration economies has also been criticised. Hoover (1937: 89-93) suggests that there are four main deficiencies in Weber's analysis. Firstly, whereas Weber argued that agglomeration economies usually only reinforce the attraction of cheap labour locations, Hoover suggests that agglomeration is also likely at material sources, trans-shipment points and markets. Secondly, Weber incorporated in agglomeration economies three distinct forces: scale economies within the firm, localisation economies (for firms within a single industry), and urbanisation economies (for firms in all industries). Thirdly, Hoover points out that Weber's model contains no mechanism for measuring the effect on the extent of agglomeration of firms being able to replace material sources when they agglomerate. And fourthly, Hoover quotes a criticism of Palander's (1935: ch. 8). Weber determines whether two firms will locate together by drawing critical isodapanes around their points of minimum transport costs. If these critical isodapanes intersect, the firms can

Figure 2–6: **Derivation of the area within which agglomeration is economic**

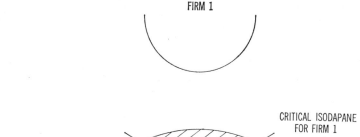

gain economies by locating together anywhere within this zone of intersection. In Fig. 2–6, the critical isodapanes intersect and so the firms can gain by locating together within the shaded area. Palander points out that while such a move is advantageous to both firms together, it is not profitable for any one firm to move unless it is certain that its partner will behave in the same way. Weber's agglomeration procedure requires co-operation from two firms which are locating at the same time. Palander also argues that each firm desires that the agglomeration be located at that point within the zone of intersection of the isodapanes which is nearest its own point of minimum transport costs: that is, the agglomerating firms are in conflict about where to locate the agglomeration, and Weber has not solved this conflict problem. Isard and his colleagues have attempted to solve competitive-co-operative situations such as this, and in one paper Isard (1967) has explained how an 'incremax' procedure could be used by the firms to reach agreement on location. The procedure is deemed fair, but it requires communication between the firms, and the fairness of the procedure demands that any firm be able to opt out of the bargaining at any time; thus an agreed fair agglomerating solution does not always occur. Isard (1956: 180) has also suggested that Weber has mis-stated the problem: since location takes place historically—some plants are already located—the question should be whether a new plant locates near an existing plant or at the point of minimum transport costs. This reformulation of the question is necessary because existing plants are unlikely to undergo the costs of relocation in order to gain agglomeration economies.

Table 2–1: **Relation between material index and location of industries**

Location of industry	Material index <1·0	Material index 1·0-2·0	Material index >2·0
At materials	2	17	3
Not at materials	16	14	1
Total number of industries	18	31	4

Source: Smith (1955: 8).

In general, Weber's is a small-scale model. It works most efficiently when analysing the location decision of one firm, partly because it does not consider the effects of firm's interdependencies, partly because it assumes that the distribution of raw materials is given. However, the distribution of resources is not a datum: resources must be created by exploration and by the discovery of potentially profitable uses. 'Features of the environment . . . become resources only if, when, and in so far as they are . . . capable of supporting man's needs' (Zimmermann, 1933: 3). Plant location decisions are determined not by the production and transport processes alone, but by the interaction of those processes with the resource creation process. That is, the distribution of resources depends in part upon firms' decisions, for firms decide how much to explore: the distribution of resources is itself part of (or even a product of) the location decision process (Fagan, 1969).

This discussion provides a formidable set of criticisms of the assumptions and methods underlying Weber's analysis. Some of the problems are readily overcome: for example, Hoover's (1948) discussion of location theory assumes tapering freight rates, analyses agglomeration economies and labour costs more fully, and discusses the influence of the relative costs of different mineral sources. But despite references to demand in this discussion (1948: 48-65), Hoover writes largely within the framework of costs: 'The greatest weakness in Hoover's work is the failure to probe deeply into locational interdependence' (Greenhut, 1956: 21). Interdependence (or monopolistic competition), variations of cost with scale, changes of input mix with scale and location, and changes in optimum location with alterations of scale have all remained largely outside Weberian analysis. The analysis of location decisions which incorporates the resource creation process is only now being started (e.g. Fagan, 1969).

Smith (1955) has evaluated the usefulness of Weber's material index as a means of differentiating material and market oriented industries in the United Kingdom. He discovered that the best results, reproduced in Table 2–1, are obtained when coal is excluded from the material index, but that, even so, the results are not satisfactory. Smith found that several other indices are equally as good as the material index at distinguishing material and market orientation. These indices are the weight of material per operative, the amount of electric power used *per capita*, and the proportion of males in the workforce. This relatively poor showing of the material index is not surprising in view of the criticisms discussed above.

The review of Weber's model yields several conclusions about the location of firms and indicates some of the assumptions which must be incorporated within a more realistic model of location choices. The most important result is indicated in Smith's paper—a general tendency for firms in which the material index is high to locate near their raw material sources. The model, as modified by Hoover, provides one important reason for the growth of towns: agglomeration economies. But in the absence of a historical model, this is not a model of the formation of towns, because most agglomeration is at labour or market sites (where it is assumed that towns exist already). Since Weber concludes that most agglomeration occurs in existing towns, his model is not a theory of town formation, although it does provide a reason for town growth.

A more realistic model than Weber's must incorporate the following assumptions: that markets are monopolistic competitive and therefore that profit maximisation rather than cost minimisation is the aim of firms; and that scale and optimum location are interdependent. In addition, the model should analyse spatial variations in labour costs, postulate tapering freight rates, and treat the individual decision taking aspects of agglomeration. If the scope of the theory is to be increased, it should incorporate the resource creation process. Finally, the theory must provide a reason for the formation of towns.

Central Place Theory

Lösch's (1959) theory of location balances that of Weber. Whereas Weber assumed point markets, Lösch postulates areal markets; Weber's analysis was concerned with the location and costs of raw materials, but Lösch ignores these in the formal development of his theory. Lösch's importance, however, extends far beyond this balancing function, for he presented new ideas about the size and shape of market areas, about the functions of towns, and about the locational equilibrium.

The model explores location patterns in general, patterns which are not specific to particular areas and times. Lösch consequently assumed a homogeneous plain which is unbounded. This condition permits him to analyse the distribution of activity in abstraction from the effects of variations in the resource endowment of regions, which generate patterns specific to individual areas. The resulting pattern is a general one, which holds on average for all countries if the distribution of raw materials is random.

The remaining important explicit assumptions are five. These are the conditions for locational equilibrium: (i) the location for the individual is a maximum profit location, (ii) locations are so numerous that the entire space is occupied, (iii) so many individuals exist that no one of them can make abnormal profits, (iv) the areas of supply, production, and sales are as small as possible, and (v) at the boundary between two economic areas individuals are indifferent about which of the two locations they patronise (Lösch, 1959: 94-7). The first

Figure 2–7: **Demand curve in a spatial market.**
  Source: Lösch (1959: 106).

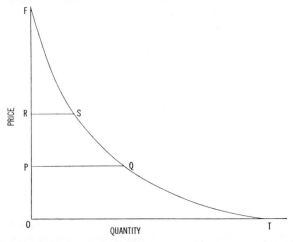

circumstance is that firms maximise income; the last is that consumers maximise income; and the second, third, and fourth imply that society maximises the number of firms.

Assume over the plain a regular distribution of self-sufficient farmers. Will one farmer be able to manufacture a good and sell it profitably to others? In Fig. 2–7 the curve *FT* is a demand curve relating price to quantity sold. The price at the factory is *OP*, so those at *P* buy a quantity *PQ* of the good. When distance costs *PR* are added to *OP*, sales fall to *RS*. At *F*, distance costs raise the price to *OF*, at which price sales are zero. The firm cannot sell goods beyond *F*, so *PF* represents the sales radius for the good. The total sales for the firm equal the volume of the cone formed by rotating the triangle *PQF* around *PQ* as axis, multiplied by the population density.

This procedure supposes that the price *OP* is known. But demand varies with price, so the firm must calculate sales volumes for many prices in order to find demand as a function of mill price. This calculation yields the curve Δ in Fig. 2–8. The firm also constructs a planning curve, π, which indicates the minimum average cost of production in a plant built to produce a given amount. Only if Δ and π intersect can a manufacturing firm exist profitably: it produces *MN* output (Lösch, 1959: 105-8). The curve Δ has been constructed under the assumption that market areas are circular. Such a shape ensures that the largest possible area is contained within a given distance of the firm. But circular market regions leave interstitial areas which are not served by any firm, whereas the assumptions require that all areas of the plain be served by firms. In addition, all firms must have the same size and shape of market area. There exist only three regular geometric figures which fulfil these requirements—hexagons,

Figure 2–8: **Sales as a function of mill price (Δ) and average costs as a function of sales (π): the scale problem.**
Source: Lösch (1959: 106).

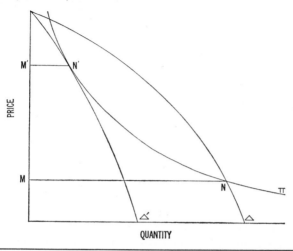

squares, and equilateral triangles. In market regions of a given area, the total demand in a hexagon is 2·4 per cent greater than in a square and 12 per cent greater than in an equilateral triangle (Lösch, 1959: 111-13). The hexagon is thus the most efficient shape for a firm's market area. Just as the shape of the market is changed from circular to hexagonal, so the area of market which a firm can command is reduced by competition from other firms until that firm can only just make normal profits (this process is required by assumption (iii)): the firm's demand curve diminishes from Δ to Δ', which just touches π (see Fig. 2–8). The firm is then at its minimum profitable size, producing $M'N'$, and the market is full (Lösch, 1959: 109–11).

The model predicts a network of hexagonal market areas for the manufactured good. If we assume that all the production sites in an industry must be either at a farm or equidistant from three farms, then only a limited number of hexagon sizes are possible. Under these conditions one firm can serve 2, 3, 4, 7, 9, 12, 13, 16, 19, 21, 25, . . . farms, the number depending on economies of scale and transport costs within the industry (Lösch 1959: 116-22). Lösch argues that it is more likely that all production sites be on farms than midway between farms because if sites are on farms local demand is more concentrated and the number of transport lines necessary to serve the production sites is lower.

Hexagonal nets are derived in this manner for each industry. Lösch proceeds then to lay the nets together so that all have at least one centre in common, and to rotate the nets until six sectors with many and six sectors with few production sites are derived. Although formal, Lösch asserts that this arrangement has several advantages: the greatest number of locations coincide; the maximum number of purchases are made locally; and the sum of the minimum distances between production sites is minimised, so that shipments and transport lines are reduced (Lösch, 1959: 124-9).

The main features of the system may be readily gathered from this summary of the analysis. The producing and selling points for each good are regularly distributed over the plain, each point having a hexagonal market area the size of which depends on transport costs and economies of scale within the industry. Selling points of different goods tend to agglomerate, technically because of the rotation of nets, and economically because of agglomeration economies. There exist in Lösch's system many of these agglomerations (central places), but their number diminishes as the number of functions within them increases; consequently the spacing of higher order central places is wider than that of lower order places.

Christaller (1966) developed his theory of central places under slightly different assumptions. His informal statement of the theory has been succinctly summarised and formalised by Dacey (1965). Assume (i) an even distribution of population in an unbounded plain, (ii) that central places provide services for surrounding hinterlands of fixed sizes, (iii) that central places are located a maximum distance apart, subject to the constraint that their market areas exhaust the plain, and (iv) that a central place provides a function of order m if and only if it also provides functions of order 1 through $(m-1)$. Dacey demonstrates that these assumptions imply that central places are located in the centre of hexagonal market areas and that each central place with function of order m provides that function to q places (including itself) which sell goods of order $(m-1)$.

There are two key differences between this system and that of Lösch. The first difference is that Christaller assumes that towns with function m also contain all functions of order lower than m; in Lösch's model, on the other hand, the degree to which functions of different orders agglomerate is deduced from the criterion that economies of agglomeration be maximised, and consequently centres of order m need not necessarily contain all the lower order functions. This difference is associated with the second: whereas in Christaller's system the ratio between the number of places of order m and the number of order $m+1$ is fixed ($=q$) for any region and all m, Lösch permitted the ratio, q, to vary as m varies. Lösch's hierarchy is far less rigid than that of Christaller, and yields a more continuous sequence of centre sizes than the distinct tiers predicted by Christaller.

Leamer (1968) has extended this form of analysis to the case of bounded markets. He used Cooper's (1963) method to determine the optimum location pattern of a given number of firms in triangular, square, and circular regions, and calculated the actual total transport cost between firms and consumers for each pattern. Leamer discovered that the actual total transport costs are approximately the same as the total transport cost which would be necessary if the same area were served by the same number of regular hexagons. Furthermore, if the number of firms is greater than ten, then those firms whose market area does not touch the outer boundary of the region have roughly hexagonal market areas. These results suggest the ready extension of Lösch's methods to bounded regions; but Leamer did not examine patterns of agglomeration of firms of different orders.

The most important feature of this theory is that it is not a theory of the formation of central places. Lösch resorts to the mechanical device of rotating nets to produce central places because he could not mathematically analyse sales patterns over space once some sellers had located. He justifies the device by claiming that agglomeration economies would cause such a pattern to evolve by means of forces within the economy which operate to minimise transport costs and to maximise local demand. But Palander (1935) has shown that agglomeration economies cannot cause towns to form unless the model postulates some mechanism whereby firms can co-ordinate their choices. Lösch does not specify such a mechanism, and so assumes away the problem of how towns form.

This conclusion can be reached in another manner. Even if agglomeration economies could cause towns to form, central place theory could not predict town formation on a non-homogeneous surface. Once it is assumed that the surface is heterogeneous, then the hexagonal nets become irregular in shape and size: they are, for example, smaller in more densely populated areas than in sparsely populated areas and smaller in areas where transport costs are high than where they are low, unless there exist extensive economies of mass-production. But as Lösch (1938) points out, it is generally impossible to arrange a set of irregular nets over an area in such a way that they all have at least one point in common: no city contains a complete set of all industries, and since the nets cannot be rotated the degree of coincidence of production sites falls markedly. On a heterogeneous plain most production would be dispersed.

Once more realistic conditions have been assumed, it becomes obvious that Lösch's theory does not constitute a model of the formation of towns. Central place theory is more important as a theory of market areas and of the size and spacing of cities. Even so, an expanded model must account for the effects of spatial variations in the costs of inputs on location decisions. Attempts have been made to generalise central place theory to take account of such heterogeneity of the earth's surface. Berry and Garrison (1958b) suggest that central place theory be reformulated in terms of the range of a good (its market area) and the threshold population of a good (the minimum population necessary to support a function). They argue that, whatever the distribution of purchasing power, a hierarchical system of central places will emerge.

Assume n types of good, ranked in order of increasing thresholds from 1 to n. The central places supplying the good of order n are A places: as many of these A centres exist as there are threshold sales to support the n-type firms. If total sales are an exact multiple of threshold sales, each of the n-type firms earns normal profits only if these firms are located either to minimise distribution costs or to minimise consumer movement. If sales are not an exact multiple of threshold sales, excess profits exist and firms are allowed some latitude in location choices.

The firms selling goods of the next lowest order $(n-1)$ are then located. These firms locate first at the A centres, which are the most efficient supply points and which offer advantages of association with the n-type firms. Other $(n-1)$-type firms locate in the interstitial areas provided the sales in these areas are large enough to support such firms. These $(n-1)$-type firms in the interstitial areas are the nuclei of next lowest order B centres. The argument and arrangement is repeated for firms selling the $(n-2)$, $(n-3)$, . . . , 2, 1 order goods. Thus every centre of order j contains sellers of goods of every order j, $(j-1)$, . . . , 2, 1.

However, this is an incomplete statement of a central place system. First, the system is not in equilibrium, because there must be consumers in the interstitial areas who are not served by any firm and because excess profits can be earned by the sellers of all goods other than the nth order good. There exists an incentive for firms to locate or to relocate in order to sell goods to the unserved consumers. Secondly, assume a more realistic process of firm establishment: that a large number of firms is created in any industry and that this number is reduced by competition to that necessary to serve society efficiently (Berry, 1967: 8-9, contains maps of this process). Then, since it is unlikely that the optimum arrangement of the $(n-1)$-type firms will include more than one or two coincidences with the n-type firms, the $(n-1)$ firms which have located at the A centres will have their market areas cut off by the surrounding $(n-1)$-type firms. Perhaps more importantly from the point of view of location analysis, 'to follow Garrison and Berry in getting rid of Christaller's severe assumption of a uniform transportation plane also removes the explicit spatial dimensions of the analysis and renders it impotent for further geographical elaboration' (Curry, 1967: 219).

The effects of heterogeneity on central place systems, which prompted the reformulation given by Berry and Garrison, have long been recognised empirically. Lösch himself realised that the simple geometry of the regular central place lattice is distorted in reality. It is distorted by resource localisation: Lösch (1938) shows how in Iowa larger towns are further apart than small ones, whereas in parts of England, where resources are more highly localised, spacing is not regularly associated with size. The regular lattice is also distorted by agglomeration economies: Bogue (1950) illustrates that population density is higher near large cities than at distances from them. Hence central functions should be more closely spaced near metropolitan centres than they are in areas more distant from large cities. Isard (1956: 270-4) redraws Lösch's hexagonal nets to take account of the effects of agglomeration. Differences in the period of settlement of areas, and so of transport rates at the time of the formation of towns, distort the hexagonal lattice even further: Morrill (1963) indicates the importance of this factor, while Neutze (1960) illustrates how the spacing of New Zealand towns depends in part on when they were established. Haggett (1965: 92-8) elaborates on these ideas.

Consequently it is not surprising that studies of the spacing of settlements have not found that towns are evenly spaced. For example, King (1962) analysed town spacing in twenty sample areas in the United States and Dacey (1960a) investigated the location of settlements in Wisconsin by measuring the distance of a town from its nearest neighbour. The nearest neighbour statistic, Rn, varies between 0·0 (all settlements cluster together) and 2·15 (uniform spacing of settlements); the value 1·0 represents a random distribution of towns. In both studies the data clearly reveal that settlement patterns approximate a random rather than a clustered or a uniform spacing. Thus King found extreme values of 0·70 in Utah and 1·38 in Missouri. Similarly, Getis (1963) found that the distribution of stores within Southeast Tacoma becomes much more regular when Euclidean space is transformed into income space (so that the area of a region is proportional to the income generated within it). Inspection of Getis's maps (1963: 18-20) indicates that even after the transformation, centres are not completely evenly spaced; the distortions due to resource localisation are not by any means the only ones.

On the other hand, the spacing of cities has been shown to be related to their size in several areas. Lösch (1959: 391) presents histograms showing that the overland distances separating Iowa cities are greater for large cities than for smaller ones. House (1953: 63) presents data for the spacing of towns in the western part of the U.S. manufacturing belt. The mean spacing in miles of towns in the 20,000-30,000 population size class is 14·6, in the 40,000-50,000 class is 28·3, and in the 75,000-100,000 class is 38·0. Thomas (1960) correlated the distance of a town from its nearest neighbour with the size of the town. For towns in Iowa he found that about one-third of the variation in spacing is explained by size and that this value has remained fairly constant since 1900. These spacing relationships are accordant with those predicted by central place theory.

Some results published by King (1961b) indicate, though, that the regularities described by Lösch and later workers may not be very typical of the United States as a whole. King drew a random sample of 200 towns from the 1950 census of the United States and related the sizes of these towns to the distances separating them from their nearest neighbour of approximately the same size. The relationship, though statistically significant, explained only about 2 per cent of the variations in spacing. (However, in the Great Plains and the Far West, $R^2 = 0·42$.) In testing five other hypotheses, King found that only one, overall population density, explained more than 10 per cent of the variation in spacing, while all six variables together explained only 25 per cent of the variation (though again the performance of the hypotheses was better in the Great Plains and the Far West). There remains scope for the improvement of the predictive power of location models. (However, Lösch's theory relates the spacing of towns to the number of basic functions in these towns, not to town populations; central place theory does not necessarily predict a close relationship between town population and town spacing.)

Several studies have traced the relationship between the population of a place and the number of functions within it. The evidence came from a variety of areas: southern Illinois (Stafford, 1963), Canterbury, New Zealand (King, 1961a), Tasmania (Scott, 1964), Snohomish County, Washington (Berry and

Garrison, 1958a), and southern Ceylon (Gunawardena, 1964). Large centres contain a greater range of service functions than small centres: the relationship between size and number of functions is curvilinear—as settlements become larger they add fewer functions for each increment of population. These relationships, with correlation coefficients between $r = +0.7$ and $r = +0.9$, are broadly compatible with central place theory.

Although it is difficult to make accurate comparisons between predictions and reality, because of heterogeneity, central place theory probably understates the number of service functions contained within a place. Lösch, in constructing his total pattern for society, merely adds the various nets of market areas together; if several production points coincide, a town is formed. That is, the resultant pattern does not allow for the fact that the production points themselves have to be served by low order sellers. This understatement by theory is greater the larger the central place and the lower the order of the good. Similarly a place contains functions which can be supported by the combined population of the place and its hinterland but not by the hinterland alone. This error is larger the greater is the population of the place in relation to the total population of the market area. It follows also that empirical studies of existing town hierarchies have not been testing central place theory but some, as yet unformulated, variant upon it. As far as central place theory is concerned, place size is defined as the number of basic service functions within a town, not necessarily as the total number of functions in the town.

Duncan (1959) makes a related point. During a statistical study of some service industries in the United States, he found that many activities are limited to larger towns even though they do not appear to sell goods to smaller towns in the hinterlands. Thus, telephone answering services occur only in cities with a population more than 25,000, but these services are unlikely to serve a non-local clientele. Similarly, parking lots and garages were only apparent in towns of more than 60,000 people, yet these services are clearly not sold outside the town. Duncan concludes that the continuing specialisation and differentiation of cities which accompany increasing size is only partly explainable by the principles of central place theory (which assumes that all services are sold outside the town). He suggests that three other principles are necessary to account for the observations he made: (i) that a larger city has more needs than a small one; (ii) that in larger cities some specialised agencies take over functions performed by households in small cities; and (iii) that in larger cities, the service portions of 'sales and service' firms separate from sales activities as functions become more specialised.

This review of central place theory suggests that the model does not account for the formation of towns. Similarly, predictions of the theory about the size and spacing of towns and the functions contained within them, although helpful, are subject to error. In some areas, the size of places accounts for up to one-third of the variations in their spacing, while the actual location of places on the ground appears random rather than even. These unexplained residuals have usually been ascribed to the heterogeneity of the earth's surface.

Dacey (1966a) has formulated a central place model which takes heterogeneity directly into account. Theory supposes that places have hexagonal market areas; but really such market areas cannot exist because no hexagonal lattice can completely cover the earth's surface. Dacey therefore incorporates in his model a displacement of the places by a random vector, where the angular and distance components of the vector are random variables. The model assumes an even distribution of places and then subjects these places to a 'shock', which causes random displacement. An empirical test of the model against the distribution of the seventy-nine largest places in Iowa indicates a relatively good fit to the data, but large displacements from the equilibrium are necessary to obtain this fit.

An alternative method of dealing with heterogeneity has been proposed by Tobler (1963). Tobler suggests that uniformity assumptions be adapted to the uneven world surface by transforming distance into non-Euclidean space. Thus, Euclidean space might be transformed so that all cells on the map had equal income or equal population density. Maps showing the states of the U.S.A. with areas proportional to population provide a crude example of such transforms. The technique is then to test central place theory on a surface transformed so that resources are evenly distributed over the new map surface.

A third possibility argues that if the heterogeneous surface of the earth has as great an effect on theory as the evidence indicates, then it might be profitable to build heterogeneity directly into the location model. Lösch argued that his theory was more general because it was based on homogeneity, but it is clear that a theory would predict more accurately and be more general if it could be solved for a generalised distribution of non-homogeneous resources, especially if the non-homogeneity assumptions induce qualitative changes in the nature of location decisions. Central place theory would be a special case of such a model.

The third means of attacking heterogeneity is more attractive than the first two. As Dacey (1966a) has pointed out, his model contains no theoretical justification for departures from the equilibrium, nor are there (yet) good theoretical interpretations of the parameters of the model. Tobler's suggestion about the use of map transforms may not be operational because when transforming distance to obtain an even distribution of population, the map loses other relationships, such as hexagonal market areas and even distances between cities (Tobler, 1963); several transformations are necessary at the same time. Accordingly, some later analyses construct models of location under assumptions of heterogeneity, while interdependence theory also assumes bounded markets.

Interdependence Theory

The group of models considered in this section explores the location decisions of firms as they are modified by competition with other firms. As in central place theory, these models abstract from costs, but whereas Lösch attempted to find the best pattern of location from the point of view of society, the interdependence models show how optimum behaviour by firms may result in socially non-

D

Figure 2–9: **Spatial relationships in a linear market**

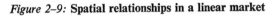
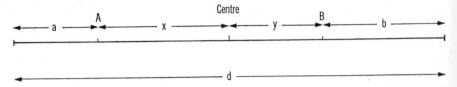

optimal behaviour. The results of these models thus constitute a criticism of central place theory: it is shown to be unlikely that a locational equilibrium is a socially optimum pattern. Central place theory does not show how the decision-making process produces the best location pattern.

In this discussion we shall review the models of Hotelling (1929) and Smithies (1941) in detail, while the contributions of other writers in this field are examined more briefly. The seminal paper was that of Hotelling; the ideas in this paper were criticised, discussed, and modified until 1941, when Smithies's paper summarised and organised the model. Except for one or two instances (e.g. Neutze, 1960, 1967; Greenhut, 1956; and Devletoglou, 1965), little use has been made of these models in location theory, largely because their conclusions are at odds with reality. Beyond their historical importance the models are useful because they provide one criticism of central place theory, because they illustrate some necessary assumptions, because they provide one key to the mechanism of town formation, and because they offer a framework within which to discuss external economies.

Hotelling assumes that buyers are spread uniformly along a line of length d, that buyers pay transport costs (of c per unit distance), that there are zero costs of production, that unit quantities of the good are consumed per unit of time per unit of distance, and that buyers prefer sellers only on the grounds of nearness. There are two sellers on the line, A and B. A's price is p_1 and he sells quantity q_1, while B sells q_2 at price p_2. Spatial relationships are shown in Fig. 2–9.

The point separating the market areas of A and B occurs where

(2–7) $p_1 + cx = p_2 + cy.$

But $a + x + y + b = d.$

Hence $x = \tfrac{1}{2}\left(d - a - b + \dfrac{p_2 - p_1}{c} \right)$

and $y = \tfrac{1}{2}\left(d - a - b + \dfrac{p_1 - p_2}{c} \right).$

Consequently the profits of the two firms are given by

(2–8) $\pi_1 = p_1 q_1$

$= p_1(a + x)$

$= \tfrac{1}{2}(d + a - b)p_1 - \dfrac{p_1^2}{2c} + \dfrac{p_1 p_2}{2c},$

and

(2–9)
$$\pi_2 = p_2 q_2$$
$$= p_2(b+y)$$
$$= \tfrac{1}{2}(d-a+b)p_2 - \frac{p_2^2}{2c} + \frac{p_1 p_2}{2c}.$$

Hotelling assumes that each competitor adjusts his price so that, at the existing price of the other, his own profit is at a maximum. That is, the firms assume that their actions call forth no reaction from their rival. Under this condition maximum profits are given by:

(2–10)
$$\frac{d\pi_1}{dp_1} = \tfrac{1}{2}(d+a-b) - \frac{p_1}{c} + \frac{p_2}{2c} = 0$$

and

(2–11)
$$\frac{d\pi_2}{dp_2} = \tfrac{1}{2}(d-a+b) + \frac{p_1}{2c} - \frac{p_2}{c} = 0,$$

for the second derivatives are clearly negative. Consequently equilibrium prices and quantities are defined by

(2–12)
$$p_1 = c\left(d + \frac{a-b}{3}\right)$$
$$p_2 = c\left(d - \frac{a-b}{3}\right)$$

and

(2–13)
$$q_1 = a + x = \tfrac{1}{2}\left(d + \frac{a-b}{3}\right)$$
$$q_2 = b + y = \tfrac{1}{2}\left(d - \frac{a-b}{3}\right).$$

By substitution we see that

(2–14)
$$\pi_2 = \frac{c}{2}\left(d + \frac{b-a}{3}\right)^2$$

at the equilibrium. The problem of location may now be examined: if A is fixed, where does B set up shop? Since π_2 increases with b, B must make b as large as possible: that is, he locates adjacent to A, on the side nearer the centre. But when B is fixed, A wishes to make a as large as possible: he locates next to B, on the side nearer the centre. The two leap-frog in this manner until the centre is reached, when no move is profitable. By contrast, the socially optimum location occurs at the quartiles, when the firms are regularly spaced (as in central place theory).

This model provides one mechanism whereby towns might be formed. But some of its assumptions are highly unrealistic. An oft-criticised condition is that a unit quantity is consumed per unit of time at each point on the line. This implies that demand is absolutely inelastic or, as Lerner and Singer (1937) suggest, that consumers have infinite incomes. A further criticism of the conditions is made by Lösch (1959: 72-5): it is highly unlikely that a duopolist would imagine that his

33

√ pricing and location policies have no effect on the policies of his competitor. Lerner and Singer also show that Hotelling's conclusion that sellers locate at the centre of the market cannot apply to more than two sellers, for if (say) three sellers locate at the centre, the middle one can then make no sales. (However, this problem can be easily overcome by the assumption of a spatial market.) Smithies's (1941) discussion takes the first two of these criticisms into account.

Smithies makes eight structural assumptions. These are (i) that there is a linear bounded market; (ii) that there exists an identical linear demand function at all points in the market; (iii) that two competing firms sell on a f.o.b. mill basis; (iv) that marginal costs are equal and zero; (v) that freight rates are uniform over the market and are the same for each firm; (vi) that firms are free to change locations instantaneously and without cost; (vii) that firms attempt to maximise profits; and (viii) that the size of the market and the costs of transport are such that sales can be made in all points of the market.

Within this environment, Smithies considers four possible situations. The first (A) is monopolistic. The second (B) exists if each firm assumes that its actions provoke an equal reaction from its competitor. The third (C) occurs when each firm supposes that its actions provoke an equal price reaction but no location reaction from its competitor. The fourth (D) situation obtains when each firm assumes no reaction at all from the other when it acts. These are clearly extreme situations, but they probably encompass actual assumptions of firms.

Examine first the conditions for equilibrium. (A): the monopolist locates in the centre, in order to minimise the loss of profits due to freight costs. If he has two plants they are located at the quartiles. (B): if a firm invades the other's territory, it loses sales in its hinterland (because of higher transport costs there), but because the other is expected to react equally, it can anticipate no gain from the invasions; these two firms locate at the quartiles. Greenhut (1956: 143-6) agrees with these conclusions. (C): each firm anticipates that moving towards the centre will enable it to gain at the expense of the other. They therefore locate closer to the centre than the quartiles. (D): the two firms think that moving towards the centre and cutting prices offers them a competitive advantage over their rival. Equilibrium occurs when the firms are nearer the centre than in (C), but they still have equal prices and equal territories.

Smithies then analyses the effect of freight rates on location decisions. He finds that the important variable is s, defined as the ratio of the cost of sending one unit of good the whole length of the market to the price intercept of the demand curve. In cases (A) and (B) location is fixed at the quartiles, so s affects prices and profits only. Firms absorb some of the freight rate and pass some on to consumers, so that prices and profits fall as s rises. In cases (C) and (D), the greater is s, the greater are the losses in the hinterland and the lower are the gains due to invasion of the other's territory. Hence the higher is s, the nearer the quartiles do the sellers locate.

Smithies's analysis demonstrates that under the normal conditions of an elastic demand curve and non-zero transport costs, two competitors separate.

They locate nearer the quartiles the greater the extent to which they assume equal reactions from competitors, the higher the freight rate in relation to the price intercept of the demand curve, and the higher are marginal costs. Hotelling's model does not provide a mechanism for town formation under Smithies's more realistic conditions.

Hotelling's argument has been taken up more recently by Neutze (1960, summarised 1967). He makes similar structural assumptions to Smithies, though with three exceptions. The first is that the market is circular, the second is that incomes in the market are rising, and the third difference is that locations, once chosen, are fixed. When demand becomes sufficient to support a seller, that seller locates at the centre of the market, as Smithies suggests. Eventually demand becomes sufficient for the market to support two sellers. Neutze indicates that the only point at which the second seller is able to gain one-half of the market is the centre. He argues that both sellers therefore locate at the centre of the market and form an embryo town.

But this argument is only partially correct. If the second seller locates some distance away from the first (central) seller, he cannot gain one-half of the market; however, sellers are then on average nearer to their customers than if they locate together, and consequently total demand and sales are larger. The second seller, by locating off-centre, enlarges the total sales of both sellers: his less than half share of these enlarged total sales is normally greater for some location away from the centre than half the smaller sales which he can obtain by locating at the centre. Neutze's argument only holds if the second firm wishes to maximise its share of the market or if, when maximising total profits, external economies at the centre are sufficiently valuable to counter greater sales away from the centre. If there are no external economies and firms maximise profits, it can readily be shown for a linear market that the optimum price and location policy of the second firm implies an off-centre location.

Greenhut (1956: 147-8) has summarised the argument so far. Industrial agglomeration is partly determined by four main factors. These are (i) the shape of the demand curve: an infinitely inelastic demand curve promotes concentration, while a more elastic demand curve encourages dispersal; (ii) the slope of the marginal cost curves: negatively sloping marginal cost curves strengthen tendencies towards dispersion whereas positively sloping cost curves promote agglomeration; (iii) freight rates: freight rates are positively associated with the degree of dispersion; and (iv) degree of competition: the greater the belief among firms that their actions will be met by equal reactions from rivals, the more those firms disperse. The models indicate dispersal of firms under normal conditions of these elements.

Sellers of the first good are therefore more or less evenly spread over the market. Neutze takes the argument one stage further by investigating the location of sellers of a second good. Two possibilities exist. The first is that these later sellers wish to locate at every second (or third, or fourth, . . .) location of the first sellers, thus forming a set of agglomerations. Figure 2–10A illustrates the condi-

35

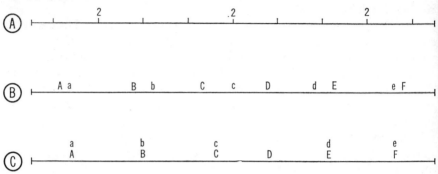

Figure 2–10: Agglomeration in a linear market. In (A) there are nine firms in industry 1; the three firms in industry 2 always locate near a firm in 1. In (B) firms in the two industries are separate; but Neutze argues that agglomeration economies cause (C) rather than (B) to occur.

tion. This possibility is much less likely than the second, in which the ratio of the number of first order sellers to the number of second order sellers is not an integer, so that not all the second sellers can locate near to first sellers. Figure 2–10B illustrates this case, where the optimum patterns of the two sets of sellers have been plotted independently. There are six sellers, $A, B, \ldots, F$, of the first good and five sellers, $a, b, \ldots, e$, of the second good. No location choices coincide. Neutze argues that agglomeration economies are sufficiently great to cause the five later sellers to mould their choices to the pattern of the earlier sellers, perhaps as illustrated in Fig. 2–10C. A further adjustment must be made to this third pattern: if seller b can exist profitably, then a sixth later seller locates at D. To test this model probably requires empirical measurement of the value of agglomeration economies in relation to transport costs.

The analysis of interdependence has recently been augmented by Devletoglou (1965). He makes the usual maximisation assumptions about the behaviour of consumers and sellers, except that some distances are too small to affect consumers' decisions: an indifference *area* rather than an indifference *line* separates the market areas of the sellers. Then in any areal market (Fig. 2–11) the zone of indifference is bounded by a hyperbola. If both firms locate at the centre of the market, the entire market lies within the indifference area, whereas if the firms separate, the indifference area becomes smaller. Firms have an incentive to separate for then they are more certain about their share of the market. Furthermore, as firms separate they reduce the area within which consumers are subject to fashion effects and so reduce the costs of maintaining inventories.

The analysis of interdependent location policies indicates that firms selling the same good should normally separate if they are to obtain maximum profits. Firms repel other firms. As in central place theory, a pattern evolves in which any one location (shopping centre) contains only one firm which sells a given good: unlike central place theory, the predicted pattern may be socially non-optimal.

Figure 2–11: **Division of market in Devletoglou's indifference zone model.**
   Source: Devletoglou (1965).

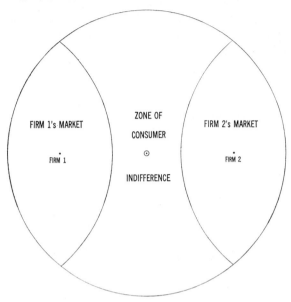

Fig. 2–12: **Effect of resources on location.**
   Source: Greenhut (1956: 60-5).

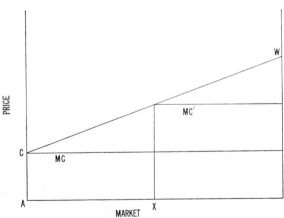

But the conclusion remains seriously at odds with reality, and some of the assumptions must therefore be altered.

Although, like central place theory, the interdependence theory of location abstracts from costs, spatial variations in processing costs can be readily built into the models. Greenhut (1956: 60-5) indicates one method whereby this may be done. Assume, in Fig. 2–12, that several firms at A produce with constant marginal costs MC. For a firm at X, marginal costs are MC'. Transport costs from A to the market are represented by CW. Should a firm locate at X it cuts off some of the market area of the firms at A. If the A firms lower their prices to meet this competition from X, prices are represented by CW along the market: no firm makes profits. But if marginal costs at X are less than the delivered price of A's goods at X, X makes a profit and cuts off the firms at A. Thus, given a low cost producing centre and a higher cost producing centre within a linear market, conditions for the dispersal of firms can be precisely stated. Where the marginal costs of production increase with distance from the established centre less rapidly than freight costs, firms disperse, provided that they compete actively to attain control over proximate markets.

Such an analysis offers one means of making interdependence models predict reality more closely. But spatial variation in marginal costs of production may not greatly modify the accuracy of the predictions of the interdependence models. In manufacturing firms, costs do vary widely over space, but in retailing, to which the interdependence models were meant to apply, costs seem to vary but little over space. For example, George (1966) has found that productivity in retailing in the United Kingdom is unrelated to the size of town. It is unlikely that cost factors in retailing are a prime cause of either the fact or the extent of agglomeration. The abstraction from costs in these models may not be very important in so far as they refer to retailing.

Even so, the models of the location of sellers of the same good are unsatisfactory as predictors of reality. Possibly the difficulty arises because they consider one good in isolation from others—if the location of firms of different types was analysed, agglomeration economies (arising from demand factors) might become more important. Certainly, the impact of multiple purpose trips on location choices has as yet received little attention in theoretical studies. A more realistic model, then, must analyse the effect of multiple purpose tripping on location, but more especially, it must investigate the effect of possible future agglomeration economies on the location of sellers.

A further necessity, revealed especially by Neutze's model, is that of determining boundary conditions for the finite market. The size of the market is vital in determining the extent of agglomeration, yet its effect has not been fully examined. Theory must analyse the impact of the size of the market and the way in which firms choose among different bounded markets. It may also be useful to envisage the bounded market and the unbounded plain as being two extreme conditions. Best results may be obtained by visualising both as special cases of the more general partially bounded market.

Conclusions on the Classical Analysis of Points
The classical theory of point location is one of the most fully developed portions of the body of location theory. Important results have been derived from it.

Weber's model of industrial location indicates that industries tend to locate near their raw materials or near their markets, depending on the size of the material index. Although the assumptions under which this conclusion is derived are questionable, the principle has broad applicability as a coarse index of location. Similarly the model points out that agglomeration economies are an important reason for the growth of towns. From central place theory are obtained conclusions about the effects of town size on the size of the market area, the spacing and the number of functions within towns, conclusions which have been empirically verified in some parts of the world. Interdependence theory throws light on the effects of competition from other firms on location decisions and shows how like firms tend to repel one another.

But, although the models are applicable to a wide variety of situations, they have not yet been integrated into a general model. Thus, there are monopolistic competition models and models assuming non-homogeneous environments, but no models incorporating both; there are models investigating cost factors and models investigating the effects of demand on location, but no models which effectively bring the cost and demand approaches together. Isard (1956) has made a partial graphical synthesis of agglomeration and scale economies and central place theory, and Greenhut (1956) has a graphical analysis of the effects of cost variations in interdependence models. But these are isolated attempts, and at best provide only partial syntheses. A realistic general theory of location must join these separate strands together more closely. Such a theory may provide deeper insights into the reasons for the formation of towns.

Perhaps a more severe limitation upon the usefulness of these point models is the fact that they have not been empirically verified or contradicted. Stevens and Brackett imply such a problem: ' . . . it is difficult to generate testable hypotheses from existing theory' (Stevens and Brackett, 1967: 7); and I (Webber, 1971) have detailed this argument with respect to central place theory. In testing a theory, we attempt to determine whether or not people actually behave in a manner or similar to that which the theory predicts. This may be accomplished either by observing actual behaviour or else by finding an area where the environmental conditions hold and then deciding whether the predictions of the theory do occur. (None of the empirical studies mentioned in this chapter has tested point theories in this sense.) The problem of testability arises because it is difficult to observe behaviour directly, while the environmental assumptions are too simplified ever to approximate reality.

All the point location models described in this chapter make assumptions about rationality in decision taking (locations are chosen either to maximise profits or to minimise costs), about firms' cost curves, and about agglomeration economies. None of these behavioural assumptions can be tested empirically. A rational location pattern may arise either if firms make rational decisions or if society 'chooses' those firms which are in the best locations from among the total number of firms which set up business: thus, observation upon individual decision taking is invalidated as a test of the theory. The assumptions about cost curves and agglomeration economies can only be examined by observing the level of costs in firms as size and location change. But, as Malmgren (1958) and Neutze (1960: 108-11) point out, such observations cannot be made because inter-firm comparisons of costs confound the effects of size with many other factors.

Testing is therefore forced to rely upon the alternative stratagem, of finding an area where the environmental conditions hold and determining whether the predictions of the theory do, in fact, occur. I have demonstrated (in Webber, 1971) that the heterogeneity of the earth's surface makes it almost, if not (in the future) entirely, impossible to test central place theory in this manner. A similar comment may clearly be made about the implication of a linear, bounded, homogeneous environment for the testing of interdependence theory. Although Weber assumes a heterogeneous environment, nevertheless that environment is unrealistic, in that it is assumed that the locations of raw materials, consumption points, and labour are given data and that these locations are unaffected by firms' decisions. It has so far proved impossible to manipulate space in such a manner that these forms of environmental assumption can be made to approximate reality.

Thus, although implicit testing of these theories has been attempted, that empirical work does not satisfy the conditions which are necessary if these theories of point location are to be verified or contradicted. The models must be developed theoretically before they can be properly tested. The difficulty arises because point models, based upon notions of individual decision taking, cannot make large-scale predictions about location patterns without the aid of gross simplifying environmental assumptions. Any further development of micro-location theory must attempt to solve this problem.

Probability Models for Point Distributions
Partly in response to the difficulties of empirically verifying classical micro-economic location theory, a new approach to location analysis has been developed in the last decade. Rather than examine the manner in which individual decision taking determines the formation and location of towns, this approach attempts to define the general forces which govern the pattern of towns. By excluding individual decision taking, the models avoid the necessity of assuming a simplified environment, and so, superficially at least, the problem of testability does not arise. The method consists in assuming a set of forces which determine the distribution of towns and deriving probability laws for town patterns from these assumptions. The probability laws may relate either to the distances between towns or to the number of towns in a randomly located quadrat. The first method is more accurate, the second is simpler, both analytically and for empirical work.

A point pattern may be classified initially as belonging to one of three kinds of distribution. The simplest case is a completely random distribution, when the location of one place has no effect on the location of any other place. The second class of models describes patterns which are more clustered than random—as if, for example, agglomeration economies induced the location of several additional places around each original place. Thirdly, distributions may be more regular than random: central place processes would create such a distribution.

Consider first a model of a completely random distribution of places. Assume that the plain is divided into equal area regions, and that on average r places occur within each region. If (i) the probability that a place is located at a point is the same all over the plain, (ii) the location of one place has absolutely no effect on the location of any other place, and (iii) two or more places cannot locate on exactly the same point, then the probability that a region contains n places is given by the Poisson distribution:

$$(2\text{-}15) \qquad Pr(n) = e^{-r}\left(\frac{r^n}{n!}\right), n = 0, 1, \ldots .$$

Dacey (1964a) contains a formal statement of the assumptions and a derivation of this model.

The distribution may arise in several ways. The simplest occurs when the places are initially laid out in accordance with the assumptions of the model, and then not altered. If the places are originally distributed according to the Poisson, and then individually and independently exposed to a risk of extermination, or if the original places are augmented by additional places located randomly, then the resulting distribution retains the Poisson form. Alternatively, if the original places are uniformly distributed, but then they are independently exposed to a serious risk of failure and elimination, the distribution tends to a Poisson form (see Skellam, 1952). The model can accommodate several different histories of town formation and decline; even so, the model has proved to be of very little use in describing actual distributions of towns. The main cause of this finding is the assumption that places are independently located: we would expect that the location of one town affects the location of other towns, either repelling them (for service functions) or attracting them (because of agglomeration economies or resource localisation). Interdependent town locations destroy the basis of the Poisson model.

The main use of the Poisson model in location analysis has been as a base against which patterns are compared to determine their degree of regularity or clustering. Assume that places are randomly distributed, with a mean of m places per unit area; then, if $\lambda = \pi m$, the probability distribution of distances, r_n, from one place to its nth nearest neighbour is

$$(2\text{-}16) \qquad Pr(r_n) = \frac{2\lambda^n(e^{-\lambda r_n^2})(r_n^{2n-1})}{(n-1)!},$$

with a mean value of

$$(2\text{-}17) \qquad E(r_n) = \frac{1}{\sqrt{m}}\frac{(2n)!n}{(2^n . n!)^2}$$

(Thompson, 1956; Dacey, 1964a). A comparison of equation (2–16) with the observed distribution of distances between towns and their nth nearest neighbours yields a simple test of regularity: a clustered distribution has a lower mean distance than a random, while a regular distribution has the highest mean distance separating nth nearest neighbours. Some uses of this technique have been outlined in the discussion of central place theory.

Clark (1956) has outlined an alternative technique based upon nearest neighbour analysis. In k-dimensional space, consider the point X_0 and its first, second, ..., nth nearest neighbours, $X_1, X_2, \ldots, X_n$. The relation of nth nearest neighbour is reflexive for X_0 if X_n is closer to X_0 than to any other points except $X_1, X_2, \ldots, X_{n-1}$. Clark shows that for randomly distributed places, the proportion of points for which the nth nearest neighbour relation is reflexive in one-dimensional space is $(2/3)^n$, and in two-dimensional space is

$$(2\text{--}18) \qquad 2Pn = \left(\frac{6\pi}{8\pi+3^{1.5}}\right)^n.$$

In clustered distributions, the proportion is higher than this; in regular distributions, the proportion falls. Dacey (1960b) used the one-dimensional relation to show that the spacing of river towns along the Mississippi River is clustered rather than random.

The second set of distributions—those more clustered than random—has a common base. Assume first that $p(z)$, the number of 'parent' places in a quadrat, has a Poisson distribution. Suppose further that around each parent place there develops a number of dependent, or 'offspring' places; $q(z)$ is the number of dependent places in a cell (note that the number of dependent places in a cell depends in part on the number of parent places in that cell). Then the probability distribution of the total number of places per quadrat is

$$(2\text{--}19) \qquad P(n) = \sum_{i=0}^{n} \Pr\{p(i)\} \cdot \Pr\{q(n-i)|p(i)\}, \, n = 0, 1, \ldots.$$

Each of the four models described here makes slightly different assumptions about the probability law which governs the number of dependent places per parent (Skellam, 1952; Harvey, 1966a).

Perhaps the simplest of these models is the Thomas Double Poisson (Thomas, 1949). Thomas assumes that the distribution of offspring places follows a Poisson form (equation (2–15)) when the probability that there exist k places in any given quadrat is

$$P(0) = e^{-m}$$
$$(2\text{--}20) \qquad P(k) = \sum_{r=1}^{k} \left(\frac{m^r e^{-m}}{r!}\right)\left(\frac{(r\lambda)^{k-r}e^{-r\lambda}}{(k-r)!}\right), \, k = 1, 2, \ldots.$$

In equation (2–20), m is the mean number of parent places per quadrat and λ is the mean number of dependants per parent. If, on the other hand, the parent dies when the offspring places develop and the number of offspring per parent follows the Poisson distribution, then the probability of finding k places in any given quadrat follows the Neyman Type A distribution (Neyman, 1939):

$$(2\text{--}21) \qquad P(k) = \frac{\lambda^k}{k!}e^{-m} \sum_{r=0}^{\infty} \frac{r^k}{r!} (e^{-\lambda}m)^r, \, k = 1, 2, \ldots.$$

If, thirdly, the number of offspring per parent follows the logarithmic distribution, then the number of places per quadrat is described by the negative binomial distribution (Anscombe, 1950; Evans, 1953):

$$(2\text{--}22) \qquad P(k) = \binom{k+j-1}{k-1} p^j (1-p)^k, \, k = 1, 2, \ldots,$$

with, by the method of moments,

$$(2\text{--}23) \qquad p = \bar{x}/s(x) \quad \text{and} \quad k = \bar{x}p/(1-p)$$

($\bar{x}$ is the mean and $s(x)$ the variance of the observed distribution of points per cluster). Fourthly, the Polya-Aeppli distribution is used to describe patterns in which the number of offspring places per parent follows the geometric distribution:

$$P(0) = e^{-m}$$

$$(2\text{--}24) \qquad P(k) = e^{-m} \left(\frac{\lambda-1}{\lambda}\right)^k \sum_{r=1}^{k} \binom{k-1}{r-1} \frac{1}{r!} \left(\frac{m}{\lambda-1}\right), \, k = 1, 2, \ldots.$$

Although the intuitive meaning of these models has been couched in terms of the ecological processes of parents and offspring (for which processes the models were originally formulated), the distributions can be readily interpreted in locational terms. One such interpretation is that a place, once developed, encourages the formation of other places nearby: for example, sub-contracting firms may cluster around a large firm which purchases semi-processed components. Alternatively, the contagious model may describe a process which arises from resource localisation: if the area provides a good site for one town, by virtue of local resources, it is also likely to provide good sites for alternative towns. Similarly, within an urban area, a site which is attractive to one firm is also likely to attract others which require similar transport facilities, labour force, and land values. In these applications, the initial attractive facility (purchasing firm, resource, transport advantage) is assumed to be located completely at random (with locations described by a Poisson distribution), while the size of the cluster of secondary firms or towns is assumed to be defined by the second distribution (Poisson, logarithmic or geometric). Contagious distributions, then, seem applicable to the analysis of places (or firms) which rely on manufacturing activity to determine their location. But apparently no empirical work has tested such an hypothesis.

The third class of distributions, point patterns more regular than random, has received more attention in the geographic literature than the previous two classes. Three distributions are important: they are based either on a one-step process in which conditions vary over space, or on a mixture of regular and random components.

First, if the study area consists of several sub-regions, within each of which the pattern of places is described by a Poisson distribution, and if the mean of these distributions varies between regions according to the gamma distribution, then the total pattern of places in the study area is defined by the negative binomial probability law (equation (2–22)). In addition to these contagious and compound models, Feller describes several other processes which generate the negative binomial distribution (Feller, 1957: 143, 164ff., 450). The fact that several processes, very different in their locational implications, can each give rise to this same probability law poses a key problem in the interpretation of empirical results (Harvey, 1968a). As Skellam (1952) has observed, while the derivation of probability models from assumed causes creates little logical concern, the reverse process, of inferring a cause from the empirical distribution, is much more dangerous. The negative binomial has been used to describe a variety of data— of innovation adopters in Sweden (Harvey, 1966a), of houses in Puerto Rico (Dacey, 1968), and of shopping goods stores in Stockholm (Rogers, 1965)—but much of the robust character of the distribution may be due in part to its being derivable from opposite sets of circumstances (Harvey, 1968a). Rogers, for example, was unable to distinguish which process, the contagious or the inhomogeneous Poisson, had generated the observed pattern of shopping goods stores in Stockholm.

Dacey (1964b) has derived a second probability model for relatively regular point patterns by adding two independent processes. He assumes first that each county has the same probability, p, of receiving a county seat: the regularity in this model thus arises from the political fact that no county can contain more than one county seat. The remaining towns in the region are distributed among counties in accordance with the Poisson distribution. The probability that any county contains x towns is given by:

$$(2\text{--}25) \qquad P(x) = (qa^x e^{-a}/x!) + (pxa^{x-1}e^{-a}/x!), \quad x = 0, 1, \ldots,$$

where $q = (1-p)$ and a is the mean number of non-county seat places per county. In testing the model against the distribution of places of more than 2500 people in Iowa, over the period 1840 to 1960, Dacey found extremely good fits for all years, with p increasing from 0·008 in 1840 to 0·830 in 1960.

But the model only operates efficiently in areas which are homogeneous, for the parameters p and a are assumed to remain constant over the region. Dacey (1966b) has constructed a third model which assumes areal inhomogeneity. He assumes that the parameter a varies according to the gamma distribution while p has a beta distribution over the region. Then the probability that a county contains x places is given by the sum of two negative binomial distributions:

$$(2\text{--}26) \qquad P(x) = (1-s)\frac{(k+x-1)!}{x!(k-1)!}v^k(1-v)^x + s\frac{(k+x-2)!}{(x-1)!(k-1)!}v^k(1-v)^{x-1},$$

where k, v, and s are parameters to be estimated. Like the previous law, this model is designed to describe the pattern of service centres in rural areas rather than in densely populated regions, because the mechanism is dispersal not contagion. Dacey discovered that the model described accurately town distributions in a 10 per cent sample of rural counties in the United States and in six trans-Mississippi states.

These probability laws comprise regular and random components; the question arises, then, of determining the relative importance of regular and random components in a point pattern. Dacey's models are too restrictive to permit this determination, because they assume a maximum of one 'regular' place per county. Medvedkov (1966) presents a more general method for measuring the regular and random components of a rural settlement pattern. The number, i, of points in each quadrat is counted; m_i is the number of quadrats which contain i points. Then the probability of finding a quadrat with i points in it is

(2–27) $\qquad P_i = m_i/Q,$

where Q is the total number of quadrats. Medvedkov uses equation (2–27) to define the total amount of information (H) in the settlement pattern:

(2–28) $\qquad H = -\sum_{i=1}^{n} (P_i \log_2 P_i);$

n is the total number of point density levels exhibited by the region. For a completely uniform (central place) field, $m_i = Q$; hence $P_i = 1$ and $n = 1$, and consequently $H = 0$. For a completely random field (distributed according to the Poisson),

(2–29) $\qquad H = -\sum_{D} \left(\frac{a^D}{D!}e^{-a}\right) \cdot \log_2 \left(\frac{a^D}{D!}e^{-a}\right)$

$\qquad\qquad \simeq 1 \cdot 95 + 1 \cdot 46 \log a + 0 \cdot 19 (\log a)^2,$

where a is the mean number of points per cell. Now, if a completely random pattern is superimposed upon a completely regular pattern, the resulting observed value of H is due solely to the Poisson component; therefore, by substituting the observed value of H in equation (2–29), the value of a (the mean number of randomly distributed points per cell) can be determined. The difference between m (the mean number of points per cell) and a is the mean number of regularly distributed places per cell.

This technique represents a useful first approach to the problem of separating regular and random components in a settlement pattern. But the model contains two flaws. First, a perfectly regular central place system does not contain an equal number of places in each square quadrat: the number of places is equal in hexagonal regions. More importantly, the model is unduly restrictive in supposing that the central place element of the settlement pattern is perfectly represented: the model would gain generality if the regular component in the pattern could be imperfectly represented.

Both Medvedkov's technique and Dacey's homogeneous county seat model can be incorporated within a more general model for patterns more regular than random. Suppose that an area is divided into n hexagonal regions. The area contains l places from a hypothetical perfect central place system which has m places per region ($l \leqslant mn$). These l places represent the imperfectly realised central place system. In addition, j towns in the area are distributed completely

45

at random. Then the probability that a region contains s places is

$$(2\text{-}30) \qquad P(s) = \sum_{k=0}^{z} \binom{m}{k} \binom{mn-m}{1-k} \binom{mn}{1}^{-1} e^{-j/n} \frac{(j/n)^{s-k}}{(s-k)!}, s = 0, 1, \ldots.$$

(Note that z is the minimum of m, s.) At $m = 1$, the model collapses into Dacey's county seat model. At $l = mn$, all the central places are present, and the model takes the form of a Poisson distribution plus a constant: Medvedkov's case. The parameters of the model may be readily interpreted: l/m is the proportion of the hypothetical central place system which is actually present, that is, the degree of 'perfection' of the actual central place system; and $l/(l+j)$ is the proportion of all places which are central places—that is the degree of regularity of the system.

Thus a variety of models is available to describe different forms of location pattern. Such curve fitting therefore has considerable descriptive value. But the analytic power of the technique has not been fully realised yet. There seem two main ways in which this curve fitting could prove useful.

Firstly, as quadrat size is altered, so the parameters of the models vary and the goodness of fit of the models changes. Such scale effects have yet to be analysed to determine the appropriate level upon which the models operate. Dacey's county seat models contain a built-in cell size—the county—but the other models discussed do not; yet, as Harvey (1968b) points out, the potentially important identification of scale and process by probability model fitting has received little attention.

Secondly, partly as a consequence of the multiplicity of models and of the experimental nature of this form of location analysis, it seems that no one has analysed the relationship between the parameters of a model and the parameters of the region being studied. In a contagious model for economic processes, what factors in the economic and physical environment are correlated with the mean number of parent towns per cell and the mean number of offspring towns per cluster? Similarly, can we correlate variability in the landscape with the degree of randomness in a rural settlement pattern? Given an equation relating inhomogeneity and the imperfection of the central place system, it may be possible to determine what pattern of rural settlement would occur in the limit of absolute homogeneity. Such work could form a major contribution to location analysis.

But these probability models, though capable of predicting actual location patterns, must remain of marginal interest to location theorists. One difficulty has already been discussed: the fact that some of the models may be interpreted in terms of several different location processes. More important is the property that these models have no explicit economic content: the nature of the economic processes which could generate such models is not specified. For example, Curry points out that a model which assumes completely random point patterns 'is neutral as to rationality . . . every decision may be optimal from a particular point of view and yet the resulting actions as a whole may appear as random' (Curry, 1964: 138). One of the most interesting and important facets of location theory— the nexus between individual behaviour and social location patterns—is completely ignored by these probability models. Until such models can be more closely related to economic processes, they must remain of limited usefulness to location theory.

Conclusions

The models described in this chapter provide several potential reasons for the formation and growth of towns. Weberian theory suggests that towns function initially as sites for agglomerated manufacturing industries; Lösch argues that towns operate primarily as service centres, whose locations are determined by social optimising forces; Hotelling's model visualises the growth of towns as the product of competitive behaviour by interdependent service firms. None of the models provides a reason for the formation of towns, though they do imply mechanisms of growth and hypotheses about the primary functions of points. Unfortunately, neither direct data nor the probability models provide incontrovertible evidence about the respective merits of these theories.

Similar conflicts about town origins characterise historical studies. Perhaps the most closely studied era of town formation is medieval Europe, but there are several interpretations of town formation in this period. Thus, Pirenne (1936: 40-57) argues that medieval towns originally comprised groups of merchants who were engaged in long distance trade; artisans later collected around the merchants in order to use the materials which they had imported. Mumford (1961: 248-56), on the other hand, suggests that medieval towns arose primarily as defensive sites; within them there then developed a market for the exchange of local agricultural and handicraft production; and finally, these developments gave rise to long distance trade. Thirdly, Ennen (1956) divides Europe into three regions: (a) the north German area, in which existed little trace of Mediterranean urban culture, so that the medieval towns represented a new phenomenon; (b) northern France and the Rhine and Danube valleys, where most Roman towns disappeared after the Empire and town sites were changed considerably during the medieval revival; and (c) southern Europe, where many of the Roman towns existed without interruption into the medieval period. Medieval historians thus identify several main theories about the origins of towns: as being due to long distance trade, local trade and production, defence (and ecclesiastical activities), and as being Roman creations.

The notion of towns as long distance trading centres has received little formal attention in location theory (except implicitly). The local trade and production theories are closely related to the models of Weber and Lösch. The hypothesis that defensive and ecclesiastical functions provide the motive for town formation introduces a novel element into location theory: that agglomerations of 'non-economic' functions provide the loci for towns. Presumably the size, spacing, and location of such functions could be analysed in terms of population density, economies of scale, and transport costs, in exactly the same way as any other function: the problem of town formation would remain—why should these different functions agglomerate? (Note that it is only when two or more functions

47

E

agglomerate that a 'point' or 'town', in the sense employed in this book, exists. Some medieval boroughs may not have been 'towns' in this sense.) In general the empirical study of medieval towns indicates the importance of continuity in town sites, throws doubt upon the notion of a purely economic explanation of the existence of towns, but does not provide positive evidence strongly in favour of one particular model.

3 Theories of Land Use

The classical theory of agricultural location is that of von Thünen (Hall, 1966). This work proposed a method of analysis which von Thünen employed in an econometric study of land use in Prussia. The method and the model were not fully developed until Dunn (1954) and Lösch (1959) discussed the ideas more generally and derived equilibrium conditions for the location patterns. Although originally formulated in terms of agricultural location, the model has been found to be applicable to land use allocation problems within cities.

Two major points of difference exist between land use theory and the theory of point location. Whereas Weber's theory, interdependence models and, to some extent, central place theory are concerned with individual firms and decisions (though at a highly simplified level), agricultural and land use models have traditionally analysed aggregated location policies. Point location models ask: 'Where does this firm locate?', but land use models ask 'What is the overall location pattern of this industry?' Although Dunn (1954) and Isard (1956) have both emphasised that agricultural location theory can be extended into an analysis of the industrial firm, the dualism of approaches between the 'Where to locate?' and 'What to produce?' questions has remained. The second main difference between the two types of model lies in their concern with rent: in agriculture and within cities, firms' location and production policies are constrained by rental payments, for, in relation to the space available, these firms consume significant areas of land. In point location theory, on the other hand, rent is normally considered an insignificant location factor.

Rent, for both agricultural and urban land, is a payment to that land equal to its marginal revenue product. The key to land rents is the value of land's marginal product, which in turn is largely determined by fertility and distance from the market. In agriculture, fertility affects yields and location affects f.o.b. prices, whereas in towns 'fertility' should be interpreted as topography (e.g. the view over Sydney harbour), while distance affects both f.o.b. prices (to producers) and commuting costs (to consumers). The basic elements in agricultural and urban land use theories are the same, but they are blended in different ways: urban land use theory analyses land in consumption as well as in production.

49

Agricultural Location Models

Two general, though closely related, types of agricultural land use model can be recognised. The first class has developed out of von Thünen's early analysis of the location of production around a market. These models are relatively abstract and are primarily concerned with the effects of location on production. A second form of model is the inter-regional equilibrium model, which is more general than von Thünen's model, in that it can incorporate variations in production costs and the existence of several markets. The von Thünen model is discussed first.

We follow the treatment of Dunn (1954). The determining element in agricultural location is competition for land, which is expressed through rental payments. The land use providing the greatest rent makes the highest bid for land, and thus displaces other uses. The rent provided by the production of a single good is given by

$$(3-1) \qquad R = E(p-a) - Efk$$

where R is rent per unit of land, k is distance from market, E is yield per unit of land, p is the market price for the good, a is the production cost per unit of the good, and f is the transport rate per unit of distance. It is assumed that the owners of land maximise their rent receipts. Then the location decision maximises the rent accruing to a piece of land for its advantage of position.

The equilibrium statement for the whole industry (Dunn, 1954: 19-24) requires eight assumptions. The conditions for equilibrium, that individuals and industries regard prices as outside their influence and that demand equals supply, can be specified by a system of equations if

(i) only agricultural goods are produced,

(ii) the incomes of consumers are known,

(iii) non-land factors of production are perfectly mobile and divisible,

(iv) yields do not vary over space,

(v) the supply of factors is adequate for all production; therefore these factors are available at constant prices,

(vi) the transport rate is constant over time and space,

(vii) the agricultural industry is supplying a single market, and

(viii) the transport network is undifferentiated over space. These conditions imply that the model examines location in an agrarian economy (condition (i)) which is static (conditions (ii) and (vi)), contains one market centre (condition (vii)), is set on an isotropic surface (conditions (iii), (iv), (vi), and (viii)), and has sufficient factors of production to meet demand (condition (v)).

Under these conditions Fig. 3–1 indicates the relationship between rent (R) and location (k) for a single good. The sloping rent line—the marginal rent

Figure 3–1: **Relationship between rent and location for a single crop**

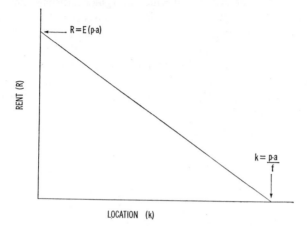

Figure 3–2: **Relationship between rent and location for two crops**

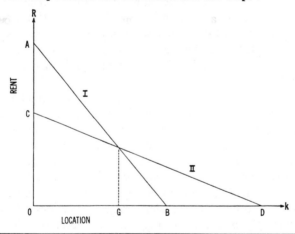

line—is the line of marginal returns. Since rent has been expressed net of production costs, the k-axis is the marginal cost line. Then rent is maximised if production takes place up to that distance at which marginal returns equal marginal costs: that is, from equation (3–1), up to that point at which

$$(3\text{–}2) \qquad k = \frac{p-a}{f} \,.$$

Figure 3–2 represents the situation in which two crops are produced (Dunn, 1954: 9–13). The use of land by the first industry is subject to an opportunity cost (the rent which the land would yield under alternative crops); this is the rent yielded by the second industry. Thus, if industry I is the inner one, the good is grown up to that distance at which marginal returns equal the marginal opportunity cost. Industry II, the outer industry, has two margins, an inner and an outer one, and its marginal cost curve follows the line ABk. Hence good II is produced in the zone GD, for marginal returns equal marginal costs at G and at D. Such an analysis implies the formation of zones of land use around the market. These zones will develop if and only if the R intercept is greater for industry I than for II (equation (3–3)) and the k intercept for II is greater than that for I (equation (3–4)):

$$(3\text{–}3) \qquad E_1(p_1-a_1) > E_2(p_2-a_2) > 0,$$

$$(3\text{–}4) \qquad \frac{p_1-a_1}{f_1} > \frac{p_2-a_2}{f_2} > 0.$$

This analysis can clearly be extended to the case of many industries.

Dunn (1954: 44-6) also discusses the relationship between distance and intensity of production. For a single land use, rent rises as the market is approached; land as a factor of production becomes more expensive relative to other factors of production. Consequently, as the market is approached, more of the cheaper factors are substituted for the relatively expensive factor, land: more factors are applied to land, and cultivation becomes more intensive. But it does not follow that, of two competing land uses, the more intensive one will be nearer the market. Von Thünen's case of forests near the city exemplifies this point. Nor is any reason supplied by this model for farm size to increase with distance from the market.

Some of the simplifying assumptions may be relaxed (Dunn, 1954: 38-70). Since transport costs per unit of distance fall as the length of journey increases, a movement of given distance away from or towards the market causes a greater substitution adjustment near the market than at a distance from it. Thus the distance-rent function is probably concave up, as in Fig. 3–3. This change does not disturb the essence of the conditions for spatial equilibrium, but one crop may now appear in more than one zone (see Fig. 3–3). The existence of multiple markets also modifies the simple rings and creates a new boundary— that between supply areas. Land may be of uneven quality: this creates analytical problems because the only accurate measure of productivity is rent, and crops may not be competing directly to locate on the same type of land.

There exists one technical difficulty in Dunn's treatment of the location problem (Stevens, 1968). Dunn's set of equations to determine simultaneously the inner and outer boundaries of each crop ring only has a solution if it is known in advance which of the potential crops are actually produced in the system. But Dunn does not present a method to define which crops are produced; and although, as we have seen, a graphical presentation of the model is simple, a mathematical determination of the actual crops produced is extremely tortuous. Stevens therefore proposes a linear programming format for the model: maximise

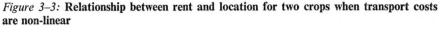

Figure 3–3: **Relationship between rent and location for two crops when transport costs are non-linear**

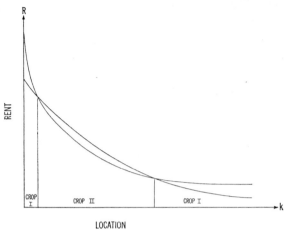

(3–5) $Z = \sum_i \sum_j R_{ij} x_{ij},$

subject to $\sum_i x_{ij} \leqslant 1$, for all j

and $x_{ij} \geqslant 0$ for all i and all j.

In equation (3–5), R_{ij} is the profit per unit area yielded by crop i at distance j, and x_{ij} is the proportion of land at distance j which is allocated to crop i. Although this formulation requires that distance be divided into discrete segments, the solution variables, x_{ij}, defining which crops are produced and where, are generated automatically. The model can readily incorporate yield, production cost, and transport rate variations over the plain, and may be employed if there exists more than one market.

The model predicts some of the effects of distance from market on the location of agricultural production. Von Thünen and Dunn both recognise that in reality there exist many centres of consumption (towns) with competing spheres of influence. It has been claimed, however, that in many areas, cities and towns are so numerous that production zones become confounded to the extent that in practice these zones cannot be differentiated. Grotewald (1959) summarises this case by pointing out that, with the development of modern transport methods, the costs of shipping are not effectively related merely (or mainly) to bulk and distance; and that, as transport costs fall, the comparative advantages of places due to environmental attributes become more important relative to advantages due to location.

As Chisholm (1962: 40) indicates, this is almost certainly true within the United Kingdom and northeastern United States. Chisholm produces evidence, though, which demonstrates that at some places and scales zoning of pro-

53

Figure 3–4: **Relationship between net output per acre in fields and distance of fields from farmsteads, in Finland.**

Source: Chisholm (1962: 55).

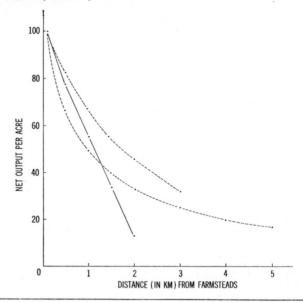

duction around regions and villages does occur. Figure 3–4 summarises data from Chisholm (1962: 54-5) relating to net output in three sample areas in Finland. Net output per hectare in fields is lower the further those fields are from farmsteads. Chisholm (1962: 62-5) then quotes evidence about the arrangements of crops in relation to yields and labour requirements around Canicatti, a settlement of 30,000 inhabitants in Sicily. Figure 3–5 illustrates some of this evidence. On a larger scale, Chisholm quotes data about imports of food into the United Kingdom: Table 3–1 contains some of these data. This evidence reveals distinct regularities in crop patterns related to distance from markets.

Complementary evidence is offered by the U.S. Department of Agriculture. This study found a regular decline in the average rent per acre of farms with distance from Louisville, Kentucky. At distances less than eight miles from the city, rents averaged $11.85 per acre; at between nine and eleven miles, the mean rent was $5.59; at twelve to fourteen miles, $5.37 was the mean rent; while at distances greater than fourteen miles, the mean rent had fallen to $4.66 (U.S. Department of Agriculture, 1918: 11). Although this 'empirical rent' was not defined in exactly the same way as rent in the models, nevertheless the results do indicate that the effects predicted by von Thünen and Dunn may be apparent in reality.

On some scales at least, then, the predicted regularities are apparent. Even

Figure 3–5: **Relationship between distance from Canicatti and proportion of land area (solid line histograms) and of crop area (dashed line histograms) devoted to several crops.**
Source: Chisholm (1962: 63).

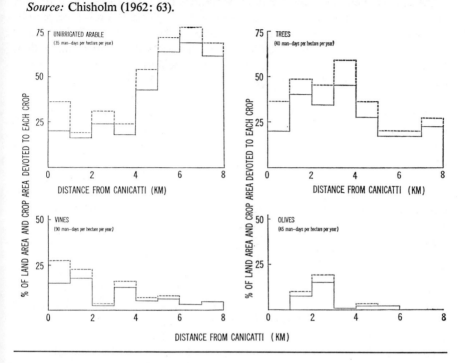

Table 3–1: **Zonation of milk-based food imports into United Kingdom**

Commodity	Weight*	% supplies imported	I	II	III	IV	Other
				% of import from zone			
Fresh milk	1034	0					
Condensed milk	372	1	85				15
Dried milk	124	46	17			82	1
Cheese	99	55	13	2	4	80	1
Fresh cream	82	11	98				2
Butter	39	91	30	5		64	1

Zones I: Belgium, Channel Is, Denmark, Eire, Netherlands, Norway
    II: rest of Europe
    III: North Africa, North America
    IV: South and East Africa, Argentina, Chile, Australia, New Zealand.
* Weight of product in metric tons per one million litres of milk.

Source: Chisholm, 1962: 99.

so, the regular gradients and patterns of the model are highly distorted in reality. These distortions have a variety of causes.

As von Thünen and Dunn realised, variations in resources cause distortions in the ideal land use pattern. Grotewald (1959) considers the resource base to be now a prime determinant of land use patterns. Thus, Hidore (1963) found a correlation coefficient of $r = +0.65$ between the location of land with less than 3° slopes and the location of cash grain farms in the north-central United States. Such an effect is clearly to be expected: however, other imperfections require more detailed analysis.

Haggett (1965: 175-6) suggests that land use gradients are also distorted by economies of scale. On the one hand, the size of farm affects the production decisions made by farmers. This point parallels the argument of Moses (1958) discussed in Chapter 2. Thus Mead (1953) discovered that, around Helsinki, large farms have a smaller percentage of their land under cultivation and consume a smaller percentage of their crops on the farm than do small farms. On the other hand, Chisholm (1962: 191) has argued that large producing areas may gain economic advantages over smaller areas because of their size: California farm marketing organisations, with their large volume of fruit and vegetable production and their standardised goods, have been able to bargain favourable transport rates to the northeast United States with the railway companies; thus they undercut Florida producers in the northeastern market, even though Florida is nearer the northeast than is California. Similarly, Harvey (1963) concludes that part of the reason why the Kentish hop industry was concentrated in mid-Kent is provided by agglomeration economies (specialised financial facilities, a skilled labour force, the localised development of service industries supplying poles and manure, specialised marketing arrangements, and trade prejudice against other areas) and by the process of cumulative change. Harvey (1966b) also argues that the failure of many medium-sized U.K. towns to develop distinctive concentric land use zones in the nineteenth century may be due to the economies of scale experienced by larger towns; these economies caused the supply areas of smaller markets to be swamped by larger hinterlands.

Further distortions occur as a result of urban-rural interactions on town fringes. Sinclair (1967) proposes that the effects of distance from urban markets on land use may now be transmitted through an anticipated rise in land values rather than through transport costs. Sinclair's idea is that since entrepreneurs near the city anticipate urbanisation, rural land values increase; consequently the relative value of the land for agricultural uses declines and the intensity of investment on that land falls. That is, land near cities may be valuable more for its anticipated price increase than for its income from agriculture. Another reason why the intensity of production near cities may be relatively low is that, because of anticipated urbanisation, farmers have less time in which to pay off long-term investments on that land: long-term investment is discouraged near the city. Kostrowicki (1964) has found a different effect: in Poland, peasant-workers (who own a smallholding while also engaged in factory work) produce less per acre than similarly sized full-time farmers. In comparison with full-time farmers these peasant-workers tend to avoid labour-absorbing crops and to employ more machinery. Gasson (1966, 1967) has investigated similar relationships in the area south of London. She discovered significant differences between the practices of full-time and part-time farmers: the full-timers display less arable and more time-consuming livestock enterprises, greater output per acre, and more complex farming systems than the part-time farmers. On the other hand, Golledge (1960) discovered that farms on Sydney's metropolitan fringe exhibited in 1954 some of the distance-size-intensity relationships which the von Thünen model predicts. Farms in the inner local government areas (LGAs), that is in the zone just being developed for residential land use, had an average size of between 5·6 and 14·4 acres and between 33·7 and 57·4 per cent of their area was cultivated; by contrast, farms in the remainder of the county of Cumberland, that is beyond the immediate fringe, were between 28·0 and 271·1 acres in size and had less than 13·9 per cent of their area cultivated. Golledge's data suggest that farm size increases and farming intensity decreases as distance from the city rises.

Harvey (1966b) criticises the von Thünen-Lösch-Dunn model because it is static and does not consider the problems of transition. Nicholls (1961) has made an extensive study of the way in which agriculture in the Tennessee Valley and South Carolina-Georgia Piedmont adjusted to industrial-urban development in the period 1860-1950. This work provides our most detailed knowledge of the transition process. The present leading agricultural counties had in 1860 significant advantages over the other counties—including superior resources, windfall gains from new cash crops, and higher rates of agricultural capital formation. But by 1900 these advantages had been more or less entirely lost as a result of labour migration. Thus subsequent divergence of patterns is not due merely to resource advantages, for labour migration could overcome these. Nicholls found that after 1900 the most rapidly industrialising counties were also those in which agricultural output and efficiency were rising most quickly. Partly this result can be ascribed to the effects of industrialisation on capital markets. With industrialisation came an influx of outside capital, which increased personal incomes and savings: consequently bank resources rose, and more loans and credit were made available to farmers. As a result, industrial counties maintained higher rates of investment in land improvements and in capital intensive enterprises (such as livestock), which in turn increased farm incomes per worker as compared with less industrial counties. Partly, also, industrialisation assists agriculture by increasing the demand for labour. As the cost of labour rises, farmers are forced to reorganise, and this they can do in one of two ways. Either small full-time farmers can become part-timers (which is not possible in the non-industrial counties) or the full-time farms can be enlarged to raise the productivity of agricultural production (and higher rates of off-farm employment quicken this process of farm amalgamation in the industrial counties in comparison with the rural counties).

Although some of these criticisms of agricultural location theory are almost classical, they have not yet been incorporated into a coherent theory of agricultural location. They do indicate, however, some of the directions in which such a theory must develop. It is a relatively simple matter to incorporate the effects of resource variations on land use patterns, but more theoretical analysis of the impact of economies of scale, rural-urban interactions, and transition processes are necessary before they can be adequately merged in a more widely applicable theory.

Some of the criticisms are taken into account in inter-regional equilibrium models. In such models, space is disaggregated into a set of regions, each of which consists of completely homogeneous points. Transfer costs are incurred only when goods are transported between regions, each region has a known demand for each good, and production costs within each region are given. An early inter-regional equilibrium model is that of Enke (1951), who used electric analogue methods to find the net price in each region, the quantity imported and the quantity exported by the regions. Samuelson (1952) employed linear programming methods to solve the same problem.

Stevens (1959) outlines a general inter-regional linear programming model. The model assumes linear production functions, and so it contains no mechanism which automatically takes economies of scale into account. Thus the size of firms within the regions has no effect on the solution. Stevens assumes a fixed demand at fixed prices: in return for this limitation, the model yields optima of production, location, and inter-regional trade. Within each region of the multi-region economy, there exists a fixed stock of immobile resources (natural, capital, and human). Transport within each region is costless. In addition to resources, the system comprises productive processes (defined by linear homogeneous production functions with constant coefficients), intermediate goods, and final goods, all of which are transportable between regions. Transport is part of the production process: it is an intermediate good which must be produced and which is itself transportable. The solution variables are shipment levels, not production levels. Thus for a system of n regions, a good in region j is produced by n different processes, one for export to each region (including j); but all the input coefficients except transport inputs are the same in each of the n production functions. Stevens also specifies a minimum consumption level in each region, to prevent any region falling below subsistence levels in the solution (this constraint is required because of the assumption that labour is immobile). And finally Stevens assumes that there is no net production of intermediate goods in the system as a whole.

The model itself is quite simple. There are four sets of constraining equations (the Appendix to this chapter presents a mathematical statement of them):

(a) In any region, the amount of a resource required in the production of intermediate goods must not exceed the local endowment of that resource.

(b) The supply of intermediate goods must equal the demand for them.

(c) The supply of transport (which is an intermediate good) must equal the demand for transport.

(d) In each region the consumption of each final good must be greater than some minimum level.

Given these constraints, maximise

$$(3\text{-}6) \qquad Z = \sum_{J=1}^{u} \sum_{e=1}^{n} {}^{J}S_{fe}^{L} \ P_{fe}^{L};$$

in equation (3–6),

${}^{J}S_{fe}^{L}$ = the number of units of final good e produced in region J and shipped to region L, and

P_{fe}^{L} = the market price of final good e in region L.

Notice that the solution is bounded at both ends (by production and consumption constraints); it is therefore possible that the model has no solution.

The main limitations on inter-regional linear programming models are well illustrated by this model of Stevens. Production functions are assumed to be linear: costs per unit are the same whether one unit or one million are produced. Demand and resources are fixed and immobile, and so inter-regional factor movements are impossible. As Harvey (1966b) points out, this implies that the model can only work effectively over short periods. These are in theory quite severe limitations, but, in return, the linear equilibrium model yields important results, since inter-regional variations in production costs can be readily incorporated into the model. It is also easy to make the model operational.

For example, Henderson (1959) has used the inter-regional linear programming model to analyse changes in U.S. agricultural production in 1955. The United States was divided into 160 regions, each a homogeneous type-of-farming area. For each area, Henderson obtained local data on the costs of planting, cultivating, and harvesting eleven chosen crops. Expected prices for each of the included crops were taken as the announced level of government price support; expected yields were set equal to the average for the region over the last five years. (Notice that in Henderson's model, transport costs enter implicitly through the use of local prices.) The net agricultural return in each region is maximised, subject to three constraints: for region i, maximise

$$(3\text{-}7) \qquad Z_i = \sum_{j=1}^{m} x_{ij} \ (p_{ij} y_{ij} - c_{ij}),$$

where x_{ij} = acreage devoted to crop j in region i; p_{ij} = price of crop j in region i; y_{ij} = yield per unit area of crop j in region i; and c_{ij} = total costs per unit area of producing crop j in region i. The constraints are that (i) the acreage devoted to each crop cannot exceed the total available; (ii) the change in land use pattern of 1955 from that of 1954 is limited between some empirically determined minimum and maximum levels by farmers' uncertainty (or, where relevant, is limited by the government's acreage allotment); and (iii) acreages devoted to crops cannot be negative. Henderson's estimates of regional production in 1955 seem closer to reality than several naïve estimates or the industry forecasts of the Department of Agriculture.

These models of Henderson and Stevens illustrate a methodological problem of location models. Stevens's model, moderately operational, may be usefully employed in theoretical analysis because the variables of location and demand are clearly identified. However, Henderson's model confounds these important variables with others in the local price structure, and thus loses theoretical value although it thereby gains operational power. It seems that we can construct theoretically useful models or operational predictive models, but not models which are both theoretically and operationally powerful.

City Land Use Models
The early theories of urban land use identified many of the elements important in more modern models. Hurd (1903) indicated that land is allocated to the highest bidder for that land, and that the value of a site (the rent it can command) depends on its location—specifically on its nearness to the city centre. Haig (1926) constructed a theory of the spatial organisation of metropolitan areas. Rent is the charge imposed for a relatively accessible site, arising from savings in transport costs. Haig's theory is that the costs of friction within a city are measured by the site rents plus transport costs, and that metropolitan areas are organised so as to minimise these friction costs. Alonso (1966: 6-9) has objected to this model because it neglects the effects of size of site and, like Weber's model, relies on a minimum cost rather than a maximum profit criterion of optimality. Wingo (1961) has constructed a model the form of which depends upon very detailed assumptions about the demand for and cost of transport within cities; the complexity of these assumptions obscures the general patterns of land use within cities. The models of Muth (1961) and Alonso (1966), while structurally simpler than that of Wingo, predict quite accurately some observed features of city land use.

Muth (1961) constructed a model of residential land use. The model assumes that a market exists and that homogeneous land extends indefinitely beyond it; that all production and sale takes place at the market; that land is used only for residences; and that transport costs increase at a decreasing rate from the market. The similarities between this model and that of von Thünen are quite obvious, and the conclusions Muth reaches are similar to those von Thünen and Dunn reach for a one industry economy.

At equilibrium, for each consumer the savings in housing costs obtained by moving a small distance out of the city must equal the increase in transport costs caused by this move. Thus

$$(3-8) \qquad -q\frac{dp}{dk} = \frac{dT}{dk},$$

where q is the household's consumption of housing, p is the price per unit of housing, T is transport costs, and k is distance from the centre. Since transport costs increase at a decreasing rate with distance, housing costs decrease at a decreasing rate with distance. The model also indicates that if transport costs fall, or incomes rise, or housing costs fall, consumers disperse and the rate of decline of housing prices decreases.

Now households are 'produced' from land and non-land factors. The producers of households—builders—combine these land and non-land factors in such a way that they maximise their incomes. Assume that builders are competitive and have identical production functions, and that the price of non-land factors is everywhere the same. Then land is substituted for non-land in the production process as distance increases (because rents fall). Therefore the price per unit of housing, the rent per unit of land, and the output of housing per unit of land all decline, while the *per capita* consumption of housing rises with increasing distances from the market.

Alonso (1966) provides a more detailed set of predictions than Muth. The model assumes (Alonso, 1966: 15-18) that all land is of equal quality, freely bought and sold, that knowledge is perfect, that consumers maximise satisfaction (if they are households) or profits (if they are firms), and that employment, goods, and services are available only at the centre of the city. The similarity to the von Thünen-Dunn model is again apparent. But unlike Muth, Alonso incorporates an analysis of firms' decisions. In Alonso's models, as in the agricultural models, the goods produced by firms are all exported to the city centre: local consumption of goods plays no part in the model.

The urban firm decides on a location and on the amount of land to be occupied in order to make greatest profits. Alonso assumes that

(3–9) $G = V - C - R,$

where G is profits, V is sales, C is non-land costs, and R is land costs; that

(3–10) $V = f_1(t, q),$

where t is location (distance from the market centre) and q is size of site; that

(3–11) $C = f_2(V, t, q);$

and that

(3–12) $R = P(t)q,$

where $P(t)$ is the price of land at distance t (Alonso, 1966: 45-6). From these assumptions Alonso derives two equations (Alonso, 1966: 50-2). The first of these is the location equation:

(3–13) $0 = \dfrac{dV}{dt} - \dfrac{dC}{dV} \cdot \dfrac{dV}{dt} - \dfrac{dC}{dt} - q\dfrac{dP}{dt},$

where $\dfrac{dV}{dt}$ is the marginal revenue lost by moving a distance dt from the centre;

$\dfrac{dC}{dV} \cdot \dfrac{dV}{dt}$ is the change in marginal operating costs caused by the change in the

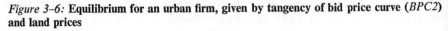

Figure 3–6: **Equilibrium for an urban firm, given by tangency of bid price curve (*BPC2*) and land prices**

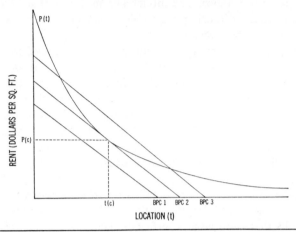

volume of business which accompanies the relocation; $\frac{dC}{dt}$ is the marginal increase in operating costs caused directly by the movement dt; and $q\frac{dP}{dt}$ is the decrease in rental payments caused by falls in the price of land with distance. The second equation is the size of site equation:

$$(3\text{--}14) \qquad 0 = \frac{dV}{dq} - \frac{dC}{dV}\cdot\frac{dV}{dq} - \frac{dC}{dq} - \frac{dP}{dq},$$

where the marginal changes are interpreted as in equation (3–13).

Equations (3–13) and (3–14) are solved simultaneously to obtain bid price functions for the firms. These bid price functions,

$$(3\text{--}15) \qquad p_f(t)[G_0,$$

define the price (p) bid by the firm (f) at each location (t) so that, when the quantity of land is optimised, the firm can achieve a constant level of profits (G_0) and no more. This is the bid price curve such that the firm is indifferent between locations. The solution to the simultaneous equations indicates (Alonso, 1966: 53-5) (i) that lower bid price curves offer greater profits to the firm, (ii) that bid price curves normally slope downward because revenue falls and operating costs rise with increasing distance, and (iii) that the slope of the bid price function is such that the savings in land costs from a relocation are just equal to the value of the business lost plus the increase in operating costs. The equilibrium for the firm is shown in Fig. 3–6: *BPC1*, *BPC2*, and *BPC3* are three bid price curves for the firm (the firm prefers the lower bid price curves) and $P(t)$ is the price structure of the land market. Equilibrium occurs when $P(t)$ is tangent with a bid price curve (*BPC2*) at distance $t_{(c)}$ and price $p_{(c)}$.

Alonso also analyses households' decisions. The general budgetary equation is (Alonso, 1966: 21)

$$(3\text{–}16) \qquad y = p_z z + P(t)q + k(t),$$

where y is income, p_z is the price of all other goods, z is the quantity of all other goods, $P(t)$ is the price of land at distance t, q is quantity of land, and $k(t)$ is commuting costs to distance t. From equation (3–16) Alonso derives (1966:71) the bid price curve:

$$(3\text{–}17) \qquad \frac{dp_i}{dt} = \frac{p_z u_t}{q\, u_z} - \frac{1}{q} \cdot \frac{dk}{dt},$$

where p_i is bid price, u_t is the utility of distance, and u_z is the utility of all else. On the right hand side of (3–17) the first term is negative because of the disutility of distance and the second term is negative because commuting costs are positive. Therefore both tastes and commuting costs cause residential prices to fall with distance from the centre. Thus the bid price curve is defined so that the income effect of cheaper land counteracts the depressing effects of commuting costs on income, and so that a given level of satisfaction can be maintained by substituting land and all else for accessibility as distance increases.

A simple four person game is used to illustrate how rent payments are determined, given bid price curves (Alonso, 1966: 77-9). The game assumes unlimited land at two locations, t_1 and t_2 (t_2 is the more distant site), held by two landlords L_1 and L_2. Each landlord seeks to maximise the price of his land; landlords do not collude. There are two renters, an urban resident, i, and a farmer, ag. The farmer is willing to pay p_{ag} at each location.

Since the farmer is willing to pay p_{ag} at each location, i must pay more than p_{ag} for either t_1 or t_2. But i is willing to offer more for t_1 than for t_2, and so i locates at t_1 and ag at t_2. The price at t_1 can now be determined. We know that p_1 must be more than p_{ag} and that i is not willing to pay more than his bid price for t_1: these data fix the price range. But, by the definition of the bid price curve, i receives more satisfaction at t_1 than at t_2 so long as p_1 is less than i's bid price for t_1. Therefore L_1 can charge the extreme point in the price range with no fear of losing his tenant. Consequently i is charged his bid price for t_1. Land is allocated to the highest bidder, who is charged his bid price for that land.

Alonso's model provides four main predictions about the structure of land uses within a city (Alonso, 1966: 83-4 and 106-15). The steeper the bid price curve the nearer to the centre of the city does a user of land locate, a conclusion paralleled in agricultural location theory. If the desire for land is strong—that is, if the wealthy buy large blocks of land—the slope of an individual's bid price curve falls as his income rises: so the rich live in suburbs, the poor in central locations. An increase in population causes greater demand for land which, by increasing prices, reduces the amount of land bought by each person. Technological improvements in transport reduce the marginal disutility of distance and in so doing cause bid price curves to slope more gently; therefore prices are lower

63

F

at the centre and higher at the periphery than before the improvement. The model demonstrates that suburbanisation depends on rising incomes and transport improvements.

A variety of data indicates that the predictions of the models of Muth and Alonso are broadly fulfilled in practice. Alonso (1966: 126) quotes Philadelphia data which show that population density and the price of land fall with distance from the city centre, that richer people buy more land than poorer, and that the rich live further from the city centre than the poor. Muth (1961) examined 1950 data for forty-six U.S. cities. He found that forty of them exhibit significant density gradients and that the average explanation of population density provided by the gradient is 45 per cent. His results also indicate that density gradients are lower the lower are transport costs, the higher are city median incomes, the later the development of the city, and the lower the proportion of manufacturing employment which is located in the Central Business District (CBD).

Several workers have studied the decline of population density with distance from the city centre. Clark (1951) fitted negative exponential functions to data on urban population densities in thirty-six European and U.S. cities over the period 1801 to 1950. This curve has the form

$$(3\text{--}18) \qquad D(s) = \exp{(a - bs)},$$

where s is distance from city centre and $D(s)$ is population density. On the other hand, Sherratt (1960) has fitted a second degree negative exponential function to data on Sydney:

$$(3\text{--}19) \qquad D(s) = \exp{(a - cs^2)},$$

and Ajo (1965) has fitted a curve of the form

$$(3\text{--}20) \qquad D(s) = \exp{(a - m\sqrt{s})}$$

to data on density levels in the rural periphery of London. Casetti (1969), in a study of eight American and British cities, compared the descriptive value of the various forms of the negative exponential function, but concluded that no one form fitted all cities better than the other forms.

More general studies have been made of the determinants of the spatial distribution of land values in cities. Yeates (1965) analysed land values in Chicago for the period 1910 to 1960. Variables included to explain land values are distance from the CBD, distance from nearest shopping centre, distance from Lake Michigan, distance from the nearest subway, population density, and the number of non-whites as a percentage of the total population. In 1910, the most important variables (in terms of the size of their standardised regression coefficients) were distance from the CBD, distance from Lake Michigan, and distance from the nearest subway; the equation explained 77 per cent of the spatial variation in land values. By 1960, the most important variables were (in order) non-whites as a proportion of total population, distance from Lake Michigan, and distance from the CBD; but explanation had fallen to 18 per cent. Daly (1967) analysed current land values in a much smaller city—Newcastle, N.S.W. (which has a population of about 0·2 million). In the inner area and central suburbs, land values were related largely to distance from the CBD and from local shops; in the main suburban areas, distance from the nearest school and beach ranked foremost; while in the outer, sparsely settled areas, height and population density were the most important controlling variables. These two studies indicate that the concentric land use models of Muth and Alonso have some use as predictors of land values, but that as time passes their power is diminishing.

This diminishing power seems to depend on two main factors. First, as transport costs fall, the gradients of land value and density decline, as Alonso predicts. As a consequence, the 'fertility' component (height, lakes, seaside) of land values becomes relatively more important, and the radial models, which do not incorporate this component, lose power. Secondly, neither of these models analyses the development and organisation of suburban employment and retail centres; but as the relative importance of CBD sales and employment in a city falls over time (Johnston, 1965, and Vance, 1960 have documented this process), so the impact of the CBD on the spatial structure of the city may fall. Although Wingo (1961) analyses the effects of suburban centres on population density, there exists no model which incorporates both a central place system and land use competition; the impact of these centres on the parameters of the city is not known quantitatively. The 'inter-regional' linear programming model of Herbert and Stevens (1960), which allocates households among city regions, may help to broaden the scope of city land use models, most notably by analysing the effects of fertility variations.

The existence of more descriptive models of city land use indicates the problems of constructing formal models of multiple-nuclei cities. The classical descriptive model of urban land use is that of Burgess (1925). Burgess, analysing the growth of great cities, illustrated the process by which the city expanded with a schema of concentric circles (see Fig. 3–7). Five zones were identified: (i) the CBD, the industrial, commercial, and transport focus of the city; (ii) a transition zone of deteriorating residential properties, which is being invaded by business firms and light manufacturing industry; (iii) a working class residential zone, occupied by families which have left the second zone; (iv) a residential zone of high class apartments and single family dwellings; and (v) a commuters' zone. Burgess argued that, as a city grew, so each zone expanded out into the next one, a process which he termed 'succession'. This model is a descriptive and more sociological version of the concentric economic models already discussed; whether one prefers a land use classification (as offered by Burgess) or a continuum of variable change (as in the economic models) depends on one's purpose.

This model has been modified by Hoyt's (1939) sector model of land use. Hoyt recognised that the structure of land uses within a city is conditioned not only by distance from the city centre, but also by accessibility to routes which radiate from that centre (see Fig. 3–7). Sectoral variations in 'fertility' could also prompt such an urban form.

65

Figure 3–7: **Upper diagram: Burgess's concentric model of urban land use; lower diagram: Hoyt's sector model of urban land use.**

Source: Haggett (1965: 178).

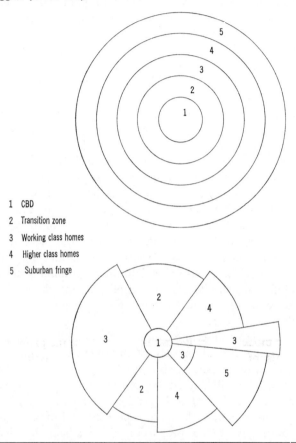

1 CBD
2 Transition zone
3 Working class homes
4 Higher class homes
5 Suburban fringe

Sociological data indicate that these two interpretations of city structure may be complementary rather than competitive. For example, Anderson and Egeland (1961) have analysed the spatial distribution of indices of social rank and of urbanisation (indices developed by Shevky and Williams, 1949: 33-6) in four American cities: Akron, Dayton, Indianapolis, and Syracuse. The index of urbanisation measures the fertility of a population, the tendency of women to work, and the physical characteristics of a neighbourhood; distance from the city centre explains 57 per cent of the variation between neighbourhoods in this index. The social rank index comprises measures of occupational status, educational status, and income; this index is shown to vary between the radial sectors of a city. These results add wider social dimensions to the economic models.

One of the most important omissions from all these land use models is an analysis of the problems of change. The transition from one land use to another, the adjustment to changing technological, cultural, and economic constraints, is apparently not easily accomplished within the market framework of cities. The high degree of social planning which is necessary to ensure smooth change within cities indicates that large external economies of transition exist, economies which firms must find it difficult to internalise. Such problems of transition, the forces which give rise to them, and the effects which they have on location patterns, remain largely unexplored by urban land use theory.

Another weakness of the models is their emphasis upon the concentric pattern, a highly structured city form which offers all the appearances of being merely a temporary phenomenon. There is evidence that pre-industrial cities exhibited only limited spatial structure: Martin (1966: 1), describing London in 1800, notes the close proximity of wealthy and poor, of residence and workplace; Hoyt (1966) points out that in nineteenth-century Chicago and New York, the houses of the well-to-do and the poor were often not spatially segregated; and Ragheb (1966) writes that present-day Middle Eastern towns are characterised by a land use admixture which makes it difficult to trace a clear spatial pattern, for industrial areas and slums, commercial and residential zones intermingle. The concentric structural form may only have had a limited history; yet evidence also suggests that relationships between distance and density (or land value) are rapidly becoming less obvious in U.S. cities. Land use models need to explain this evolution of city structure, not merely describe present patterns.

Conclusions

These theories of land use, though they employ slightly different approaches, yield some common conclusions. Around a market centre rents decline because distance (transport and commuting) costs increase. These changes in rent levels are seen as the prime determinants of location patterns around the market. Industries in which profit declines rapidly with increasing distance locate nearest the market. As transport costs rise, so the advantages of the centre as compared with the periphery also rise: the rate of decline of rents with distance depends on the transport rate. Urban models indicate, in addition, that the rich live in the outer suburbs, where population density is lowest, and that, as the population of a city rises, so does the average density of population within that city.

Some common difficulties also face the models. Like much of location theory, they are static and fail to investigate how change takes place and how impediments to smooth adjustment may produce permanent distortions to the ideal pattern. The interaction between urban and rural types of land use is ignored in both urban and agricultural models. But perhaps the most important problem is the failure to examine scale or agglomeration economies and the way in which these induce the development of local nuclei within the land use rings. Therefore the models are simplistic in predicting only concentric land use zones rather than also the existence of smaller nuclei which interrupt the smoothness of these gradients. Land use patterns around a city are visualised as depending on the size and the location of the market; the fact that the location and development of these zones may influence the location and growth of the central market (and of subsidiary markets) is ignored.

The manner in which entrepreneurs determine the rent actually paid for land needs to be investigated more fully. Alonso's (1966: 77-9) game treatment is plainly unsatisfactory. Firstly, Alonso states that since the farmer is willing to pay p_{ag} at each location, i is forced to pay more than this to secure either site. This is not necessarily true, for the farmer can only purchase one of these sites. Suppose, for example, that there are two sites, I and II; i would make a profit of three units at I and one unit at II, whereas ag would make a profit of two units at either site; bids can only be made in whole units. Renters bid in order to maximise profits. If they can only bid for one site, then, even though they are completely uncertain about the other's bidding, i bids one unit for site I and ag bids one unit for site II.

Secondly, Alonso suggests that landlords can charge the extreme upper rent in the price range without losing their tenants. In a sense this is true. But in the same sense, tenants can refuse to pay more than the minimum bid without fear of losing their landlords. Introspection suggests that bargaining yields an agreed rent midway between the minimum bid and the maximum possible bid. This idea is supported by experimental evidence presented by Siegel and Fouraker (1960): bargaining by players of equal strength results on average in agreement at a position midway between the two extreme possibilities. (Such a system is not fully determinate.)

If the number of tenants equals the number of sites, this analysis indicates (i) that a firm is allocated to that site at which it makes its greatest profit, provided no other firm makes its (higher) greatest profit at the same site, and (ii) that rents paid are usually half the profit that a firm can make at the allocated site— though this value does depend on relative bargaining abilities. (Such a rent making procedure does not alter the structure of land use in Alonso's model; it merely alters rent levels.) If there are two firms but only one site, the firm making the greatest profit receives the site, by bidding a sum equal to the profit which the second firm could make at the site. Bargaining with the landlord, if fair, indicates an agreed rent midway between the profit of the locating firm and the profit of the second firm. As even more firms compete for the site, the agreed rent paid is midway between the profit made at the site by the winning firm and the profit which could be made by the next highest bidder. As the models assume conditions nearer perfect ease of entry, so the rent paid for a site approaches the maximum profit which any firm can make at the site. In such a continuous bidding and bargaining model, rents reach their maximum possible value only if there is an indefinitely large number of firms and perfect ease of entry. These land use models thus require the assumption of perfect competition in order that rent levels be fully determinate and maximised.

One obvious point of comparison between point location theory and land use theory is the lack of probabilistic land use models. There have been only very limited attempts to develop stochastic land use models to perform the descriptive role played by point probability models. This lack of development undoubtedly reflects in part the fact that no other science has evinced interest in this form of problem (in contrast to the interest of ecologists in point patterns). In addition, such probabilistic land use models must be more complex than point models, because land use models have to assume some point location pattern and then describe land uses around those points. Lacking probability statements, descriptive land use theory is less powerful than descriptive models of point location.

Appendix to Chapter 3

This Appendix gives a mathematical statement of the constraints of Stevens's (1959) inter-regional linear programming model.

In the equations and inequations, let

$r_c a_{id}^L$ = number of units of resource c required in region L to produce one unit output of intermediate good d;

$i_d a_{ih}^L$ = number of units of intermediate good d required in region L to produce one unit output of intermediate good h;

$i_d a_{fe}^L$ = number of units of intermediate good d required in region L to produce one unit output of final good e;

$i_m^L a_{ih}^J$ ($i_m^L a_{fe}^J$) = number of units of the intermediate good, transport, required to ship one unit of intermediate good d (final good e) from region L to region J;

$^L S_{id}^J$ = number of units of intermediate good d produced in region L and shipped to region J;

$^L S_{fe}^J$ = number of units of final good e produced in L and shipped to J;

$^J S_{im}^L$ = number of units of transport services produced in J and shipped to region L;

E_{rc}^L = maximum locally available supply of resource c in region L;

C_{fe}^L = assumed minimum level of consumption of final good e in region L; and

P_{fe}^L = market price of final good e in region L.

There are four sets of constraining equations:

(a) the amount of a resource required in the production of intermediate goods must not exceed the local endowment of that resource—

(A3–1) $\quad \displaystyle\sum_{J=1}^{u} \sum_{d=1}^{n} r_c a_{id}^L \cdot {}^L S_{id}^J \leqslant E_{rc}^L$

$(L = 1, \ldots, u; c = 1, \ldots, n)$;

(b) the supply and demand of intermediate goods must be equalised:

$$(A3\text{--}2) \qquad \sum_{J=1}^{u} \sum_{h=1}^{n} i_{d}a_{ih}^{L} \cdot {}^{L}S_{ih}^{J} + \sum_{J=1}^{u} \sum_{e=1}^{n} i_{d}a_{fe}^{L} \cdot {}^{L}S_{fe}^{J} - \sum_{J=1}^{u} {}^{J}S_{id}^{L} = 0$$

$(L = 1, \ldots, u; d = 1, \ldots, n; d \neq m)$;

(c) the supply of and the demand for transport (an intermediate good) must be equalised:

$$(A3\text{--}3) \qquad \sum_{J=1}^{u} \sum_{h=1}^{n} i_{m}^{L}a_{ih}^{J} \cdot {}^{L}S_{ih}^{J} + \sum_{J=1}^{u} \sum_{e=1}^{n} i_{m}^{L}a_{fe}^{J} \; {}^{L}S_{fe}^{J} - \sum_{J=1}^{u} {}^{J}S_{im}^{L} = 0$$

$(L = 1, \ldots, u)$; and

(d) the consumption of each final good in each region must be greater than some minimum, that is

$$(A3\text{--}4) \qquad -\sum_{J=1}^{u} {}^{J}S_{fe}^{L} \leqslant -C_{fe}^{L}$$

$(L = 1, \ldots, u; e = 1, \ldots, n)$.

Given these constraints, maximise

$$(A3\text{--}5) \qquad Z = \sum_{J=1}^{u} \sum_{e=1}^{n} {}^{J}S_{fe}^{L} \cdot P_{fe}^{L},$$

where

$$\qquad {}^{J}S_{fe}^{L} \geqslant 0, \text{ for all } J, L, e.$$

4   Growth

Most theories of regional and national growth are spatially general: they do not generate patterns of activity over space. Economists have traditionally not been interested in space and few geographers or location theorists have analysed regional growth in a spatial context. The theory of the location of economic development has correspondingly remained less comprehensive and coherent than either theories of point location or theories of non-spatial economic growth. Geographers and economists have evinced a greater interest in urban growth processes, but even so, less attention has been paid to spatial aspects of growth mechanisms than to static models of location and land use. Sufficient results have been obtained, though, to permit a sketch of existing ideas on spatial growth and to suggest a way in which they may be integrated in a model of the location of growth under certainty.

This chapter analyses answers to two questions. The first is: what factors prompt the speed and direction of growth at a point in a country? The second asks: what factors inhibit or promote the spread of that growth throughout the economy? Although logically distinct, the analyses must occasionally be confounded. The techniques necessary to integrate these answers are developed in Chapter 9, which investigates spatial dispersal effects under uncertainty.

Both urban and regional growth mechanisms are analysed, and data are presented for both urban and regional systems. The rationale for this combination of what have traditionally been regarded as distinct model forms is the essential similarity of the central ideas in the two cases. The main models discussed may be regarded as urban or as regional growth models with only relatively minor adjustments of emphasis as the scale changes: in turn, the analysis of urban growth in terms of regional growth processes apparently increases our understanding of urban growth mechanics.

The notion of growth comprises two elements. The first aspect of growth is the accumulation of total output or population—the growth of the aggregate. The second component is an average: output *per capita*. These components are logically distinct, for there is no *a priori* reason why growth of the aggregate should necessarily be accompanied by growth of *per capita* output. The bulk of this discussion follows the main emphasis in the literature and relates to aggregate growth, though some aspects of growth of the average are considered.

Determinants of Growth

Assume a closed economy at a subsistence level. The economy contains no capital: the inhabitants are too poor to save. Consequently all goods are made by hand. Bensusan-Butt (1960: 15-33) develops a model of capital accumulation in this economy by assuming that growth starts as a result of a chance occurrence, such as an unusually good harvest. The farmers may eat the surplus, sell it for consumption by non-farmers, or save it (that is, use it to buy machinery). Provided that the last—saving—occurs, permanent change (growth) results. Thus, Butt suggests, the factor setting an economy in motion may be a freak event which offers temporary windfall gains. The problem of the initial start is not a difficult one.

A major determinant of national rates of economic growth is the 'desire' for improvement. The ability of individuals to perceive that self-improvement is possible and the desire to attain higher living standards are the principal foundations of growth. Adam Smith (1759) stressed the role played by personal drive and ambition in promoting economic expansion, and more recently Hirschman has made a similar point: 'Once economic progress in the pioneer countries is a visible reality, the strength of the desire to imitate, to follow suit, to catch up obviously becomes an important determinant of what will happen among the nonpioneers' (Hirschman, 1958: 8).

Psychologists have recently begun to quantify the relationship between personal ambition and national growth. Ambition—the 'need for achievement' —is defined as a disposition to seek out situations in which one can evaluate oneself against a standard of excellence and to derive satisfaction from doing a job well. The need for achievement in the national ethic can be measured in statements from the popular literature (including songs and drama) of the country. Using this technique, Bradburn and Berlew (1961) found a close relationship between the need for achievement as exemplified in a period's literature, and the increase (about fifty years later) in coal imports into London above the level expected (i.e. the increase over and above the average rate of increase of coal imports in previous years); import of coal into London was the only quantifiable measure of English economic growth during the period studied, 1500-1830. Cortes (1961) has found similar, though less impressive, evidence of the effect of need for achievement on Spanish economic growth between 1500 and 1730. McLelland (1963) used children's stories to measure need for achievement in thirty-nine countries in the 1950s; he discovered a significant positive correlation ($r = +0.43$) between need for achievement and the deviations of the actual rates of growth of electricity production (1952-8) from the levels expected given 1952 output levels.

While it would be tempting to infer from these results that regional (or even urban) rates of growth are affected similarly by the need for achievement of the local population, there are no data to support such an inference. In addition, we might expect fewer differences in levels of ambition between regions at a point in time than between nations or than between different periods in a nation's history. In the absence of data about the implications of regional achievement motives, the remainder of this discussion must analyse traditional technical features of an economy as determinants of growth.

Assume that the entire economy is growing—that capital accumulation, propensities to save and consume, and population growth are such that the whole is expanding. Given that these elements are equal over the entire economy, the analysis now examines other causes of regional differences in the speed and nature of growth. This is done by outlining the export base theory and then determining the additions necessary to make it a more complete model.

The export base model of regional and urban growth has a long history. 'Progress does not take place unless the colony possesses markets, where it can dispose of its staple products . . . The prime requisite of colonial prosperity is the colonial staple' (Mackintosh, 1923: 14). More recently, North (1955, 1961) and Perloff and Wingo (1961) have urged the export base thesis in respect of American regional growth. North argues that in the United States the regions always aimed at producing goods for export; subsistence economies only developed when transport to markets was lacking. Regional growth, then, was typically promoted by the export of goods—such as petroleum from the southwest, amenities from Florida, timber from the northwest, and agricultural goods from the Plains. As the examples show, the export base need not be a primary activity, nor even necessarily a manufacturing activity; but common to all the bases is a close relationship to raw materials. In this model, a prime cause of regional differences in exports and growth rates is the location of raw materials—though in relation to demand, costs, and technology. A very similar model has been proposed for urban growth: Weimer and Hoyt (1939) suggested that there exists for any city at any given point of time a relationship between the growth of basic employment or income (that is, employment in or income from export industries) and the growth of all employment or income in the urban area. Andrews (1953a, b, c, 1955) has outlined the main ideas of the model.

This approach can be connected to international and inter-regional trade theory through the idea of comparative advantage. (The inter-regional equilibrium models discussed in the previous chapter are clearly relevant to this approach.) Such an analysis (e.g. Isard and Peck, 1954) emphasises the effects of distance on trade. Using a multi-country and multi-commodity model, Isard and Peck show how the trade between two regions may be expected to decline as the distance between them increases. Beckerman (1956) has presented data on trade between the OEEC countries which support this suggestion. As North indicates, an argument based on resources must analyse location as well.

North then argues that the growth of a region depends on the success of its exports in the national and international economy. The development of exports promotes local industrial growth through the establishment of raw material oriented industries which process exports, of service industries tied to the export sector, of market oriented industries and of footloose industries. The importance of resource advantages depends on their ability to support a stream of nationally wanted production, on the extent of locationally associated linkages, and on the succeeding growth of market, service, and footloose industries (Perloff and Wingo, 1961).

The role of resources in promoting growth usually receives less emphasis in urban development models. But North's discussion of regional growth and that of Pred (1966: 46-83) on American metropolitan growth contain obvious similarities. Pred ascribes to the extension (and location) of the American railroad net the main role in determining the rate at which cities grew in the second half of the nineteenth century. As transport facilities improved, cities could produce goods for increasingly extensive areas, and the relative accessibility of cities to the entire U.S. market became of greater consequence to their rates of advance. As does North, Pred emphasises production for export, based on comparative advantage (location near the U.S. market and access to this market through railroads).

North's detailed analysis of American regional growth until 1860 (North, 1961) illustrates his argument. Regional specialisation began in the period 1790-1814, with the northeast concentrating on trade and associated services, the south heavily committed to cotton, and the west (across the Appalachians) starting to supply food to the south via the Mississippi River (North, 1961: 47-53). After the Napoleonic Wars, although the immigration of people and capital was significant, it was the growth of cotton exports that was decisive to the expansion of the American economy, especially until 1840. In a plantation economy cotton exhibited substantial comparative advantages over other crops, and North employs an argument from Baldwin (1956) to claim that the limited social overhead investment, lack of popular education, and general lack of urbanisation in the south were all direct or indirect results of the region's dependence on cotton exports (North, 1961: 122-34). The northeast had initially to provide services: to finance, transport, insure and market cotton, but gradually, as transport costs fell and the effective size of markets increased, so the northeast was able to begin supplying manufactured goods to the rest of the United States. The initial emphasis on textile and clothing manufactures extended (via backward linkages) into the manufacture of machinery, and (via forward linkages) into trading in these goods (North, 1961: 156-76). The west, after early development as a subsistence economy (because of isolation from markets) entered the market economy by sending food down the Mississippi River system to the south. 'The major determinant of the pace of westward expansion before 1860 continued to be the profitability of the traditional staples: wheat, corn, and their derivatives' (North, 1961: 136), but after 1845 the eastern market became relatively more important than that of the south as eastern urbanisation intensified and overland transport costs fell. Thus, North argues, the timing and pace of economic development in a region was controlled by, firstly, the success of the region's exports, and secondly,

74

the degree to which growth due to exports was transmitted to the rest of the economy (i.e. the value of the multiplier). Perloff and Dodds (1963: 138) echo the general import of these conclusions.

The development of the exporting region may be treated using Metzler's (1950) multiple region model of income and trade. Consider the short run, during which there are no changes in technology, wages, prices, resources, or the distribution of income. The initial accounting equation is

(4-1) $\qquad Y = E + X - M,$

where Y is net regional product, E is spending on investment, consumption and government, X is exports, and M equals imports.
But

(4-2) $\qquad E = a + bY$

(4-3) $\qquad M = c + eY$

(4-4) $\qquad X = \bar{x},$

where a is expenditure when Y is zero, b is marginal propensity to spend, c is the level of imports when Y equals zero, e is the marginal propensity to import, and $\bar{x}$ is the given level of imports. Substitute equations (4-2), (4-3), and (4-4) in equation (4-1):

$$Y = a + bY + \bar{x} - c - eY,$$

which becomes:

(4-5) $\qquad Y = \dfrac{a - c + \bar{x}}{1 - (b - e)}.$

The change in equilibrium income which results from a change in exports (or from a change in a or c) is

(4-6) $\qquad \dfrac{dY}{dx} = \dfrac{1}{1 - (b - e)}.$

This equation measures the degree to which the total income in a region (the export base plus the subsequent activities) varies in response to variations in the sales made by the export base. The level of this index, the multiplier, depends on b and e, where $b - e$ may be defined as the marginal propensity to spend locally. Metzler's model, then, neatly summarises the ideas of the export base school, even though it is merely a short-run model whereas the development model is long-run.

The export base theory may be justified by two observations. The theory maintains firstly that export production is the basis of regional prosperity and, secondly, that export industries in a region are located independently of the consumers in that region. The export industries are consequently vital to the growth of a region and their growth is not dependent on the growth of the local market;

but in growing they provide a market for service, market, and footloose industries. The real foundation of a regional hierarchy is thus the regional export industries.

But the model has been extensively criticised and other factors besides exports have been thought to determine growth. The most important criticisms are that the export base model is an over-simplification of reality; that the model is superficial, in that it does not analyse any causes of regional comparative advantage apart from the effects of resources and multipliers; and that econometric measurement indicates that changes in the level of exports are of relatively minor importance in determining total growth.

Schultz (1953: ch. 10) discusses the evolution of agricultural income disparities in the United States during economic growth. He suggests that the increasing regional income differences are caused largely by the way in which the U.S. economy has developed and are not primarily the results of the physical characteristics of the land itself. Schultz's view is that differences in the suitability of the land for farming are not an important factor in shaping the course of economic development. In fact, Schultz reverses the causative chain: the economy evolves in such a manner as to give some land a comparative advantage over other land in its potential to adjust to economic development, not as a consequence of the productivity of that land, but because of its nearness to a centre of development. Though not a criticism of the export base concept itself, Schultz's work (and some later data reported in the next section) does censure the model's emphasis on resources as a source of the export base.

North and Perloff are not the earliest writers on economic growth to emphasise the role played by fixed natural resources. The notion of a fixed supply of land extends back in classical growth theory at least to Ricardo, whose pessimistic views about development stemmed largely from his obsession with fixed land resources and diminishing returns from agriculture. But two facts indicate that the assumption of fixed resources may not be a useful one for dynamic economic models. The first of these facts is the continued history of western European expansion since the fifteenth century, an expansion which has drawn larger and larger resource areas together into one economic system; exploration of the moon merely continues a process begun five centuries ago. Secondly, the resources available to a community are obtained only by investment, and, just as investment in education increases labour resources, so investment in exploration and knowledge increases 'natural' resources. Land is not in fixed supply, but that supply expands or contracts with knowledge and investment.

Tiebout (1956) has criticised North's statement of the export base model. He points out first that other items besides export incomes affect a region's income: in the United States the most important of these receipts are business investment and government spending. Tiebout also suggests that growth is subject to an important feedback effect, especially in larger regions: the exports of region A depend in part on the income of A's market; but the income of A's market, by the export base model, depends in part on exports to region A (that is, on A's income).

Thirdly, the quantitative importance of exports in determining regional incomes depends in part on the size of the region: an individual exports everything, the United States relatively little. These three points indicate that regional economic growth is not a process as simple as the export base model indicates.

Pfouts (1957) illustrates some of Tiebout's arguments. An economy's trade balance (B) is the difference between its exports (x) and imports (M); assume that both imports and consumption (C) are linearly related to community income (Y):

(4–7) $M = c + eY$

(4–8) $C = a + bY,$

where the marginal propensity to import and to consume are set at e and b respectively. Pfouts shows that an increase in exports relative to imports of dB causes total community income to rise by

(4–9) $dY = dB/[1 - b + be].$

That is, exports, though important, are only one variable out of three which determine community income; the other two are the marginal propensity to import and the marginal propensity to consume. North's theory is fully extended when he argues that these other two variables, the propensities to import and to consume, both depend on the level and type of exports.

Another criticism may be advanced against the export base concept. This reproach depends on the fact that the export base is not independent of other activities within the region. Tiebout (1956) argues that location theory—which explains the creation of the export base—only works if factor costs can be determined. But factor costs depend in part on the nature of the residentiary activities: for example, on the cost of living, on agriculture, and on the economies of scale available. Tiebout quotes the example of the failure to develop Alaska as indicating the importance of factor costs. A further instance is the argument that America dominates world trade in commercial aeroplanes in part because residentiary demand for these aeroplanes is so large as to offer scale economies not available to European producers.

As Tiebout's criticisms predict, exports sometimes make only a relatively minor contribution to regional and national growth. Whereas the observations of North and of Perloff and Wingo are qualitative, an econometric estimate by Chambers and Gordon (1966) challenges the idea of the supremacy of exports. They examine the growth of Canada from 1901 to 1911, and find that the spectacular expansion of Prairie agriculture during this period contributed only 5-8 per cent of the increase in Canadian real income of 23 per cent *per capita*. Clearly, factors other than rising primary exports must be sought to explain the rise in *per capita* incomes. Chambers and Gordon argue that the key to success was technological change, based on education. On the other hand, Borts (1960), in an analysis of the factors influencing regional wage levels in the United States, found strong support for a model of growth founded on the export base concept. In a later study, Borts and Stein (1964) hold that equally as important as the export base in determining regional growth in the United States were regional wage levels.

Pfouts has presented two additional tests of economic base theory, using data on the growth of American cities. He argues that if basic employment increases, the total employment of a city increases too, and conversely; on the other hand, in the short run if basic employment increases, the ratio of basic to non-basic employment ($B:NB$) should fall, and conversely. Thus, over a relatively short period, the change in the value of the ratio $B:NB$ in a city should be negatively related to growth of employment in that city. In fact, for twenty-eight U.S. cities of population between 100,000 and 300,000, the correlation between $B:NB$ changes and growth over the period 1940 to 1950 was almost significantly positive (Pfouts, 1957). Using slightly more sophisticated techniques, Pfouts and Curtis (1958) found a non-significant relationship between these variables among the central cities of forty standard metropolitan areas over the period 1940-50. Although Pfouts's measurement of the economic base is open to objection (Andrews, 1954a, b, c; Blumenfeld, 1955), his results do throw doubt upon the value of the simple base model.

The idea that the export base is *the* fundamental determinant of regional and urban growth is clearly not tenable. Evidence indicates that growth of export incomes may account for less than one-third of growth of total incomes in some regions. The success of the export base may itself be influenced, at least in part, by the nature and scale of residentiary activities. The export base model can only operate completely efficiently in the short run, when the nature of the export sector and comparative advantages are unlikely to change (Thompson, 1965: 29-30). In the longer run, the model is circular.

Hirschman (1958) points out that in non-spatial growth theory, ideas have been changing about what is necessary for economic growth. Up to about 1930 natural resources were thought vital; the role of capital dominated theory in the 1930s, whereas now major emphasis is placed on the importance of entrepreneurial activity and innovation as proximate causes of growth. The argument put forward here is essentially that regional growth theory must progress from an emphasis on exports and resources—perhaps to entrepreneurial and managerial factors.

Concentration and Spreading
One part of the explanation of the degree of concentration of activity in a region is the factors which cause that region to grow at a particular speed and in a particular direction. But another essential portion of the explanatory process is an analysis of the factors promoting and hindering the spread of progress into other regions of the economy. The models which have been constructed in this explanation refer more specifically to space and location than do the export base explanations of the nature of growth. Although these models have typically been

Figure 4–1: **A positive feedback economic system. Arrows indicate the direction of the effect; signs indicate whether correlations are positive or negative.**

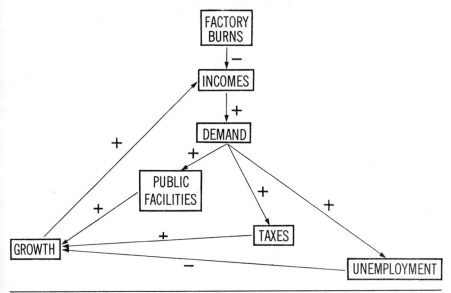

constructed to explain regional growth, some insights into urban growth processes may be gained by determining their applicability to city development.

Perhaps the fundamental fact of regional growth which must be explained by our models is the relative stability of inter-regional variations of activity. The rank order of regions with respect to density levels remains relatively constant over long periods of time. Clark (1967: 289-91) points out, for example, that the regions in late eighteenth-century Europe which were densely populated were also, with limited exceptions, the regions of high population density in 1961. The two main exceptions to this rule are Ireland and southern Italy. Clark ascribes their failure to develop to their poor access to European markets.

Myrdal (1957) has analysed the causes of this stability in terms of spread and concentration effects. He argued that the inherited theoretical approach of economics is inadequate, partly because it assumes that systems tend to a stable equilibrium. On the contrary, it appears that development is characterised by circular and cumulative causation (Myrdal, 1957: 11-22). An example of such a cumulative circle is: because people are poor, they become sick, and because they are sick they work less effectively and so become poorer. Myrdal's point is that change does not necessarily call forth a reaction which operates in the opposite direction to that first change, but rather that a change normally calls forth a supporting change; consequently an equilibrium is not established, but instead greater movement occurs in the direction of the first change. In systems language, whereas the usual assumption is of negative feedback, Myrdal believes that

79

G

economic systems are normally characterised by positive feedback. Figure 4–1 illustrates such a cumulative process. If a factory burns down, regional incomes and demand fall. As a consequence unemployment in other businesses rises, the tax rate has to rise or the quality of public facilities must fall, all of which tend to reduce the rate of growth even further (Myrdal, 1957: 23-6).

Such a cumulative positive-feedback process promotes concentration of rapid growth in a few regions. The traditional equalising factors which were thought to cause growth to spread are migration, capital movements, and trade. Myrdal (1957: 27-9) argues, though, that in reality these are ineffectual promoters of regional equality. Migration away from a low income area, though it increases the value of resources per head in that area, also harms the region because those migrating tend to be in the most productive age group and to be the most enter-prising members of the community. (Neutze, 1962, also makes this point, but Okun and Richardson, 1961, dispute it.) Capital movements also increase inequality between regions, for they siphon capital off to regions where returns are high (i.e. to regions of rapid growth). Myrdal argues too that relatively developed areas have, by definition, a comparative advantage over less developed areas: hence the poorer regions are likely to stagnate industrially as a result of trade. These three elements then, are factors which enhance the concentration of activity and growth in a few regions, not factors which weaken that concentration.

Although he is concerned to analyse the process of regional concentration, Myrdal also discusses spread effects (1957: 31-5). These are effects by which some of the impetus of growth in a region is transmitted to other areas. Rising demand within the growing region requires that at least some goods (notably raw materials) be produced in another region: the subsequent increase of income generates some new consumer industries there. The growth process thus begins in a second region. Another important cause of diffusion is the development of external diseconomies of scale in the growing region, which forces firms to look outside that growth pole for suitable locations. (But the growth of Megalopolis and of the London region reveal that external diseconomies may impinge only a little on firms' decisions.)

Pred (1965; 1966: 12-85) has presented a model of American metropolitan growth over the period 1860 to 1914 which relies upon Myrdal's analysis. Pred interprets metropolitan growth in terms of initial advantages (early accessibility to the national market through the railroad net, local innovation, and the de-velopment of an early capital market) and of circular and cumulative causation. Cities, like regions, grow by circular mechanisms; different rates of growth reflect initial advantages. Similar principles govern the diffusion of growth in both urban and regional systems, even though particular causes may differ between the systems.

A similar analysis of regional growth has been presented by Hirschman (1958: 183-201). He assumes that economic development does not appear everywhere at the same time. This initial premise is easy to accept: at the very least, innova-tions are at first spatially concentrated. Hirschman then analyses the forces which

encourage or limit the spread of progress away from the area of early development. Assume that there are two areas within the economy, one progressed (i.e.
the location of the innovation: 'North'), and one backward ('South'). Some progress trickles down to South, for North increases its purchase and investments in
South and absorbs some of South's unemployment. On the other hand, polarisation effects are also apparent. First, Northern goods undersell South's manufacturing output and exports, which are, by definition, inefficiently produced;
secondly, Northern manufacturers may demand the erection of a tariff wall
which, if established, causes prices to rise in South without generating a corresponding increase in incomes there; and thirdly, migration to the North tends to
be of South's most enterprising men. Even if polarisation is the predominant
effect, however, Hirschman suggests that North must eventually develop South
—if only because of the congestion in North and the problems caused by a small
home market (due, in turn, to depressed Southern incomes).

The value of increasing returns has been analysed both theoretically and
empirically. 'The superiority of one country over another in a branch of production, often arises only from having begun it sooner. There may be no inherent
advantage on one part, or disadvantage on the other, but only a present superiority of acquired skill and experience' (Mill, 1848, vol. 2, bk V: 495). Young
(1928) analyses 'present superiority'; he assumes true Adam Smith's dictum that
the division of labour depends on the extent of the market, and points out that
the extent of the market (its size and income) depends on the increasing returns
of roundabout production (that is, on the division of labour). Smith's statement
thus becomes that division of labour depends on the extent of the market which,
in turn, depends on the division of labour. In this cumulative process and the
incident increasing returns, Young thinks, lie the main possibilities of economic
progress, apart from that progress which comes as a result of new knowledge.

Similarly, Wensley and Florence (1940) analyse the cumulative growth process
which has caused industrial concentration in the English Midlands. The initial
industries in the region and their labour force provide a market for market
oriented industries, which augment the local market, which in turn attracts more
industries, and so on. The advantages which an area acquires for an industry,
once established, intensify a positive feedback process which is moderated only
by scarcity of land and by difficulties of labour supply.

On the other hand, Rosenstein-Rodan (1943) suggests why spread effects might
be weak. He argues that nineteenth-century concepts of industrialisation may
not be applicable to the present generation of developing countries. One reason
for this is the increasing proportion of total capital which is absorbed by over-
heads and fixed assets: a rising proportion of fixed capital increases risks and so
reduces the mobility of resources. For Rosenstein-Rodan, a major element in the
social profitability of an enterprise is external economies, which do not figure at
all in the profitability comparisons of private investment. Some examples of
external economies which he quotes include the training of labour and the complementarity of industries: whereas one individual firm might gain but a small

81

market for its goods, an entire planned complex of industries would create jobs and so provide much of its own market.

In effect these writers construct two main arguments. There are first the trickling down (spread) effects: increased purchases in the poor regions, migration to the growth pole, and diseconomies of scale and agglomeration in the growing region. Secondly, polarisation effects include the underselling of other regions' goods, tariffs, differential migration from the underdeveloped areas, agglomeration economies, and, according to Myrdal, capital flows to the growth pole. Some of these factors must now be investigated further in order to determine the fundamental forces affecting the degree to which development polarises. It must be remembered that the analysis assumes a system in which knowledge is perfect.

All writers agree that polarisation is enhanced by extensive agglomeration economies—especially if these economies are available over a wide range of output before diseconomies set in. As in town growth, apparently, economies of agglomeration are a major cause of the degree of concentration of activity. These agglomeration economies are (i) transfer economies, offered to linked firms through transport cost savings, (ii) external economies of scale to a firm in one industry as localised output in that industry rises, and (iii) external economies of scale available to firms in many industries (such as transport, labour, and commercial overhead services). Included within agglomeration economies, therefore, is the polarisation effect of the goods made in the developed region underselling goods made in less developed regions. Similarly, Myrdal's argument that the flow of capital to developed regions enhances polarisation, is an argument about the effects of agglomeration economies; for capital flows to where its price (and so the demand for its services) is high, and its price is highest where it is most productive, that is, where industry is most efficient (where agglomeration economies are most fully developed).

A second element affecting polarisation is the degree to which the growth region purchases goods from other regions. The extent of the diffusion caused by such purchases depends primarily on the marginal propensity to import. (The connection with the export base model through this mechanism explicitly links this growth model to location.) Since the growth pole has a comparative advantage in producing industrial and service goods, its demand from other areas is mainly for agricultural goods and industrial raw materials. It follows that, except for a few vital raw materials and fuels (such as petroleum), the marginal propensity of the growth pole to import is relatively low. The extent of dispersal of growth due to external purchases is relatively low. Perhaps a major difference between urban and regional growth arises from the greater dispersal of urban growth: the marginal propensity to import is higher in towns than in regions.

The third determinant of polarisation is the degree of inter-regional migration and the differences between the migrating and non-migrating cohorts in ages and skills. Since knowledge is assumed to be perfect, people migrate in response to the real wage differentials which have been created by development in one region of the country. To this extent, real wages are equalised over the economy. On the other hand, migration is inhibited by the cost of moving, of packing, transporting, and re-establishing a household. Over a perfect system, then, real wages are not exactly equal, but rather reflect the costs of migrating, by means of a real wage gradient away from the developed area: the further an area is from the development pole, the lower are wages there.

In a perfect system, differences in migration rates between portions of the population may arise in several ways. The demand for skilled labour in a developing economy rises more rapidly than the demand for unskilled labour. Therefore the ratio of the demand for skilled labour to the demand for unskilled labour is higher in the growth pole than in the underdeveloped regions of the economy, and the difference in ratios increases with increasing differences in degree of development. Correspondingly, real wages for skilled labour rise more rapidly than real wages for unskilled labour in the developed region; the difference in wages is greater than it is in the underdeveloped regions. Therefore skilled labour is more attracted to the development pole than is unskilled labour. The developing agglomeration attracts skilled labour away from the poorer regions to a relatively greater extent than it attracts unskilled labour.

The effect of age on migration may be analysed in a similar manner. A migrant invests money in relocating, an investment which may increase slightly with his age (for a person's goods and chattels normally increase to some extent with his age). To this investment there corresponds a return, which is the future annual flow of increased income—the annual value of the difference in real wages between the two regions, discounted into the future. Given a fixed retiring age, the older a migrant is, the less time he has to recoup his investment, and so the less likely it is that he finds it worthwhile to make the investment decision to migrate. Similarly, people in those occupations in which wage differentials are least are the people least likely to recoup an investment in migration. Therefore the growth pole attracts migrants from the less developed regions who include proportionately more of the younger and more skilled workers than their numbers in less developed regions would indicate. To this extent, Myrdal's point about the detrimental effects of emigration is valid.

The degree to which development polarises within an economy depends on three factors. Polarisation is enhanced by: extensive economies of agglomeration, a low marginal propensity to import the products of other regions, and a low demand for unskilled immigrants together with a relatively wide wage differential for skilled as compared with unskilled workers. Such an analysis is clearly similar to the supra-national scale model of Prebisch (1950, 1959), in which he develops the contrast between the urban-industrial heartland nations and the countries of the 'periphery'.

The model of Myrdal and Hirschman is also relevant to the question of the dynamic adjustment of agriculture which was discussed in the previous chapter. Schultz (1953: ch. 9) argues that economic development takes place within specific locational matrices (which are primarily urban-industrial in character) and that the existing economic organisation of agriculture operates most effect-ively in locations favourably situated with respect to such matrices. Hoselitz (1953, 1955) has also provided a documented discussion of the relationship between urbanisation and the development of the surrounding regions. While recognising that some cities had parasitic relationships with their hinterlands, he found that, in medieval Europe, growth in most cities strongly affected the non-urban regions located near them. Local rural development was stimulated by (i) rising urban demand for labour, which encouraged commuting from rural areas, (ii) rising demand for the industrial raw materials of the surrounding regions, and (iii) increasing demand for food from the countryside. More recently, Nicholls (1956, 1960) has explored the implications of industrial development in the Tennessee Valley and Piedmont for agriculture. The more industrial counties are characterised by greater resources per farm, larger farms, better factor com-binations, and higher farm incomes per worker than the less industrial counties. Nicholls ascribes the beneficial effect of industrialisation to the creation of a local demand for non-farm jobs and the influx of outside capital. While particular causes vary with time and scale, the analyses of Hoselitz and Nicholls are clearly contained within the framework of the growth pole model.

The model of polarisation has not been empirically tested at this generalised level; rather, testing has concentrated on four main aspects of it—the idea of cumulative causation, and the measurement of inter-regional flows of capital, commodities, and labour. Several writers have commented that economic development tends to concentrate in the areas which are already most advanced. Some examples are regional development in Europe (Economic Commission for Europe, 1955: 136-77), Britain (Caesar, 1964), Mexico (Nicholson, 1965: 164-9), and Uganda (O'Connor, 1963). The concept is also stressed in studies of the United States—both of regional (Perloff and Wingo, 1961) and of metropolitan (Pred, 1965) growth. Baer (1964) has documented the means used in Brazil to maintain inter-regional income differences. Although the particular structures of the positive feedback system may not have been established, the fact that concen-tration induces further concentration seems to have been agreed by most empirical workers. Similarly, several studies have demonstrated the existence of the inter-regional flows necessary to support polarisation. Williamson (1965: 7) has reported that capital transfers in Indonesia are predominantly from the outer islands to the central, more developed areas, while Robock (1963: 108) has documented private transfers from the poor north to the booming southeast of Brazil. Smith (1953: 93-121) has argued that goods manufactured in the indust-rialising growth regions of the United Kingdom during the early nineteenth century depressed the smaller scale and less efficient industry of the more back-ward areas. And Hathaway (1960) and Williamson (1965: 6) indicate that in the United States and Indonesia the volume of labour flows, their direction and their selectivity, are roughly in accordance with those predicted by the model. Okun (1967) also presents data for the United States which confirm Myrdal's notion that migration is a force for widening interstate differences in incomes *per capita*

Table 4-1: Association between national *per capita* income and regional income inequalities within states, 1960

Income group	Members of group	Mean group inequality V_w	Mean group inequality M_w
I	Australia, N.Z., Canada, U.K., U.S.A., Sweden	·139	·117
II	Finland, France, W. Germany, Netherlands, Norway	·252	·201
III	Ireland, Chile, Austria, Puerto Rico	·335	·290
IV	Brazil, Italy, Spain, Colombia, Greece	·464	·381
V	Yugoslavia, Japan	·292	·223
VI	Philippines	·556	·296
VII	India	·275	·194

Source: Williamson, 1965.

(though he disagrees with Myrdal's hypothetical cause of the observation). The theory seems, then, to have some empirical validity: indeed, the model and the evidence about it have sufficient force for it to be used as a policy prescription for the efficient allocation of resources over space (Lefeber, 1964).

Myrdal (1957: 34) argued that spread effects become more important than polarisation effects as incomes rise in a country, because high income countries have better transport and communications networks than do poorer countries. Williamson (1965) supported this notion by pointing out that external economies in the North may begin to diminish over time; that the central government may begin to develop regional income equalisation policies; and that the relative demand for skilled as compared with unskilled labour diminishes in the North in relation to the South. To test this hypothesis, Williamson measured the weighted coefficient of variation of regional income *per capita*, by two formulae:

$$(4-10) \qquad V_w = \frac{1}{\bar{y}} \sqrt{\sum_i (y_i - \bar{y})^2 \frac{f_i}{n}},$$

and

$$(4-11) \qquad M_w = \frac{1}{\bar{y}} \sum_i |y_i - \bar{y}| \frac{f_i}{n},$$

where f_i = population of the *i*th region, n = national population, y_i = income per head in the *i*th region, and $\bar{y}$ = national income per head. Table 4-1 contains Williamson's results: the cross-section data indicate that, with the exception of the Philippines, medium income countries exhibit wider variations in regional income than either high or low income countries. Williamson also examines regional income variations within the individual states of the U.S.A. Noting that the lowest income state (Mississippi) has *per capita* incomes above those of the medium income countries listed in Table 4-1, he expects and finds a negative correlation between income and inequality for both 1950 and 1960.

85

Conclusions

The two theories examined in this chapter represent, with their extensions, significant generalisations of many of the present ideas about regional growth. The relatively simple export base model has to be augmented in order to accommodate the other factors influencing growth and in order to incorporate an analysis of the effects of residentiary activity on exports and growth. Nevertheless the model points up one factor—exports, based on resources—which helps mould growth. Once this initial growth has taken place, the cumulative causation hypothesis of Myrdal and Hirschman indicates that development may remain concentrated rather than being transmitted through the whole system, and that the degree of polarisation may increase during economic development. Location theory under conditions of certainty can therefore predict the existence of regions of relatively intense activity and can suggest some of the factors which promote this concentration. Regional wage differentials in such an economy should be relatively small and, as economic development proceeds, should first increase and later decrease in magnitude.

On the other hand, these growth models yield few explicit conclusions about the location of these concentrations, their size and spacing, and the activities present within them. Implicitly, the models do provide some information about these aspects of growth. For example, the greater the polarisation effects as compared to spread effects, the greater the degree to which activity is concentrated in one or a few regions, and so, presumably, the greater is the average size of those concentrations and the larger is the average distance between them. At a more formal level, though, spacing relationships are less obvious. To the extent that developed areas maintain underdeveloped peripheral regions around them, as sources of primary goods and as markets, concentrations disperse. In comparison with distant areas, regions close to the development pole are subject to greater competition from that pole and so are less likely to develop in their own right. Yet, in so far as much of the trade of developed regions is with other developed regions—Duncan et al. (1960) and Berry (1966) provide evidence to this effect—the developed regions gain an advantage from being close together.

Some hints have been provided about the possible locations of regional concentrations. Hicks (1948: 166) and Pred (1965) have both argued that an early start is of great advantage to developing regions, whether this start occurs through the spatially random processes of chance innovation (Hirschman, 1958) and freak harvest (Bensusan-Butt, 1960) or through good location with respect to areas of emigration (such as the location of New England) or because of the advantages of a useful resource base. Ullman (1958) has suggested that development areas are likely to be located near the spatial centre of an economy. On the one hand, fringe areas are often remote from the rest of the economy; on the other, they must by definition have less area and so a smaller probability of developing a large local market than a central area. However, Ullman does recognise that fringe areas display the advantage of a protected local market, a factor which Perloff et al. (1961: ch. 11) argue has encouraged the rapid growth of California. In addition, the growth of fringe areas is enhanced by cheap sea transport; this is one important factor which has promoted the development of Australia's coastal belt. But a formal analysis of regional location under certainty has not yet been attempted.

Similarly, little has been written of the industries which concentrate within regions. An implication of the North and Perloff and Wingo model is that the regional export industries must be capable of being transported over relatively long distances—that is, they must be of relatively high value in relation to their cost of transport—and must be capable of being sold at a distance (it is difficult to envisage such service industries as retailing providing an export base). Once regional development has begun, the Myrdal-Hirschman model implies that those industries concentrate to the greater extent in which agglomeration economies are greatest and in which access to a large local market is most vital. Furthermore, the probability of a high degree of concentration is greatest among those industries which use the least land in their production processes. Thus the most concentrated industries should be those characterised by goods which are valuable in relation to freight rates, by extensive agglomeration economies, by the need for large local markets, and by production functions which require only little land.

The main ideas of spatial growth theory appear then in the status of received doctrine, being approved both theoretically and empirically. This is especially true when some of the extensions of the export base model are brought within the analytical framework. But the theory has been applied solely to growth and to the formation of regions of concentrated activity, not to any of the more detailed questions—of the location, size, spacing, and nature of these concentrations— which must properly be treated by a fully developed theory. (Of course, as Chapter 2 makes clear, this criticism is less relevant to urban growth theory than to regional growth models. This is one point of contrast between the two model forms.) As we shall see later, there remains room for further development of these models, even within the realm of the factors causing concentration.

5   Decision Making in Uncertainty

The previous three chapters have analysed the location patterns which theory predicts would develop in an economy in which knowledge is complete. In such a system the decision-making criterion is clear—to maximise the discounted net rate of return from an investment—and normally provides a clear indication of what action to take. (There may, however, arise some confusion about long and short run decisions.) Furthermore, in such theories of choice there is a one-to-one correspondence between actions and their consequences. But when it is assumed that knowledge within the system is imperfect, and therefore that entrepreneurs are uncertain, neither of these conditions remains true. In the first place, there is a multiplicity of theories of rational choice, each of which seems applicable to only a limited range of situations (though it is not always clear to precisely what range of conditions the theories do apply). And secondly, there is no necessary correspondence between an action and its consequence; consequences are not certain and therefore are not uniquely related to actions.

There has long existed in location theory a dichotomy between theories of the actual behaviour of firms and theories of the rational behaviour of firms. In much of economics it is often supposed that firms actually do behave rationally. The theory of location no longer pretends that the models which assume certainty are theories of behaviour: rather that these theories may account for the location of activity once social and economic pressures have adjusted location patterns to best serve the needs of that society. However, location models which assume uncertainty can pretend that they account for the actual behaviour of firms. The models of choice which are discussed in this chapter may therefore be regarded either as models merely describing rational behaviour or as models claiming to describe actual behaviour. This chapter begins by assuming only that these are models of rational behaviour, and analyses and describes in some detail those models which appear most useful to location theory; it is left to the final section of the chapter to defend the notion that entrepreneurs may actually behave in the rational manner described by the criteria of choice.

Uncertainty is introduced into location models in order to extend the range and accuracy of the predictions derived from those models. 'In this [classical economic] theory there is no room for uncertainty. The theory assumes that people decide how to consume, produce, and invest with full knowledge of what the outcome of their decisions will be. Uncertainty is either ignored or explicitly "assumed away". It is obvious that the resulting theory is not very realistic, and probably not very useful' (Borch, 1968: 9). But what phenomena and behaviours are introduced into location theory by the assumption of uncertainty?

Phenomena Related to Uncertainty
Before analysing criteria of choice under uncertainty, it may be useful to describe some of the features of economic organisation which may be associated with uncertainty. This description will provide some idea of the facts which a theory of choice must at the very minimum explain. Arrow (1951) discusses some of these facts, though not in a spatial context.

Gambling and insurance are obvious examples of phenomena which by their very definition are concerned with uncertainty. In gambling, an individual shows a preference for the combination of a small probability of a large gain and a large probability of a small loss to the certain event that his income will be larger than the mathematical expectation of his gamble. Gambling events require that an individual's utility for money is such that the small probability of a large gain is more valuable than the almost certain event that he loses. The fact that individuals may like gambling (that is, obtain utility from the act of gambling itself, not merely from the possibility of gain) has posed serious problems for the theory of choice in uncertainty. In insurance, of course, one is acting differently: the almost certainty of a small loss is preferred to the very small probability of a large loss.

Arrow (1951) also discusses a second type of phenomena, events which are not related to uncertainty by definition, but which nevertheless have no other conceivable explanation. Included within this class are legally guaranteed incomes, variations in the rate of return on securities, and the fact that firms hold inventories larger than those demanded simply by economies of bulk purchasing. The importance of these phenomena seems to require statistical evaluation, from which comparisons with the predictions of choice theories could be made.

The third class of events is more interesting to location theorists. These are phenomena the relationship of which with uncertainty may be disputed. It has been argued that both the existence of profits (in the sense of a residual left after all factor payments, including interest on capital, have been made) and limitations on the size of firms are due to uncertainty.

Thus Knight (1921: ch. 2) contends that under pure competition there would be no profits: in a static society there can by definition be no profits, and if innovations occur, these can offer small temporary profits only if there are frictions retarding the rate of adoption of those innovations. Similarly, Shackle (1955: ch. 8) argues that, since production involves a time lag between the decision to manufacture and the making of sales, production is subject to uncer-

89

tainty, and decisions have to be made about courses of action the consequences of which are uncertain. These two inter-related uncertainties have profit as their reward: profit would not exist without uncertainty. But as Arrow (1951: 408) points out, the statistical evidence on the magnitude of pure profits can only be described as negligible.

A second event which may be related to uncertainty is the fact that firm size is limited. In perfect markets with certainty, there is no place for management, except in the sense of establishing initial plans; since the firm is a managerial rather than a technical organisation, there is correspondingly no limit to the size of firms under certainty. Depending on the point of view, there exists then only one firm or no firms at all (Heady, 1960: 535). By contrast uncertainty does appear to pose some limits to the size of firms through the operation of managerial diseconomies of scale: where knowledge of change and the future is uncertain, management must function continuously. As uncertainty increases so the number of decisions which must be made by management also increases; the greater the number of decisions per unit time period, the less perfect they become because the supporting knowledge upon which each is based becomes less perfect. Consequently diminishing returns from management are the result of imperfect decisions and the misdirection of resources relative to price and production outcomes (Kaldor, 1934). If entrepreneurs measure uncertainty by the dispersion or the range of expected outcomes, then uncertainty limits firm size in another manner (Heady, 1960: 538-42). Suppose that the odds of success are five to one: if the outcome is favourable, $5 are returned for every dollar invested, whereas in unfavourable outcomes the investment is lost. Thus the range of outcomes from an investment of $100 is $600 and from an investment of $10,000 is $60,000. While the rate of earnings on the investment is constant, the range of outcomes and the possible loss increase as the size of the investment rises. Hicks has argued (1948: 200) that 'As the planned size of the firm increases, the possible losses become steadily greater; and people will usually become less and less willing to expose themselves to the chance of such losses.' Uncertainty may also limit firm size through the principle of increasing risk. This principle suggests that as a firm expands by the use of borrowed capital, the chance of loss of its own capital increases (Kalecki, 1939: 95-106; Steindl, 1945). A firm has to pay interest on borrowed capital; if its rate of return is not equal to the market rate of interest, payments for borrowed capital reduce still further the return on the entrepreneur's own capital. Although the odds of success remain the same—or even improve if there are economies of scale—the possible loss of the firm's own capital increases.

Thus uncertainty poses a limit to the optimum size of firms. But location theorists are more interested in plant size than in firm size. In a perfect spatial economy, even without technical diseconomies to scale, plants must be limited in size, because of transport costs on marketing goods and obtaining raw materials. In an economy with perfect knowledge, even though the firm is of unlimited size, there will be several plants in each industry, scattered over space. Correspondingly, uncertainty and plant size are not necessarily related, though if most firms own only one plant, uncertainty, by limiting firm size, may reduce plant size below the optimum output level which occurs under certainty. The greater the uncertainty, the greater may be this limitation.

Closely associated with these ideas about the existence of firms is the point made by Isard (1969: 57-9): that with the introduction of uncertainty it becomes useful to analyse the allocation of government authority and power among regions and to examine the spatial distribution of decision-making power. Some theoretical aspects of planning, particularly in relation to uncertainty, are discussed in Chapter 10. But the location of decision-making 'plants' may be analysed in exactly the same terms (transport costs, density of demand, and agglomeration economies) as any other plant. In empirical situations, the values of these variables may be different for decision making and other plants—for example, transfer costs may be low and agglomeration economies high—but the principles remain very similar. Hence the location of decision making is not discussed explicitly in this book.

A third set of phenomena which occur under conditions of uncertainty comprises behaviour which arises from the gradual extension or contraction of knowledge over time. At any one point in time, our knowledge is in error and our perception of the environment does not constitute a simple linear transformation of that environment: some resources are unknown, distances are distorted, risks may be improperly appreciated. A psychologist studying perception is analysing a fact which arises from uncertainty. But knowledge becomes more accurate, and the increments of accuracy are spread among a population. The diffusion of an innovation—the spread of a new piece of information—is also closely associated with uncertainty.

A fourth fact which has been related to uncertainty is Pareto non-optimality in decision taking. Tisdell (1963) assumes two products manufactured by firms whose production decisions are made n periods before the output is produced; a given distribution of inputs between the firms; a fixed aggregate level of inputs; and a convex technical transformation function for each firm. If firms predict different price ratios for the two products, then the economy's output is less than that possible: if firms act on the basis of different price ratios, the Pareto conditions for maximisation of welfare are not satisfied. Furthermore, the greater the variations in price ratios, the greater is the reduction of output as compared to the maximum. Uncertainty reduces social welfare.

Uncertainty and its Consequences

If a theory of choice under uncertainty is erected, this theory presupposes that the consequences of a choice in uncertainty can be described. To describe uncertain choices quite clearly demands some reference to probability: what is probability? This question is one to which no single answer commands general agreement; therefore no single method of describing consequences or of ordering these consequences is generally agreed to be best. Fortunately, this disagreement about the

91

bases of decision making may not be too serious for location theory, because statistics—sometimes described as the science of decision making under uncertainty—has provided important conclusions despite the fact that statisticians disagree about the foundations of the subject. As Savage points out, 'catastrophe is avoided, primarily because in practical situations common sense generally saves all but the most pedantic of us from flagrant error' (Savage, 1954: 1).

The mathematical theory of probability is itself well defined and subject to little disagreement. The basis of the theory is the definition of a probability measure: a probability measure on a set S is a function $P(B)$ attaching to each event, B, within $S(B \subset S)$ a real number such that

1. $P(B) \geqslant 0$ for every B,

2. If $B \cap C = 0$, $P(B \cup C) = P(B) + P(C)$, and

3. $P(S) = 1$.

The first criterion implies that probabilities are non-negative; the second that, if two events are mutually exclusive, the probability of one or other or both of these events occurring is the sum of the probabilities of each event; and the third criterion indicates that the probability of the certain event is 1. This axiomatic system, ascribed to Kolmogorov (1950), is in little dispute, in contrast to the interpretation of probability, which is controversial. There are three main views about the intuitive meaning of probability.

The first of these views has been called the necessary theory of probability. This theory has been advanced by Keynes (1921) and Carnap (1950), who suggest that probability measures the degree to which one proposition necessarily implies another, out of logical necessity; probability theory is thus held to be an extension of logic. This theory will not be used in this book for two reasons. The first reason is that, since the theory abstracts from human opinion (it relies only on logical necessity), it seems peculiarly ill-suited to use in models of locational decision taking. Secondly, as Savage (1954: 61) claims, the development of a necessary theory of probability remains highly incomplete.

The second view, the objectivistic one, is an empirical interpretation of probability. Von Mises (1941) argued that probability measures the degree of frequency with which an event occurs: the probability of an event occurring can be found only by measuring the number of times it occurs and the number of times it fails to occur. No other evidence is allowed. But the theory contains three difficulties. Firstly, it can apply only to repetitive events: it is not meaningful in terms of the objectivistic view to make the statement that the probability of my dying in the next decade is 0·25. Either I die or I do not. In this relative frequency theory a once and for all event cannot have a probability distribution. Secondly, and following this argument, it is impossible in objectivistic terms to compute the expected income of acts and to choose to maximise this expected income, because each act can have associated with it only one possible consequence: the expected value of an act is the value of its (yet to be observed) consequence. This deficiency is particularly unfortunate in the analysis of location decisions, where the idea of expected values is often useful. Thirdly, Savage (1954: 62) has accused the objectivists of circularity. Probability measures assume an infinite sequence of independent events, an idealisation the value of which and the errors inherent in which can only be determined by experience. But it is the purpose of probability theory to analyse the concept of experience, and the theory cannot be supported by alluding to experience until the concept has itself been analysed. The relative frequency theory has consequently not been used.

Instead the later analyses are mainly predicated on the theory that probability is a measure of degree of belief. The theory asserts that if I say that the probability of my dying in the next decade is 0·25, then I believe that this is the probability of my dying; that is, probability measures the degree of confidence one has in a particular proposition. An important implication is that two people may disagree about the probability of a hypothesis being true even though they have used the same evidence. Assuming six reasonable postulates about behaviour, Savage (1954: 1-55) shows how the axiomatic probability system can be constructed from a simple ordering of acts with respect to preference.

The theory that probability measures degree of belief is therefore used as a crude approximation of the way in which people actually behave. Such a use is closely associated with applications of Bayes's Theorem. The degree to which one believes that a proposition is true depends on the *a priori* belief which one has in the truth of proposition and on the evidence culled to investigate the proposition. Bayes's Theorem indicates how these two elements should be compounded to yield an *a posteriori* probability that the proposition is true. Let the symbol $P(A|B)$ mean the probability that A (the proposition) is true, given that B, the evidence, is true. Suppose that it is known that one of the mutually exclusive hypotheses, $H_1, H_2, \ldots, H_n$, is true and that the event X has occurred. Then the probability that the hypothesis H_i is true given the evidence, X, is

$$(5\text{-}1) \qquad P(H_i|X) = \frac{P(X|H_i) \cdot P(H_i)}{P(X)}.$$

The use of the theory requires, then, that people entertain *a priori* probabilities. Arrow (1951) points out that, although this period's *a priori* probabilities are the last period's *a posteriori* probabilities, the process has to start somewhere: there must be some point at which people formulate degrees of belief without reference to evidence. This is usually thought to be accomplished by the Principle of Insufficient Reason (Bernoulli, 1738). This principle states that if there is no evidence that one event is more probable than another, the two events should be judged equally likely. But criticism has been brought against this principle (Arrow, 1951; Savage, 1954: 64-6), on the grounds that it can lead to divergent, non-unique views. This is probably a major theoretical difficulty in a personal theory of probability, though in practical applications it need not hinder the development of useful results (because *a posteriori* probabilities converge after only a few applications of Bayes's Theorem to evidence).

Classification of Uncertain Decision Situations

In order usefully to analyse choice in uncertainty, and in particular to draw locational conclusions from this analysis, we must classify (and therefore, simplify) the range of decision situations in which an individual may be placed. Isard (1969: 160-221) has described such situations in terms of behavioural assumptions, which relate to an individual's abilities, tastes, attitudes and standards, and of structural assumptions (which describe the individual's knowledge of the external situation).

Isard (1969: 161-88) has defined a decision situation as involving an individual in a choice problem described by five aspects. First, the individual perceives alternative courses of action. Secondly, he realises that some outcomes may result from his action, the exact outcome depending on the acts of other individuals or on the state of the environment; only one prospect can be associated with each combination of actions and state of the environment. Thirdly, the individual exhibits preferences among the outcomes, and chooses that outcome which he most prefers. In situations which are characterised by a unique association of acts and outcomes (i.e. certainty), this third aspect automatically implies a choice of action. But under uncertainty, an individual's actions depend also on a fourth aspect—his objectives, which embody his concepts of the optimal state of affairs and define his optimising behaviour. Finally, when confronting other individuals, one has some guiding principles, moral and procedural rules, which delimit one's range of acceptable outcomes. Having thus defined a decision situation, Isard can describe an extremely wide range of human types; and this generality accords well with his attempt to derive a general equilibrium statement. In this book, the aim of which is to produce low level predictions of specific locational behaviour, the rules about individual behaviour must be more closely defined, as is done when discussing choice procedures below.

The structural conditions specify the second element in a description of decision situations. Isard (1969: 190-200) classifies decision situations by two criteria into 26×20 cases (though some of these cases are empty).

The first criterion relates to an individual's knowledge of properties which are independent of any other participant. It comprises four sub-criteria:

(i) The number of possible plays (i.e. the number of actions which are made). Most location decisions are one-play situations, for the locator normally intends that he choose a location only once; but some cases—such as the collection of information—do require many plays. Later in this chapter simple sequential decision taking is analysed, but most decision situations are assumed to involve only one play.

(ii) The number of moves per play. This sub-criterion is relevant only to bargaining situations, and so will be treated as merely one facet of bargaining.

(iii) The degree of knowledge about the environment. Isard classifies individuals as having no knowledge at all about what state of the environment will occur (they are uncertain), or as knowing the probabilities associated with each state of the environment (they have probabilistic knowledge), or as knowing for certain which state will occur. This classification of knowledge as certain, risky (probabilistic), or uncertain (no probabilities) was introduced into economics by Knight (1921), and has become a traditional view. But recently the dichotomy of risk and uncertainty has been questioned: for instance, Borch, introducing the proceedings of a conference on risk and uncertainty (Borch and Mossin, 1968), comments that there is no need to distinguish risk and uncertainty, and that the distinction played no fundamental role in any paper given at the conference. Savage (1962: 14) comments that it is impossible to define the situation of knowing nothing, that is, of complete uncertainty. In this book, therefore, we shall not employ the distinction between risk and uncertainty.

(iv) Classification of action spaces as having a finite or a continuous range of actions. But this distinction is mainly of technical (mathematical) interest, and it will not be employed in classifying decision situations.

Isard's second criterion describes the individual's knowledge of properties which relate to the other participants. The two sub-criteria which he employs are the degree of knowledge of other participants' action choices and objectives, and the nature of possible agreements and threats. For simplicity it is normally assumed in this book that firms are homogeneous, unless the analysis provides a reason why firms should differ: inter-firm differences are an outcome, not an assumption of the analysis. Thus we make the heroic (but traditional) assumptions that firms have complete knowledge of each others' preferences and objectives. The nature of possible threats and bargains becomes important only when bargaining can take place: in location decision taking, the possibility of bargaining is a more important criterion than the nature of the bargaining which is permitted. Thus the classification which follows omits the nature of bargaining as a criterion.

Isard's discussion yields three criteria which are useful in classifying locational decision-taking situations. These are (i) whether decision taking is once-and-for-all or sequential: for simplification of analyses, sequential decision taking is treated as a completely separate topic, and so the analyses of location decisions assume that each firm takes only one action; (ii) the degree of environmental knowledge (certain or uncertain); and (iii) whether or not bargaining is permitted. But in addition, it is useful to characterise situations as being purely competitive (what one firm gains, the other loses) or mixed motive (there is some competition between firms, but they can improve the outcomes by co-operating). Differences also arise according to whether there is only one firm or several.

The resulting classification of uncertain location decision situations is presented in Table 5-1. This table contains many fewer cases than Isard's classification, because sequential decision taking is omitted (and treated as a separate topic), because firms are assumed to know each others' motives and preferences, and because the sub-classifications of bargaining situations are not included. Whereas Isard intends his discussion of decision taking to relate to political and

H

Table 5-1: **Classification of uncertain location decision situations**

Case no.	No. of firms	Degree of competition	Possibility of bargaining
I	1	—	—
II	$\geqslant 2$	Competitive	—
III	$\geqslant 2$	Mixed motive	None
IV	$\geqslant 2$	Mixed motive	Permitted

Note: In purely competitive situations, it is never an advantage to bargain: hence there exist in the classification no 'competitive-bargaining permitted' classes.

social, as well as to economic, environments (so that bargaining forms a most important component of his analyses), this book is limited to location decisions, to which bargaining has only slight applicability. Unless firms are large, they cannot bargain about location decisions, for small locating firms cannot communicate with other locating firms (especially when some of those firms may not have decided whether or not to exist).

Most economists have assumed that the main source of uncertainty to a firm is uncertainty about market prices (see Borch and Mossin, 1968). While this is a natural assumption from the point of view of a businessman, it hinders rather than helps an analysis of location choices under uncertainty. Prices are not fundamental independent variables, but are determined by other forces in the economy; and it is these forces which are the basic sources of uncertainty. Siroyezhin (1968) suggests that there exist two main sources of uncertainty in a Soviet economy—(i) uncertainty about the production function (that is, uncertainty about the state of nature), and (ii) uncertainty about consumer behaviour. These two sources are labelled in Table 5-1 as uncertainty about the environment. In a capitalist society there is a second, completely different source of uncertainty: although the locator may know the other participants' preferences and objectives, an element of uncertainty is introduced by the existence of other firms, because each firm's optimum location depends on the location of those other firms. Interdependencies between firms create uncertainty. In Table 5-1, the nature of this second element of uncertainty is classified by the 'degree of competition'.

Table 5-2 represents a schematic location game, in which a participant's uncertainty is due to both the state of the environment and the other participant's choice. Location case I (one player) is represented by a single vector: the outcome depends on the choice made and on the state of the environment. Such a matrix (or vector) is solved by a two-stage procedure. The first stage is to analyse the sub-matrices (sub-vectors) which correspond to each action pair (action) of the players: the $m \times m$ (m) values of R_{ijkl} in each sub-matrix (sub-vector) are replaced by a single value, which is the player's expected outcome from that particular action pair (action). In case I, the player then chooses the action having the

Table 5–2: **General uncertain location game**

Action of Player A	Ba				Action of Player B		Bn		
State of nature	E_1	E_2	..	E_m	....	E_1	E_2	...	E_m
A_a $\quad E_1$	R_{aa11}	R_{aa12}	..	R_{aa1m}	....	R_{an11}	R_{an12}	...	R_{an1m}
$\quad\quad E_2$	R_{aa21}	R_{aa22}	..	R_{aa2m}	....	.	....		.
.	.	.	..	.	....	.	....		.
.	.	.	..	.	....	.	....		.
$\quad\quad E_m$	R_{aam1}	R_{aam2}	..	R_{aamm}	....	R_{anm1}	R_{anm2}	...	R_{anmm}
.	.	.	..	....	R_{ijkl}	.	....		.
.	.	.	..	....		.	....		.
.	.	.	..	....		.	....		.
A_n $\quad E_1$	R_{na11}	R_{na12}	..	R_{na1m}	....	R_{nn11}	R_{nn12}	...	R_{nn1m}
$\quad\quad E_2$	.	.	..	.	....	.	....		.
.	.	.	..	.	....	.	....		.
$\quad\quad E_m$	R_{nam1}	R_{nam2}	..	R_{namm}	....	R_{nnm1}	R_{nnm2}	...	R_{nnmm}

Note: Each R_{ijkl} represents an outcome to player A and an outcome to player B, depending on choices and environments.

highest expected outcome, and the game is solved. The method by which players discover the expected value of such sub-matrices or sub-vectors is discussed in the following section. In cases II, III, and IV, there then remains a simplified $n \times n$ matrix in which uncertainty is now effectively due solely to the actions of the other player; this matrix is solved in the second stage of the analysis (by methods outlined in the next but one section).

Choice with Environmental Uncertainty

Having decided what probability is, and thus what a description of uncertainty is, a model of location must then specify how choices are made among the alternative acts available. Arrow (1959) indicates that in economic theory the subjective certainty model is the norm. This model assumes that people behave as if they thought that one state of nature were to occur with absolute certainty. The model, though widespread, is not very useful in analysing the effects of uncertainty. For example, several phenomena related to uncertainty, at least in part, such as diversification of assets and flexible fixed capital, are not explainable in these terms. In general the model fails to account for conservative behaviour, a form of action which, as will be shown, is relatively common under uncertainty.

The models which analyse location policies under uncertainty will use the theory that persons and firms maximise the expected utility of their actions. This criterion of choice has been shown to be rational, given seven axioms, by Savage (1954). Since the theory is the foundation of most of the location models which follow, it is outlined here. This outline is followed by a briefer discussion of some alternative decision making models which have been used or proposed in economics.

The axioms of Savage's system are (Savage, 1954: 17-104):

1. Events can be ordered so that
(a) either x is not preferred to y, or y is not preferred to x, and
(b) if x is not preferred to y and y is not preferred to z, then x is not preferred to z.

2. If a person would not prefer consequence f to consequence g, either knowing that B is true or knowing that B is not true, then that person does not prefer f to g.

3. If one act f has a consequence g and another act f' has a consequence g', then the act f is not preferred to f' if and only if the consequence g is not preferred to g'.

4. If a person is deciding which of several events will occur and is given a prize for deciding correctly, that person's decision is not affected by the size of the prize. Arrow (1951) objects to this axiom on the grounds that individuals will not make indefinitely large bets at the same odds. Furthermore, if there is a cost attached to evaluating acts, a small prize may not be worth bothering about; for larger prizes, the person evaluates the acts properly, and so his decision may, in fact, change as the prize alters in value.

5. Among the acts being compared there is at least one pair of acts for which the consequences of one are definitely preferred to the consequences of the other. From these five axioms it is possible to derive a qualitative probability, that is, a probability ordering based on the relation 'not more probable than'.

6. If an event B is less probable than an event C, there exists a set of mutually exclusive hypotheses such that the union of any hypothesis with B is less probable than C. Given the relation 'not more probable than', axiom 6 implies strict agreement between qualitative probability and numerical probability. These six axioms of behaviour have therefore been used to deduce a personal probability measure which obeys the three axioms of mathematical probability.

7. If every possible consequence of an act g is at least as attractive as the act f considered as a whole, then f is not preferred to g. Define utility as a function which assigns real numbers to consequences in such a way that an act f is not preferred to an act g if and only if the utility of the expected value of the consequences of f is not preferred to the utility of the expected value of the consequences of g. Then the attractiveness of an act is measured by its utility, and so a person acts rationally if he decides in favour of an act the expected utility of which is as large as possible.

Thus, given a set of acts, $a_1, a_2, \ldots, a_i, \ldots, a_n$, a set of states of the environment, $E_1, E_2, \ldots, E_j, \ldots, E_m$, together with their associated probabilities, $P(E_j)$, and a set of utilities of outcomes, R_{ij}, which depend on both acts and states of the environment, then an act a_i is preferred to an act a_k if and only if

$$(5\text{-}2) \qquad \sum_{j=1}^{m} P(E_j) \, R_{ij} > \sum_{j=i}^{m} P(E_j) \, R_{kj}.$$

This decision model (maximise subjective expected utility) is applied to case I (one firm, uncertain knowledge of the environment) and its implications for location decision taking are there fully explored. In the remaining cases, II, III, and IV, the expected utility of each joint outcome set (depending on the choices of both participants) is assumed to have been computed as in case I. This simplification permits us to separate the implications of uncertainty about rivals' behaviour from the effects of uncertain knowledge of the environment. In effect, knowledge of the environment in cases II, III, and IV is assumed to be of the 'certainty equivalent' kind: this fact explains why Table 5–1 contains no cases with certain knowledge of the environment.

There are several possible sources of error in this model (Edwards, 1954). The model may be wrong if people do not compute the expectation of an event by multiplying probabilities and values, or if these products are not added. Thus people may choose among acts in order to maximise some function of probabilities and values, $f(p_1, x_1; p_2, x_2; \ldots ; p_n, x_n)$, a function which need not be of the form specified by the maximised expectations model. Another source of error occurs if the decision makers enjoy gambling; and choose for thrills as well as for values.

Several measurements have been made of the relationship between actual and estimated probabilities. Preston and Baratta (1948) found that people over-estimate low probabilities and underestimate high probabilities: estimated and actual probabilities are equal about $p = 0.2$. Edwards (1955) made experiments using bets: if the subjects can win or break even (but not lose), their estimated probabilities are greater than the objective probabilities, whereas if the subjects cannot win, their estimated probabilities equal the actual probabilities. Such interaction between probabilities and utilities creates considerable problems for the decision model: axiom 4 above is being broken.

Atkinson (1957) has analysed inter-personal differences in risk-taking behaviour. He assumes a motive to achieve success (M_s), a motive to avoid failure (M_f), and subjective probabilities of success (P_s) and failure $(P_f = 1 - P_s)$. If the incentive value of achieving success is inversely related to the subjective probability of succeeding (i.e. $1 - P_s$) and the incentive value of avoiding failure is the negative of the subjective probability of succeeding $(-P_s)$, motivation is measured by $P_s (1 - P_s) (M_s - M_f)$. People whose motivation to achieve success is greater than that to avoid failure are most motivated when $P_s = 0.5$, so they prefer intermediate probabilities of success. On the other hand, people who are more motivated to avoid failure than to achieve success prefer probabilities of success which are near zero or unity. Although our location models do not take into account such inter-personal differences, it is important to remember that individuals do vary in the extent to which they accept risk taking.

Partly as a result of these difficulties, alternative models of decision making under uncertainty have been proposed in economics and statistics. Neyman and Pearson (1933) and Wald (1939, 1950) specify a model in which probability is not used to discriminate among hypotheses as to their truth; the choice is based upon the consequences of each action. In an economic context another interesting model, which does not use probability either, has been developed by Shackle (1949, 1955). Both these theories will be briefly described. (Note that Isard (1969: 116-221) describes many possible decision criteria in addition to the three examined here.)

To illustrate the Neyman-Pearson model, assume two hypotheses about the state of nature, H_1 and H_2. One action dominates another action if the expected return to the first action is at least as great as the expected return to the second action under each of H_1 and H_2 and is actually greater than the expected return to the second action under one of these hypotheses. An action a is admissible if no other action dominates it. The decision rule is that a rational choice is restricted to admissible actions (Neyman and Pearson, 1933; Chernoff and Moses, 1950; Arrow, 1951). But as Arrow (1951) points out, though reasonable, this rule hardly ever leads to definite decisions about which action to take. One major advantage of Savage's model over this theory is consequently that Savage's criterion is operational: it can actually be used to predict location choices and so can be used to construct location theories.

Shackle views probability as relative frequency. The development of his theory is motivated by the fact that relative frequency cannot be used in economic models because it cannot refer to the outcome of an individual event. In the relative frequency view, probability is only valid when applied to a large number of trials, each conducted under the same conditions, and when a few initial losses do not preclude the possibility of more trials (Shackle, 1949: 2-9). Typically, as Shackle points out (1955: ch. 1), location decisions are once and for all events, never to be repeated (or repeated only rarely); so relative frequency is irrelevant to location decisions. But this objection does not apply if probability is thought to measure the degree of belief that a proposition is true. Under the degree of belief hypothesis, probability is clearly applicable to a single trial.

Shackle measures the possible outcomes of an action by their desirability and by the strength of the claims of the possibilities to be true. The latter is measured by the degree of potential surprise—the extent to which an individual would be surprised if an outcome actually occurred (Shackle, 1949: ch. 2; 1955: ch. 2), while the desirability is measured by both the possible gain and the possible loss (1949: 2-9; 1955: ch. 2). Shackle then finds the maximum stimulation associated with a gain from an action (this stimulation increases as the size of the gain increases and as the degree of potential surprise falls) and the maximum stimulation associated with a loss from that action (1949: 10-58). The possible actions are then ordered on an indifference map of stimulus gain and stimulus loss to determine which action should be taken.

Some difficulties associated with the model may be noted. Shackle largely bypasses the problem of how the degrees of potential surprises are accorded to outcomes (O'Connor, 1954). Arrow (1951) comments that, although the idea of simplifying the problem is sound, this particular simplification is both complicated and arbitrary. Furthermore the model does not accord well with introspection: Shackle (1953: 65) says that if a leading cricketer's score 'turns out to be 50, or 49, or 81, or 2, or . . . even nought, I shall not be in the least surprised . . .', so that the degree of potential surprise accorded to each score from zero to eighty-one (at least) is zero. But even so, I may much prefer to bet that this player makes fifty than that he makes zero (see also Carter, 1954). A further difficulty is that the model is hardly operational: it is nearly impossible to construct models of location using Shackle's criterion of choice.

Although the criterion that firms maximise expected utility contains difficulties, it is more operational than these other two criteria. And given our emphasis upon deriving location patterns rather than on creating general equilibrium theory, this is a considerable advantage. But before the criterion is used, a utility function must be defined, to relate the utility ($u(x)$) of a sum of money (x) to the amount of that sum. Both Borch (1968: 34-46) and Isard (1969: 178-83) discuss the shape of the utility function. Unfortunately, as Isard points out, there exists little empirical evidence upon which to decide the shape of utility functions. Traditionally, it has been assumed that money is subject to a diminishing (but positive) marginal utility. In the models developed in this book, we shall assume that the utility of a sum of money equals that sum:

(5-3) $u(x) = x,$

except when the implications of diminishing marginal utility are discussed, when it will be assumed that:

(5-4) $u(x) = \sqrt{x}.$

Uncertainty through Interdependencies

Under some conditions, Savage's model is not useful. The first of these conditions occurs when *a priori* probabilities are not known, but this case is ignored, for such a degree of ignorance is almost undefinable and very infrequent. Secondly, the use of probabilities in a maximised utility model is inappropriate when a player's uncertainty is due to the behaviour of rivals or competitors. Location models with interdependent firms are treated with the theory of games (von Neumann and Morgenstern, 1944; Luce and Raiffa, 1957). This treatment covers cases II, III, and IV.

The theory assumes a set of outcomes which are well specified and over which individuals have a consistent pattern of preferences. The assumptions about utility and the ordering of preferences are consistent with those of Savage (1954). This is important, for it implies that the various location models to be constructed are consistent one with another. The theory further assumes that the players in a game make choices without knowing the choices of others, but make these choices

101

Table 5–3: **Two person zero sum game matrix**

A's choice	B's choice Ace	Deuce	Minimum of row
Ace	1	2	1
Deuce	4	3	3
Maximum of column	4	3	

in order to maximise expected utility. Again, these assumptions are consistent with the Savage model. In the words of Williams (1954: 23): 'the sensible object of the player is to gain as much from the game as he can, safely, in the face of a skilful opponent who is pursuing an antithetical goal'.

The solutions to some games are clearly determined. The simplest of all games is the two person zero sum game, which is played between two players and in which the gains of one player are the losses of another. The two players are completely competitive, as in case II. Such a game is reproduced in Table 5–3. If A and B guard their cards and they each play one card simultaneously, the game fulfils the model conditions. Should A and B both play Aces, B pays A one unit of utility; if A plays the Ace and B the Deuce, B pays A two units; and so on. To every such game there corresponds a pair of strategies, one for A and one for B, such that A's strategy is the best against B's play and B's strategy is the best against A's play. Such a pair of strategies, called an equilibrium, occurs in the simplest case when, if a matrix contains an entry X which is simultaneously the minimum of its row and the maximum of its column, A plays the row containing X and B plays the column containing X. The value of the game is defined to be X. In Table 5–3, the equilibrium occurs when A and B both play the Deuce. Such a strategy is usually interpreted to mean that B chooses in order to minimise the maximum loss he can make and A chooses in order to maximise his minimum gain: the equilibrium strategy is the best certain outcome for each player. Luce and Raiffa (1957), Williams (1954), Dryden (1964), and Blackwell and Girshick (1954) discuss this and more complicated games. Lieberman (1960) has performed experiments upon college students which indicate that the prescribed minimax decision is made frequently.

More interesting, but more difficult to solve, are non-zero sum games. In such games the gains of one player are not simply the losses of the other: advantages accrue to players who co-operate. These are the mixed-motive games of cases III and IV. Such games are typical of oligopolistic situations (Shubik, 1959). One form of this game is bilateral monopoly, where there is one buyer and one seller in a market. Von Neumann and Morgenstern (1944) assume that the players agree to act co-operatively to maximise their joint return and that they then divide this return among themselves in the form of side-payments. Firms are expected to collude if they thus gain at least as much as they can obtain competitively. The division of the joint return is not uniquely determined: the solution consists of the set of returns which dominate all others but which do not dominate each

Table 5-4: **General Prisoner's Dilemma**

Player 1's Act	Player 2's Act	
	A	B
A	R, R	S, T
B	T, S	P, P

Table 5-5: **Specific Prisoner's Dilemma**

Player 1's Act	Player 2's Act	
	A	B
A	5, 5	2, 6
B	6, 2	3, 3

Note: Player 2's reward is listed after Player 1's reward.

other. This non-uniqueness of the division reduces the usefulness of the model. The Nash (1950, 1953) solution to the non-zero sum game is an attempt to overcome the indeterminacy of the von Neumann-Morgenstern model. Nash suggests that players divide the joint return fairly, as though the return had been divided by a referee. Such a 'fair' return is based on the relative strengths of the players, strength often being measured by the relative potential loss in profits caused by a threat not to co-operate. If strengths are equal, profits should be equally divided, a result which has been empirically verified by Siegel and Fouraker (1960). Braithwaite (1955) presents a solution which is in many respects similar to Nash's. Isard (1969: 222-370) discusses existing co-operative procedures in much greater detail; but bargaining is not of sufficient importance in location theory to justify such treatment here.

Some games have both co-operative and competitive solutions. A classic game of this type is Prisoner's Dilemma (Rapoport and Chammah, 1965). The general matrix is shown in Table 5-4 and a specific matrix in Table 5-5: in this game, $S < P < R < T$. The competitive strategy is (B,B) offering returns (P,P), a strategy which is rational if the game is played a finite number of times. Obviously, though, if they can agree (and bind each other) to co-operate, strategy (A,A) yields greater returns. Experimentally, Rapoport and Chammah (1965: 33-49) found that the proportion of co-operation (the percentage of plays which are (A,A)) increases as R and P increase and as $T (= -S$, in their experiments) falls. Deutsch (1958) has also examined the manner in which people play Prisoner's Dilemma. He discovered that co-operation increased when players could communicate and when plays were made simultaneously; and that preliminary statements inciting players to greater degrees of competitiveness reduced co-operation. Deutsch concluded that a player's motivation has an important bearing upon the manner in which he plays Prisoner's Dilemma. Another, slightly different, game with both competitive and co-operative solutions is the Cournot duopoly problem, discussed in game terms by Isard and Smith (1966) and Funck (1966).

Game theory, in its various forms, is a versatile tool, and one which has been used to analyse choices in many different situations. Thus Langham (1963) analysed in game terms the decision of Louisiana rice farmers to press the U.S. government for greater acreages or for higher prices. Stevens (1961) cast the Hotelling location model into zero sum game form; similarly Isard and Dacey

103

(1962) and Isard and Reiner (1962) have proposed that game theory be used to predict the locational behaviour of firms, while Isard (1967) has used the theory to analyse typical Weberian models. Gould (1963) applied Wald's minimax criterion to analyse the games of Ghanaian farmers against Nature. Danskin's (1962) study of optimum convoy routing and size illustrates the possible application of the model to transport nets and flows (though in a pathological context). The fullest discussion in location terms is that of Isard (1969).

Perception of the Payoff Matrix

We have yet to specify the manner in which the data in the payoff matrices are obtained. Although clearly important in models with uncertainty, the problem of data collection has received little attention in the analysis of location decisions. Data collection is closely related to the manner in which individuals perceive their environment: that is, 'in daily practise, we all subordinate reality to the world we perceive, experience, and act in. We respond to and affect the environment not directly, but through the medium of a personally apprehended milieu. This milieu differs for each of us . . .' (Lowenthal, 1967: 1). Or, more directly, 'Understanding of the sources of variance in environmental perception is essential to an understanding of variation in man's environmental behaviors' (Sonnenfeld, 1967: 42).

The large and complex real world must be simplified and adjusted by individuals in order that information about that world be efficiently stored by them. These adjustments are distortions in the sense that a person's conceptual space does not correspond directly with 'objective data' (Stea, 1969). But although mental maps are being measured (Gould, 1966; Gould and White, 1968), and although some workers have studied people's perception of 'natural' hazards (drought and flood) in the United States (White, 1961; Kates, 1962; Burton and Kates, 1964; Saarinen, 1966), there is no widely recognised body of theory in geography which enables us to establish (or assume) a particular relationship between perception and environment, comparable perhaps to the relationship between utility and money. The 'mutual interrelation of real environment, perceived environment and human activity emerges in a shadowy, or at best halting manner. It becomes apparent that this is an extremely difficult field to handle in behavioural research . . .' (Brookfield, 1969: 61). This is unfortunate, for it would be fascinating to compare theoretical location patterns for perceived and more 'objective' environments.

Lack of knowledge precludes us from examining fully the implications of variations in environmental perception for location theory. Instead, some notions relevant to perception will be analysed at separate points in the discussion. Thus, the nature and implications of gradual learning about the environment (the development of experience) and some models of environment searching procedures are reviewed at different points in the analysis. The implications for location theory of an individual having to collect his own data are also investigated.

Rationality: The Concept of Maximum Profit

So far in this chapter an interpretation of probability has been announced, on the basis of which two theories of choice have been described, one relevant when *a priori* probabilities are given and one which applies to interdependent firms' uncertainties. These theories take as their criterion of choice the principle that a rational act is that one out of all the available acts which maximises expected utility. Such theories can clearly be applied as logic-like criteria whereby the consistency of one's views may be judged. In this book, though, the theories will be used in a more contentious way—as crude approximations to the actual decision criteria used by economic operators: that is, the following models of location under uncertainty assume that people act to maximise expected utility. This assumption will now be defended; in the course of this defence the concept of maximum profits will be redefined (see also Webber, 1969). (The assumption that the utility of money is a linear function of the amount of money makes the decision criterion 'maximise expected utility' equivalent to the criterion 'maximise expected profits'.)

Each of the major models of location theory assumes rational behaviour. Some function (profits) is maximised under given stated conditions. In Weber's theory maximum profits are held to be identical to minimum costs; in the interdependence approach and in Lösch's theory, maximum profits are effectively considered to be maximum sales. Once the profit function has been defined, the process of maximisation is simple and subject to well-defined mathematical rules.

The difficulty occurs, though, of defining the profit function. In the real world, information is not always available to the firms to permit them to analyse the manner in which their profits vary over space. For every possible location, firms must be able to find the prices and freight rates on raw materials, to determine production costs, and to evaluate the sales which can be made. The location of all other firms and consumers must be known. Brown (1960) indicates that firms can trade profits in one period for profits in another and have options about the manner in which profits are distributed, while stockholders also have diverse aspirations. Although bad decisions are easily ruled out, usually a very large number of good ones remain. Clearly, except where one factor is so important as to dominate all others, the location decision, like any other production decision, requires costly evaluation by the firm.

Therefore it is not surprising that location models have been criticised for retaining the maximisation concept. Three main strands of criticism may be identified. First, there are writers, often concerned with actual location choices, who argue that many firms consider 'non-economic' factors in deciding on locations and that many firms make mistakes. Secondly, some analysts have concluded that firms do not really attempt to maximise profits at all. And thirdly, the models have been criticised for being deterministic, whereas more accurate predictions can be made by stochastic models. Each strand of criticism will be considered in turn.

105

It has often been observed that interview studies which attempt to evaluate location choices find many firms which have located with respect to non-economic factors. Some businessmen are reputed to locate to take advantage of social facilities for themselves or for their families. The case of the (former) Morris motor works at Cowley—selected to take advantage of an available manor—is frequently cited. Similarly, an interview study of firms in country towns in New South Wales found that many firms (especially those set up by local entrepreneurs) were sited in a given town 'because I lived here' (Webber, 1967: 64). Mueller, Wilken, and Wood (1961: 14-18) report that 50 per cent of the Michigan industrialists they interviewed gave 'personal or chance' reasons for locating in Michigan. Evidence suggests that few private capitalists undertake comparative cost or profit analyses (McLaughlin and Robock, 1949: chs. 2 and 3; Klemme, 1959: 71-7; Luttrell, 1962).

But several elements suggest that such non-optimum choices are less important as criticisms of maximising models than may at first sight appear. As Estall and Buchanan (1961: 18-19) point out, choice on the basis of a golf course is perfectly rational if the locations being compared offer similar profits. Furthermore, Tiebout (1957) has shown that the predictions of maximising models may be accordant with reality even though businessmen may not choose rationally, because the firms in poor location suffer reduced profits when compared to firms in better locations. Thus the poorly located firms tend to go out of business. Tiebout argues that society chooses the firms in the best locations: the argument depends on (i) more firms establishing than are needed to satisfy the demand and (ii) firms being unable to condition their own success. Thus the argument applies most strongly to industries in which there exist many small firms. Of the U.S. firms existing at the beginning of 1956, 7·9 per cent had failed by the end of that year; of these, 60 per cent were less than five years old and 90 per cent had liabilities of less than $100,000 (Summers, 1962). These data suggest that in at least some sectors of the economy, condition (i) is fulfilled.

On the basis of a careful study of Florida industry, Greenhut and Colberg (1962) argue that non-economic factors have been over-rated in importance. They too find firms which claim that the choice of location was motivated by personal managerial considerations; these factors are classified into 'personal factors with pecuniary gain' and 'personal factors without pecuniary gain'. It is only the latter which truly represent non-economic forces, and they find that these factors predominate only rarely.

I have argued similarly (Webber, 1967). Locating in the home town of an entrepreneur is in many cases a profit maximising choice. Several factors affect the location of the first plant of a firm. One of these is the personal cost of relocating, such as the loss of friends: this is a so-called non-economic motive. Another is the cost of obtaining knowledge about distant locations when the firm has only limited capital. This knowledge is largely of two kinds—acquaintance with local businessmen, which permits credit, supplies, and markets to be obtained more easily, and knowledge of demand, which allows a better choice of industry. The

Greenhut and Colberg study (1962: 77-80) found that personal factors with a pecuniary advantage (i.e. friendship with customers or suppliers) was more important in determining the community which was chosen than in affecting the decision to locate in Florida: it was a primary factor in determining the choice of a community in thirty-eight firms (20 per cent of all plants which were not branches or relocations), the second factor in nine firms, and the third in forty-nine firms. Jervis (1957: 200-1) pointed out one reason why personal knowledge is important to small firms in England: most small and young firms have to use banks to finance expansion (because they have not been able to accumulate reserves), and advances are made on securities or, in the case of new firms, on the basis of known personal qualities.

The criticism that the location pattern in a society reflects non-economic choices is thus often overstated, except perhaps in economies dominated by a small number of relatively large firms. Only in a few cases do non-economic forces significantly cause a firm to locate in a poor position, and even then social forces may operate to remove the firm. But even though this is true, it is also true that our concept of maximum profit location decisions must be enlarged and redefined to take account of some of the problems mentioned.

The second criticism is that entrepreneurs are satisficers not optimisers. Simon (1957: 196-206) has argued that optimisation requires information and decision processes which operate at the highest level. Since information must be imperfect, because of time uncertainties, firms cannot operate at the level required for optimisation. The capacity of the mind is small in relation to the size of the problems to be solved. Simon's alternative is to suggest that men try to obtain satisfactory rather than optimal patterns of behaviour. 'Most human decision-taking, whether individual or organisational, is concerned with the discovery and selection of *satisfactory* alternatives; only in exceptional cases is it concerned with optimal alternatives' (March and Simon, 1958: 140-1). Hamilton (1967: 364-8) echoes this point. Margolis (1958) presents a similar model, which is based on the assumption that firms aim to make satisfactory profits, that is, a level of profit equal to their aspirations. These aspiration levels relate to a finite time period, must be sufficient to keep the firm viable, and are above current profit levels. Margolis also suggests that the past and present experiences of the firm limit the range of alternatives which it perceives (but such a suggestion can never account for qualitatively different behaviour). Siegel (1957) also argues that success raises aspiration levels. The satisficing model assumes that when a sequence of possible outcomes is presented to a firm, the entrepreneur chooses the first that is acceptable. Isard (1969: 211-16) discusses several forms of this satisficing model.

Haggett (1965: 181-2) indicates that regular land use patterns are distorted by sub-optimal behaviour. He quotes Wolpert's (1964) findings. Wolpert studied farming patterns in an area of central Sweden and found that labour productivity in Swedish farming is below the optimum. Less than half the area evidenced labour productivity levels within 70 per cent of the optimum. Wolpert suggests that this low productivity and regional variations in levels of productivity may be ascribed to (i) satisficing rather than optimising behaviour by the farmers, (ii) regional variations in knowledge associated with the diffusion process, and (iii) uncertainty. Hobbs, Beal, and Bohlen (1964: 1-7) claim that an abundance of research evidence reveals that profit maximisation is only a secondary goal of farm managers: many farm managers are more oriented towards security, ease, and convenience than to maximum profits (Dean, Aurbach, and Marsh, 1958; Hoffer and Stangland, 1958).

But as an argument against a maximum profit theory of location patterns, the criticisms appear to rest on a misunderstanding. Firstly, Tiebout's point (1957) may again be made: socially optimal location patterns will tend to evolve as a product of economic forces if not as a product of conscious private decision. Secondly, the fact that information is not perfect means that, unless lucky, the firm will not make objectively optimal decisions; but it does not mean that the firm is not trying to optimise on the basis of available information. Thus Wolpert's farmers may be doing the best they can, given their level of knowledge. We must separate the intentions from the consequences of an act; such a view again requires that our concept of maximum profits be enlarged and redefined.

Such a confusion of intentions and consequences is frequently made. Suppose that an expected profits maximiser is offered two bets, each of which costs $1.00: (i) $10.00 with probability 0·9 or $0.00 with $p = 0·1$, and (ii) $5.00 with probability 0·7 or $2.00 with $p = 0·3$. The rational, optimising decision is to take the first bet. Now suppose that the 'wheel is spun' twice and that the first bet yields $0.00 while the second yields $5.00. Then it is said that the person's choice turned out to be wrong or incorrect: after the event, the choice is regarded as suboptimal. Such a view is wrong: the choice must be evaluated with respect to the information available when that choice was made, and subsequent events do not alter the correctness or otherwise of the decision. (Of course, in more complex situations, the correct choice at one point in time may be to collect more information.) *Ex ante* and *ex post* optimality are not equivalent.

Much recent geographic and economic work has evidenced an increasing movement into probabilistic laws, reflecting stochastic processes, away from the earlier deterministic models. In deterministic systems, development in time and space can be completely predicted once the initial conditions and relationships are known. Thus, when we have defined economies of scale, transport costs, and the density of population, we can completely determine the position and relations of Lösch's hexagonal nets. On the other hand, probabilistic or stochastic models build random variables into their structure, variables which summarise events the net effect of which is random.

Morrill (1963) suggests a three-fold rationale for the use of stochastic models in location analysis. Firstly, there are basic uncertainties in the pattern of human behaviour: the models can allow for the fact that a few firms may not try to maximise. Secondly, stochastic models can allow for problems of individual choice when several alternative courses are of equal value: the golf-course effect is built in as a random variable. And thirdly, probabilistic models of location recognise that location theory is unable to predict or to take account of many small effects. As a simple example, Morrill (1967) constructs a transport flow model which assumes a Poisson distribution of errors by individuals: choosing the best route involves zero error; choosing the second best route is one error; choosing the third best route is two errors; and so on. In trying to predict the evolution of location patterns in a region, a deterministic model can use only known determinants of location, and thus may be seriously in error because of unknown effects; a stochastic model contains random variables to account for these unknown effects. Even so, the analysis of new variables in order to increase the range of variables whose effect is known is often most easily accomplished through the use of deterministic models, because of their simpler mathematics.

These three strands of criticism can ultimately be resolved into the criticism that most location theories are related to an environment within which information is perfect. Location theory has so far been largely a static construction. Lösch defends the fact that his theory is static by pointing out: 'Dynamically there is no best location, because we cannot know the future' (1959: 16). However, it is clear that if location theory is to predict patterns more accurately, it must adopt the assumption that entrepreneurs are uncertain. It is at least arguable that, despite Lösch, economic operators do try to take into account future conditions. Consequently it seems worthwhile to determine the extent to which such influence may be analysed and therefore to which the introduction of expectations may improve the predictions of location theory.

However they are approached, decisions with imperfect information are different from existing models of decision under certainty. The basis of this difference lies in the term 'maximum profits'. In traditional analyses, the use of the term is relatively simple: a maximum profit location is that site amongst all others at which the profits of the firm are highest. An uncertain firm tries to maximise profits safely; the firm's motives include high profits, but—equally importantly—secure profits as well. A necessary condition for long-run maximum profits under uncertainty is that the firm stays in business. The usefulness of this concept in location theory arises because firms realise that their profits depend in part on the location of later sellers and consumers. They must therefore try to secure a location which will be reasonably good (and which, at the very least, will allow them to stay in business) no matter what other firms decide. (This vague formulation can be tightened when particular decision situations are discussed, for the relationship between security and maxima can then be closely specified.)

Thus the fact that at any one point in time a firm is not at the optimum location does not mean that the firm was not using this enlarged concept of profit maximisation. Obviously, unless they are very lucky, firms cannot be optimising choices with respect to perfect information; but they can still be optimising their choice with respect to such information as they have. In other words, although a choice may be sub-optimal when examined after the event (i.e. after other firms have located), it may well have been optimal before the event. *Ex post* sub-optimal behaviour does not imply satisficing behaviour.

There is no *a priori* reason why firms should not be able to find an optimal *ex ante* location. Indeed, it can be proved that such a location can, at least in theory, be determined. Define first a 'Turing machine' (Turing, 1937): this is an archetype machine. Into the machine is fed a tape input; the tape is read, whereupon the machine moves the tape, either one space to the left or one space to the right. A symbol is printed on the tape: this symbol constitutes output. Such a machine can continue indefinitely any mathematical series which can itself be produced by a machine (no matter how complicated). This result proves that machines are not limited by the intelligence of their designers. Similarly, it can be proved that Turing machines can be made to construct other machines, including machines more complex than themselves (von Neumann, 1951). Von Neumann (1956) has also shown that by multiplexing and duplication it is possible to obtain an answer from a machine which is correct to an arbitrarily high probability, even though the components of the machine are unreliable.

These results form the basis of the cybernetic view of a planned factory (Beer, 1959: 128-41). The normal situation in which several departments of the factory are in conflict about where to locate can be simulated electronically. The model contains several machines, each simulating one department of the firm. The machines are linked. The decision process then consists of each machine proposing states (locations) to the others, which either accept the proposals or reject them and propose counter-states. Satisfactory limits are fed into each machine and when all machines satisfy these limits the location bargaining ceases: a location has been chosen. By setting the limits arbitrarily high, an optimal rather than a satisfactory state may be obtained. Thus no matter how complicated are the real world and decisions about it, an optimal *ex ante* plan of location may be evolved.

But the enlarged idea of optimal decision taking must take account of another factor. Part of the process of making an optimal *ex ante* decision involves collecting the data upon which to base this decision. The firm has to decide how much information to collect and where to collect it from. This imposes further novel elements on the theory of the optimal *ex ante* decision.

Collecting Information: Sequential Decision Making
The question of how much information to collect before a location decision is made is a problem in sequential decision making. Irwin and Smith (1957) present an experiment typical of sequential problems. Subjects were shown a sequence of cards and asked whether the mean of the entire set was greater than or less than zero. The subjects were paid for correct decisions and charged for each card looked at. The number of cards looked at increased as the prize increased and fell as the cost of looking increased.

Some subsets of sequential decision-making problems are well covered by statistical theory. Thus Chernoff (1959) has analysed the sequential design of experiments when samples are large (i.e. when the cost of experimentation approaches zero). And Bross (1953: 135-40) presents an optimal procedure for the sequential inspection of factory samples. Marschak (1954) analyses the case of a manager who decides whether or not to pay to be told the exact value of an uncertain variable which affects his profits; Marschak shows that the value of asking is the variance of the uncertain variable. But these are non-spatial designs.

Cherry (1961) and Goldman (1953) present introductory discussions of information theory, which might seem potentially useful in analysing information collection. Thus Danskin (1962) discusses the allocation of military reconnaissance to various regions. The uncertainty in a map (about enemy deployment of missiles) is the mathematical expectation of the individual uncertainties of the possible events that missiles and/or decoys are placed in the regions. Then the information yielded by a reconnaissance is defined as the change in the uncertainty of the map which results from that reconnaissance. The reconnaissance effort is directed to maximise this information yield. But such an approach seems difficult to apply to optimal site searches, where the findings in one region affect the expectations of the findings in another and where the cost of searching must enter the analysis more explicitly. And the measure of information used in the mathematical treatment of information theory refers to the total content of a message: the firm, unlike the military, is not interested in maximum message content, but only in particular values of the message.

Isard (1969: 344-69) discusses sequential decision making in some detail. But since his discussion relates largely to predictions of the behaviour of pairs of players who are involved in many plays of mixed motive games (such as the Prisoner's Dilemma), his conclusions do not assist us.

Flood (1960) discusses a more useful technique. He assumes the 'polar explorer's problem'. The explorer searches for the point of greatest thickness of ice. Thickness is measured by expensive borings, but the discovery of added depth has known value. The Box-Wilson technique is to bore in several places, observe depths, fit a polynomial surface to these observations, maximise this equation, and from this find the point of greatest depth. The technique can fail badly if the explorer assumes that there is one peak when there are really several peaks. Furthermore the model must also specify how many observations are to be made and where they are to be made.

Consider therefore a highly simplified problem. An entrepreneur, located at one end of a linear market, wishes to find his optimal location. He knows that the profitability of sites varies randomly along the line: the profitabilities are approximately normally distributed within the limits of $\pm p$. The cost of sampling is cd, where c is a constant and d is distance from the entrepreneur's home site. There being no trend in profitability, the firm's best first sample is its cheapest—i.e. at $d = 0$. A second sample is taken at $d = 1$. From these the firm can estimate the mean profitability of sites and the standard deviation of profitabilities. The standard error of these estimates can be computed. These data tell the firm the

111

expected profitability of the next site to be sampled (at $d = 2$). If this expected profitability is greater than the maximum profitability of the sites already sampled plus the discounted future value of the cost of sampling ($2c$), the firm takes this third sample. Otherwise the firm locates at the best of sites 1 and 2. The procedure continues until the expected gain from sampling is less than the cost of sampling. The firm takes an $(n+1)$th sample if

$$(5\text{-}5) \qquad \frac{1}{\sqrt{2\pi\sigma^2}} \int_{x=-p}^{p} x \cdot \exp\left[\frac{-(x-\bar{x})^2}{\sigma^2}\right] dx - \max(x_1, x_2, \ldots, x_n) \geqslant nc,$$

where x is the profitability of sites, σ is the standard deviation of profitability, $x_1, x_2, \ldots, x_n$ the profitability of the 1st, 2nd, $\ldots$, nth sites, and nc is the discounted cost of sampling the $(n+1)$th site.

Another simple case may be examined. Suppose that an entrepreneur is making a decision and that he wishes his decision to be accurate. Assume further that information is costly to collect and that this cost increases with distance—because information has to be transmitted over space. Suppose that in general there are diminishing returns from extra information, for the costs of processing the information rise and each additional increment of information contributes less and less to the accuracy of the decision. (It is not assumed that this applies to every piece of information, merely that an entrepreneur thinks that the situation occurs on average.) The most profitable amount of information which an entrepreneur should obtain may be deduced from these data.

Let the cost of collecting one unit of information at a point be

$$(5\text{-}6) \qquad c = ad,$$

where d is the distance of the point from the entrepreneur and a is a constant. If information is randomly spread over the area and is available on average in unit amounts per unit area, generally πd^2 units of information are located within distance d of the entrepreneur. Hence the total costs of gathering the information within distance d are the number of units within d multiplied by the average cost of collecting those units:

$$(5\text{-}7) \qquad C = \frac{2}{3}ad \cdot \pi d^2 = \frac{2}{3}a\pi d^3.$$

Let the total return on information gathered be

$$(5\text{-}8) \qquad R = b\sqrt{i},$$

where b is a constant and i is the number of units gathered. Therefore the return on collecting the units of information within d is

$$(5\text{-}9) \qquad R = b\sqrt{\pi d^2}.$$

Hence the profit on information gathering is

$$(5\text{-}10) \qquad P = R - C = b\sqrt{\pi d^2} - \left(\frac{2}{3}\right)\pi ad^3.$$

Therefore, the equation

(5-11) $d = +\sqrt{b/2a\sqrt{\pi}}$

defines the maximum profit decision of the firm.[1]

Thus there is a definite and limited area within which it pays the firm to gather information. Furthermore this area is smaller the higher are the costs of sending information and the less extensive are the returns from information gathering. The amount of profit to be gained through more accurate decisions by collecting information falls as distance increases. Therefore if entrepreneurs try to maximise their profits, they have knowledge of only a limited area around them and are ignorant of circumstances outside this area.

A more complete model may be developed. Assume an areal set of possible locations for a firm. Observations are made on the profitability of the firm at different sites, yielding values of the form $(x+t)$ where x is the actual profitability and t is a normally distributed error term. Observations are subject to a cost, which is the product of a constant factor (c) and distance (d). After some observations the firm can fit a polynomial surface to the observations and can calculate the standard error of this surface. For any possible site the firm then has an estimate of its profitability and of the standard deviation of possible profitability values. The firm knows the expected profitability of the best site. The value of taking a new observation is therefore the resulting change in expected profitability at the best site and the change in uncertainty about the actual profitability of this site. Thus if the utility of the change in uncertainty can be valued, the gain to the firm from making the $(n+1)$th observation is

(5-12) $P_{n+} = (E_{n+1}-E_n) + f(\sigma_n-\sigma_{n+1})-cd_{n+1},$

where P_{n+1} is the profitability of the $(n+1)$th observation, E_{n+1} and E_n are the expected profitabilities at the best sites after $(n+1)$ and n observations respectively, f is a function to be determined, $(\sigma_n-\sigma_{n+1})$ is a measure of the change in uncertainty resulting from the $(n+1)$th observation, and d_{n+1} is the distance of the $(n+1)$th observation from the home site of the entrepreneur. The observation is made if P_{n+1} is positive, and is made so as to maximise P_{n+1}. To do this the firm must make E_{n+1} large, d_{n+1} small, and (if f is a monotonically increasing function) σ_{n+1} small.

As in the previous models, the more observations that have been taken the less

---

[1] From equation (5-10), the rate of increase of profit with respect to the distance over which information is gathered is

$$\frac{dP}{dd} = b\sqrt{\pi}-2a\pi d^2.$$

Profit is at a maximum or minimum when this function equals zero, i.e. when
  $d = \pm\sqrt{b/2a\sqrt{\pi}}.$
But
$$\frac{d^2P}{dd^2} = -4a\pi d,$$
and since a and π are both positive, the equation (5-11) defines the maximum profit decision for the firm.

likely it is that a further observation will be made. And the more distant a point is from the observer, the less likely it is that profitability will be sampled at that point. But this is not because of satisficing behaviour in Simon's sense; rather, firms are making optimal *ex ante* decisions in view of the costs of collecting information.

These are highly simplified models of information gathering. But they do point up an important result: they provide another reason why decisions may not be optimal when viewed after the event. By showing why information should be collected sparingly, the models indicate why location in the home town of an entrepreneur may be an optimal decision before the event. It is usually uneconomic to try to collect all the information necessary for an accurate decision, but an *ex ante* optimal decision is not necessarily accurate.

A further consequence of the models may be illustrated by means of an example. Suppose that n firms are selling a good in a system; they are all selling over the entire system—their market areas are not spatially separated. There is room for one more firm in the system. From the point of view of society and given hindsight we can define the optimum location for that $(n+1)$th firm. But if several firms are considering locating in the system their optimum *ex ante* location need not coincide with the defined social optimum. And if the entrepreneurs are in different locations, the optimum *ex ante* location of each firm may be different from that of each of the others, because entrepreneurs collect information only about limited areas about them. Thus the optimum location before the event of firms of a given type depends not only on the input-output and production cost relationships of the firms, but also on the location of the entrepreneur who is setting up the business.

Some sequential location decision making has been described in terms similar to these models. For example, Bird (1968: 14-15) writes of Governor Phillip's rejection of Botany Bay as the site for an Australian penal colony in terms which suggest that once Port Jackson was found, no other harbour was examined. 'I did not think myself at liberty to continue my research after I had seen Sydney Cove. Had I seen the country near the head of the harbour I might have been induced to have made the settlement there . . .' (Phillip, 1790: quoted in Bird, 1968: 29). The possibility of finding a better site than Sydney Cove was clearly not worth the effort of looking for it, especially as Phillip was being pressed to establish a settlement quickly.

Conclusions

At several points in this chapter some of Isard's (1969) results have been discussed. That book represents the first major attempt by anyone in the 'spatial disciplines' to generalise classical location theory into uncertainty, and so, before discussing the plan for the remainder of the analysis, the relations between Isard's intentions and the intent of this book are briefly explained.

Isard's book falls into two distinct sections. The first of these attempts to extend classical partial equilibrium location theory by analysing the location of decision taking and by presenting decision criteria under various conditions and degrees of uncertainty. Isard is concerned not so much to draw specific locational conclusions as to extend decision-making criteria through his thorough classification of decision situations. That is perhaps the first contrast between Isard's book and this: I intend not to examine decision criteria for their own sake, but to draw specific locational conclusions from the application of these criteria to decision situations. Consequently this discussion is less general than is Isard's. While extending decision criteria, Isard examines in detail the impact of bargaining on decisions in mixed-motive games; he illustrates his discussion by analysing agglomeration in the Weberian and Hotelling models. In contrast to the emphasis which Isard gives to bargaining processes, I treat most location decisions as if communication between the participants were impossible, a notion which is justified by the observation that small firms cannot communicate with other potential locators, because these others may not exist at the time the decision is made.

The second section of Isard's book culminates in his statement of a general equilibrium model for location. This statement extends previous models by explicitly including decision taking, government and planning activities, and commodities (such as love, respect, and achievement) which are normally omitted from economic models. Despite generality in this sense, the statement still assumes certainty. This assumption causes a contradiction in the analysis—if the environment is certain, then decision taking, government, and planning would not exist and should have no place in Isard's statement. Indeed, it is difficult to create a Walrasian type of general equilibrium statement for a spatial economy with uncertainty, because this needs assume that the market can compute 'the best' for an infinite number of prices and markets (Borch, 1968: 107). In contrast, this book remains within the traditional bounds of partial equilibrium analysis and 'economic' goods. The point is to attempt to derive specific locational conclusions.

The variety of locational decision situations has been simplified to fit the decision criteria available. The art of such model making is, of course, to simplify without losing the essential elements of the real situation. Consequently an important part of the theory presented in the latter half of the book (if such a loose collection of models can be dignified by the name of a theory) is the allocation of criteria to simplified situations. One part of the simplification has already been described: it consists in treating the portion of uncertainty which is due to the environment before, and independently of, the analysis of the effects of other firms on decisions. The second element of simplification—the allocation of models to cases—is presented briefly, by way of a plan of the remainder of the book.

Chapters 6 and 7 examine point locations under uncertainty. At the simplest level, one firm situations are analysed, slightly more complex are purely competitive games with no bargaining (case II), but most attention is focused on case III—mixed motive games with no bargaining. Chapter 6 introduces the

115

topic with some simple models, while Chapter 7 is devoted to a more formal and detailed exposition of a simple location model. It is contended that point locating firms' decisions can be efficiently analysed as interdependent location games, where a large portion of the uncertainty is caused by the behaviour of other firms.

In Chapter 8 are analysed land use and growth models, which are closely related under uncertainty. The simplest games contain one constituent (case I), which are more important than in analyses of points, for an important element of uncertainty in land use decisions is the state of the environment. In more sophisticated analyses, other firms are introduced, but bargaining is not permitted (cases II and III). Several additional models are cast outside the game framework: to analyse the impact of uncertainty upon the spatial variations in production costs.

Chapter 9 examines the impact of changes in the amount known about the environment. Learning and innovation diffusion processes affect location patterns substantially.

The final chapter compares location patterns under certainty and uncertainty. The planning process, with some bargaining (case IV), functions as a partial bridge between location decisions under certainty and uncertainty.

6 Uncertainty About Rivals: Some Simple Models

Most models which analyse the implications of uncertainty about rivals' behaviour concern location decisions rather than production decisions. This emphasis implies that uncertainty about rivals' choices is more relevant to the analysis of the decisions of manufacturing and service (point locating) firms than to the decisions of agricultural (land using) firms; this chapter reflects this emphasis. Nevertheless, two models of choice for land using firms uncertain about rivals' behaviour are presented. But these are isolated instances, and most extant analyses assume that uncertainty about the state of the environment is more important to land using firms than is uncertainty about the behaviour of other land using firms.

A Simulation Model

Morrill (1960, 1963, 1965) has attempted to simulate aspects of the spread and growth of urban settlement in a developing economy (Sweden, 1860 to 1960). Morrill's models concentrate upon three spatial processes—central place location, industrial location, and migration—which give rise to the observed patterns of population density and settlement distribution. Within this framework, Morrill introduces two elements which yield useful insights into locational processes. The first of the elements is the explicit use of a time dimension: the location patterns evolve over time, and are not merely static or timeless. Secondly, Morrill attempts to introduce uncertainty explicitly into the model.

The simplest model Morrill discusses (1963; 1965: 45-54) relies for its dynamic upon population migration in an initially empty area. Central places are then located to serve these migrants. The original system contains one unit of population at one given place; subsequent development is subject to the following rules: (i) both time and space are simplified into discrete units (generations and cells, respectively); (ii) all places exhibit the same natural population increase during each generation; (iii) of each additional two units of population in a centre, one stays in the centre while the other migrates; (iv) the distance and direction of migration are governed by probability, the probability of a move of a given distance declining as a power of that distance; (v) there is a limit to the size of a place, such that settlement n distance units from the origin can contain no more than n people—a rule which reflects the effects of competition between towns; (vi) a place can be settled any number of times (provided that rule (v) is not contradicted).

The model is very simple, and later Morrill (1965: 55-109) designs more general models which incorporate migration from outside the system, inter-area variations in the probability matrix which governs migration, flows of people from country to town, manufacturing industry, and transport route location. Nevertheless, the original model illustrates most of the insights which Morrill gains from this historical simulation. First, although the resultant patterns reveal some symmetry, even on a homogeneous plain there exist gaps and islands of settlement concentration. Development seems to occur along radials rather than continuously about a frontier. This result occurs because Morrill treats all decisions as probabilistic and partly affected by random processes. Morrill considers that uncertainty has no systematic or regular effect (a view which we shall later dispute) and therefore that the effects of uncertainty can be summarised by the migration law (rule (iv)); but even with such a minimum assumption, patterns differ in this model from those in an evolutionary model under certainty. Some concentration arises from this effect of uncertainty. Secondly, Morrill finds that the treatment of the settlement process as evolutionary rather than timeless reduces the number of central places in the system below the optimum static number. The rigid location of old places and the process of random assignment of functions to towns prevent space being divided most efficiently into town hinterlands; it also reduces the number of outlets for each function below the timeless optimum. Time and inertia cause inefficiencies.

Morrill's models indicate that dynamic location models will yield patterns different from those predicted by static theory. But clearly we must experiment with such models in order to determine the effects of different conditions upon settlement patterns. (Unfortunately, Morrill does not seem to have experimented with different parameter values in his simulation models.) The models are predictive, in the sense that they illustrate how particular processes yield patterns accordant with aspects of reality. But additional explanation is necessary: the economic and social pressures which result in the particular mathematical processes must be analysed. Thus, Morrill assumes that towns exist: theory must therefore prove that towns are a necessary feature of social and spatial organisation. Similarly, the factors which determine the particular matrix of migration probabilities need to be examined. The models which are constructed in this book to describe the impact of uncertainty on location are analyses of economic processes rather than mathematical predictors of reality.

Some Simple Location Games

The theory of games is increasingly being used to explore location processes under uncertainty. Like game theory generally, these location games have proved

Table 6-1: **Relative advantage to Bidder I from his bid choices**

Bidder I chooses	A	B	C	Bidder II chooses AB	AC	BC	ABC	Min.
A	0	0	0	0	0	−1	−1	−1
B	0	0	0	0	−1	0	−1	−1
C	0	0	0	−1	0	0	−1	−1
AB	0	0	1	0	0	0	1	0
AC	0	1	0	0	0	0	1	0
BC	1	0	0	0	0	0	1	0
ABC	1	1	1	−1	−1	−1	0	−1
Max.	1	1	1	0	0	0	1	

most useful in a two person context and so have sometimes been employed to analyse the interdependence approach to location. Some esoteric location problems have been analysed with the aid of game theory; thus Danskin (1962b) uses the theory to determine the optimum routing of convoys, the number of ships in a convoy and the number of protection vessels necessary, while Berkovitz and Dresher (1960) design a game theory model to allocate limited numbers of bombers and fighters against possible enemy tactics. Again, Rothschild (1947) has used the analogy of war to solve some aspects of the price structure problem in oligopolistic markets. He assigns to firms the motives of maximum profits and, equally importantly, of secure profits and concludes that, in oligopolies, prices are more stable than would be expected on the basis of other models, firms are larger than the optimum, and reserves are typically re-invested within a firm rather than being used in response to returns.

Stevens (1961) has analysed less pathological models more closely applicable to location theory. His first model is a reformulation of the Hotelling (1929) problem with two perfectly mobile sellers. When demand is inelastic the sellers locate at the centre of the market, but with moderately elastic demand sellers gain an advantage from locating at the quartiles. These results reinforce those obtained in Chapter 2.

Stevens then discusses a more novel problem. He assumes that there are three service franchises for sale along a turnpike. There exist two buyers who have equal funds and who make sealed bids for the franchises. The sites are sold to the highest bidder. This situation is normally of non-zero sum game form, but to simplify, Stevens assumes that each seller attempts to maximise his advantage over his competitor. The players can bid for one, two, or all three of the locations, and any strategy (combination of bids) uses up all the funds available. The locations are equally profitable; the players have the same amount of funds. From these assumptions may be derived Table 6-1, which shows the relative advantage of the several strategies to player I. The table indicates that there are three strategies, *AB*, *AC*, and *BC*, which are at once the minima of their

Table 6–2: **Payoff for Bidder I, in relative advantage of profitability**

Bidder I chooses	400 ABC	040 ABC	004 ABC	310 ABC	301 ABC	031 ABC	220 ABC	202 ABC	022 ABC	130 ABC	103 ABC	013 ABC	211 ABC	121 ABC	112 ABC	Min.
4A	0	1	2	1	2	0	1	2	0	1	2	0	0	0	0	0
4B	−1	0	1	−1	−2	1	−1	−2	1	−1	−2	1	−2	−2	−2	−2
4C	−2	−1	0	−4	−2	−1	−4	−2	−1	−4	−2	−1	−4	−4	−4	−4
3A1B	−2	2	2	−1	0	1	2	2	0	2	2	0	1	1	0	−2
3A1C	−2	2	2	−1	0	1	2	2	0	2	2	0	1	1	0	−2
3B1C	0	−1	1	0	−1	0	0	−2	1	−2	−2	1	−1	−1	−2	−2
2A2B	−1	1	4	−1	−2	0	0	1	1	1	4	4	4	2	4	−2
2A2C	−2	2	2	−4	−2	2	−1	0	1	2	2	0	−1	2	1	−4
2B2C	0	−1	1	0	0	−1	−2	−1	0	−4	−2	1	0	−2	−1	−4
1A3B	−1	1	4	−1	−2	2	−1	−2	4	0	1	4	−2	1	1	−2
1A3C	−2	2	2	−4	−2	2	−4	−2	2	−1	0	1	−4	−1	−1	−4
1B3C	0	−1	1	−2	0	−1	−4	0	−1	−4	−1	0	−2	−4	−2	−4
2A1B1C	0	2	4	−2	−1	1	−4	1	0	2	4	2	0	1	2	−4
1A2B1C	0	2	4	0	−1	1	−2	−2	2	−1	1	4	−1	0	1	−2
1A1B2C	0	2	4	−2	0	2	−4	−1	1	−1	1	2	−2	−1	0	−4
Max.	0	2	4	1	2	2	2	4	4	2	4	4	4	2	4	

rows and the maxima of their columns. Consequently an optimal strategy for each player is to make a random choice of any two of the three locations and to bid for those two. The game is fair, in that one player will obtain one location, the second another location, while the third location is allocated to a player on the basis of a device which gives each player a probability of one-half of gaining that location.

This is an interesting conclusion; the precise strategy is not an intuitively obvious solution. But it seems to depend on the restrictive assumptions of the model. If the players are permitted to divide their funds in any manner at all among bids for the three locations, then (except that no player allocates all his funds to a bid for one site) all bids are equally likely, for all have a row minimum of −1 and a column maximum of +1. The game therefore tells us very little about location strategies, except that firms never bid for only one of the three franchises.

A more useful location game occurs when the sites are not equally profitable. Stevens analyses this case in two ways. First, if one location is twice as profitable as another and the players distribute their funds equally among the franchises bid for, then both bid with all their funds for the best location. The second case assumes that funds are distributed among bids in accordance with the profitability of the locations: again, both bid for the best location. The situation may be analysed more generally by permitting the players to distribute their funds among the bids as they like and by assuming that the value of the locations is in the ratio $3:2:1$. If they have funds of four units, Table 6–2 holds. The optimal strategy for each player is to allocate all his funds to the bid for A, the best site. Unfortunately, as it stands, the model is not generally useful, for it implies that the bidders would be willing to pay unlimited amounts for the privilege of locating at A. This unsatisfactory result is due to the fact that profitability is not related to the amount bid for the sites.

Other location games have been developed, though often in an introductory way. Greenhut (1957) argues that the von Thünen-Weber least cost search ignores the game-like interdependence of firms. Such interdependence and its associated uncertainty make the move to the quartiles in Smithies's (1941) model daring; Greenhut suggests rather that firms are more likely to be conservative in choices. Similarly, Isard and his co-workers have analysed some simple games. Isard and Dacey (1962) and Isard and Reiner (1962) have proposed that game theory be used to predict the behaviour of firms, but apart from analysing some simple two person zero sum matrices, they have not demonstrated the pattern generated by this behaviour nor have they indicated the value of the game model. Isard (1967) has used game models to analyse typical Weberian problems, but, like Stevens's (1961) analysis, these models do not greatly increase our understanding of these situations.

The most extensive statement of game-like decision models for interdependent firms is that of Isard (1969), but in general he is not concerned to draw specific locational conclusions from his models. However, he does discuss the contributions of game theory in Weberian and Hotelling frameworks (Isard, 1969: 430-90). In particular, Isard presents some decision criteria which may be used to solve the agglomeration problem for firms which operate within a Weberian system and to permit firms to achieve optimal solutions to the Hotelling problem of two sellers in a linear bounded market. These criteria all depend on bargaining by the firms. It is this explicit introduction of bargaining and compromise procedures which defines Isard's contribution to these models. But such procedures are of use only to large firms; small firms are typically unable to communicate with each other, especially when locating in sequence. Thus, bargaining procedures seem inapplicable to a wide range of locational situations.

The formal game models used in location theory have so far largely presented only alternative formulations of existing models of patterns under certainty. They have not shed much additional light on the way in which these certainty models work.

A Market Shares Model

In this section a simple model of location is analysed. The model assumes that firms attempt to maximise their share of the market. Such a decision criterion is little used in economics: generally a maximum profit criterion is more useful. But if we assume zero marginal costs of production, an absolutely inelastic demand and fixed prices, then a variant of the Hotelling model develops in which a maximum share of the market is equivalent to maximum profits.

Alternatively the model may be regarded as simulating the location of firms in which economies of scale are so large that profits are a monotonically increasing function of size within the range of sizes permitted by the market. This re-analysis of the simple interdependence model yields useful conclusions about location policies in a discontinuous market.

Five 'towns' are assumed to exist in a linear market. They are located one at each end of the market, one at each quartile, and one at the centre. Two firms exist; a firm sells only to those towns to which it is nearer than the other firm. The towns may be envisaged as being the sites of primary and secondary production, when the model may be interpreted as analysing the location of pairs of firms which sell services to primary and secondary producers. The model thus describes the location policies of service firms which decide to locate as if they felt that some other firm is locating at the same time. That location is chosen which maximises the firms' share of the market.

The five towns, A, B, C, D, and E, contain respectively a, b, c, d, and e per cent of the market (where $a+b+c+d+e = 100$). A general result may be proved about such a system: it is never to the advantage of a firm to locate outside a town.[1]

Thus once a set of towns has been formed, the conditions under which new towns may be established are limited. Firms which have zero marginal costs of production and infinitely inelastic demand curves and which maximise their share of the market will never cause new towns to be formed when they locate on a market. Thus, once some towns have been formed, new towns may be established only because of resource advantages at particular places, or because the demand curves of firms are elastic, or because there is some evenly spread population between the towns. The same result occurs, of course, if A, B, C, D, and E are visualised as developed regions or as shopping centres within towns. If demand is concentrated for some reason at points, firms acting under these assumptions locate only at those points, never at sites between them.

This result simplifies the analysis of location policies in a discontinuous market, for we need only analyse the results of location at the already existing towns. The analysis is most easily accomplished in general rather than in specific form, and to simplify without significant loss of generality it will be assumed that towns A, B, C, D, and E contain respectively a, b, c, c and c per cent of the market (where $a+b+3c = 100$). The relevant zero sum matrix is reproduced in Table 6–3. The matrix is constructed as follows. If both firms locate at A, they share the entire market, each obtaining $\frac{1}{2}(a+b+3c)$ per cent. If the first firm locates at A and the second at B, the first is nearer town A only, and so receives only a per cent of the market. The rest of the table is filled in similarly.

Comparison of row E with row D shows that the value of locating at E for player I is always less than the value of locating at D, no matter where player II

---

[1] See the Appendix to this chapter.

Table 6–3: **Percentage of sales accruing to Player I**

Player I locates at	Player II locates at				
	A	B	C	D	E
A	$\dfrac{a+b+3c}{2}$	a	$a+\frac{1}{2}b$	$a+b$	$a+b+\frac{1}{2}c$
B	$b+3c$	$\dfrac{a+b+3c}{2}$	$a+b$	$a+b+\frac{1}{2}c$	$a+b+c$
C	$\frac{1}{2}b+3c$	$3c$	$\dfrac{a+b+3c}{2}$	$a+b+c$	$a+b+1\frac{1}{2}c$
D	$3c$	$2\frac{1}{2}c$	$2c$	$\dfrac{a+b+3c}{2}$	$a+b+2c$
E	$2\frac{1}{2}c$	$2c$	$1\frac{1}{2}c$	c	$\dfrac{a+b+3c}{2}$

Note: $a+b+3c = 100\%$.

Table 6–4: **Percentage of sales to Player I at admissible locations**

Player I locates at	Player II locates at		
	A	B	C
A	$\dfrac{a+b+3c}{2}$	a	$a+\frac{1}{2}b$
B	$b+3c$	$\dfrac{a+b+3c}{2}$	$a+b$
C	$\frac{1}{2}b+3c$	$3c$	$\dfrac{a+b+3c}{2}$

locates. Player I will never locate at E; similarly, neither will player II. Without loss of generality, we may assume that $a+b \geqslant c$, in which case location at D is never preferable to location at C. That is, locations D and E are dominated by location C: only locations A, B, and C are admissible choices. The original 5×5 matrix has become the 3×3 matrix of Table 6–4.

Now in such a matrix of admissible strategies, a location is chosen if and only if it is at once the maximum of the row minima and the minimum of the column maxima. Thus location A is chosen by both players if and only if

$$\min \left(\frac{a+b+3c}{2}, a, a+\tfrac{1}{2}b \right) > \min \left(b+3c, \frac{a+b+3c}{2}, a+b \right),$$

$$\text{and } \min \left(\frac{a+b+3c}{2}, a, a+\tfrac{1}{2}b \right) > \min \left(\tfrac{1}{2}b+3c, 3c, \frac{a+b+3c}{2} \right),$$

$$\text{and } \max \left(\frac{a+b+3c}{2}, b+3c, \tfrac{1}{2}b+3c \right) < \max \left(a, \frac{a+b+3c}{2}, 3c \right),$$

$$\text{and } \max \left(\frac{a+b+3c}{2}, b+3c, \tfrac{1}{2}b+3c \right) < \max \left(a+\tfrac{1}{2}b, a+b, \frac{a+b+3c}{2} \right);$$

that is, if

(6–1) $a > b+3c$.

The firms locate at A if and only if more than 50 per cent of the market is contained in A. Similarly, B is chosen if and only if

$$a < b+3c \text{ and } a+b > 3c;$$

that is, if and only if

(6–2) $3c-b < a < 3c+b$.

Firms locate at B only if A and B contain together more than one-half the market and if A alone contains less than half the market. Again, C is chosen if and only if

$$a+b < 3c \text{ and } a+b > c;$$

that is, if

(6–3) $c < a+b < 3c$.

Provided that A and B together contain a greater share of the market than C, firms locate at C if and only if A and B together account for less than one-half the market. A random choice between A and B is made (with $p = 0.5$) if

$$a = b+3c,$$

and a random choice is made between B and C (again with $p = 0.5$) if

$$a+b = 3c.$$

This model precisely specifies the location choices of the two firms. But it does not yet show how location patterns will evolve. This evolution is most conveniently analysed in three stages. Firstly, if more than 50 per cent of the market is at A, the first firms locate at A, so that the proportion of the market which is at A increases, and all following firms must locate at A also. Secondly, if more than 50 per cent of the market is contained in A and B, but A itself comprises less than half the market, the first firms locate at B; this increases B's share of the market, and later firms must locate there too. Finally, if less than half of the market is located in A and B, the first and all later firms must locate at C. Thus one of the three towns will contain all the service firms in the market and therefore one of them will gradually increase its share of the market. The model assumes that there is initially a best site; by locating at this site a firm will improve it for later firms; therefore the initial best site is the only one at which firms locate. The force for concentration is powerful, but all this assumes an inelastic demand and no diseconomies of scale.

A More Complex Market Shares Model

This section analyses a model similar to that examined previously. A line market containing five towns—one at each end, one at each quartile, and one at the median—is assumed. The policies of two identical firms which locate at the

Table 6–5: **Schematic matrix of market shares to Player I**

Player I locates at	Player II locates at					
	1	2	. . . .	J	. . . .	N
1	$\frac{1}{2}$.			a	. . . .	
2	. . . .	$\frac{1}{2}$.		b	. . . .	
.	. . . .					
.	. . . .					
J	1–a	1–b	. . . .	$\frac{1}{2}$	. . . .	1–c
.	. . . .					
.	. . . .					
N	. . . .			c	. . . .	$\frac{1}{2}$

Note: $1 \geqslant a \geqslant 0$; $1 \geqslant b \geqslant 0$; $1 \geqslant c \geqslant 0$.

same time with the same fixed price are examined. These firms are assumed to attempt to maximise their share of the market. The crucial difference between this model and the previous one is that demand is assumed to be elastic: as prices rise, lower quantities are sold.

In any payoff matrix, such as Table 6–5, no matter where player II locates, player I can always gain at least half the market by locating at the same site. When both firms locate at one of the sites 1, 2, ..., J, ..., N, each firm gains half the market. Thus, in any column, the maximum share is at least 50 per cent; and in any row, the minimum share is less than or equal to 50 per cent. But the equilibrium strategy occurs when the maximum of a column equals the minimum of a row. Hence the equilibrium strategy guarantees each player half the market. The game is consequently fair.

It can be proved that players always locate in one of the five towns, never outside those towns. It is assumed that the market is arranged as in the previous model. Sales at any point in the market are given by

$$(6\text{–}4) \qquad D = \frac{n-d}{n}.m,$$

where n is a positive constant, d is distance from the seller to the point, and m is the size of the market at that point. Without loss of generality, it may be assumed that the distance between each town and its nearest neighbours is unity. The market in towns C, D, and E is assumed equal to c. The proof (in the Appendix to this chapter) assumes that firms can sell to all the towns in the market from any point.

This proof means that, if markets are discontinuous, demand curves are linear (either elastic or inelastic), and firms try to maximise their share of the market, those firms always locate in the already existing towns. No new towns, no new shopping centres, no new regions of concentrated activity are created by the actions of uncertain sellers in this simple situation. In the model, new

125

Table 6–6: $D = \dfrac{4-d}{4}$m: **Market shares of Player I**

Player I chooses	Player II chooses A	B	C	D
A	0·50	$\dfrac{a}{a+b+1\cdot50c}$	$\dfrac{a+0\cdot375b}{a+0\cdot75b+2\cdot25c}$	$\dfrac{a+0\cdot75b}{a+0\cdot75b+2\cdot50c}$
B	$\dfrac{b+1\cdot50c}{a+b+1\cdot50c}$	0·50	$\dfrac{0\cdot75a+b}{0\cdot75a+b+2\cdot25c}$	$\dfrac{0\cdot75a+b+0\cdot375c}{0\cdot75a+b+2\cdot50c}$
C	$\dfrac{0\cdot375b+2\cdot25c}{a+0\cdot75b+2\cdot25c}$	$\dfrac{2\cdot25c}{0\cdot75a+b+2\cdot25c}$	0·50	$\dfrac{0\cdot50a+0\cdot75b+1\cdot00c}{0\cdot50a+0\cdot75b+2\cdot75c}$
D	$\dfrac{2\cdot50c}{a+0\cdot75b+2\cdot50c}$	$\dfrac{2\cdot125c}{0\cdot75a+b+2\cdot50c}$	$\dfrac{1\cdot75c}{0\cdot50a+0\cdot75b+2\cdot75c}$	0·50

Note: Location E is dominated and never played: sales at E are therefore omitted from this table and Table 6–7.

towns can be formed only by the location of resource-oriented industries or if there is a spread of agricultural population between the towns. In reality, of course, diseconomies of agglomeration may also promote dispersal—but only if profits, not market shares, are maximised. These market share models indicate clearly how uncertain interdependent sellers act to promote town growth and the concentration of activity.

The graphs, Figs. 6–1 and 6–2, have been drawn to illustrate location policies in such a market. The proportion of the market at C, D, and E has been assumed to be equal (to c); the proportion of the market at A is a and at B is b. The graphs show the location decisions of the firms as the sizes of a and b are allowed to vary. Policies for two demand curves have been calculated: the first is for the curve

$$(6–5) \qquad D = \frac{4-d}{4}.m,$$

where d is the distance of a town from the seller and m is the population of that town, and the second is for the curve

$$(6–6) \qquad D = \frac{2-d}{2}.m.$$

Tables 6–6 and 6–7 have been calculated using these demand curves. These tables provide the zero sum game matrices which are used to solve the location games; from them may be derived the conditions under which the firms locate at the various towns. Table 6–6, for the demand curve (6–5) yields the location conditions:

(i) firms locate at town A if

$$a > b+1\cdot50c$$

$$(6–7) \qquad a > 2\cdot25c$$

$$a > 2\cdot50c-0\cdot75b;$$

Table 6–7: $D = \dfrac{2-d}{2}m$: Market shares of Player I

Player I chooses	Player II chooses			
	A	B	C	D
A	0·50	$\dfrac{a}{a+b+0\cdot50c}$	$\dfrac{a+0\cdot25b}{a+0\cdot50b+1\cdot50c}$	$\dfrac{a+0\cdot50b}{a+0\cdot50b+2\cdot00c}$
B	$\dfrac{b+0\cdot50c}{a+b+0\cdot50c}$	0·50	$\dfrac{0\cdot50a+b}{0\cdot50a+b+1\cdot50c}$	$\dfrac{0\cdot50a+b+0\cdot25c}{0\cdot50a+b+2\cdot00c}$
C	$\dfrac{0\cdot25b+1\cdot50c}{a+0\cdot50b+1\cdot50c}$	$\dfrac{1\cdot50c}{0\cdot50a+b+1\cdot50c}$	0·50	$\dfrac{0\cdot50b+c}{0\cdot50b+2\cdot50c}$
D	$\dfrac{2\cdot00c}{a+0\cdot50b+2\cdot00c}$	$\dfrac{1\cdot75c}{0\cdot50a+b+2\cdot00c}$	$\dfrac{1\cdot50c}{0\cdot50b+2\cdot50c}$	0·50

(ii) firms locate at B if

$$a < 1\cdot50c + b$$

(6–8) $$a > 3\cdot00c - 1\cdot33b$$

$$a > 2\cdot33c - 1\cdot33b;$$

(iii) firms locate at C if

$$a < 2\cdot25c$$

(6–9) $$a < 3\cdot00c - 1\cdot33b$$

$$a > 1\cdot50c - 1\cdot50b;$$

and (iv) firms locate at town D if

(6–10) $$a < 1\cdot50c - 1\cdot50b.$$

The combination of these conditions yields the graph, Fig. 6–1.

Table 6–7, derived from the demand curve (6–6), provides the location conditions:

(i) firms locate at A if

$$a > 0\cdot50c + b$$

(6–11) $$a > 1\cdot50c$$

$$a > 2\cdot00c - 0\cdot50b;$$

(ii) firms locate at town B if

(6–12) $$a > 0\cdot50c + b$$
$$a < 3\cdot00c - 2\cdot00b$$

(iii) firms locate at town C if

$$b < 1\cdot50c$$

(6–13) $$a < 3\cdot00c - 2\cdot00b$$

$$b > 1\cdot00c;$$

Figure 6–1: **Location policies (location at *A*, *B*, *C*, or *D*) in linear market depending on size of markets at *A* (*a*) and *B* (*b*). The demand curve is *D* = (4-d)m/4.**

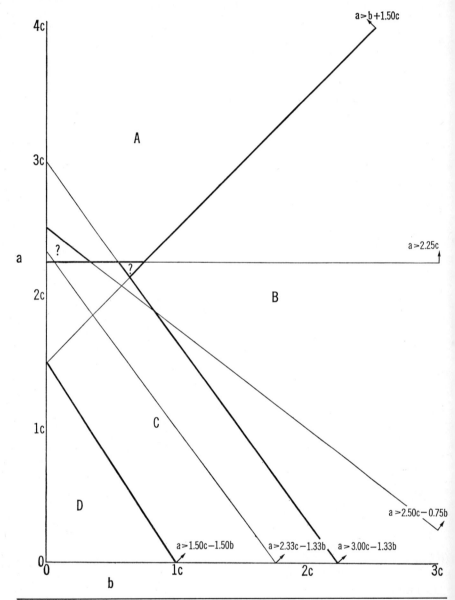

Figure 6–2: **Location policies in linear market depending on *a* and *b*. Demand, D= (2–d)m/2.**

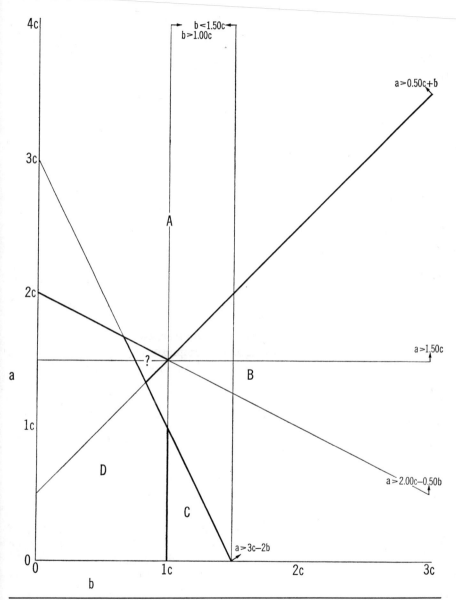

Table 6–8: **Relative frequencies with which locations are chosen**

Location	Inelastic	Demand curve $\dfrac{4-d}{4}$	$\dfrac{2-d}{2}$
A	0·200	0·469	0·625
B	0·400	0·209	0·181
C	0·350	0·247	0·026
D	0·050	0·075	0·168

Note: The limits over which a and b are assumed to vary are: $0 \leqslant a \leqslant 5c$ and $0 \leqslant b \leqslant 2c$.

and (iv) firms locate at D if

$$a < 2{\cdot}00c - 0{\cdot}50b$$

(6–14) $a < 3{\cdot}00c - 2{\cdot}00b$

$$b < 1{\cdot}00c.$$

These conditions have been graphed to produce Fig. 6–2.

The graphs illustrate that when demand curves are elastic, the conditions governing optimum location policies are complex. Both Fig. 6–1 and Fig. 6–2 contain zones, indicated with question marks, where location policies are confused. In these zones there is no simple optimal choice, but rather an optimal combination of policies (including random strategies). This complexity contrasts markedly with the relative simplicity of the case in which demand is inelastic. Under uncertainty, then, optimal location policies do not necessarily yield determinate location patterns.

A comparison of the strategies indicated by Fig. 6–1 with firm's strategies when demand is inelastic indicates that location policies are more extreme when demand is elastic than when it is inelastic. Thus the percentage of the market necessary in A to induce firms to locate at A is lower when demand is elastic than for inelastic demand. As the demand schedule becomes more elastic, the proportion of the market in towns C, D, and E necessary to induce location at D becomes smaller. These differences are even more pronounced when demand is very elastic (see Fig. 6–3). Table 6–8 has been constructed to illustrate this point: it shows the proportion of the possible combinations of a and b between $a = 0$ and $a = 5c$ and $b = 0$ and $b = 2c$ which result in location at the different towns. The proportion of the combinations in which A is chosen rises from 20 per cent when demand is inelastic to over 60 per cent when demand is very elastic. Similarly, D is chosen on 26·8 per cent of the possibilities when demand is elastic, but only on 5 per cent of the occasions when the demand schedule is inelastic. By contrast, the proportion of the combinations on which B or C is chosen falls from 75 per cent when demand is inelastic to about 20 per cent when demand is elastic. Locations which are central to the entire market area are less likely to be chosen if demand is elastic than if demand is inelastic. The models provide several conclusions. If firms in a discontinuous market maximise sales under conditions of fixed prices, then those firms locate within already existing concentrations. Town systems, once formed, are stable. Secondly, precise conditions for the location decisions of the firms have been determined. These conditions parallel those of Weber (Friedrich, 1929: 62-7), who found that firms only locate at a raw material or market site if the weight of the goods produced or consumed in production at that site accounts for more than half the total weight of goods produced or consumed in production. In this model though, towns generally do not have to contain more than 50 per cent of the market to attract service firms—only when demand is inelastic does the extreme town, A have to comprise half the market before attracting firms. Increasing elasticity of demand prompts increasingly extreme location patterns. Thirdly, the model shows that in the absence of diseconomies of agglomeration, one of the towns in the system will grow at the expense of all the others, and will progressively cumulate advantages. And finally, since both sellers locate in the same town, the location pattern is not optimal from the point of view of society. But the conditions under which these results have been established are restrictive. Chapter 7 is devoted to a formal generalisation of the maximum profit case.

Inter-Industry Interdependence

The first game models discussed analyse the effects of the interdependence of firms in the same industry. A model of inter-industry interdependence is analysed here to pave the way for the more general model of the following chapter. In contrast to the previous models, which are strictly competitive, the inter-industry model is co-operative: that is, it is not zero sum. The model is based upon the ideas of Schelling (1960). Schelling argues that the use of formal models of games in non-zero sum situations may cause erroneous predictions of reality, because a prime characteristic of actual solutions is that they are suggested to the players by the conditions of the game. Solutions tend to be prominent or conspicuous outcomes; their prominence is due to the game environment. An interesting application of this argument lies in the role of natural features as focus points for agreement on national boundaries. A physically obvious feature such as a river may be a more prominent (and so more readily acceptable) boundary solution than a more rational, though less conspicuous, unused zone away from the river.

Assume two individuals in an economic system, each of whom has to make an irreversible decision to locate. Assume further that costs and sales are invariant with location, except that the two must locate together to prevent the costs of communication between them becoming prohibitive. The firms cannot communicate before they locate. In planning a location, they can only randomise their choice and hope to coincide, but they will win, in the sense of both choosing the same spot, very rarely. However, a system may contain some indicators which aid choices of this kind. Assume that the economic system contains many cities, one of which, A, is larger than any other. As in the previous models, it is supposed that the activity in these cities is based on the exploitation of resources.

Schelling (1960: 53-80) points out that, in such a co-ordination game, the one firm cannot locate where it expects the other to be, because the other bases its choice on the expected location of the first firm. To co-ordinate predictions, the firms must identify the one course of action upon which their expectations of each other's behaviour can converge. A rule has to be agreed upon by tacit consent. The two firms must therefore predict the other's decision and predict the other's expectation of their own decision, using the only guide available— the number and size of cities. The only city which can act as a focus of ex- pectations in Schelling's sense is the largest one, A, the only one which is prominent among the others. Therefore, two—or more—individuals, acting in ignorance of each other but having to agree on a common location, establish at the point which becomes the focus of expectations by virtue of its qualitative differentiation and uniqueness. If size is the differentiating criterion, the firms locate in the largest city.

Now this model may be simply transcribed into the terms of location theory. Three conditions which conform to the assumptions of the model are: the establishment, individually, of the buying offices of one firm and the selling offices of another; the location of the first firm in a new industry; and the location of a firm and the workers in its industry. If these cases can be analysed in the terms of this game model, some of the attraction of industry to large cities might be explained. It forms an initial model of urbanisation economies under uncertainty.

Consider first the location of buying and selling offices. If the industry is a new one, it may be assumed that the buyers have not yet decided to act as such. Therefore the sellers locate their offices in ignorance of the buyers' choices, though in anticipation of an expected choice. Costs of communication rise with distance between the firms: the assumptions of the model are typically fulfilled by the situation. Hence the first selling office is located in the largest city (or in a city renowned for its concentration of similar industries), a choice which is repeated by the buying offices and, possibly, by other selling offices. But communication costs within a firm also rise as does the distance between the offices and producing plant of the firm. Consequently, if the costs of communi- cation within a firm rise more steeply with distance than the costs of production fall, the large city becomes an attractive site for manufacturing as well as for buying and selling. The advantages of the largest city for buying and selling help make that city an attractive site for some manufacturing plants.

Secondly, the conditions of the model apply to the location of a new firm in a new industry. A new industry is characterised by rapid technological change: a firm must be able to copy new designs and to incorporate the innovations of other firms in the industry. The firm therefore locates close to the anticipated location of these later firms. The conditions of the model are satisfied, and the firm establishes in the largest city, the only site which offers a better than random chance of 'winning'. The later firms also locate in that city, to be close to the first firm and because they too anticipate that this will be the site chosen by later firms.

The location chosen by firms during the early period of economic development is similar. Hirschman (1958: 185) indicates that entrepreneurs overestimate the economies of agglomeration available in developing regions: 'What appears to happen is that the external economies due to the poles, though real, are consistently overestimated by the economic operators.' However, this conclusion may be misleading, for firms may locate at the development poles not merely to obtain the economies already available there, but also to take (future) advantage of the more extensive economies which develop later as more firms establish at those poles. If firms predict the future locational pattern of society, and locate in accordance with that prediction, it may appear as if the economies already available at the poles are being overestimated. Since firms expect other firms to locate at the poles, they must also establish there to minimise the costs of gathering information and to maximise external economies. Of course, the firms' predictions have the status of self-fulfilling prophecies.

Thirdly, the model may be used to analyse the location of firms with respect to labour. Labour has traditionally been regarded as a static element in society, whose location is given and whose efficiency is known: this assumption is made most extremely in Weber's model. But the decision of labour to locate may be visualised as a continuing process, for decisions to live and work elsewhere or to remain at the same point are being remade (at least implicitly) every time a new factory is set up. Thus the labour pool in a city is not merely existing there, it is continually deciding to stay in the city. Furthermore, firms and their potential labour force communicate poorly, for potential workers cannot inform potential firms of their locational preferences. The conditions of the model hold.

Therefore the firm and its potential labour force must agree, without communication, on a common focus of expectations. The firm must analyse the location decision of each potential element of its labour force, and each potential worker must consider what he expects the firm to decide, what he expects each of his fellow workers to do, and what he expects the firm and the other workers to expect of him. The focus of expectations is stability—the labour force remains in the city and the firm locates at the source of labour, which, in the model, is the largest city.

Some of the assumptions of the model may now be relaxed. The two players may not decide at the same time. If the first firm thinks that a second is locating at the same time, or may be locating at the same time, its choice must be made in accordance with the anticipated choice of the other. The first firm therefore locates in the largest city and the second follows in order to reduce the costs of communication between them. If, on the other hand, the first knows that the second firm will not locate until later, it can choose any location it wishes, sure in the knowledge that the second will follow. The necessary condition that the first firm locates in the largest city is consequently that either the seller thinks that the second is establishing at the same time, or the seller is afraid that the second may be locating at the same time. The first seller must be ignorant of the choice and the timing of the decision of the other.

The assumption that costs do not vary over space may also be relaxed. Make the extreme assumption for the model: that costs rise as does the size of city. The firms maximise individual profits by locating in a small city. But there are many such small cities, and two firms locating at the same time are unlikely to chance on the same one. Therefore these firms must expect high costs of communication between them if they choose a small city. Although the game has now become one of mixed strategy, provided that the need for co-operation is greater than the cost of competition—i.e. that the costs of communication between two spatially separated firms are greater than the increase in production costs due to locating at the focus of expectations—the two firms locate in the largest city.

A limited amount of bargaining is also possible. If one of the 'players' is a group of individuals, the members of which cannot communicate among themselves, the assumption that each individual in the group may bargain with the other player does not affect the outcome of the game. Each individual worker and the firm may regard a move as the most profitable choice, but each worker expects the other workers to retain the focus of expectations. Deciding tacitly, the individuals in the group can only agree on the common policy of behaving as the focus of expectations dictates.

Generalised, this simple model provides some useful conclusions. Two firms are attracted to the largest city in an economic system if they must agree on a common location and if the first player is uncertain of the timing of the choice of the other, even though production costs may favour a small city and even though, if one of the 'players' is a group of individuals, the individuals can each communicate with the other player. As the uncertainty is relaxed, the tendency to concentrate in the large city is less evident: for instance, if the two firms can communicate, they can agree on a mutually most profitable location. The growth of the largest city is reinforced by uncertainty. Everyone's expectation of what everyone expects of everyone is a conservative location criterion, but then, the concentration of people in a few large cities is a conservative or least risk phenomenon.

Land Use Models for Interdependent Firms

As was pointed out at the beginning of this chapter, land use analysis under uncertainty has traditionally regarded the major source of uncertainty as due to the state of the environment rather than to the actions of rivals. This emphasis follows the main body of economic doctrine which assumes that agriculture is a competitive industry, that is, an industry in which the policy of rivals is a datum. Consequently most land use models are either one person models (if they analyse individual production decisions) or models for the entire industry (such as von Thünen's). Few models analyse land use decisions in terms of two person games, but two such models are described here.

The first of these models is due to Moglewer (1962). He analyses farmers' choices among wheat, corn, soybeans, and oats in the United States over the period 1948 to 1958. The model framework comprises one farmer who operates as a rival to all other farmers (and buyers are introduced to make the game zero sum). The demand curve for the ith crop is determined by regressing q_i (quantity bought) on p_i (price) in the Cobb-Douglas schedule:

$$(6\text{--}15) \qquad p_i^{-E_i} \cdot q_i = c_i,$$

where E_i is the elasticity coefficient and c_i is a constant. Moglewer assumes that one farmer's production has no effect on the price of a crop, and then the payoff to a single farmer is

$$(6\text{--}16) \qquad M = \sum_{i=1}^{4} Y_i \, L \, x_i \left(\frac{y_i}{K_i}\right)^{1/E_i},$$

where $K_i = c_i / \overline{Y_i} \, \overline{L}$, Y_i is the individual's yield of the ith crop, L his total acreage, x_i is the fraction of his acreage in the ith crop, y_i is the fraction of the other farmers' acreage of the ith crop, $\overline{Y_i}$ is the others' yield of that crop, and $\overline{L}$ is their total acreage. The values of the yield are taken to be those of the year for which decisions are being made. This assumption gave better results than setting expected yields equal to the previous year's yield.

Given these payoff functions (equation (6–16)), the game can be solved. Moglewer finds that in any one year the deciding farmer should select one of the four crops by chance (with known probabilities) and plant all his acreage to that one crop. By thus solving for each farmer, the actual acreage devoted to each crop may be determined. The correlations between predicted and actual acreages for the ten years are 0·69 for corn, 0·70 for oats, 0·49 for wheat, and 0·36 for soybeans. Moglewer ascribes the two poor results to the existence of government wheat acreage controls and the very rapid expansion of soybean acreage. These are quite high correlations considering the simplicity of the model.

Despite Moglewer's success with this model, there is evidence that many farmers do not operate in this manner; they do not behave as if they were engaged in a game against rivals. One important piece of evidence of this kind is the existence of agriculture product cycles. Allen (1959: 31-9) illustrates a wide variety of product cycles (marked cyclical variations in the amount of a crop produced), including coffee (up to World War I, since when Brazilian government intervention has curtailed the cycle), potatoes in the United Kingdom, pigs, cattle and sheep (in several European countries) cycles. These product cycles are usually analysed in terms of the 'Cobweb' theorem (Ezekiel, 1938;

135

Table 6–9: **Matrix of received rents**

Owner I	Owner II	
	Not rent to negro	Rent to negro
Not rent to negro	$100, $100	$80, $110
Rent to negro	$110, $80	$90, $90

Note: Figures are monthly rentals earned by the two owners; owner I's rental is the first figure of each pair.

Hooton, 1950).[2] Although this theorem does not predict all aspects of product cycles accurately, it does provide a mechanism for self-generating cycles.

From our point of view, two pre-conditions for product cycles are particularly important. These are, firstly, that there is a time lag between the implementation of decisions and the maturation of those plans (i.e. commitments are made before a farmer knows what other farmers have decided), and secondly, that a large proportion of farmers ignore the expected actions of other farmers, so that they expand or contract output simultaneously. The first pre-condition is generally important in the analysis of uncertainty: production and location patterns are most strongly affected by uncertainty when firm commitments are made in ignorance of others' choices. The second pre-condition implies that the form of Moglewer's model does not occur frequently: farmers often do not take rivals' actions into account when making decisions.

A second attempt to analyse land use decisions in terms of inter-personal interdependence is Smolensky, Becker, and Molotch's (1968) prisoner's dilemma model for the expansion of negro ghettoes in the United States. Assume two owners, with houses to rent. Two negroes offer themselves as tenants. Maintenance costs are constant, irrespective of who rents the houses, but rents offered depend on the tenant's race. The negro pays a premium rent so long as he is the only negro in the area; if more than one negro enters the area, they demand rents lower than those paid by whites. If negroes live in an area, rents paid by whites are reduced. The resulting game matrix is reproduced in Table 6–9: if the owners co-operate, they exclude negroes; if they compete, they both take negroes as tenants.

Smolensky and his co-workers interviewed 177 real estate agents who rent apartments in Chicago. Although they found evidence that the agents (and especially the small ones) expected that a prisoner's dilemma game would face them, those who had actually confronted the situation did not think that

---

[2] In simple terms, the Cobweb theorem predicts a production cycle in the following manner. Assume that producers expect current prices to hold in the future. If prices are high, supply is encouraged. Farmers' production plans mature at the same time, and so supply of the good is greater. Prices are driven down, and supply is discouraged. This reduced supply in turn causes prices to rise, initiating a new sequence of the cycle. The degree to which such a cycle is dampened, oscillates indefinitely, or oscillates with ever increasing amplitude depends upon the shape of the demand and supply curve in theory, and is affected in practice by chance fluctuations of yield and the returns from other crops.

the game accurately modelled the problem: the actual rent matrix is not of prisoner's dilemma form. The model therefore fails to account for the pattern of spread of the ghettoes.

These models represent novel ways of analysing the uncertain decisions of land use entrepreneurs. But clearly the analyses are only partially successful. While Moglewer's predictions could perhaps be improved if he used a less simple assumption system, his analysis cannot be extended to all farmers, many of whom appear to make decisions independently of rivals' behaviour. Smolensky's model is even less successful than this. These results help to support the traditional analysis of land use decisions in terms of uncertainty about the state of the environment rather than about rivals' actions.

Conclusions

The models developed in this chapter are exploratory, setting up some features of location under uncertainty which will be analysed more formally in the next chapter. Even so, the models, though as yet unrelated to one another, illustrate some main features of the impact of uncertainty on location. Both the model of inter-industry interdependence and the models of within industry interdependence show how the decision-making criteria used cause firms to foster the growth of existing towns, especially large ones. The third model also indicates that uncertainty may cause firms to locate in large towns even though the costs of production may be lower in small towns. Such location policies are socially non-optimal. Moglewer's model indicates how uncertainty about rivals' behaviour may cause diversified production within an industry: the industry produced all four crops in any one year rather than concentrating all activity upon the one most profitable good. The analysis of product cycles illustrates the importance of prior commitment to firms which are uncertain: firms decide without knowing the choices of rivals and without being able to alter their decisions as knowledge becomes available. A comparison of the models reveals the importance of communication between firms if location choices are to be optimal. Yet such communication must be imperfect, because a firm which is locating cannot communicate with all other potential firms. Location decisions must be socially imperfect in the real world, unless the state helps to co-ordinate choices.

Appendix to Chapter 6

Firms will always locate in existing 'towns' in the market shares models, as this Appendix proves.

In the simpler market shares model, demand is inelastic. It may be proved that it is never to the advantage of a firm to locate outside an existing town by noting that in a two person zero sum game, a location strategy is chosen if it is a maximin of the game: that is, if and only if the strategy is the maximum of the row minima. (Since the game is symmetrical the maximum of the row minima is also the minimum of the column maxima.) Therefore to prove that one location is never the best, it is sufficient to show that the minimum return at that location is less than the minimum return at some other location.

Consider first location between A and B. The share of the market obtained at this location is $b+c+d+e$ per cent when the other firm is at A; 50 per cent when the other firm is at the same location; and a per cent when the other is at B. Now, if a is less than $b+c+d+e$, the minimum of these is a per cent, while if a is more than $b+c+d+e$, the minimum is $b+c+d+e$ per cent. But, if a is less than $b+c+d+e$, the minimum sales for a firm at B is either $a+b$ per cent (when the other firm is at C) or 50 per cent (when the other firm is also at B); and if a is greater than $b+c+d+e$, the minimum share of the market gained by a firm at A is 50 per cent (when the other firm is also at A). Thus the minimum share of the market gained by a firm located between A and B is always less than the share gained by a firm at some other location. The same argument applies, of course, to locations between D and E.

Consider, now, location between B and C. If A and B together contain more than half the market, the minimum share of the market obtained at this location is $c+d+e$ per cent, when the other firm is at B; but a firm at B gains a minimum share of 50 per cent or $b+c+d+e$ per cent. On the other hand, if A and B contain less than half the market, a firm sited between B and C can ensure for itself a minimum share of $a+b$ per cent (when the other firm is at C), whereas a firm at C obtains a minimum share of either 50 per cent or $a+b+c$ per cent. Again, location between the two towns yields a lower minimum share to a firm than location at a town site. And a similar argument shows that firms never locate on sites between C and D. Since the matrix is symmetrical, the other firm never prefers a location outside a town either. This completes the proof.

In the more complex market shares model, it is assumed that demand is elastic. Sales at any point in the market are given by

$$(6A-1) \qquad D = \frac{n-d}{n} \cdot m,$$

where n is a positive constant, d is distance from the seller, and m is the size of the market at a point. The distance between each town and its nearest neighbours is unity. The market in each of towns C, D, and E equals c. Assume that firms can sell to all the towns in the market from any point.

Consider first the case of a firm which locates $(1-w)$ from A and w from B $(1 > w > 0)$. Suppose that

$$n \geqslant 3+w,$$

i.e. that firms can sell to all the towns in the market from any point. If player I locates between A and B and player II locates at A, II can sell to A only. His sales are

(6A–2) $\quad \dfrac{n-0}{n}a = a.$

On the other hand, player I sells to B—

(6A–3) $\quad \dfrac{n-w}{n}b;$

to C—

(6A–4) $\quad \dfrac{n-1-w}{n}c;$

to D—

(6A–5) $\quad \dfrac{n-2-w}{n}c;$

and to E—

(6A–6) $\quad \dfrac{n-3-w}{n}c.$

Thus, player I's share of the market is

(6A–7) $\quad \dfrac{(n-w)b + (3n-6-3w)c}{na+(n-w)b + (3n-6-3w)c}.$

If both players locate at the same site between A and B, they receive half the market each. And if player I locates between A and B while player II locates at B, player I's share of the market is

(6A–8) $\quad \dfrac{(n-1+w)a}{(n-1+w)a + nb + (3n-6)c}.$

Now, it has already been shown that, if a strategy is an equilibrium strategy, then its value must be one-half of the market; that is, the minimum share which a player can receive by locating between A and B must be one-half if this location is an equilibrium strategy. Therefore, both inequations (6A–9) and (6A–10) must be satisfied before a player locates between A and B rather than at A or B:

(6A–9) $\quad \tfrac{1}{2} < \dfrac{(n-w)b + (3n-6-3w)c}{na+(n-w)b + (3n-6-3w)c}$

(6A–10) $\quad \tfrac{1}{2} < \dfrac{(n-1+w)a}{(n-1+w)a + nb + (3n-6)c}.$

Inequation (6A–9) implies

(6A–11) $\quad a < \dfrac{(n-w)b + (3n-6-3w)c}{n},$

and inequation (6A–10) implies

(6A–12) $\quad a > \dfrac{nb+(3n-6)c}{n-1+w}.$

139

It is readily shown that, if

$$n \geqslant 3+w,$$

then inequations (6A–11) and (6A–12) are incompatible. Since these inequations cannot both be satisfied at the same time, it is impossible for the minimum share which a player can gain by locating between A and B to be one-half of the market. This cannot therefore be an equilibrium strategy. This result, that players do not choose to locate between A and B, can be duplicated for larger values of n.

Consider now location at a site between B and C, $(1-w)$ from B and w from C. Suppose that

$$(6A–13) \quad n \geqslant 2+w.$$

Inequation (6A–13) implies that if player II is at towns A or B or C while player I is located between B and C, the players between them sell to the entire market. Player I's share of the market if II locates at A is

$$(6A–14) \quad \frac{3(n-1-w)c + (n-1+w)b}{na+3(n-1-w)c + (n-1+w)b},$$

if II locates at B is

$$(6A–15) \quad \frac{3(n-1-w)c}{(n-1)a + nb + 3(n-1-w)c},$$

and if II locates at C is

$$(6A–16) \quad \frac{(n-2+w)a + (n-1+w)b}{(n-2+w)a + (n-1+w)b + (3n-3)c}.$$

If they both locate at a site between B and C, player I's share of the market is one-half. For location between B and C to be an equilibrium strategy, inequations (6A–17), (6A–18), and (6A–19) must be satisfied:

$$\tfrac{1}{2} < \frac{3(n-1-w)c + (n-1+w)b}{na+3(n-1-w)c + (n-1+w)b}$$

implies

$$(6A–17) \quad a < \frac{3(n-1-w)c + (n-1+w)b}{n};$$

$$\tfrac{1}{2} < \frac{3(n-1-w)c}{(n-1)a + nb + 3(n-1-w)c}$$

implies

$$(6A–18) \quad a < \frac{3(n-1-w)c - nb}{n-1};$$

and

$$\tfrac{1}{2} < \frac{(n-2+w)a + (n-1+w)b}{(n-2+w)a + (n-1+w)b + 3(n-1)c}$$

implies

(6A–19) $\quad a > \dfrac{(3n-3)c - (n-1+w)b}{n-2+w}.$

The inequations (6A–17) and (6A–19) are compatible if

(6A–20) $\quad b < \dfrac{(6n-6-3w+3w^2)c}{2n^2-4n+3nw+2-3w+w^2};$

and the inequations (6A–18) and (6A–19) are compatible if

(6A–21) $\quad b < \dfrac{3(n-1-w+w^2)c}{1-w}.$

But the substitution of (6A–20) and (6A–21) in the inequations (6A–17) and (6A–18) respectively imply negative values for a. Since a town cannot have a negative population, the inequations (6A–17), (6A–18), and (6A–19) form an incompatible set. Therefore location at a site between B and C is never an equilibrium strategy. The result that players never locate at a site between B and C can be duplicated for larger values of n.

The third case is location between the towns C and D, at a distance $(1-w)$ from C. Assume that if player I is located between C and D while player II locates at either A or B or C or D, they sell to the entire market—

$$n > 3-w.$$

If player II locates at C, player I's share of the market is

(6A–22) $\quad \dfrac{(2n-1-2w)c}{(n-2)a + (n-1)b + (3n-1-2w)c}$

while if II locates at D, player I's share is

(6A–23) $\quad \dfrac{(n-3+w)a + (n-2+w)b + (n-1+w)c}{(n-3+w)a + (n-2+w)b + (3n-2+w)c}.$

For location between C and D to be an equilibrium strategy, the share gained when both locate at the site between C and D (one-half) must be less than the share gained when II is at C or D. This implies inequations (6A–24) and (6A–25):

(6A–24) $\quad a < \dfrac{(n-1-2w)c - (n-1)b}{n-1}$

(6A–25) $\quad a > \dfrac{(n-w)c - (n-2+w)b}{n-3+w}.$

These inequations are compatible when

(6A–26) $\quad b > \dfrac{c(2n-3w - 3+2w^2)}{1-w}.$

But the substitution of the minimum value of b permitted by (6A–26) in inequation (6A–24) reveals that (6A–26) is only true when a takes negative values. Thus for permitted values of a, (6A–24) and (6A–25) are incompatible; firms prefer location at C or D to location at a site between C and D. Location at any site beyond D, the quartile, is dominated.

7   A Least Risk Model of Town Formation

In this chapter is developed a least risk model of the formation of towns. In the previous chapter some exploratory models of location under uncertainty were examined, but now a more formal location model which purports to explain some aspects of the formation and growth of point agglomerations is constructed. Like the previous models, the games analyse the location choices of firms which sell the same good. This model is similar in many respects to that of Neutze (1960); although the manner of analysis is different (e.g. the decision variable is profit here, whereas Neutze's is essentially a market shares model), the initial idea of examining interdependence in a bounded market as the basis for a formal location model was provided by Neutze's work.

Assumptions

It is assumed that the firms know the conditions of the game. Strict assumptions are made at first; the effect of relaxing them is noted later. There are ten conditions.

    1. The market is linear and bounded. A bounded market area may approximate reality more closely than an unbounded market area, except possibly for firms which sell over the whole world. The effect of varying degrees of bounding is analysed later. The calculation of sales and profits is easier in a linear than in a circular market, and the analysis is more definite.

    While the assumption of a linear market allows relatively simple calculation, it poses the problem that three sellers never locate together because the middle one could make no sales. This is one of Chamberlin's (1950) objections to the Hotelling model. To overcome this difficulty it is assumed that, if several firms locate at the same point, they are equidistant from all consumers. Thus, if n firms locate at the same point and sell identical goods at the same price, they each sell to one nth of the market in each direction. This condition is more realistic than the assumption that consumers react to infinitely small differences in sellers' locations, and it permits a more useful analysis of location patterns in the relatively simple straight line market.

2. Purchasing power is evenly spread over the market. If purchasing power is unevenly distributed, a concentration of activity would already exist, and the model would be assuming the presence of the feature it is trying to explain. An even distribution of purchasing power implies that consumers do not engage in multi-purpose trips and that sellers do not buy from one another.

3. Demand curves are negatively sloping, the standard assumption of economic theory.

4. Production costs are identical at all points along the market. This condition facilitates comprehension of the argument by excluding the effects of the distribution of resources on town formation; it does not imply that resource distributions have no effect on town formation.

5. All firms have identical cost curves when normal profits are included in costs. This simplifying assumption is adopted purely for ease of exposition. In the discussion of the firms' decision whether or not to locate in a particular market, it is assumed that average cost curves are 'U' shaped; but when analysing the decision where to locate, it is supposed that marginal costs are zero. (This assumption is adopted because of its simplicity.)

6. The goods sold by firms are indistinguishable except by their location. Firms are competing directly for sales: this is one extreme of the range of conditions in reality between absolute competition and absolute complementarity. Later discussion relaxes the assumption.

7. Firms cannot change locations. Some firms may be able to change locations at virtually no cost to themselves (for example, ice-cream vendors on a beach), but most firms find relocation costly, because buildings and plant are both long lived and imperfectly mobile. This condition may therefore be more realistic than the assumption of perfect mobility and is later made more general.

8. There is only one transport medium on the line; it serves all points equally well. Firms cannot gain transport economies by locating together. Transport rates are the same for all firms and are directly proportional to distance. The effect of agglomeration economies which accrue from the use of the transport medium is analysed later.

9. Sellers attempt to maximise profits safely. Similarly, consumers minimise costs by patronising the nearest seller. These conditions entail the assumptions that consumers and sellers obey the axioms of Savage's personalistic theory of probability and that utility is measured by profits (for sellers) or by income (for consumers). We shall briefly examine the impact of non-linear utility functions on location decisions.

10. Sellers locate in ignorance of each other and without communicating. This condition introduces into the static model the readjustments which a firm makes if it expects other firms to establish later. It therefore injects an element of competitive interdependence.

It is difficult to examine the effects upon firms' decisions created by their not knowing how later firms are going to behave. A complete analysis of sequential location policies by firms requires that a firm review all possible future contingencies and their impact on its location choice. This extended review is avoided here by assuming that, although firms normally do locate in sequence, their location decisions take account of the fact that other firms may be locating at the same time. Thus many games assume that firms imagine that other firms are locating at the same time. This assumption is not meant to imply that a large proportion of location choices is in fact made simultaneously, but rather that decisions made in such circumstances simulate the adjustments which firms make to their decisions if they expect other firms to locate in the market at a later period.

These conditions are obviously not general and do not reflect reality. As a consequence the analysis can be simple and the deductions clear. Furthermore, by excluding external economies and resource variations, the model can investigate more readily the behaviour of competitively interdependent firms. Later discussion examines the effects of competitive interdependence, external economies and resource variations on town formation under more realistic conditions.

The Decision to Locate

The first question which a firm must answer is whether or not location within the bounded market can be profitable. Only if the firm can make profits somewhere does it proceed to analyse alternative locations in order to find the one at which profits are highest. Since the plain is homogeneous, the entrepreneurs who are deciding whether or not to locate are not uncertain about demand curves and cost curves, for knowledge of the demand schedule of one person and the cost schedule at one location suffices for all consumers and locations. The decision whether or not to establish a plant in the market is made on the basis of certain knowledge about cost and demand schedules.

Assume that the demand curve at any point for the products of a firm is

$$(7\text{-}1) \qquad q = A - B(p + rd),$$

where q is quantity sold, p is mill price, d is the distance of that point from the mill, r is the transport rate, and A and B are positive constants. Individual demand curves are linear and negatively sloping; but, if consumers pay transport costs, total sales over the firm's market area as a function of price are

$$(7\text{-}2) \qquad Q = 2 \int_0^s q \, dd,$$

that is,

$$(7\text{-}3) \qquad Q = 2(As - Bps - \tfrac{1}{2}Brs^2),$$

where s is the distance from the firm to the point at which sales fall to zero. From equation (7–1),

$$(7\text{-}4) \qquad s = \frac{A - Bp}{Br}.$$

144

Figure 7–1: **The decision whether to locate by comparison of marginal costs and marginal revenue**

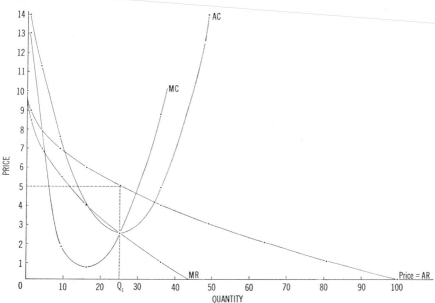

Substitution of (7–4) in (7–3) provides the market demand schedule facing the firm:

$$(7\text{–}5) \qquad Q = \frac{A^2}{Br} - \frac{2Ap}{r} + \frac{Bp^2}{r},$$

a demand function which is not linear with respect to price. Multiplying (7–5) by p yields the total revenue curve, from which changes in revenue due to changes in output are given by

$$(7\text{–}6) \qquad MR = \frac{dR}{dQ} = \frac{A^2/B - 4Ap + 3Bp^2}{2(Bp - A)}.$$

By assumption the average cost curve is 'U' shaped:

$$(7\text{–}7) \qquad AC = X - YQ + ZQ^2,$$

where X, Y, and Z are constants. Equation (7–7) yields the marginal cost curve

$$(7\text{–}8) \qquad MC = \frac{dC}{dQ} = X - 2YQ + 3ZQ^2.$$

The firm produces most profitably at that output for which marginal cost equals marginal revenue, when equation (7–8) has the same value as equation (7–6). If, at this output level, average cost is less than average revenue (price), the firm can make profits and may establish a plant in the market. Figure 7–1

145

Figure 7–2: **Comparison of costs and revenue, using sales radius rather than output as abscissa**

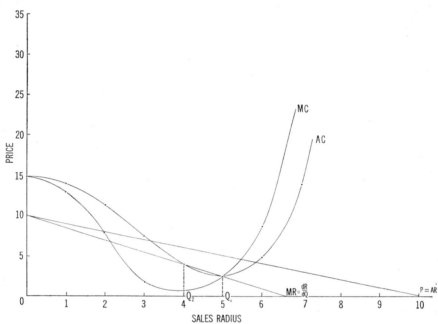

illustrates such a situation: *MC* equals *MR* at output Q_1, when *AC* is less than price.

For location analysis, though, Fig. 7–2 is more useful than Fig. 7–1. In the second diagram, the quantity axis has been replaced by an axis which represents the size of the firm's market area. From equation (7–4)

(7–9) $$p = \frac{A - Brs}{B},$$

which when substituted in (7–3) yields

(7–10) $Q = Brs^2.$

The relationship (7–10) permits a sales radius axis to be substituted for a quantity axis. In Fig. 7–2, some changes are noticeable: both the demand curve and the marginal revenue curve are straight lines, while the 'U' shaped cost curves have become more complex. The graph again yields a profit maximising sales area, marked Q_1—this is the size of market necessary for the most profitable operation of the firm. The graph also illustrates that a market area larger than Q_2 is required before average costs fall below price: the market area must be of size Q_2 before any firm is profitable. Thus, in making the decision

Figure 7–3: **Comparison of cost and demand curves for one firm with those which arise when two firms locate at the centre of the market**

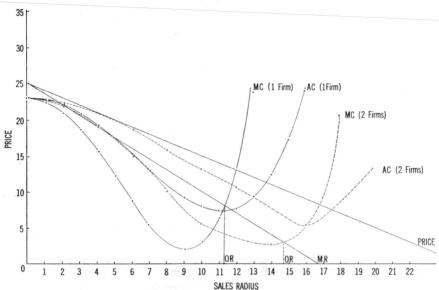

whether or not to locate in the market, a firm has only to consider whether the market is larger than Q_2 or not; if it is, the firm may produce profitably in that market.

It is therefore a simple process to decide whether or not a firm can make profits in a given market area. The analysis can also be extended to determine the forces affecting which industries may be profitably located in a given market. The greater the demand per unit area for the goods of an industry, the higher is the intercept of the demand curve with the price axis, and the smaller is the minimum profitable size of market area. The lower the costs of transporting a product, the less steep is the demand curve and the smaller is the minimum profitable sales radius. Industries in which economies of scale do not cause very large firms (in which cost curves are 'U' shaped rather than relatively flat) are also the industries most able to exist in relatively small market areas. Thus, industries in which demand per unit area is high, transport costs are low, and scale economies are limited can exist profitably in market areas smaller than those required by industries characterised by low demand per unit area, high transport costs, and extensive economies of scale.

But while this analysis indicates whether a firm can make profits in a market, it does not reveal whether or not firms actually will locate in that market. The problem from the firm's point of view is that if it can make profits in the market, so can other firms; the firm does not know whether other firms will be locating

Table 7–1: **Game matrix for decision to locate**

Firm A's decision	Firm B's decision	
	Locate	Do not locate
Locate	−10, −10	25, 0
Do not locate	0, 25	0, 0

Note: Figures are notional levels of return to each firm under each outcome; *A*'s return is listed first in each pair.

in the market at the same time. Thus, if two firms analyse a market and find that Fig. 7–2 holds, they might both locate in the market, because they are ignorant of each other's decision. But then, of course, the situation is represented not by Fig. 7–2 but by Fig. 7–3 if they both locate at the same point. One of the firms is consequently forced out of business.

Several possible strategies are available to a firm thus placed, strategies which depend in part on the nature of the firm. The firm may analyse the situation from a game-like viewpoint or from a probabilistic stand, or may attempt to reduce the risks (i.e. the possible losses) associated with the establishment of a plant. Each possibility yields conclusions of locational significance.

The firms are faced with game matrices of the type shown in Table 7–1. If both locate in the market, losses are made; if only one establishes, that firm makes a profit; if neither locates, both gain zero. Two main forms of behaviour commend themselves. First, it is in the interest of both players to find each other and to agree on a common location policy. The obvious elements of this policy are a random choice to determine who locates in the market and a division of the profits among the two firms, so that each takes half the profits. Such a policy has the advantages of being rational, fair to both players, and a combined optimum. But it suffers from two problems: communication costs must be incurred in order that firms find each other, while the fact that two players communicate and agree does not preclude the possibility that a third firm is locating in the market. This action is therefore risky and may consequently be replaced by the 'fanfare' strategy. The firm, *A*, wishes to locate in the market and to deter others from acting similarly. One solution is for *A* to publicly commit itself to the policy of establishing a plant in the market. If the firm announces its intention to locate and publicly commits itself—say, by buying land—then the matrix of choices and payoffs for a second firm is no longer represented by Table 7–1. Once firm *A* is committed, *B*'s decision to locate in the market has a payoff of −10, while its decision not to locate in the market has a payoff of 0. The second firm, *B*, thus finds that its best policy is never to locate in the market. Once a firm has publicly committed itself to locating in the market, no other firm can contemplate locating profitably in the market while that market remains small. Such a policy can clearly be successful, but its usefulness depends on several factors, the most important of which is the ability of the firm to publicly commit itself. The commitment has to be made public through the mass communication

148

media, since the firm has no idea who its rivals might be. Where communication is poor, the commitment must therefore be ineffective; if mass media are efficacious, they are concerned with large events rather than small ones, and so permit large firms to publicise their commitment more readily than small firms. The value of fanfaring to a firm depends, then, on the effectiveness of communication media and on the size of the firm.

Alternatively, a firm may attempt to calculate the probabilities that two, three, four, or more firms may locate in the market, to determine its profit under each circumstance, and thus to estimate its expected profitability. The firm has several guides to help it estimate these probabilities: the greater the population in the market the more likely it is that some other firm will have perceived the possibility of making a profit; the more rapid the rate of growth of an industry, the greater the probability that other firms will be locating too; the greater the amount of patented innovation in the firm's methods and product, the less likely are competitors. The higher the probability that other firms are establishing, the lower is the expected profitability of the location, and so the greater is the delay before firms locate in the market. This delay is therefore greater the larger the population of the market, the higher the rate of growth of an industry, and the less the amount of innovation in a product. But despite these aids in estimating probabilities, firms can make large errors and therefore are likely to be conservative in deciding to locate.

The extreme conservativeness predicted by the probabilistic approach suggests that a third method of analysing the market may be useful. Firms may attempt to reduce the losses which would occur if other firms were locating at the same time. The most obvious method of accomplishing this is to make a gradual commitment to the industry: a firm may gradually develop the function, perhaps initially on a part-time basis and with the minimum of specialised equipment. Then, should another firm be locating at the same time, the loss incurred is small. This gradual commitment to a line of action is similar to that advocated by Hart (1941: ch. 4) as a method of planning output levels. Hart suggests that firms make provisional output decisions and adjust these decisions according to events. This policy is most successful when the average cost curve is relatively flat—that is, when little specialised equipment is used.

These various modes of analysis lead to different predictions about behaviour. The game mode indicates that large firms may make public commitments to locate if mass communication is possible; but since most firms begin small this solution is not available to many firms. The probability mode, though subject to error, reveals the conservativeness associated with an uncertain market; if adopted, it is likely to be supplemented by the third mode, that of minimising possible losses by making a gradual commitment to the industry. This combined approach is the one most likely to be used by small firms (that is, the majority of firms). It indicates that firms locate later in a market under uncertainty than in certainty, that these firms are smaller, and that they are relatively unspecialised, at least when they commence operations.

Figure 7–4: **Relationship between profit and location for single firm, depending on firm size**

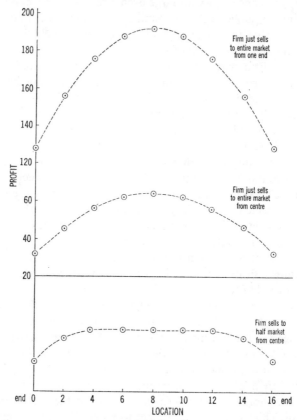

The Location Decision of the First Firm
Having decided to establish a plant in the market, the firm must then decide where to locate this plant. Some elements of the location decisions of small firms have already been deduced. They are made by firms which are small relative to firms operating under certainty, and the decisions are conservative, in that there is some delay between the time when plants first become profitable and the time when plants are located in the market. These firms are afraid that other firms may be establishing at the same time: if one firm sees a profitable opportunity, so may other firms. Therefore a firm must regard it as likely that other firms are locating at the same time, and must try to choose a location which is optimal under this uncertainty. The firm is uncertain about the number of firms which locate in the market and about the location policies of these other firms. Consider now the thought experiments which the firm makes before it locates.

150

Table 7–2: **Profits in two-seller game**
(Maximum sales area equals one-half of the market area)

Firm A locates at	2/8 (Quartile 1)	3/8	Firm B locates at 4/8 (Median)	5/8	6/8 (Quartile 2)
2/8	8·0, 8·0	11·5, 11·5	14·0, 14·0	15·5, 15·5	16·0, 16·0
3/8	11·5, 11·5	8·0, 8·0	11·5, 11·5	14·0, 14·0	15·5, 15·5
4/8	14·0, 14·0	11·5, 11·5	8·0, 8·0	11·5, 11·5	14·0, 14·0
5/8	15·5, 15·5	14·0, 14·0	11·5, 11·5	8·0, 8·0	11·5, 11·5
6/8	16·0, 16·0	15·5, 15·5	14·0, 14·0	11·5, 11·5	8·0, 8·0

Note: A's profit is listed first in each pair.

When only one firm locates in the market, policy is relatively simple. If the firm's optimum sales area is larger than the market, that firm has to locate at the centre in order to maximise profits. The two upper curves of Fig. 7–4 illustrate this case by showing the relationship between profits and location. Thus, large firms which can commit themselves locate at the centre of the market because they expect to be monopolists. If, on the other hand, a firm maximises profits by selling to a sales area smaller than the actual market area, that firm has a greater latitude in its choice of a location, as the lowest curve of Fig. 7–4 demonstrates. In such circumstances, there exists a range of equally good locations, but the centre is never worse than any other location.

The decision of a firm which expects another firm to locate at the same time is more complex. Three main types of situation may be identified. They are analysed by means of two-person games matrices, which show profits to the firms for location at the quartiles, the median, and the points midway between the quartiles and the median (it is never profitable to locate nearer the ends than the quartiles).

The first case is represented by the matrix, Table 7–2, in which the maximum sales area of a firm is small in relation to the market. The best combined policy occurs with one firm at each quartile, when both firms receive a profit of 16 units. But if firm A chooses quartile 1, there is a 0·50 chance that B, locating in ignorance of A, also chooses the same site. There is a 0·50 chance that both firms locate at the same quartile, and so earn a profit of only 8 units. The choice of a quartile location thus yields an expected profit of

$$(0.50 \times 8) + (0.50 \times 16) = 12.00.$$

This expectation is greater than the certain gain derived from locating at the centre (8), and even if the worst comes to the worst (location choices coincide), the quartile is as profitable as the centre. A firm in this state acts rationally by choosing a quartile location.

Table 7–3 represents a second case: when the maximum sales area for a firm is the same size as the market area. The best combined policy is, as in the previous

Table 7–3: **Profits in two-seller game**

(Maximum sales area equals the market area)

Firm A locates at	2/8 (Quartile 1)	3/8	Firm B locates at 4/8 (Median)	5/8	6/8 (Quartile 2)
2/8	28·0, 28·0	31·5, 39·5	38·0, 46·0	43·5, 49·5	48·0, 48·0
3/8	39·5, 31·5	31·0, 31·0	37·5, 39·5	44·0, 44·0	49·5, 43·5
4/8	46·0, 38·0	39·5, 37·5	32·0, 32·0	39·5, 37·5	46·0, 38·0
5/8	49·5, 43·5	44·0, 44·0	37·5, 39·5	31·0, 31·0	39·5, 31·5
6/8	48·0, 48·0	43·5, 49·5	38·0, 46·0	31·5, 39·5	28·0, 28·0

Note: A's profit is listed first in each pair.

case, location of one firm at quartile 1 and the other at quartile 2, which yields both a profit of 48 units. However, such a pattern is unstable, for, if one locates at position 2 and the other at position 6, both firms have an incentive to move nearer the centre. If A is located at $Q1$ and B at $Q2$, A increases its profit from 48·0 to 49·5 by shifting to position 3, whereupon B gains by shifting to position 5. Firms uncertain about rivals' policies do not choose the quartiles, but rather tend to positions intermediate between the quartiles and the median. Again, though, there is an 0·50 probability that two firms, deciding independently and in ignorance of each other's choice, choose the same location. Therefore the expectation of profit to each firm from choosing a location at position 3 or position 5 is

$$(0·50 \times 31·0) + (0·50 \times 44·0) = 37·5.$$

This expectation is greater than the profit of 32 units which can with certainty be made at the centre. In this state, then, most firms opt for location midway between the quartiles and the median, though some conservative firms may choose the centre because its certain profit of 32 is greater than the minimum (31) which can certainly be obtained between the quartiles and the median.

The third case is illustrated by Table 7–4. In this table profits have been calculated on the assumption that the maximum sales area of the firm is twice as great as the market area: the firm can sell to the entire market from any point on the line. Optimum combined location policies for the pair are again represented by location at the quartiles; but when firm B is at location 6, the best location for A is not quartile 2 but the median, to which strategy B's best reply is also the median. (Note that these 'movements' are not actual movements, but represent conceptual moves of a firm engaged in a thought experiment: once located, a firm is immobile.) For both firms, location at the median is the best response to any location decision of the other firm. The two firms therefore locate at the centre of the line, and each makes a profit of 96 units, 16 less than the profit which they could obtain by agreeing on a common location policy.

Table 7–4: **Profits in two-seller game**
(Maximum sales area equals twice the market area)

Firm A locates at	2/8 (Quartile 1)	3/8	Firm B locates at 4/8 (Median)	5/8	6/8 (Quartile 2)
2/8	88·0, 88·0	71·5, 125·5	86·0, 126·0	99·5, 121·5	112·0, 112·0
3/8	125·5, 71·5	94·0, 94·0	93·5, 111·5	108·0, 108·0	121·5, 99·5
4/8	126·0, 86·0	111·5, 93·5	96·0, 96·0	111·5, 93·5	126·0, 86·0
5/8	121·5, 99·5	108·0, 108·0	93·5, 111·5	94·0, 94·0	125·5, 71·5
6/8	112·0, 112·0	99·5, 121·5	86·0, 126·0	71·5, 125·5	88·0, 88·0

Note: A's profit is listed first in each pair.

If a firm has a convex-up rather than linear utility function, behaviour becomes more conservative. Assume that

(7–11) $u(x) = \sqrt{x}$.

To illustrate this point we may simplify the structure of the matrices, Tables 7–2, 7–3, and 7–4: they contain an optimum (when the two firms separate) of a^2, a minimum (the two firms locate at the same off-centre site) of value b^2, and the median, of value c^2 (when both firms locate there). The values of the locations can be ordered:

$$a^2 \geqslant c^2 \geqslant b^2.$$

Suppose now that the expected profit at the centre is less than the expected profit at the non-central point (i.e. that $\frac{1}{2}(a^2+b^2) > c^2$). The difference in expected profits between the two locations is

(7–12) $\frac{1}{2}(a^2+b^2-2c^2)$.

If the firm maximises expected utility rather than expected profits, the value of the three sites is a, b, and c, and the difference in expected utility between the two locations is

(7–13) $\frac{1}{2}(a+b-2c)$.

The difference in expected utility (7–13) is always less than the difference in expected profits (7–12). That is, if the utility function is convex-up, a firm which maximises utility is more likely to locate at the centre of the market than is a firm which maximises profits.

The decision-making criterion which we have used (and shall continue to use) to solve the two person game matrices is a rational one, given some assumptions about individuals' preferences and expectations. But it is a complicated criterion to use; it does not yield intuitively obvious results. Therefore some high school students have played similar games in order to determine whether, faced with such matrices, people actually do make the choices predicted by the

153

Figure 7–5: **Spatial relationships: two firms in a linear market**

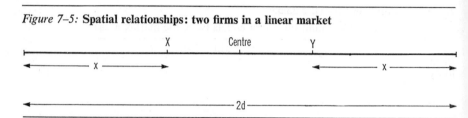

decision-making criterion. The experimental methods and results are fully described in the Appendix to this chapter.

The students were presented with four matrices, one of which was zero sum while the other three were non-zero sum matrices (one of the form of Table 7–2, one like Table 7–3, and one like Table 7–4). The games were impersonal, that is the students were told that they were playing against me and that I had already made my choices. In the zero sum game, 85 per cent of students made the minimax choice; in the non-zero sum games, the predicted choices were made by 85 per cent of players in the matrix which required quartile location, by 70 per cent of students in the matrix requiring location midway between quartile and median, and by 55 per cent of students in the matrix which required location at the median. The choices were different from those which would have been made had the students chosen at random. Although the decision-making criterion is not used by everyone, a majority of students did make their choices in accordance with that criterion.

These specific cases may be readily generalised to include a wider range of circumstances. Assume a linear market of length $2d$, on which are located two firms at points X and Y. X is sited a distance x ($x \leqslant d$) from the left hand end of the market, and Y is sited x from the right hand end of the market. Figure 7–5 illustrates spatial relationships. These firms relocate if a move by either one is profitable, assuming that the other remains put: as in Prisoner's Dilemma, the firms advance to short-run optima in an attempt to gain an advantage over their competitors. The logical and experimental evidence about games of Prisoner's Dilemma played only a few times (Rapoport and Chammah, 1965) indicates clearly that short-run optima readily attract firms from long-run stable solutions. (When one firm decides first and a second later, that first firm has to expect the later one to take full advantage of the first firm's immobility; the first firm has therefore to locate at the point which is the optimal to the rival's location. This policy is in fact identical with the search for short-run optima in games with simultaneous choice.)

The mathematics of the analysis are contained in the Appendix to this chapter. For two firms, the analysis indicates that, as the sales radius of the firms increases, so the optimum location approaches the centre, until, when the sales radius equals the length of the market, the firm locates at the centre of that market (this is the case represented by Table 7–4). If the locating firm expects two competitors, its policy is more complex: if the firms can sell over

Table 7–5: **Location policies of firms in linear market**

s	1 Firm	2 Firms	3 Firms	4 Firms
½d	0·5 −1·5	0·5 : 1·5	0·4 : 1·0 : 1·6	1·0 : 1·0 : 1·0 : 1·0
¾d	0·75 − 1·25	0·58 : 1·42	1·0 : 1·0 : 1·0	1·0 : 1·0 : 1·0 : 1·0
d	1·0	0·67 : 1·33	1·0 : 1·0 : 1·0	1·0 : 1·0 : 1·0 : 1·0
2d	1·0	1·0 : 1·0	1·0 : 1·0 : 1·0	1·0 : 1·0 : 1·0 : 1·0

Note: The market is of length $2d$; s = the maximum sales radius of the firms. The table identifies the locations of firms, and expresses these in units of d from the right-hand end of the line. For one firm, if $s<d$, that firm has a range of equally profitable locations from which to choose.

more than three-quarters of the market area from the centre, the firms can never find an equilibrium pattern but rather continue jostling indefinitely for locations (because the middle firm's market area is too small when the two outer firms are at their optimum locations, and so that middle firm then relocates outside one of the outer firms). As in the case of three sellers, four firms are unable to find a stable optimum location pattern for themselves. But whereas for three firms instability occurs if the firms' maximum sales area is greater than three-quarters the length of the market, four firms are unstable if the maximum sales areas are longer than half the market. Similarly, as five or more firms locate on the market, instability occurs at even smaller firm sizes. A firm which uses these results when thinking out its location decision is unable to decide that any one location is best, from the point of view of maximising sales. There is no optimum location policy in such cases. (This conclusion applies *a fortiori* to a firm which is expecting its competitors to locate later rather than at the same time.)

A relatively large firm which expects two or more competitors must therefore replace the criterion of maximum sales with some other criterion for location. One obvious replacement is maximum share of the market. If firms attempt to maximise their share of the market, the game is subject to a definite conclusion —firms locate at the centre of the market. Similarly, if firms look to other facts, they expect that firms in other industries locate at the centre; hence the centre offers economies of urbanisation to the firm. Thus, when patterns are unstable when judged by the criterion of maximum profits, firms must look to decision criteria outside the formal game; these criteria, of maximum shares and urbanisation economies, indicate location at the centre of the market.

Table 7–5 summarises the results of these location experiments. The location decisions of uncertain firms are more conservative than those made by certain firms. The decision to locate is made later and is normally more oriented towards the relatively safe central location under uncertainty than in certainty. The actual location depends on the size of the optimal sales area in relation to the size of the market and on the number of competitors which the firm expects to enter the market at the same time. If firms expect no competitors, they usually locate at the centre of the market, irrespective of size. Firms whose optimal

155

sales area is small in relation to the market locate at or near to the quartiles, unless they expect three or more competitors to be locating at the same time, when they are more attracted to the centre. Large firms whose optimal sales area is twice the size of the market always locate at the centre. The location policy of firms whose optimal sales area is about the same size as the market depends on the number of competitors expected: if one competitor is expected, a position between the quartile and the median is chosen; if two or more competitors are expected, the firm locates at the centre.

The larger the firm, the more likely it is to locate at the centre. The greater the probability which a firm attaches to the events of zero or more than two competitors, the more likely is that firm to choose a central location. But, partly because of their size and partly because of their methods of committing themselves to locations, large firms are less likely to expect other competitors than small firms. Small firms, unable to deter other firms, must expect several competitors to be locating at a similar time. Thus, large firms locate at the centre because they expect to become monopolists; small firms locate at the centre of the market because they expect several other competitors. (A small firm which locates at the centre of the market is in the wrong location only if no more than one competitor locates in that market.)

A seller trying to optimise his location decision in a linear bounded homogeneous market, on which he cannot change sites, locates at the centre of that market. Firms are uncertain about both the number of competitors locating at the same time and the location policies of those sellers. The centre is the least risk location: it is chosen because firms are uncertain about rivals' policies. The even spacing of firms which occurs under certainty is replaced under uncertainty by the more conservative policy of centralisation.

Two conditions define the uncertainty facing sellers and the effects of that uncertainty on their decisions. The firms decide on a location without knowing the others' choices and without even knowing how many firms are locating at the same time or are going to locate in the future, because they cannot communicate. This uncertainty is given positive content by the assumption that firms cannot change locations (or, in reality, that plants are long lived). If a poor choice is made, the firm cannot avoid the consequences, but must suffer reduced profits. Location at the centre is less likely as these conditions are relaxed.

If firms can communicate with each other, they may agree on common location policies. Profits are higher if the firms agree to locate symmetrically; for two firms, this implies that one is near each quartile. Smithies (1941) has shown that two sellers locate near the quartiles if demand curves are negatively sloping and sellers are certain and mobile. Similarly, if three or more firms are locating in the market, they position themselves evenly over the market, at the social optima. Similarly, Isard (1969: 454-61) has shown that 'split-the-difference' or 'incremax' bargaining procedures (see Isard, 1969: 308-28, for details of the procedures) may be applied to Hotelling location games; sellers can then bargain to find more profitable locations away from the centre. The fact that firms are not in communication ensures that such bargaining procedures cannot be used by firms to find and agree on higher profit, socially optimum sites.

The second element in the model which causes conservative behaviour is the fact that it is impossible to relocate plants: fixed investments are long lived. If firms cannot revise their choices, they must decide on a location that is best over the entire range of possible alternatives chosen by other firms. The progressive relaxation of this assumption, by supposing that relocation is costly and then that mobility is perfect, reduces the risk of a location at the social optima. Even if the firm's anticipations about the number and behaviour of rivals are wrong, the firm is able to adjust its own behaviour at little expense. As mobility becomes more perfect, the risk of a location near the certainty optimum falls.

Therefore the tendency for sellers to locate at the centre of the market and to form an embryo town rises as does uncertainty. When uncertainty is at a maximum (the firms cannot relocate and cannot communicate) they locate at the centre. When uncertainty parallels reality—when relocation is costly and when firms cannot communicate (because they do not know each other)—a central location is still very likely. But when uncertainty is low (mobility and communication are perfect) the firms are more attracted to the higher profit, less conservative locations.

More Realistic Conditions

Some of the more restrictive assumptions must now be relaxed. Replacing the assumptions of a linear bounded market, of indistinguishable goods and of a homogeneous plain, does not diminish the tendency for firms to locate in central towns.

Few markets are linear. In a circular market, there is an infinite number of maximum profit locations (all the points at the optimum distance from the centre) but the choice of a maximum profit location off centre still entails the risks that other firms locate nearby and reduce sales, and that the expected number of firms does not materialise. The uncertainty incentive to locate at the centre remains. Similarly, in irregularly shaped market areas, there are some risky locations which yield maximum profits under certainty (the exact number depends on the shape of the market area and on the expected number of competitors) and one relatively safe central location. The firms in an areal market are unlikely to choose a certainty maximum profit location because it is optimal only for a limited range of conditions. In a long-run bet, such as the choice of a location, firms must play safe.

Absolute bounding occurs infrequently; in its extreme form the assumption is indefensible in terms of reality. However, most regions have some type of boundary. Political and physical boundaries (the sea, rivers, mountain ranges, and deserts) hamper the movement of goods and services. The difference between absolute bounding and bounding caused by such variations in purchasing power over the plain is one of degree, not of kind. Differences in resources also cause bounding. The realism of this degree of bounding can be established empirically: single towns which dominate a fairly clearly bounded market area are common. In New Zealand, with the exceptions of the twin centres of Napier and Hastings on the one hand and of Palmerston North and Wanganui on the other, every centre with a population of 20,000 or more serves a market region which is fairly clearly bounded by variations in purchasing power (Neutze, 1960: 136). Neutze suggests that this is true of many of the smaller towns too. Every State capital city in Australia serves a region which is bounded for political functions by State boundaries and for other functions by almost continuous zones of low population density. Similarly, the towns in Queensland with a population of more than 20,000 are, with the exception of Toowoomba, all serving clearly defined agricultural and dairying regions which are surrounded by grazing areas of relatively low productivity. For some purposes at least, the assumption of a bounded region is closer to reality than Lösch's assumption of an unbounded plain. (Furthermore, it will be shown after the discussion of innovation diffusion in Chapter 9, how partially bounded markets may arise on an otherwise homogeneous plain.)

The assumption that resources vary over space and that population density is not even permits the analysis to retain the condition that the market is bounded to some extent. It is intuitively evident that the certainty maximum profit sites lie in the area of dense purchasing power or of low costs, and it is proved in Chapter 6 that uncertain firms locate in such areas of dense purchasing power, not between them. Location at the centre of such areas is less risky than location at these certainty optima. So long as the market is bounded by low population density or by high production costs, the firms are likely to choose the safe location.

Once it has been assumed that resources vary over space, then it must also be assumed that site conditions vary. The availability of water at a point, the possibility of flooding, facilities for defence, and suitable ground for building are all site factors which may influence a firm to locate a small distance from the geometric centre of the market area. Sellers may therefore not locate at the exact centre of a market area, but the availability of good sites close to the centre attracts the expected competitors as well as the seller from that centre. Site variations of this kind ease the location decisions of sellers, freeing them from the need for an absolutely precise mathematical analysis of locations.

Products may not be entirely alike. Most goods in the modern world vary between firms even if nominally alike: no two firms sell the same margarine or shirts. Sellers attempt to differentiate goods qualitatively in order to steepen the demand curve for their products, and thus to obtain greater safety and higher profits (Chamberlin, 1950: chs. 4 and 5). The more different the products of the sellers are, the less the competition between firms, and so the greater the extent to which firms are monopolists and therefore to which their certainty maximum profit location is at the centre. The qualitative differentiation of goods increases the attraction of the centre.

External economies have so far been excluded from the model. Economies in the use of the transport mechanism, multi-purpose trips, and sellers buying from one another all increase the value of the central location as compared with dispersed sites. External economies increase the value of agglomeration to both consumers and sellers, and provide an additional reason for location at the centre.

The model may now be restated more generally. Assume an areal market in which demand is rising. Firms attempt to maximise profits safely. Sellers are locating in this market, but they cannot communicate with other potential sellers who may be locating at the same time. It is costly to change locations. These conditions have been defended as being realistic.

As each firm reviews its decision it finds one or more locations away from the centre which yield maximum profits under certainty. But a firm is unlikely to choose one of these sites; instead it may decide on a central location. The off-centre location is risky, because it is optimal only under limited conditions (the maximum profit site under certainty changes for each combination of number of sellers and firm size, and indeed may not exist at all under some conditions), for a later firm may cut off the market area of a firm in an eccentric location, and because the firm may anticipate qualitative differentiation of the sellers' products. The centre is by far the safest long-run location. In the first firm's thought experiment, sellers therefore tend to locate together at the centre of the market and to form a town. The essential conditions are that firms are uncertain about the number of rivals and about those rivals' policies, and that firms cannot relocate. Central location is less likely as uncertainty falls. The availability of external economies at the centre provides another type of reason for firms to choose the central site.

The Location Decisions of Later Sellers

The analysis thus far indicates that the first seller in a market is likely to locate at the centre of that market. An exactly similar mode of analysis may be applied to the first sellers in every industry, with the exception that, as firms in the centre sell to one another, the centre becomes progressively a higher profit point than the rest of the market as well as a minimum risk location for these sellers. Thus a town is formed at the centre of the market consisting of the first sellers in each industry and of firms whose choices coincide in time with those of the first sellers. The growth of this central town is assured by the location within it of certain sellers of new goods, of sellers of more specialised goods, and eventually (if cost curves are 'U' shaped) of firms which sell to the growing market within the town.

If economic development in the market (a rise in population density and in income per head) proceeds more rapidly than technical change (an increase in the most profitable scale of the firm), then a second seller of the good with the smallest optimum sales area eventually locates in the market. Under the strict assumptions, the location of these later sellers depends on their size and on the expected number of competitors. If a firm expects no competitors to be locating at the same time, it locates at a point

159

M

Figure 7–6: **Spatial relationships: one firm located, one firm deciding and expecting two competitors**

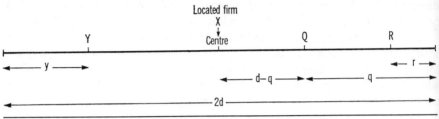

$$(7\text{-}14) \qquad y = \frac{2s+d}{5}.$$

If a firm expects one competitor, it still locates at the point y in equation (7–14), for then one firm locates on either side of the central firm. If a firm expects two competitors, policies are more complex. One firm locates on one side of the centre, the other two locate on the opposite side of the market. Figure 7–6 illustrates the situation. The firm Y locates in the manner defined by equation (7–14). The two firms Q and R have optimum locations:

$$(7\text{-}15) \qquad q = \frac{r+d}{2}$$

(that is, Q locates midway between R and X), and

$$(7\text{-}16) \qquad r = \frac{2s+q}{5}.$$

Equations (7–15) and (7–16) may be solved simultaneously to yield the location choices of the firms:

$$(7\text{-}17) \qquad q = \frac{2s+5d}{9} \text{ and}$$

$$(7\text{-}18) \qquad r = \frac{4s+d}{9}.$$

However, the situation is unstable if $s > 0·6d$. Exactly similar policies apply to four firms.

The firm can readily generalise over these results. Unless its sales area is larger than six-tenths of the market area, the firm's best policy is to locate at the position y, as defined in (7–14), for this is optimal when there are zero or one competitors, and is part of the optimal strategy even when two competitors are expected. Large firms which expect two or more competitors locate at the centre of the market, for they have to replace the maximum sales criterion by that of maximum share of the market. Under the strict assumptions, then, sellers distribute themselves over the market (though not so evenly as if they were certain).

But since a town already exists at the centre before these later sellers locate, the model must include agglomeration economies. The central town is an area of denser demand than the remainder of the market, and so attracts sellers to a greater extent than the strict model implies. If firms wish to tap this large market, they must locate in the centre of the market area: any off-centre location, no matter how close to the centre, yields up the entire dense market to the already existing central firm. Firms may be attracted to the centre, but the attraction is *to* the centre, not merely towards it.

If a firm locates at an off-centre location, y, it makes sales S_y; in comparison, sales at the centre are S_c. Normally, as we have seen, S_y is greater than S_c. Therefore a firm only locates at the centre if the additional sales at that point due to the greater density of demand are at least equal to $S_y - S_c$. But the demand curve at a point is, from equation (7–1):

$$q = A - B(p + rd).$$

Therefore sales at the point $d = 0$ are

(7–19) $q = A - Bp.$

Equation (7–19) would measure sales made within the centre, were there no agglomeration economies; for agglomeration to occur, sales at the centre must be larger than this by the amount $S_y - S_c$. Therefore sales made within the town (assuming that town to be a point) must be, as a ratio of the sales made at any other point:

(7–20) $q_c = 1 + \dfrac{S_y - S_c}{A - Bp}.$

Equation (7–20) measures the income density in the town in relation to the income density at other points such that agglomeration occurs.

Equation (7–20) has been applied to the location policies of these second sellers. If a firm expects no competitors, agglomeration takes place if

(7–21) $q_c = 1 + \dfrac{6ds - d^2 - 4s^2}{10s}$ $(s \leqslant d)$

$q_c = 1 + \dfrac{s^2 - 4ds + 4d^2}{10s}$ $(s \geqslant d).$

Similar equations may be developed for the case of a firm which expects one competitor to be locating at the same time. Figure 7–7 illustrates some results. As the size of the optimal sales area of the firm increases, so a smaller increase in demand at the centre is necessary to attract the firm. A firm which expects a competitor to be locating at the same time is less attracted to the centre at given income densities than a firm which does not expect any competitors; for, if a competitor locates too, the central market has to be shared among three rather than between two sellers. But the diagram indicates that only a relatively small increase in income density at the centre is necessary to attract firms from off-centre locations. Clearly, the early sellers, unless they have very small market

161

Figure 7–7: **Population at centre as a proportion of population at other points which is necessary to attract a firm to the centre, as a function of s, the maximum market area of the firm**

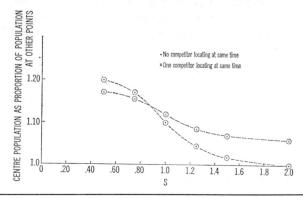

areas, locate at the centre of the market rather than away from the centre. At least the first two sellers in all but the smallest industries locate at the centre; the first because it is uncertain, the second because demand is higher in the town than outside.

But as the number of firms in an industry which locates at the centre increases, so the advantages of a central location relative to non-central locations diminish. Some sellers locate near the edge of the market to sell goods to local consumers. As demand density rises, firms may make profits while selling to spatially smaller market areas; some firms therefore find it profitable to sacrifice the dense, but competitive, central market in order to sell to a compact, more monopolistic, local market.

Formally, the location equations are those of (7–14) to (7–18). But in even a slightly variable environment, these equations are likely to be modified. The first firms to locate away from the centre are those with the smallest optimum market areas—because they are the firms least attracted by the high density of the centre (as Fig. 7–7 illustrates), and because they can most easily establish local monopolistic markets. But in such firms the variation in sales caused by small shifts from the optimal location are very limited. For example, if $s = d/2$, optimal location is $2d/5$; whereas if $s = 3d/4$, the optimum occurs at $d/2$ (the quartile). The loss of sales of the small firm caused by a shift from the optimum location to the quartile is only 15 per cent. Therefore small site advantages in the region of the quartile are likely to attract such small firms. The attractiveness of such sites is enhanced if firms realise that by locating in a position which is quite good for all firms, they can reap future increases in sales as the local demand density rises. Even though there exists no centre to act as a minimum risk location (because it is occupied) and even though these later sellers no longer have a common minimum risk location, the fact that the variation of sales about the optimum is so small implies that sellers are potentially able to agglomerate at one point rather than being forced into a diffuse location pattern. Even if agglomeration economies are very small, and may perhaps be limited to slight variations in the density of demand, secondary towns will develop about the main central town. (This process is later repeated as third order towns are established around the towns at the median and quartiles.)

The settlement history in a single market region follows a simple pattern. The first firms in each industry locate at the centre because of uncertainty. The 2nd, 3rd, . . . , nth firm in each industry locates either near the quartile or the centre, depending on the density of demand and the number of firms at the central market. Eventually, as demand densities over the entire market rise, some firms in each industry locate near the quartiles, forming two new towns, one each side of the median. Agglomeration of these firms is a function of small variations in sales levels around the optimum location and greater demand density in the new town (even if this only arises because of sales to the other firms in the town). The formation of later towns about the first and second order towns depends on similar processes. Uncertainty, in the sense of lack of knowledge about rivals' reactions, is a key variable in the establishment of the first, central town, but plays a lesser role in the development and location of later towns.

Spatially Separated Market Areas

The analysis of location in discontinuous markets would appear, given the nature of the real world, an important component of location theory. Yet apart from Ackley (1942), little account has been taken of this circumstance. Here only some simple cases are analysed: the formal assumptions of the one market case are retained, with the exception that we assume a string of linear markets separated by empty areas rather than only one market area. A completely general and formal development is difficult: several separate cases are analysed instead. Geometric methods are used.

First, assume two linear markets of equal length, separated by an empty area which is as long as one of the markets. A firm locates on this market: it may feel that it is the only firm in the market, or it may expect competitors. The analysis of this uncertain decision supposes firms of three sizes: those which can just sell over the entire market from one end, those which can sell over the entire market only from the centre, and those which can sell only over one-half the market from the centre. This implies that firms are large compared to those in the previous analysis.

The mathematics of the analyses are contained in the Appendix to this chapter; only the conclusions of those analyses are reported here. A large firm, able to sell over the entire market from any point, which expects no competitors, locates at the inner end of one of the regions, but if another firm is expected, the optimum location is the centre of one of the regions. A firm which can sell over the entire market only from the centre of that market locates at the centre of one of the regions, whether or not it expects a competitor; smaller firms exhibit

163

similar policies. Generally, if firms expect competitors to locate in the market, those firms locate at the centre of a region rather than at the inner end of one region or at the centre of the entire market. If three linear regions exist, the first firm, no matter what its size, locates at the centre of the central region, and later firms locate at the centre of the two peripheral regions (in the absence of agglomeration economies).

This analysis of location policies in discontinuous markets reveals that if firms sell to consumers in several spatially separated regions, those firms tend to locate at the centre of one of the regions. The existence of discontinuous markets augments the concentration of sellers at the centres of those markets. The concentration of sellers at a few points under uncertainty clearly does not depend merely on the existence of one market area, but evolves also when several markets exist. As we found when analysing the case of demand concentrated in points (in Chapter 6), so, when markets are discontinuous lines, firms locate within the areas of dense demand, not in the empty interstitial areas.

Location of Wholesalers

The fact that the market is relatively continuous, within bounds, implies that the locating firms sell directly to consumers. But these firms, which may be called 'retailers', must themselves be served for a variety of functions by firms which we may call 'wholesalers'. Now these wholesalers may also be regarded as competing amongst themselves for a market which is made up of retailers. It is clear that the market for wholesalers is discontinuous, comprising a set of spatially separated agglomerations of retailers.

The analysis of location policies in spatially separated markets reveals that if wholesalers' locations depend on retail markets, those wholesalers locate in central towns too; and this is true whether the wholesalers use market shares or total sales as the decision variable. Since town formation is symmetrical about the market centre, there will be one, or three, or five, etc., retail agglomerations in the market. Therefore, early wholesalers locate in the central town; they are followed by wholesalers in the second and third order towns. These location decisions enhance town formation.

But the location pattern of wholesalers is not merely a scaled down version of the pattern of retailers. Thus if the retail pattern has forty sellers, distributed twenty in the central town and ten in each of the two second order towns, then, if there are four wholesalers, they may not be distributed among the towns in the ratios 2:1:1. To illustrate the point, assume that the market is sixteen units in length and that the demand curve and transport costs are such that a wholesaling firm can just sell over the entire market from the median. Retailers buy from the nearest wholesaler.

If the wholesalers could communicate and bargain, they would agree to locate two at the median and one at each quartile; each firm would make the same volume of sales. But under the assumptions of lack of communication and immobility, the four wholesalers are in a non-zero sum game; and considering the probability of coincidence of location choices, the expected sales at the centre are almost twice those at the quartile to a firm which expects the others to choose a location with probabilities in accordance with market sizes. Under these conditions all four wholesalers locate at the centre. Uncertainty forces wholesalers to congregate at the central town to a greater degree than the retailers are concentrated there.

But this assumes that retailers locate independently of the manner in which they expect wholesalers to locate. Retailers, however, can easily visualise the outcome of this process and realise that those at the quartiles will suffer higher costs than those at the centre once the wholesalers are located. Thus there exists an added incentive, a new agglomeration economy, to prompt retailers to locate at the centre. The existence of a chain of suppliers, each link in which sells goods to a firm nearer the consumer, reinforces the factors which cause firms to agglomerate. (This result, of course, is closely related to the analysis in the previous chapter of tacit bargaining situations with prominent points.) Other cost relations between retailers and their suppliers are examined in the next chapter.

Development over Time

The general pattern predicted by the analyses so far is simple. Under uncertainty the first sellers of a good locate at the centres of markets. Whether there be one market or several, the centre of a market is the preferred location. Later sellers establish first of all at the centres of other markets and then, when these sites have been occupied, sellers locate either at the centre of a market (alongside another firm of the same type) or at a quartile in the market. The choice between an occupied centre or an empty quartile depends partly on the size of the firm and on the number of competitors which the firm expects to be locating at the same time.

But over time changes occur in the variables which affect these location decisions. Through economic development, several conflicting tendencies operate. Income densities rise, so firms can exist with progressively smaller market areas; transport costs fall and scale economies within the firm may become greater, so firms require increasingly large market areas; the number of firms in the centre rises, so the size of this location and its attraction for sellers increases; the number of sellers of the good in the centre increases, and this progressively repulses later sellers of the same good. The analysis of the effect of these changes illustrates how location patterns within an area change over time and reveals some of the causes of differences in location patterns between industries. This analysis follows the main lines of that in Neutze (1960).

The effect of a fall in transport costs is examined in Fig. 7–8. In the lower diagram, transport costs are assumed to be high: the sales radius is limited and both demand and cost curves are compressed to the left. In the upper diagram, on the other hand, transport costs are lower, and cost and demand curves are more extended. The diagram illustrates that as transport costs fall, so the

165

Figure 7–8: **Graphs to illustrate the effect of a fall in transport costs on firm spacing**

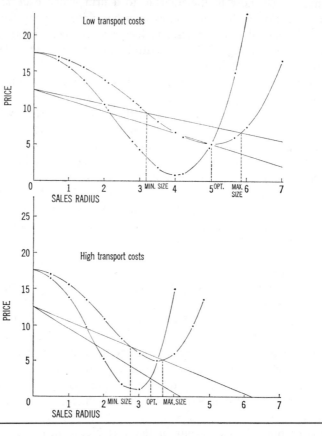

optimum firm size, as measured by the size of its market area, increases. Similarly the minimum profitable and maximum profitable firm size also increase. The diagram shows, too, that at optimum size the profit made per unit of good is greater when transport costs are low than when they are high. Thus, other things being equal, industries in which transport costs are high are characterised by closely spaced plants; as transport costs fall, firms spread out. In a region in which transport costs are high, towns are close together.

Figure 7–9 illustrates the effect of demand density on firm size and spacing. In the upper diagram, demand is at a low density, whereas in the lower diagram the demand curves are shifted upwards, as though the density of demand had risen. An upward shift in demand density effects an increase in the maximum and optimum sizes of the firm and a decrease in the minimum size of the firm. As demand density rises, the amount of profit made per unit sold at the optimum firm size increases. Thus, if an industry is competitive, and firms are near their minimum size, an increase in demand density calls forth a decrease in firm

Figure 7–9: **Graphs to illustrate the effect of demand density on firm size and spacing**

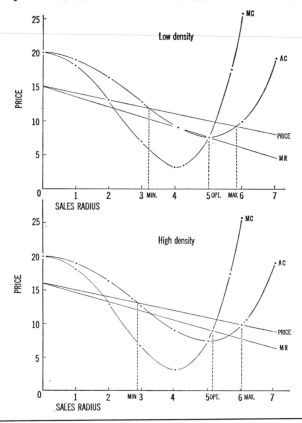

size—the minimum size market area which a firm can profitably enter falls. If the industry is monopolistic or monopolistic competitive, and firms are at their optimum size (or larger), an increase in the density of demand is associated with an increase in the size of firms.

The effect of a change in the structure of costs within a firm is examined in Fig. 7–10. In the lower diagram are shown demand and cost curves and the minimum, optimum, and maximum sizes of firm. In the upper diagram, scale economies are assumed more extensive: the marginal and average cost curves are shifted to the right. As a result of this change, the minimum size of firm falls while the optimum and maximum sizes increase. As scale economies develop, the minimum size of market area which a firm can profitably occupy falls, but the optimum size of market area rises. Prices are lower and the profit made per unit sold is greater at the optimum when scale economies are extensive than when scale economies are more limited.

If economic development is mainly associated with falls in transport costs,

Figure 7–10: **Relationship between economies of scale and firm spacing**

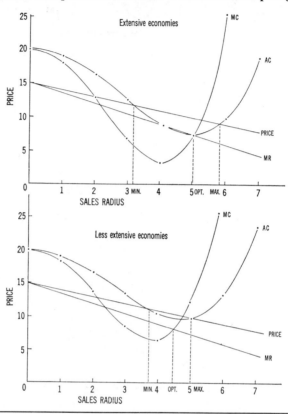

the market areas of firms increase in size over time, whether those firms are at the minimum or optimum sizes. If firms are as small as is profitable and development is largely in the form of rising demand density and increasing economies of scale, the market areas of firms fall in size; on the other hand, optimally sized firms increase their market areas over time. Provided that firms are reduced by competition to their minimum profitable size, their size increases as transport costs, demand density, and scale economies fall. Firms are most likely to be made small by competition if there are several of them in any one market area— that is, if firm size is small in relation to market areas. If, on the other hand, market areas are well separated (so that there is little competition between firms in different markets) and if firms are large in relation to market areas (so that there is little competition within a market), then firms are likely to be nearer their optimum size and development is associated with a rise in the sales radius of firms.

Similarly the spatial pattern of industries at any one point in time depends on density of demand, transport costs, and economies of scale. Those industries have the largest optimum market areas for which transport costs per unit of good sold are low, demand density is high and scale economies are well developed. The minimum market area in an industry is larger the lower are transport costs, demand density, and scale economies. Because of these relationships, industries exhibit different spatial patterns: firms in some industries are closer together and sell to smaller market areas than firms in other areas. A hierarchical system of towns within a region develops when the decision-making model is superimposed upon these various location patterns.

The Pattern Simulated

The model as so far outlined has introduced two concessions to reality. Firstly, the firms are uncertain about the number and location policy of their rivals and, secondly, markets are bounded. The analysis of firms' location choices within this context indicates that the first firm of an industry which establishes in a market locates at the centre of that market. If firms sell to several spatially separated market areas, they again locate at the centre of one of these markets. Later sellers locate at the centre or at the quartiles. The definiteness and simplicity of these conclusions depend largely on the fact that markets are bounded and sellers are uncertain.

The use of bounded markets in the analysis brings into effect one aspect of environmental variance. If resources vary, so the density of the primary producing population, which depends on resources for its location, varies also, and bounding introduces this variation in a simplified form. The model has yet to introduce environmental variance as it affects costs. Before examining facets of this necessary generalisation, however, the pattern predicted by the model is simulated. (Many more simulations need to be performed, though, before statistical relationships between variables and location parameters can be established.)

In this simulation one region of length 360 units was assumed. Within this linear market there is a series of bounded markets and empty areas. These markets and spaces vary in length from two to ten units, lengths being determined by random numbers. On these markets are located a set of industries, each of which has a linear demand curve with respect to distance inclined at 45°: sales may be made in one direction to a distance (in units) equal to the price intercept of the demand curve (in units). The sales made by an industry in one direction equal the area beneath this curve. The maximum quantity which can be sold is assumed equal to the optimum quantity, while the minimum quantity of sales necessary for profitability is one-half the optimum. Optimum sales for the first industry are four units, which implies a demand curve with respect to distance of

$$D = 2 - d,$$

where d ($d \leqslant 2$) is the distance over which sales are made (in one direction). All the firms in an industry are assumed to have the same demand curve and the same minimum sales level necessary for profits. Industries locate on the market

169

Figure 7–11: Location patterns in some markets of the simulation, assuming no sales outside each bounded market. In the market of length 4 units, industries 1 and 2 are missing from the central town; in the market 6 units long, industries 3, 4, and 5 are missing from the centre; in the 8 unit length market, industries 5, 6, and 7 are missing; and in the longest market, the central town lacks industries 6, 7, and 8.

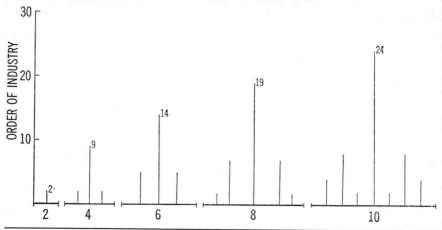

in order of increasing size: the increment in sales at the optimum between successive industries is one unit for the first industry, and increases by one unit between successive industries. The initial sequence of sales optima is therefore 4, 5, 7, 10, 14, 19, 25, . . . There exist ten industries at each of the first five sizes, nine at each of the second five sizes, eight at the following five sizes, and so on, until there is only one industry of each of the forty-sixth and larger sizes. Thus there are ten industries of size four units, but only nine of size nineteen units.

A firm locates in any market if sales are larger than the minimum necessary; the first firm in an industry which locates in a given market establishes at the centre. If location at the quartiles is profitable, given that the first firm exists at the centre, the second and third sellers locate at the quartiles. If, when the second and third firms are in position, the central firm is unable to make minimum sales, that firm is removed. If profitable, the fourth and fifth firms in an industry locate at the outside octiles, and the sixth and seventh locate at the inner octiles. Firms are removed from the quartiles if they become unprofitable after firms have located at the octiles. No more than seven firms in one industry located in any one market. Having thus located the first industry, the firms in the next smallest industry are located in the same manner. Eventually, even though other markets may be accessible, a firm in an industry cannot make minimum sales from a market; the growth of towns in this market then ceases and the market is served, if at all, by higher order firms from other markets. Typical results for some standard size markets, assuming no sales to other markets, are presented in Fig. 7–11.

Figure 7–12: **Relationship between the number of towns and the number of functions in those towns for the simulation**

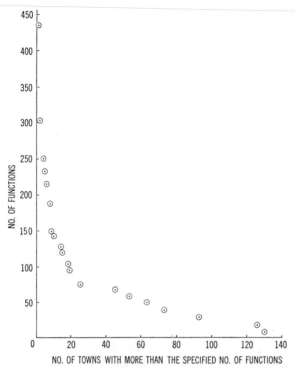

Because of the steep slope of the demand curve, no good is sold to the entire occupied market. Portions of the market are not served by sellers of the first industry, while the one firm of the highest order industry sells to only 70 per cent of the market in the worst simulation. These results probably reflect steep demand curves and widely separated markets. Furthermore, the simulation precludes sellers from selling within their own towns. The diagrams in Fig. 7–11 illustrate how towns contain most, though not necessarily all, of the industries which are of order less than the highest order industry in the town. Once sales are permitted to market areas beyond the firms' immediate local market, central towns grow relative to the other towns in the market, yielding patterns for which Figs. 7–12 and 7–13 show typical results. Figure 7–12 illustrates the town hierarchy which developed in one simulation: the distribution of town sizes is similar to the rank size distribution, though there exist distinct steps within the hierarchy. Figure 7–13 illustrates the relationship between spacing and town size: again, the simulation yields size-spacing relationships which are similar to those found in reality.

171

Figure 7–13: **Relationship between number of functions in towns and the spacing of those towns for the simulation. Distance is measured to the nearest neighbour of greater than or equal to the town's size.**

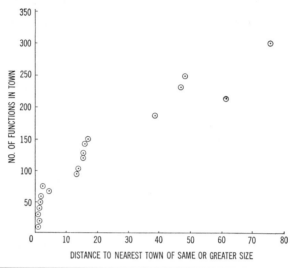

DISTANCE TO NEAREST TOWN OF SAME OR GREATER SIZE

Actual Location Patterns

Some data about actual town patterns have been collected to determine (to an initial approximation) whether the model is consistent with reality. The area chosen for the analysis of the location of towns within bounded regions is part of the market area of Keswick, a market and holiday town in the northwest of the English Lake District. Figure 7–14 illustrates some salient physical features of this region. The boundary of Keswick's market area is provided by areas of zero population. Except in the main valleys the slopes are too steep and the land too high to permit economic permanent occupation by man (Monkhouse, 1960). The boundary zone is everywhere above 500 feet, except in the northwest, where a narrow belt of low land between Bassenthwaite Lake and Skiddaw Forest constitutes the boundary. The highland zone is almost continuous and is generally at least one mile wide. The zone of low population density which bounds the market area of Keswick thus originates in physical conditions rather than in Keswick's economic organisation of its hinterland.

But within this market area there exist several smaller villages and hamlets, each serving a limited market area with low order goods and services. It is the location of these villages and of Keswick with respect to the low order market areas which is the subject of this analysis.

First, local spatial variations in the physical environment are assessed. In this region, land above 1000 feet or with a slope greater than 1:5 is not permanently usable: its only possible use is as extensive summer grazing for sheep (Monkhouse, 1960; Smailes, 1961: 294-302). Similarly, rough pastures on lower

Figure 7–14: **Physical setting of the Keswick market area.**
Source: Ordnance Survey, one inch to one mile tourist map of the Lake District, 1966.

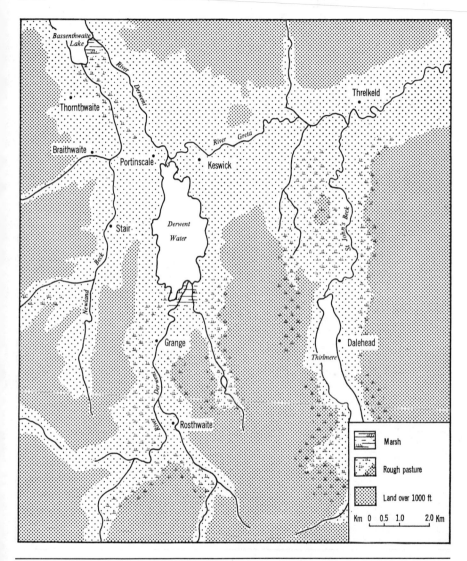

land, marshes, and lakes are not permanently occupied. All land in these categories has been classified as 'poor'; the remainder is 'good'. Although this classification is coarse, it has the merit of being simple, and land can be classified by inspection of the 1:63,360 sheets of the Ordnance Survey. The assessment of land quality is based upon the relevant one-inch map.

Figure 7–15: **Evaluation of land by cells and predicted and actual location of villages, Keswick region.**

Source: As for Fig. 7–14.

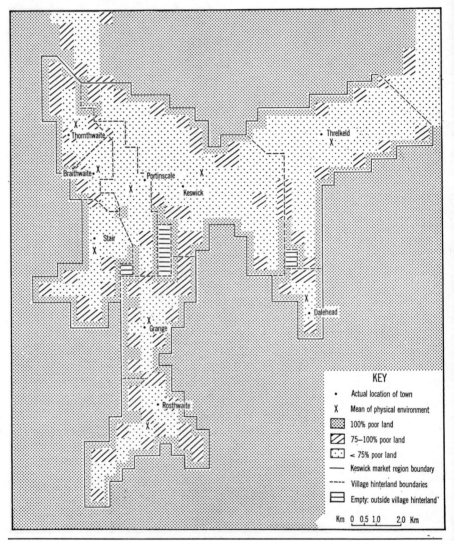

Figure 7–15 illustrates the variation in land quality in the region. The percentage of the land which is poor in each $0.25km^2$ square is calculated to form the basis for Fig. 7–15. Within the area may be delimited the boundaries of smaller regions, though they are less extensive and less obvious than the boundary of the entire Keswick market area. The boundaries between the villages in the west are not obvious from Fig. 7–15 but in fact they follow unbridged portions of rivers.

Table 7–6: **Errors of prediction of village location**

Town	Average diagonal	Error	Error as % of diagonal	Probability
Stair	2·95 M	0·68	23	0·21
Braithwaite	1·80 S	0·22	12	0·06
Thornthwaite	2·55 S	0·45	18	0·12
Rosthwaite	2·85 M	1·00	35	0·49
Grange	2·70 M	0·30	11	0·05
Portinscale	4·05 L	0·70	17	0·12
Keswick	6·00 L	0·90	15	0·09
Dalehead	1·60 S	0·75	47	0·88
Threlkeld	4·70 L	0·50	11	0·05

Note: L, M, and *S* refer to the classification of market areas into large, medium, and small on the basis of the length of their average diagonals. The average diagonal is defined as the average of the longest and the shortest diagonal in the market region. 'Probability' is defined as the probability of an error less than that observed in a circular market region of the given diagonal (= diameter) under the assumption of random choice of location.

The only boundaries which are not physically obvious on the source map are the boundaries of the village of Threlkeld and the boundary between Braithwaite and Thornthwaite. Most of the villages serve clearly bounded market regions.

Within each market area, the percentage of the land which is not poor is known. From these data, the mean location of the relatively good land may be calculated. The mean has been calculated from the formula

$$(7\text{--}22) \qquad (\bar{d}_n, \bar{d}_e) = \left(\frac{\sum_i n_i x_i}{\sum_i x_i}, \frac{\sum_i e_i x_i}{\sum_i x_i} \right),$$

where n and e are distances north and east of the assumed origins and x is the amount of good land in each distance zone from the origin. If population at the time of town formation was distributed in accordance with the quality of the land, then the mean location with respect to good land is also the mean of the (former) population distribution. Distribution of resources is used to determine the mean rather than present population, because it is possible that population distribution has been affected by the location of the town (see Bogue, 1950). The model predicts that this mean is the chosen location of the town in the market. These mean locations are shown on Fig. 7–15. Some villages are close to the mean location of their region (taking into account land quality): examples are Grange and Braithwaite. On the other hand, Dalehead and Portinscale are distant from their respective means.

Table 7–6 presents the prediction errors in more detail. The third column of the table relates the error of prediction to the size of market area. In the three smallest market areas, the errors are considerable, with an average of 26 per cent; predictions in the medium size market areas are also subject to wide error, the average being 23 per cent; on the other hand, in large market areas, towns tend to be only 14 per cent of the market's linear dimensions away from the mean location with respect to land quality. The average error for all nine villages is 21 per cent. Although the errors are quite large, the relationship between the magnitude of the error of prediction in a region and the size of that region is in the direction expected. If random variations in physical features attract towns away from the centre of their regions, those variations have similar absolute but greater proportionate effect in small than in large market regions. And inspection of the one-inch Ordnance Survey map indicates that good sites seem to have attracted towns from their mean locations. All the towns except two (Rosthwaite and Thornthwaite) have been attracted from the predicted location to good crossing and bridging points on the rivers.

The table also presents the probabilities that the errors would be less than those observed had towns been located purely at random. (Circles have been used in this calculation, and so the given probabilities overstate the actual ones.) For several market areas, the probability of such errors occurring by chance is small: whereas, if locations were random, 16 per cent of towns would be located with less than 20 per cent error, the observed proportion of towns within this limit is 67 per cent. A Kolmogorov-Smirnov test on the distribution of errors indicates that the actual distribution is different from the distribution which would arise if towns were randomly located, at $p = 0.01$. Thus towns are nearer the centre of their bounded markets than chance alone would indicate.

These observations are compatible with the predictions of the model. The market area of Keswick is well bounded and the smaller market areas of the villages are mostly clearly bounded by physical variations (and the concomitant variations in population density). The villages are located on average some 20 per cent of their regions' average linear dimensions away from the mean location of good land within these regions. This error in the prediction has apparently been caused by the attraction of the villages towards points which offer good site facilities. As we should expect, the relative error in the prediction is smaller the larger the market region. It is also true, though, that these observations are compatible with other models—for example, a market shares model of location fits these observations.

Appendix to Chapter 7

In this appendix are developed the mathematics necessary to support some of the conclusions expressed in the foregoing chapter, while the details of some game experiments are described. The game experiments are described first, then

Table 7A–1: **Your share of the market (of 50 cents)**

My choice	Your choice				
	1	2	3	4	5
	50%	85%	75%	60%	50%
	15%	50%	60%	50%	35%
	25%	35%	50%	35%	25%
	35%	50%	60%	50%	15%
	50%	60%	75%	85%	50%

Note that in the fourth matrix, my aim is to reduce the percentage you obtain to a minimum.

the location decision of the first firm is generalised, and, finally, we examine firm behaviour in spatially separated market areas.

Decision-Taking Behaviour

The models of town formation employ a particular theory of decision taking. The decisions predicted by this theory are logical, given certain axioms. However, the criteria of choice and the actual decisions are not obvious in the absence of a complex mathematical argument. It is important therefore to decide whether people's intuitive choices conform to the criteria used in the models.

A group of forty sixth formers from a high school in Canberra are the subjects of these experiments. The students were told that they would be paid up to $1 for assistance, which would be needed for half an hour. The general written instructions for all the experiments were:

On the accompanying sheets are four different experiments; the first three experiments each contain two tables, one labelled YOUR PROFITS and one labelled MY PROFITS. The fourth experiment contains only one table. You will be paid in cents the amount of money in the YOUR PROFITS tables, depending on your choices and on my choices.

The students were instructed to perform the fourth experiment first. This experiment contains a two-person zero sum game which is designed to simulate a market shares model. The game matrix is reproduced in Table 7A–1. The matrix was accompanied by the instructions:

a) The Fourth Matrix.
Do this one first. I have made a choice, between 1, 2, 3, 4, and 5. I am not going to tell you that choice. You must choose a number, 1, 2, 3, 4, or 5. The sum of 50 cents is to be divided among us. I have chosen my number in order (I think) to minimise the amount of money you are given. You must choose in order to try and maximise the amount of money I must give you. Remember that when I made my choice, I did not know your choice, and that you are not going to know my choice when you make your choice. Write down the number of your choice.

The optimum choice is the minimax decision, 3. Payment was made on the basis of my choosing 3. (But the students were not told the 'correct' choice nor were they paid until the entire set of experiments had been completed.)

The students were divided into two groups, each of twenty. The division

Table 7A–2: **The first matrix**

My choice	YOUR PROFITS Your choice					MY PROFITS Your choice				
	1	2	3	4	5	1	2	3	4	5
1	4	6	7	7½	8	4	6	7	7½	8
2	6	4	6	7	7½	6	4	6	7	7½
3	7	6	4	6	7	7	6	4	6	7
4	7½	7	6	4	6	7½	7	6	4	6
5	8	7½	7	6	4	8	7½	7	6	4

Table 7A–3: **The second matrix**

My choice	YOUR PROFITS Your choice					MY PROFITS Your choice				
	1	2	3	4	5	1	2	3	4	5
1	7	10	11½	12	11½	7	8	9½	11	11½
2	8	8	10	11¼	11	10	8	9	11¼	12
3	9½	9	8	9	9½	11½	10	8	10	11½
4	11	11¼	10	8	8	12	11¼	9	8	10
5	11½	12	11½	10	7	11½	11	9½	8	7

Table 7A–4: **The third matrix**

My choice	YOUR PROFITS Your choice					MY PROFITS Your choice				
	1	2	3	4	5	1	2	3	4	5
1	11	15½	16	15	14	11	9	10½	12½	14
2	9	11½	14	13½	12½	15½	11½	11½	13½	15
3	10½	11½	12	11½	10½	16	14	12	14	16
4	12½	13½	14	11½	9	15	13½	11½	11½	15½
5	14	15	16	15½	11	14	12½	10½	9	11

was random, for the students in one group were chosen by random numbers. One group performed a set of experiments not reported here; the second grou were given the following instructions:

(b) The First Three Matrices.

I have chosen a number (without knowing your choice); you must now choose number (and I am not going to tell you my choice). In these matrices, if you get a hig gain, that does not necessarily mean that I gain only a little (for the money is provide by the University). *e.g.:* in the first pair of matrices, if you choose 5 and I choose 1, w both get 8 cents. Thus, I have made my choice in order to get as much for myself a I can; you must make your choice in order to get as much for yourself as you car

Table 7A–5: **Results of minimax experiment (Table 7A–1)**

Location	1/5	2/4	3	Total
Number of times chosen	1	5	34	40
Expected number of times chosen (random)	16	16	8	40

Table 7A–6: **Results of non-zero sum game experiments**

| Number of times chosen in | Location | | | |
	1/5	2/4	3	Total
Matrix 1	17	2	1	20
Matrix 2	1	14	5	20
Matrix 3	7	2	11	20
Random choice	8	8	4	20

Whereas in the previous game, I was out to minimise the amount I gave you, in these matrices, we want both of us to gain as much as we can. I have made my choice. The numbers in the cells are the numbers of cents you are given at the end. What number do you choose in matrix 1? second matrix? third matrix?

The games are reproduced as Tables 7A–2, 7A–3, and 7A–4.

These matrices are modified versions of Tables 7–2, 7–3, and 7–4. The tables have been modified in order to make the games roughly equal in value. The decision-making criterion used in Chapter 7 indicates that choices should be 1 or 5 in Table 7A–2, 2 or 4 in Table 7A–3, and 3 in Table 7A–4. Choices consistent with these indicate support for the decision-taking model of firm location.

In Table 7A–5 are reported the results of the minimax decision experiment, the matrix of which is Table 7A–1. Of the forty people who performed the experiment, thirty-four (85%) made choice 3, the minimax choice, which theory predicts is optimal. The results stand in marked contrast to the results which would have been expected had the students chosen randomly: Chi-squared is $106 \cdot 12$, which, with two degrees of freedom, is significant at a probability less than $0 \cdot 1\%$. Despite the complicated mathematics necessary to prove that this choice is optimal, people are able to find the minimax decision and, having found it, regard it as the best choice.

The results of the other three experiments are reported in Table 7A–6. Optimal choices were made by 85% of people in matrix 1, 70% in matrix 2, and 55% in matrix 3. Again, the majority of students chose in the manner predicted by the decision-making criterion. The choices made are different (Chi squared is significant at p less than $1 \cdot 0\%$) from those which would be expected if people had chosen randomly. Furthermore, the choices are significantly different

Figure 7A–1: **Spatial relationships, two firms in a linear market**

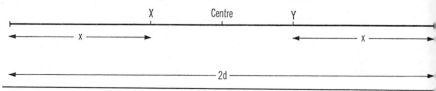

between the matrices: the students altered their choices in response to the changes in the matrices. Furthermore, 35% of the students made all their choices in accordance with the predictions, and a further 40% made only one choice not predicted by the model. The distribution of the number of students who made zero, one, two, or three choices which accord with the predicted choices is significantly different from the distribution which would be expected if choices were random: Chi squared equals 11·47, which is significant at a probability of 1·0%. The students chose 'better' than random.

These experiments indicate that the sample of students tended to make decisions in the manner predicted by the decision-making model used in Chapter 7. In the zero sum matrix, most students used the minimax criterion of choice. In non-zero sum matrices, the students made the predicted decision more frequently than chance alone would indicate: a majority chose in accordance with the model. (However, the third matrix, which requires the most conservative decision, reveals the existence of a significant proportion of students who chose the quartile location. These are long-run maximisers, who refused to use the logic of short-run maximisation which advocates central location.) Generally, though, the results lend support to the notion that the decision-making model may approximate the decisions made by a majority of people.

Location Decision of the First Firm

Figure 7A–1 illustrates spatial relationships. Assume that s, the distance from the firm to the furthest point at which sales can be made, is such that a firm located on a quartile can sell to at least half the market (i.e. $s \geqslant \frac{1}{2}d$). Smaller values of s eliminate the problems caused by competitiveness in location. A firm thus sells to a distance x towards the end of the market, and to a distance $d-x$ towards the centre. Substituting these values in equation (7–5) yields the sales obtained by the firm at X:

(7A–1) $\quad S_x = (A-Bp)d - \frac{1}{2}Br(2x^2+d^2-2dx).$

If X moves to a distance $x+\Delta x$ from the end of the market, its sales are

(7A–2) $\quad S_{x+\Delta x} = (A-Bp)\left(d+\frac{\Delta x}{2}\right) - \frac{1}{2}Br\left(2x^2+\frac{5(\Delta x)^2}{4}\right.$

$$+3x\Delta x+d^2-2dx-d\Delta x\bigg),$$

Figure 7A–2: **Spatial relationships, three firms in a linear market**

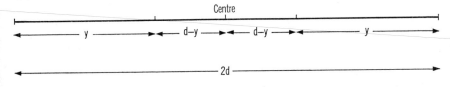

---

while at a distance $x-\Delta x$ from end of the market, sales are

(7A–3) $\quad S_{x-\Delta x} = (A-Bp)\left(d-\dfrac{\Delta x}{2}\right) - \tfrac{1}{2}Br\left(2x^2-3x\Delta x\right.$

$$+ \dfrac{5(\Delta x)^2}{4} + d^2 - 2dx + d\Delta x \bigg).$$

Now, X is the optimum location for the firm if, first,

$$S_x \geqslant S_{x+\Delta x},$$

that is, if

(7A–4) $\quad \dfrac{5\Delta x}{4} + 3x - d \geqslant \dfrac{A-Bp}{Br}$.

But Δx is infinitesimal and s is defined as $\dfrac{A-Bp}{Br}$,

and so condition (7A–4) becomes

$$3x - d \geqslant s.$$

The second necessary condition which must be satisfied if X is the optimum location for the firm is

(7A–5) $\quad \begin{array}{l} S_x \geqslant S_{x-\Delta x}: \\ s \geqslant 3x-d. \end{array}$

Obviously, conditions (7A–4) and (7A–5) can only both be satisfied simultaneously if

$$s = 3x - d.$$

Thus the optimum location for each firm is given by

(7A–6) $\quad x = \dfrac{d}{3} + \dfrac{A-Bp}{3Br}$.

As s, the sales radius of the firm, increases, so the optimum location of the firm approaches the centre, until, when $s = 2d$ (the sales radius equals the market area), the firm locates at the centre of the market.

If a firm anticipates two competitors, its thought experiment of the location game is more complex. Assume that one firm locates at the centre and that the

181

other two locate one on either side of the centre, at a distance y from the end of the line. The market is of length $2d$. The firm on the left hand side of the market sells goods to a distance y to its left and $d-y$ to its right (see Fig. 7A-2). From equation (7-5), therefore, sales at y are:

$$(7A\text{-}7) \qquad S_y = (A-Bp)\left(\frac{y+d}{2}\right) - Br\left(\frac{5y^2+d^2-2dy}{8}\right).$$

Location at y is optimal for the firm if location at $y+\Delta y$ and at $y-\Delta y$ yield lower sales than at y. By a similar argument to that used in the case of two firms, location at y is optimal if

$$(7A\text{-}8) \qquad y = \frac{d+2s}{5}.$$

Equation (7A-8) defines the optimal location for the firm in terms of the length of the market and the distance over which the firm can sell goods. The larger is s in relation to d, the closer to the centre does this firm locate: when $s = 2d$, the firm locates at the centre. This initial analysis indicates that, just as when there are two sellers, three sellers locate at the centre of the market when their maximum sales area equals the length of the market area.

But the two outer firms never reach the centre while the original central firm remains at the median; for as the two outer firms approach the centre, they reduce the market area of that central firm. Sales of the central firm as a function of the location of the two outer firms are

$$(7A\text{-}9) \qquad S_x = (A-Bp)(4y-2s) - Br(4y^2+s^2-4sy);$$

while one firm remains at y, sales of the original central firm at a point j (j is nearer the end of the market than y) are, for optimum j

$$(7A\text{-}10) \qquad S_j = (A-Bp)\left(\frac{6y+2s}{10}\right) - Br\left(\frac{s^2+y^2}{10}\right).$$

Sales at j are greater than sales at y if

$$(A-Bp)(22s-34y) > Br(39y^2+9s^2-40sy),$$

that is, if

$$(7A\text{-}11) \qquad s > \frac{3}{2}y.$$

By substituting (7A-11) in (7A-8) we find that the central firm is forced from the median to a position near one end of the market if

$$s > \frac{3}{4}d.$$

If condition (7A-11) holds, the firm which is now the middle one of the three relocates to a site midway between the firm at j and the firm which has not moved. But then the firm at j also shifts towards the centre, which in turn causes a

Figure 7A–3: **Spatial relationships, four firms in a linear market**

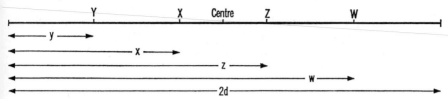

Figure 7A–4: **The location decision of a large firm in two spatially separated markets**

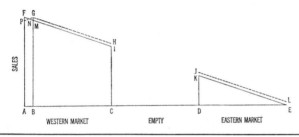

readjustment in the location of the middle firm. This process continues until the firms reach the situation of one at the median and two firms at a distance y from the end of the market. The situation is thus totally unstable. The condition for instability is expressed by inequation (7A–11). Clearly, if the firm's optimum sales area is longer than three-quarters of the market area, this thought experiment does not offer very useful conclusions to a firm which is deciding on a location.

Consider now the case of four firms. The spatial relationships between these firms are illustrated in Fig. 7A–3. Given the location of X, Y's sales are

$$(7A\text{--}12) \qquad S_y = (A-Bp)\left(\frac{x+y}{2}\right) - \tfrac{1}{2}Br\left(\frac{5y^2+x^2-2xy}{4}\right),$$

and S_y is at a maximum when

$$(7A\text{--}13) \qquad y = \frac{2s+x}{5}.$$

But, given the location of Y and Z, X's best location is defined by

$$(7A\text{--}14) \qquad x = \frac{y+z}{2}:$$

midway between Y and Z. Conditions (7A–13) and (7A–14) are paralleled for Z and W;

$$(7A\text{--}15) \qquad z = \frac{x+w}{2}$$

183

(7A–16) $\quad w = \dfrac{10d-2s-x}{5}$.

The equations (7A–13) to (7A–16) can be solved simultaneously, to yield the stable optimum pattern of firm location, in terms of $2d$, the length of the market, and s, the sales radius of the firms. This solution is

$$y = \frac{d+3s}{7}$$

(7A–17) $\quad x = \dfrac{5d+s}{7}$

$$z = \frac{9d-s}{7}$$

$$w = \frac{13d-3s}{7},$$

for $s \leqslant 2d$.

When the firms are thus placed, X can make sales:

(7A–18) $\quad S_x = \dfrac{Br}{49}(32ds-15s^2-4d^2)$.

But suppose that X relocates to a point J, which is closer to the right hand end of the market than Y $(j < y)$.
The optimum is

(7A–19) $\quad j = \dfrac{2s+y}{5}$,

and at this point, J makes sales of

(7A–20) $\quad S_j = \dfrac{Br}{50}(206sy-59s^2-101y^2)$.

Sales at j are greater than sales at x if $S_j \geqslant S_x$: that is, if

(7A–21) $\quad s \geqslant d/2$.

Condition (7A–21) is therefore the condition that a location pattern for four simultaneously locating firms is unstable.

Spatially Separated Market Areas
This section analyses the location decisions of firms in spatially separated markets. First we discuss decisions in two markets, and later extend the analysis to the case of three separated markets.

Figure 7A–4 illustrates the decision of a firm which can sell over all the market from any location and which expects no competitors. Assume that the firm contemplates location at A; its sales are then $AFIC+DKE$. On the other hand, if it compares location at B with location at A (B is an infinitely small distance from A), the firm finds that sales in the AB zone are the same for both

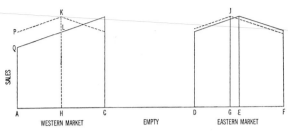

Figure 7A–5: **Location decision of second large firm in two spatially separated markets**

sites, but that sales to the right of the firm are higher when at B than at A. So B with sales $PGHCA+DJLE$ is preferred to A. A further shift, a small distance to the right of B, results in another rise in sales to the right and a drop in sales to the left. A move to the right of distance ΔB causes a rise in the demand curve to the right of

$$\frac{\Delta B \times AF}{AE},$$

and a fall in the demand curve to the left of the same amount. Thus the increase in sales from the move is

$$\frac{\Delta B \times AF}{AE}(BC+DE)$$

while the loss of sales to the left is

$$\frac{\Delta B \times AF}{AE}(AB).$$

Moving to the right remains profitable so long as AB is less than $BC+DE$, that is, until the firm reaches C. Thus optimal location for a large firm which expects no competitors is one of the ends of the markets, near the centre. While location in the central empty area is as profitable as location at one of the market ends, such a location entails greater risk, with no addition in profit to compensate.

Suppose that this first firm chooses a location at the inner end of the western market, at C. Then a second firm locates at the median of the eastern market, as Fig. 7A–5 illustrates. This is proved by showing that it is unprofitable to move from E in either direction. Assume that the firm contemplates a small shift, to G: then sales in the GE zone are the same at G as at E, sales in the DG zone increase by

$$\frac{GE \times AF}{GJ}(DG),$$

and sales in the EF zone fall by

$$\frac{GE \times AF}{GJ}(EF).$$

Figure 7A–6: **Comparison of location at centre of entire system and at centre of one market, for large firms**

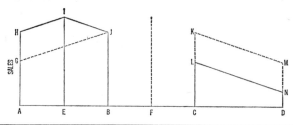

But *EF* is more than *DG*, and so sales at *G* are less than sales at *E*, a conclusion which also holds for shifts to the right. However, when the second firm has located at *E*, the first firm would make greater sales at *H* than at *C*. Thus if a second firm is expected later, the first firm optimises by locating at the median in one of the markets.

The first firm may expect a competitor to locate at the same time. Clearly, as when Fig. 7A–5 holds, the best combined location pattern consists of one firm at the median of the eastern market and one at the median of the western market. But since both firms may locate at the same median, we must show that the expectation of sales from the choice of a median location is better than the choice of the centre of the whole region. In Fig. 7A–6: since the probability of coincident locations is 0·50, it has to be shown that the average of sales at *E* with one firm and at *E* with two firms is greater than the sales made at *F*. Now if one firm is at *E* and the other is in the eastern market, sales at *E* are *AHIJB*; if both are at *E*, sales of one firm are $\frac{1}{2}(AHIJB+CLND)$; if both firms locate at *F*, sales of one firm are $\frac{1}{2}(AGJB+KMDC)$, that is *AGJB*. Thus the expectation of gain at *E* is

$$(7A–22) \qquad E_E = \tfrac{1}{2}AHIJB + \tfrac{1}{2} \cdot \tfrac{1}{2}(AHIJB+CLND)$$

$$= \tfrac{3}{4}AHIJB + \tfrac{1}{4}CLND,$$

which, omitting sales in the eastern market, is

$$(7A–23) \qquad \frac{33}{24}AE \times EI.$$

Sales at *F* are given by

$$(7A–24) \qquad S_F = \tfrac{1}{2}AB \cdot \tfrac{1}{2}EI + \left(EI - \frac{EB}{AD}EI\right)$$

$$= \frac{32}{24}AE \times EI.$$

The expectation of sales at the centre of one market is greater than expected

Figure 7A–7: **Location decision of medium-sized firm in two separated markets: the firm imagines that it is locating alone**

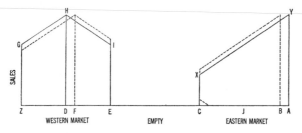

sales at the centre of the whole area. A firm expecting another firm to locate in the market at the same time locates at the centre of one of the markets.

Provided large firms expect other firms to locate in the market, whether at the same time or closely in the future, these firms maximise their sales by locating at the centre of one of the markets. The centre of the whole system, in the empty area, is not chosen. Only if the firm does not expect any other competitors does it not locate at the centre: but such eccentric location is risky, especially if the firm's prediction about the number of competitors is wrong.

The location policies of a medium-sized firm, which can sell to the entire market only from the centre, may be analysed in a similar manner. Figure 7A–7 depicts the situation of a firm which thinks that it is locating alone. If the firm locates at A, sales are $ACXY$, but a shift to B clearly increases the sales. The firm finds that shifts to the left remain profitable until it reaches the centre of that market, when its decision is represented by the diagram in the western market. At the centre, D, sales are $ZGHIE$; a small shift to the right, to F, results in a gain of sales of

$$(7A\text{–}25) \qquad \left(\frac{2DF}{AZ}AY\right)(FE) + \tfrac{1}{2}\left(\frac{2DF}{AZ}AY\right)(DF) - \left(\frac{2DF}{AZ}AY\right)(DZ)$$

$$= \left(\frac{2DF}{AZ}AY\right)\left(DE + DF + \frac{DF}{2} - DE\right)$$

$$= -DF/2.$$

Location at F is less profitable than location at the centre of the market. This first firm locates at the median of one of the markets. And, similarly, the second firm also locates at a median position, though in the other market.

But the firm may expect another seller to be locating at the same time. By the arguments already produced, the best combined location policy for these firms is for one to locate at the centre of the eastern market and one at the centre of the western market. However, because of uncertainty, both firms may locate

187

Eigure 7A–8: **Decisions of two medium-sized firms in two separated markets**

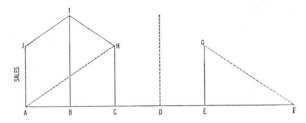

Figure 7A–9: **Decision of large firm in three separated markets**

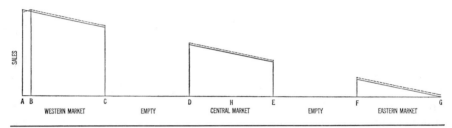

at the same site. Refer to Fig. 7A–8: at *B* the expected sales are

(7A–26) $\frac{1}{4}$(AJIHC)+$\frac{1}{2}$(AJIHC)

while at *D* the expected sales are

(7A–27) $\frac{1}{2}$(AHC+FGE) = AHC.

But triangle *AHC* equals triangle *HAJ* (because *AC* = *HJ*, *CH* = *JA*, ∠*ACH* = ∠*HJA* = 90°), and so *AJIHC* > 2*AHC*; consequently expected sales at *B* are greater than expected sales at *D*. A firm which expects a second firm to establish at the same time locates at the centre of one of the markets.

There is little need to analyse the location decisions of small firms in detail; they may readily be proved to be similar to the cases already examined. The general result of the entire analysis is that firms, if they expect other firms to locate in the market, whether later or at the same time, choose a site at the centre of one of the two markets which comprise the region. These results therefore indicate that the concentration of firms at the centres of market areas is enhanced if those firms are considering location in relation to a wide area, which is made up of several markets. By this process the central location in a market grows at the expense of quartile locations in that market.

Consider now location policies of firms which locate in three spatially separated market areas.

We analyse first the policies of large firms which can sell over the entire market region from any point in that region. Figure 7A–9 illustrates the case. A firm at

Figure 7A–10: **Decision of second large firm in three spatially separated markets**

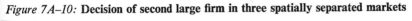

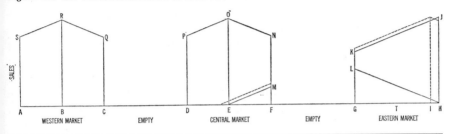

Figure 7A–11: **Location decision of medium-sized firm in three markets**

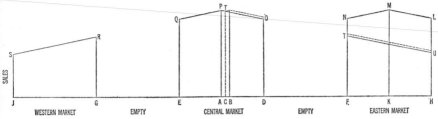

the end of the market, *A,* which contemplates a small move to *B* finds that the demand curve rises over the range *BC, DE, FG,* and falls by the same amount over the range *AB.* Therefore a move to the right remains profitable for so long as the area to the right of the firm is larger than the area to the left. The firm moves to the centre of the entire region, *H.* The decision of a second firm is analysed in Fig. 7A–10.

If that firm locates at *A* with the first, its sales are

$$\tfrac{1}{2}(JSRG+EQPOD+FTUH),$$

that is *(APOD+FTUH).* Now if the second firm moves to *B,* it loses sales *APTC* and gains the sales indicated by the dotted line through *TOTU.* The net gain is

$$-\frac{AB.AP}{S}\left(4+\frac{AB}{AD}\right):$$

the move is not profitable. The diagram shows that this remains true for all locations: the centre of the eastern market does not offer such high returns as the centre of the central market. A similar conclusion is reached when the policy of a firm which expects another competitor to locate at the same time is analysed. Large firms, able to sell over the entire market region from any location, choose to locate at the centre of the central market.

Figure 7A–11 is used to analyse the location policies of a firm which can only sell to the entire market region while at the centre of the central market. Assume

189

Figure 7A–12: **Decision of small firm in three separated markets**

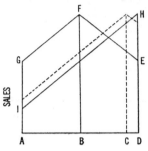

a firm at *H*. Moves to the left—to *I*—cause an increase of sales, shown by the dotted lines above *JK* and *ME*, so long as the market to the left of the firm is greater than that to the right: the firm locates at the centre of the market, *E*. At *E* the firm makes sales (*DPONF*+2*LGH*). Now assume a second firm at *B*: it makes sales *ASRQC*. Since this second firm can make no sales in the central market while it is located anywhere in the western market, the median, *B*, is the best location within that western market. Again, sales at *E*, adjacent to the first firm, are (*OEFN*+*LGH*), clearly less than sales at *B*. The second firm locates at *B*. But if a firm at *B* can make profits, so can a firm at *T*: the three firms locate, one at the centre of each market. Hence a firm which expects later competitors to locate in the market finds that its best location is the centre of the central market. The centre is also chosen if the firm believes that one or two other firms are locating at the same time.

Finally we analyse the decision of a firm which can only sell over one-half of the entire region from the centre. Figure 7A–12 illustrates the case. If the firm locates at one end of the eastern market, at *D*, its sales are *DHIA*, but clearly a small move, to *C*, creates larger sales. Moves to the west remain profitable so long as the distance to the western end of the market is greater than the distance to the eastern end. The firm therefore locates at the centre of the market, at *B*, and makes sales *AGFED*. Later firms choose the centre of the other markets. The same conclusion applies if the firm thinks that others are locating simultaneously.

8   Uncertainty about the State of Nature: the Costs of Uncertainty

The previous two chapters have analysed firms' decisions as they are affected by the uncertainty of those firms about rivals' behaviour. It was argued that the concentration of firms in towns is partly a function of this uncertainty as it affects decisions to locate within bounded markets. The uncertainty is due directly to game-like competitive or semi-competitive behaviour by the firms. But the returns which a firm can expect are uncertain also because of general variation within the economy: price and yield variations are caused by the fluctuations of weather through time and space, by changes in the rate of growth of the economy, by innovations and fashion, and by other similar stochastic elements within the system. This chapter analyses the manner in which these stochastic elements cause uncertainty to vary over space and how this pattern of uncertainty influences the evolving patterns of location within society. Whereas previous chapters analysed the individual decisions, and the influences upon them, this one deals with the more 'macro' approach: of analysing the way in which costs and returns vary over space as a function of uncertainty about the state of the environment.

The Location of Uncertainty

Stochastic uncertainty is caused by variations of two kinds. First there are variations in yields and outputs from year to year, caused mainly by variations in the weather and in other natural events. In some countries there seems to be some regular pattern in the variability of weather: for example, there is a general tendency for rainfall in Australia to become more uncertain inland. But the pattern of variation differs between countries, and it appears impossible to formulate a general rule about the patterns of weather (and, therefore, of physical output) variability which applies equally to all countries. Consequently, it is assumed that physical output variability is randomly distributed over space.

    The second element of uncertainty, variability of prices, takes the forefront

o

Table 8–1: **Victorian canning fruit farms, 1957-60: variations in gross value of production ($A)**

Fruit type	Changes in GVP caused by price changes* 1958-59	1959-60 Compared to 1957-8	Changes in GVP caused by yield changes† 1958-59	1959-60 Compared to 1957-8
Peaches	−828	−1047	−144	−480
Apricots	−109	−273	−774	−387
Pears	−519	−702	−469	+48
Total	−1456	−2022	−1387	−819

* Yields constant at 1957-8 levels.
† Prices constant at 1957-8 levels.

Source: Bureau of Agricultural Economics, 1961: 16.

in the analysis. Even in agriculture, an industry in which physical output variability is normally high, price variability is often an important component of uncertainty. Thus, Table 8–1 indicates that price changes caused a greater variation than yield changes in the gross value of production on Victorian canning fruit farms over the period 1957 to 1960.

Assume a plain which is homogeneous in all respects except that environmentally induced variability is randomly distributed over it. Variability is defined as being randomly distributed when the variance at a point is independent of the variance at any other point. Thus although points on the plain display different values for the variability caused by the environment, sections drawn across the plain exhibit no overall trend in variability. The spatial pattern of variability does not contain a range of values sufficiently large to offer significant resource advantages to any one point. Assume that knowledge about the environment and the market is limited. Therefore two notions are inherent in uncertainty: first, 'objective uncertainty' refers to the spatial pattern of price and output variability which actually exists and, secondly, the general term 'uncertainty' implies the state of mind of the entrepreneur as he attempts to make a decision. Assume that uncertainty varies, is measurable, and is some unspecified (though monotonically increasing) function of objective variability.

Over this plain is distributed a consuming population. For any point on the plain, a firm can calculate the total transport costs incurred in selling to that consuming population. As the total transport costs of a firm rise, we shall say that the firm is locating further from the market. Assume that a good is produced at points on the plain for this market and producers pay transport costs to the market. Let the price over the market be p per unit of good and let the average cost of transport from a point on the plain to the market be a per unit ($p \geqslant a \geqslant 0$; a is constant over short time periods at a point). If the price over the market falls 50 per cent, the new price at the point of production is

(8-1) $\quad \dfrac{p}{2}-a = \left(\dfrac{p}{2}-a\right)\left(\dfrac{1}{p-a}\right) \times 100\%$ of the old price

$\quad\quad\quad = \left(\dfrac{1}{2}-\dfrac{a}{2(p-a)}\right) \times 100\%.$

The new price is clearly less than 50 per cent of the old price, by an amount which is greater the smaller is p in relation to a.

More formally, the variance of received prices in relation to the average price at the point of production is

(8-2) $\quad Y_p = \dfrac{\text{Var}(p-a)}{(p-a)} = \dfrac{\text{Var}(p)}{\bar{p}-a}.$

Y_p is an increasing function of a. As a increases, so does the variance of received prices in relation to the average received price. Since transport costs, a, rise with distance, the further a point is on average from the consumers, the higher is the variation of prices in relation to the average received price at that point: the further a firm is from its market, the greater are percentage price changes. The coefficient of variation of received prices rises with distance from the market; if the uncertainty facing an entrepreneur is in part a function of the coefficient of variation of received prices, the more distant a point is from the market, the more uncertain are returns there.

International data are available to establish whether the pattern of variability in reality is consistent with this model. (The data reported in this chapter are discussed more fully in Webber, 1967.) The model predicts that if a producing country pays the freight charges on its exports, the variability in the price and value of its exports increases the further that country is from its markets. A second factor, not included in the model, which qualifies the variability of export prices and values is the type of commodity exported; on the basis of inter-country correlations on the structure of exports, countries have been classified into three groups—those that export manufactured goods, those that export minerals and beverages, and those that export other agricultural or forest products.[1] The variability of the value of a country's exports is defined as the standard deviation of the percentage year-to-year changes in the value of exports. A similar definition is applied to the variability of export prices.

[1] A classification procedure, leading to the use of analysis of variance techniques, has been preferred to correlation because it makes less stringent demands upon the accuracy of the data. The classification of countries is (a) distant from markets: United States, United Kingdom, Japan (manufactures exporters); Argentina, Israel, Australia, New Zealand, South Africa, Jamaica, Ecuador, Peru, Burma, Pakistan, South Korea, Philippines, Thailand (food exporters); Chile, Trinidad and Tobago, Iraq, Indonesia, former Central African Federation, Costa Rica, Brazil, El Salvador, Guatemala, Ceylon, India, Ghana (minerals and beverages exporters); (b) close to markets: Canada, West Germany, Belgium, Italy, France, Netherlands, Norway, Sweden, Austria, Finland, Portugal (manufactures exporters); Panama, Ireland, Greece, Denmark, Honduras, Mexico, Spain, Turkey, Cyprus, United Arab Republic, Algeria, Morocco, Tunisia (food exporters); Venezuela, Colombia (minerals and beverages exporters). Data are from UNDESA (1951-63).

Table 8–2: **Effects of type of exports and location on export instability**

Commodity exported*	Distance from market† High	Distance from market† Low	Mean
Manufactures	8·34	8·32	8·33
Minerals and beverages	12·08	8·89	11·62
Food	17·07	11·99	14·53
Mean	14·00	10·21	12·20

* For commodities exported, two digit codings of Standard International Trade Classification (UNDESA, 1958-61) are used to compute correlation coefficients between all pairs of countries. Countries are allocated to those groups with which their average correlation coefficient is highest. The use of three groups is arbitrary.

† Distance of a country from markets is defined as the average distance over which its exports are moved, weighted by the value of trade sent to the various destinations. Distances between major trading ports are from Hutchinson (1958) and data on yearly distribution of exports from International Monetary Fund [IMF] (1951-61).

Notes: The main effects of distance and commodity group are both significant at $0·05 > p > 0·01$.

Data for variability of the value of exports refer to the period 1951 to 1961 (IMF, 1951-61; UNDESA, 1951-61) and comprise the value of exports, free on board.

The pattern of value instability is summarised in Table 8–2. Both commodities exported and distance from market are significantly associated with variability in the value of a country's exports. The probability that this is a chance relationship among the fifty-four countries is less than 5 per cent. Allowing for the effect of the type of commodity exported, the further a country lies from its markets, the more variable is the value of its exports. Only among the exporters of manufactured goods does distance from market not affect the stability of export earnings. As expected, countries which export manufactured goods exhibit a lower variability of export values than do countries which export mainly mineral or agricultural goods.

Data on the variability of export prices[2] are more limited by the availability of price series to a fixed base. Evidence has been published for seventeen non-manufacturing countries for the decade after 1950.[3] These data indicate that whereas the variability of export prices in countries close to their markets is 8·11, it is 13·53 in countries more distant from markets. This difference in means is significant at $0·05 > p > 0·01$. A proportion of the pattern of instability of export earnings is due to a pattern of price variability rather than simply to variations in the quantum exported.

There exists a clearly defined pattern of variability of both the prices and values of exports among countries which mainly export non-manufactured

[2] The annual price of exports is defined as the weighted average price, as published by IMF (1951-61).

[3] These countries are Australia, Brazil, Ceylon, Colombia, Costa Rica, Denmark, Ecuador, Guatemala, India, Indonesia, Ireland, New Zealand, Peru, Philippines, Spain, and Venezuela.

goods. At greater distances, the variability is higher: distance explains (statistically) some 20 per cent of the inter-country variations in variability. If uncertainty is positively associated with income variability, then the uncertainty in a country is greater the further that country is from its markets. At least part of this uncertainty is due to the effects of location on price variability. This conclusion is compatible with the theoretical pattern of uncertainty.

This background pattern of uncertainty is now used, together with some models of choice, to examine the location of production over space. The immediate task is to examine how stochastic uncertainty affects production and location choices. This is accomplished by three models—of the allocation of inputs to competing enterprises, of the scale of output of the firm, and of the costs of inputs to a firm. The first of these models is concerned with a problem normally analysed in agricultural location theory, the second and third with problems in industrial location. However, each model is applicable to a greater or lesser degree to all types of firm.

The Allocation Problem

Under certainty a farmer's allocation decision is relatively simple. The farmer's problem is to maximise profits—the difference between outputs (returns) and inputs (costs). Often, because of capital shortages, there is an upper limit to the amount of inputs which he may apply to his crops. Thus assume a maximum level of inputs to the two crops, A and B of P. Suppose that there are two known production functions

$$Y_A = f(Q) \text{ and } Y_B = g(P-Q),$$

where Y represents output and Q is the input allocated to A (both expressed in money terms). Total output is maximised when

(8-3) $$\frac{d(Y_A+Y_B)}{dQ} = 0$$

and

(8-4) $$\frac{d^2(Y_A+Y_B)}{dQ^2} < 0.$$

Under uncertainty the farmer's decision is more difficult. Each year a different production function occurs, as prices change and natural conditions alter. The farmer does not know the production functions that will occur; he merely knows which ones have occurred in the past. The farmer has to predict which production function he thinks will occur and then he must maximise his allocation of inputs according to this prediction.

A commonly used model of uncertain decision taking in such circumstances is the criterion that firms maximise expectations. Given the behavioural axioms outlined in Chapter 5, this is a rational criterion upon which to decide. In an experiment (that is, some production decision of the farmer) assign a real number according to some rule (the value of output, perhaps) to each event

195

Table 8–3: **Minimax decision: profits per acre**

Choice	Poor year	State of nature Good year	Minimum
Crop A	5	10	5
Crop B	−20	40	−20

(harvesting period) of the sample space. Such an assignment of real numbers is a random variable; the random variable in this case is the value of output in each year. Over a period of k years, the farmer's average income is the average value of the random variable, X. The average value of the random variable is the expectation of X: if X may take the values $x_1, x_2, \ldots, x_k$, and the event that each occurs has the probability $f(x_1), f(x_2), \ldots, f(x_k)$, respectively, then the expectation of X is

(8–5) $E(X) = x_1 f(x_1) + x_2 f(x_2) + \ldots + x_k f(x_k).$

Use of such a maximised expectation model yields a decision which is socially optimal when viewed before the event (i.e. before prices and yields actually occur). But the model requires that farmers know or can estimate the probabilities associated with the outcomes; and if a poor result occurs in one year, the farmer who uses this simple model may be bankrupted. These problems have led some (such as Gould, 1963) to use the minimax decision-making criterion in such games against Nature. If one of the players is Nature—the farmer is trying to decide which crops offer the highest safe income—the farmer who uses the minimax criterion is assuming that Nature is choosing a strategy (of prices and weather) which minimises outcomes to the farmer. Since most of us assume that Nature is indifferent rather than actively malevolent, the farmer's minimax decision is conservative. Such a criterion offers a decision which is not socially optimal and which, given that the firm can stay in business, does not maximise long-run profits for the firm. But maximum profit in the long run for the firm requires as a necessary condition that the firm stays in business. The firm may not make a bet according to the odds because a failure would bankrupt it.

An example illustrates the point. Assume for simplicity that there is a fixed level of inputs per acre and that this fixed level offers the profits shown in Table 8–3, depending on the weather. The farmer can choose crop A or crop B or some combination of both. If the season is poor, crop A is better; if the season is good, crop B ought to be grown. According to the minimax criterion the farmer devotes all his land to A, and over a long period of time he can expect an average profit of 7·5 per acre if good and poor years are equally likely. But if the farmer knows that good seasons occur in five years out of ten, he may try to maximise the mathematical expectation of his decision. The expectation of A is 7·5 per acre per year and of B 10·0 per acre per year. The farmer therefore chooses B, and he thus earns more on average than if he had used the minimax criterion. There exists an incentive for firms to estimate the probability of a poor season.

There also exist other decision-making criteria for this situation. Isard (1969: 116-59) discusses these in detail, and they have been mentioned in Chapter 5. Cowling and Perkins (1963) analysed the decisions of English farmers to use different varieties of sugar beet in the period 1956-60. They compared the actual decisions with those predicted by the Laplace (maximise expectations with equal probabilities assigned to each outcome), maximin, maximin regret, maximax, and Hurwicz criteria. Although the data did suffer some deficiencies, Cowling and Perkins concluded that the Laplace criterion was the most accurate predictor of decisions and that the maximin criterion was not accurate. This evidence suggests that some farmers do attempt to estimate probabilities, even if only simply.

But Cowling and Perkins did not explicitly consider the ability of firms to withstand poor results. Similarly, the ability of a firm to withstand a poor year while growing B has been omitted from the calculations made on Table 8–3. Farms are typically small firms, without the capital reserves necessary to weather a series of losses. If it does not have the reserves to carry a poor season while growing B, the firm may go bankrupt, and is not then maximising its long-run profits.

Suppose that a firm can withstand only a fixed number of losses. Let this number of losses be $(s-1)$: then the sth loss bankrupts the firm. Assume that the probability of a good year is p and of a poor year is q ($q = 1-p$). The firm goes bankrupt in the nth year if $(s-1)$ losses occur in the previous $(n-1)$ years and one loss occurs in the nth year. Now the probability of a given arrangement of $(s-1)$ losses in $(n-1)$ years is

$$q^{s-1} \cdot p^{n-s}.$$

But there are $\binom{n-1}{s-1}$ such arrangements, and so the probability of $(s-1)$ losses in $(n-1)$ years is

$$\binom{n-1}{s-1} q^{s-1} \cdot p^{n-s}.$$

Finally, the probability of a loss in the nth year is q. Hence the probability that a firm which can withstand $(s-1)$ losses goes bankrupt on the nth year after a production decision is made is given by:

$$(8\text{–}6) \qquad \Pr = \binom{n-1}{s-1} q^{s} \cdot p^{n-s}.$$

The expectation of a decision is the sum over n years of the products of the probability of going bankrupt in any one year and the value to the firm of its decision if it does become bankrupt in that year. If it falls bankrupt in year n,

197

the firm has made s losses (each worth a) and $(n-s)$ profits (each worth b). Consequently the expected value of a decision is

$$(8\text{-}7) \qquad E = \sum_{n=s} q^s p^{n-s} \binom{n-1}{s-1} [(n-s) b - sa].$$

This series is summed over the relevant time period for the firm. If the time horizon for summation is infinite, the series has the value

$$(8\text{-}8) \qquad E = \frac{bps}{1-p} - sa.$$

Normally, though, it is unreasonable to suppose that firms decide with respect to infinite time horizons, and so the series is assumed to be finite. In this case, an adjustment has to be made to equation (8-7) in computing E. At the end of r years (r is the firm's time horizon), the firm may not be bankrupt; thus part of the expected value of a decision is the sum of the products of the probabilities of making 1, 2, . . . , $(s-1)$ losses and the values of these events. For a firm which is making a decision with respect to a finite time period, the expectation of a decision is given by:

$$(8\text{-}9) \qquad E' = \sum_{n=s}^{r} q^s p^{n-s} \binom{n-1}{s-1} [(n-s)d - sa] +$$

$$\sum_{t=1}^{s} q^{s-t} \cdot p^{n-s+t} \binom{n+t}{s-t} [(n-s+t)b - (s-t)a].$$

Alternatively, a firm's planning horizon may be limited, not by an abrupt cut-off point, but by a gradual discounting of future income streams. Thus, in this year the value of income I is assumed to be I; the same income in the following year is worth now only $I(1+j)^{-1}$, where j is the rate at which the future is discounted $(0 \leqslant j \leqslant 1)$; income I in the third year is now worth only $I(1+j)^{-2}$; and so on. Under this assumption the expectation of a firm's decision is

$$(8\text{-}10) \qquad E'' = \sum_{n=s} q^s p^{n-s} \binom{n-1}{s-1} [(n-s)b - sa](1+j)^{1-n}.$$

Equation (8-10) is conceptually neater than (8-9), but is more difficult to work with empirically; unfortunately neither equation (8-9) nor equation (8-10) has a simple mathematical expression for its finite sum. This, together with discontinuities in the functions, implies that deductions from the equations about allocation are most easily made with the aid of computed numerical results.

Equation (8-9) has been applied to the data in Table 8-3. Figure 8-1 results. This figure shows the expected values of different decisions as the level of reserves held by the firm varies. Calculations have been made for six of the possible decisions: to grow only crop A, to plant 80, 60, 40, 20 per cent of the land to A, and to raise only crop B. The expected profits over ten years have been calculated. If the farmer plants all or 80 per cent of his land to A, he can

Figure 8–1: **Graph to show expectation of different decisions (how much input to allocate to crop *A*) under various sizes of reserves**

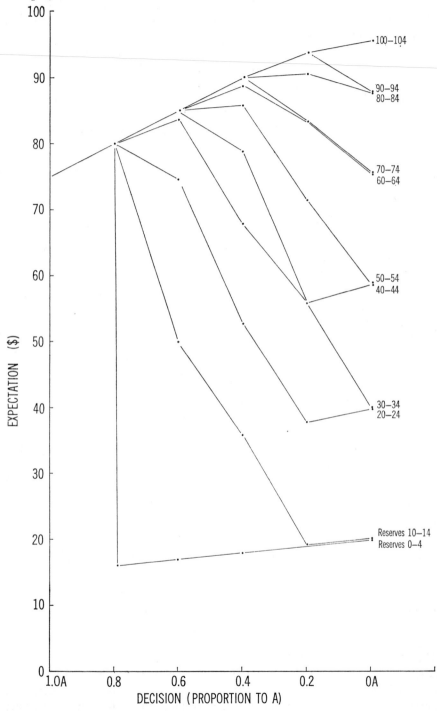

never make a loss, and so over ten years his profits are 75 units and 80 units per acre respectively. For the other alternatives, the value of a decision depends on the reserves with which the farmer can meet losses. As these reserves increase, the decisions all become more valuable. This is one of the most obvious effects of uncertainty: when reserves are low and the probability of bankruptcy relatively high, decisions made by firms are of low expected value. But as firms hold larger and larger reserves, the value of production decisions increases.

The figure shows another important result, however. As the level of reserves held by the firm changes, so the most profitable decision changes. If reserves are between 0 and 24 units, the best decision is to plant 80 per cent of the land to A and 20 per cent to B, which offers an expectation of 80 units per acre. For reserves of 25-49 units, the best choice is to plant 60 per cent of the land to A; 40 per cent of A is optimal when reserves are 50-74 units, and 20 per cent of A when reserves are 75-99 units; while if the firm's reserves are 100 units or more, the firm chooses best to grow only crop B. Thus, if reserves are very low, the firm's optimal decision is similar to (though not quite as conservative as) the minimax decision, but at high levels of reserves, the best decision is that suggested by the simple expectation criterion.

In reality, firms may be unable to estimate very closely the probabilities associated with particular events. Consequently they must either be more conservative in their choices than Fig. 8–1 suggests or they must be conservative in their estimates of these probabilities. But the general conclusion is clear. The larger the reserves which a firm can command in relation to the probability and the size of losses, the more likely that firm is to use the simple expectations approach to decision taking. When reserves are small in relation to probable losses, the firm maximises its long-run profits by staying in business—that is, by using the minimax criterion.

Therefore, provided that the size of reserves held by a firm is not related to location, the likelihood of minimax decision taking increases as the coefficient of variability of the production function rises. But the minimax decision is less close to the socially optimal decision than is the simple maximised expectation decision. It follows that production patterns are less optimal (from society's point of view) and yield lower average incomes per acre in areas where uncertainty (the coefficient of variability) is high than where uncertainty is low. Imposing this deduction on the earlier spatial uncertainty pattern yields the conclusion that production patterns are more nearly socially optimal and give higher production per acre near the market than at distances from the market. As distance from market increases, so the productivity of production patterns falls, for those patterns tend more and more to the conservative extreme.

The Scale of the Firm
A similar model, based also on the binomial theorem, may be used to analyse the problem of scale when firms are uncertain. As firms become larger, their possible losses also become larger; if they remain too small, their earnings are

Table 8–4: **Returns as a function of investment and weather**

Capital investment	10	20	30	50	100
Return (good year)	10	20	30	50	100
Return (poor year)	−1	−2	−3	−5	−10
Expected return p.a. as % of capital	45%	45%	45%	45%	45%

Note: Good and bad years are assumed equiprobable.

small. A firm, in deciding how large to become, must balance these opposing tendencies. The following model examines the impact of uncertainty on the optimum size of the firm, and analyses the manner in which optimum sizes vary with location.

When deciding on its scale of operations, a firm first finds the optimum combination of goods and the optimum techniques of production at each output level. Suppose that, having done this, the firm considers that Table 8–4 holds. The firm may invest varying amounts of capital. The returns in any year are a function of the size of the investment and of the type of year (good or bad). If good and bad years are equiprobable and the firm does not go bankrupt, the expected return on the investment over a period of years is not related to the size of the investment. The odds of success remain the same, irrespective of scale. Normally, though, a firm has limited reserves and so may possibly become bankrupt. Such limited reserves pose a limit to the size of the firm.

Given limited reserves, the expectation to the firm at each scale may be calculated from equations (8–8), (8–9), or (8–10), depending on the assumptions. Since the more useful series (8–9) and (8–10) do not appear to have simple sums, the analysis is conducted with the aid of computed examples. Let us suppose that the firm has reserves of ten units in addition to its capital investment. If it invests ten, a poor year yields −1; consequently ten poor years are necessary to bankrupt the firm. Similarly, five poor years bankrupt the firm if it invests twenty units of capital. From these data may be calculated the optimum size of the firm, given reserves of ten units. Equation (8–10) has been used.

Figure 8–2 illustrates the results of these calculations for several levels of capital investment. The firm maximises its expected return over a ten-year period by investing slightly less than thirty units of capital (ten of which units are held as reserves). Smaller and larger firms offer lower returns per unit invested over the ten-year period than firms which invest thirty units.

This analysis has assumed that firms have capital to invest but only a fixed level of reserves to sustain them against losses. More likely is the situation where firms have a fixed amount of capital (the limit which they can borrow from uncertain lenders), and require the optimum allocation of this capital to the two uses—reserves and plant investment. This allocation may be readily calculated from these data. Curves of the form of Fig. 8–3 are obtained. At first, with large reserves, a firm is too cautious; as plant investment increases, so output increases and so does the probability of bankruptcy. To the left of the horizontal

201

Figure 8–2: **Rate of earnings on capital as a function of the size of investment, assuming that Table 8–4 holds. (Reserves are fixed at ten units.)**

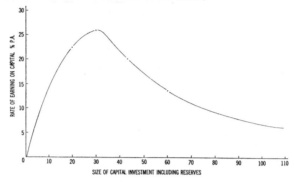

Figure 8–3: **Returns as a function of the allocation of capital to reserves, if Table 8–4 holds**

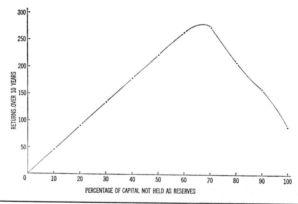

axis, output increases faster than the probability of bankruptcy; at the right, the probability of failure increases faster than output. The optimum allocation is clearly defined: the firm should invest two-thirds of its capital in plant and hold one-third in reserves. At the optimum allocation of capital to reserves, all firms, no matter what their size, make the same expected return on capital investment: a return of 28·75 per cent. Thus when firms are able to vary the amount which they hold in reserves, firm size has no effect on the rate of earning on capital if a table such as 8–4 holds.

But for our purposes the usefulness of the model lies in examining the effect of increasing uncertainty on the optimum size of the plant. Uncertainty is defined as the coefficient of variation of outcomes: it consequently increases as the mean of the outcomes falls (and the range of variation remains constant). As firms locate further from the market average returns fall because of increasing trans- port costs. Assume that the rate of investment falls in the same way as do returns

Figure 8–4: **Relationship between expected earnings on capital as a function of reserves and ratio of earnings in good and bad years**

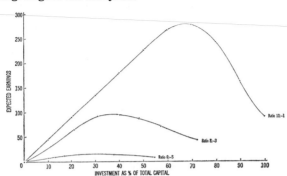

in a good year: when the season is good, firms everywhere earn 100 per cent on their total capital. With increasing distance from the market, returns in a good and a bad year fall at the same rate as capital investment falls. Returns in a good year as a proportion of the capital invested are not affected by location; by such an assumption, influences other than uncertainty are excluded from the analysis.

Figure 8–4 shows how earnings and the optimum allocation of capital to reserves and 'productive' investment vary with distance from the market. This evidence yields important conclusions about the effects of uncertainty on location patterns.

First, as the coefficient of variation of returns rises, so the optimum allocation to 'productive' investment becomes smaller. Where the ratio of returns in a good year to returns in a bad year is 10:−1, the optimum allocation of capital is 33 per cent to reserves; when the ratio is 8:−3, firms do best to allocate 65 per cent to reserves; and when the ratio of returns is 6:−5, 80 per cent of capital is held in reserves at the optimum allocation. Thus, as firms locate further from the market, so a greater proportion of their capital is held in reserve. Even though uncertainty may not influence financial size in this model, it does reduce the physical size of plants. As distance from the market increases, plant size falls, because a rising proportion of investment is held in reserve.

The figure indicates, secondly, that as uncertainty rises, the optimum investment becomes less valuable. The best sized firm can expect to earn 28·75 per cent on capital in the most certain point, but this falls to 9·50 per cent and 1·85 per cent in the more uncertain locations. Even though capital is not perfectly mobile over space, it is clear that capital which is formed at locations distant from the market has a strong incentive to shift to central market locations. Since, given similar opportunities, earning rates fall with distance, rates of investment in uncertain, distant parts of the market must be lower than investment rates near the market.

203

In Chapter 5 we argued that uncertainty limits firm size. Returns to management diminish as a consequence of imperfect decisions and the misdirection of resources relative to price and production outcomes. As possible losses become greater, people are usually less willing to expose themselves to the chance of such losses. Now, a firm, in setting up a business, borrows capital (this capital may, of course, be borrowed from the person setting up the firm). As uncertainty rises, the risk of losing large loans rises too, and so increasingly large rates of interest are necessary to obtain loans; on the other hand, as uncertainty rises the expected rate of return on capital falls (as the model has just shown). Therefore firms can borrow decreasing amounts of capital with increases in uncertainty: firm size is negatively associated with uncertainty. The firm, in using its loan, allocates funds to plant investment and reserves—as uncertainty rises, the proportion of total capital which is used as reserves rises too. Plants away from the market are smaller than plants nearer the market both because firms are smaller and because reserves absorb a larger proportion of total capital. In addition, more distant firms earn less on their capital than central firms. Therefore as distance from the market increases, rising uncertainty forces firms to become smaller and also, because of lower returns, fewer: economic activity tends to concentrate at the centre of its market.

Grayson (1960) has described some aspects of the uncertain drilling decisions made by oil and gas operators in the United States. Exploratory wells, located in areas not known to contain oil, have a low probability of success; development wells, on the other hand, are drilled in country already known to contain oil or gas, and thus have a national average probability of success of $p = 0.8$. The firms typically shared investment in wells as a means of reducing the risk of large losses. Grayson (1960: 190) points out that whereas the six small firms had on average in 1957 themselves invested only 52·5 per cent of the total cost of exploratory wells, they invested 57 per cent of the cost of development wells. A reduction of uncertainty is associated with a willingness to invest larger sums of money. The three large firms interviewed individually invested an average of 60 per cent of the cost of exploratory wells and 65 per cent of the cost of development wells. Larger firms, with greater reserves, are willing to invest more than small firms in ventures of similar riskiness.

Schwartzman (1963) has also investigated the relationship between uncertainty and firm size. He used as an index of uncertainty the ratio of markdowns in U.S. department stores to total sales of an industry (markdowns represent overestimates of demand). The index of firm size is the aggregate size of a fixed number of the leading firms in an industry. The ratio of markdowns to total sales in an industry was found to be highly correlated with firm size in that industry.

Supply Uncertainties

The preceding discussion reveals that a firm which provides a particular good for a given market has its location choices constrained by uncertainty. As it locates further from this market, its optimum size falls and its rate of earning on total capital is reduced. Consequently firms which have regional choice of location tend because of uncertainty to locate near the centre of their market. By so doing their investments become larger, safer, and more profitable.

But a firm considers not only the uncertainties of demand and ways of combating these; it also analyses supply uncertainties. Firms are motivated to secure adequate flows of the factors of production. We examine now the impact of uncertainties on the supply of capital, labour, and raw materials. The argument reinforces the conclusions already reached: development proceeds most easily and rapidly near the centre of the market.

One reason lies in the conditions affecting the supply, demand, and price of capital. Capital is unlikely to move long distances, especially when communications media are not well developed. In general, moving capital is costly—of time and money—and under the assumptions of this discussion, the risks involved rise as the distance over which capital is moved increases, because both buyers and sellers are largely ignorant of conditions at a distance from themselves. Risks caused by uncertainty severely limit the distance over which capital is moved, and much capital is therefore only available to local users.

However, the development of capital markets may be asymmetrical. First, the greater coefficient of variation of prices away from the market creates a higher objective uncertainty there. The level of capital flows away from the market is therefore lower than the level of flows towards the market. Secondly, the supply of capital is related at least in part to known demand: in the centre the greater demand for capital (by more and larger firms) creates a larger supply of capital than exists away from the market centre. Thirdly, once some firms have located at the centre, the costs of banking become lower in these areas of relatively dense settlement: financial information about the whole market is cheaper to obtain at the centre (the point of minimum transport and communications costs), a higher population density permits the establishment of larger banks, and the technical costs of arranging large loans are lower per unit lent than the unit costs of arranging small loans. Finally, even if capital were formed in relation to population, the centre, with its greater population, would form more capital than non-central locations, and a firm which requires a large initial capital investment may only be able to borrow such a sum at the centre. Therefore capital is more readily available at the centre than elsewhere in the system.

Even in a modern developed economy, in which banking and other lending institutions are nationally organised, the price of capital may vary significantly over space in response to the costs and uncertainties attendant upon lending. Thus Lösch (1959: 461-8) found that the interest rate in the United States in the 1930s rose as did distance from the eastern financial centres. Figure 8–5 illustrates one piece of evidence produced by Lösch. Lösch (1959: 463) also reports that in June 1928 the Federal Reserve Banks demanded the following rates of interest from their borrowers: in towns with a population more than 100,000, 5·3 per cent; of 15,000 to 100,000, 6·2 per cent; and of under 15,000,

Figure 8–5: **Increase in rate of interest with distance from New York, 1919-25.**
Source: Lösch (1959: 462).

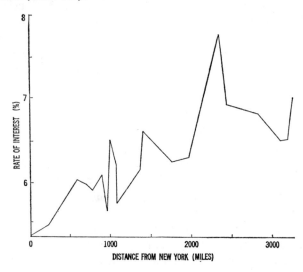

Figure 8–6: **Increase in the rate of interest with distance from Houston, Texas, 1936.**
Source: Lösch (1959: 465).

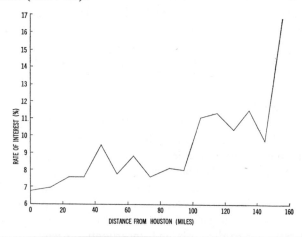

7·0 per cent. Figure 8–6 illustrates the increase of the rate of interest with distance from one financial centre. The assumption of uncertainty has been necessary to models of capital flow in the historic past: even in the middle and late nineteenth century, flows of capital were limited in the United States, both between regions and between industries. Davis (1966) estimates that despite substantial locational

206

advantages in the South, shortage of finance prevented major development of the cotton textile industry in that region until the 1870s. Similarly, the United Nations Department of Economic Affairs [UNDEA] (1949: 39) says of the period 1928-31 that:

after several years of uneasy international transactions and internal economic disturbances an epoch came to an end. The very motive for capital movements changed. Normally, such movements are determined in large measure by interest rates. When the security of investments, rather than their yield, became the decisive factor, however, capital showed a tendency to move from countries where interest rates were high to countries where they were low.

Uncertainty causes capital to be more attracted to the centre than it would be in a certain environment. This permits more rapid progress at the market centre than at other points in the system.

Secondly, firms in an uncertain economy are motivated by a desire to secure raw material supplies. Materials may be in irregular supply because the transport system is inefficient or because the sources of supply are unable to operate continuously. Such irregularities impose production and planning problems on managers and cause wastage through the failure to operate valuable capital equipment intensively. Firms may hold stocks of raw materials as a means of maintaining continuous production, but this reaction ties up capital. Furthermore, if the supplier is a local monopolist, the buying firms have only weak bargaining power: raw materials then command a higher price.

Several possible patterns of behaviour are implied. A firm may attempt to reduce uncertainty of supplies by buying the rights to operate the source or by securing the source itself. The firm has overcome the bargaining problem and has greater control over the production of raw material. Alternatively the firm may try to reduce irregularities and stocks by locating near the supplier. Thirdly, a firm may buy from several suppliers or sources. If price is the problem, there is now more competition to sell; if uncertain supply, the irregularities of each source may cancel out.

The first reaction implies no particular locational behaviour by the firm. However, this strategy is not useful by itself if the irregularities are due to the transport net. Location near the supplier enhances the attractiveness of raw materials as a site of production, but places the firm in a weak bargaining position and does not help to overcome the irregularities due to production methods at the source. (If the raw material is agricultural, the bargaining position of the firm does not deteriorate as a consequence of location at the source.) The third reaction implies a drastic reduction in the value of raw material locations and, given the likelihood that the centre is near the minimum transport cost point to the several sources of supply, increases the probability that firms locate at or near the origin. This solution is the most comprehensive means of overcoming supply problems and is therefore the most likely to occur theoretically. But the actual choice in a given situation depends on the specific problems of supply and on the other external relations of the firm.

207

Thirdly, firms may require that services are constantly available. Business services may be used only irregularly—though at unpredictable intervals of time—and may be needed at short notice. A firm may be too small to be able to employ a range of professional and repair services continuously, and so it relies on specialist firms to supply these services when required. Typically, however, such services must be supplied and used quickly (e.g. for the repair of specialised machinery). This entails close spatial contact with the service firm. In turn the specialist has to service several customers if the function is to be profitable. The external economies of uncertainty suggest location at the centre.

The firms which use external economies most are normally the small firms in the economy, those without an output large enough to justify the overhead costs of the specialised service. Large plants, which have a greater volume of output, may feel freer of dependence on the origin. However, not all firms are able to adjust by increasing their size: some industries are characterised by small plants. In any case, new firms are typically small for a time, and so they tend to locate at the centre. If the firm relocates elsewhere after it has grown larger and more independent, all the information (about suppliers, labour, markets, and credit facilities) which it has accumulated about the centre is wasted. Provided that some firms are conservative in relocating in order to preserve information, the attraction of the centre as a location of new, small plants promotes the overall growth of the region.

Not only firms, but also entire industries, locate in the established core during the period of their initial development. In a new and rapidly evolving industry, firms are uncertain about the market for the products of the industry and, perhaps more importantly, firms are uncertain about that part of the market which they may hope to capture. This characteristic high uncertainty of new industries is caused by rapid technological and stylistic development. Firms in the new industries are small, partly because the market is small and partly because capital and the market are minimising their risk of loss by fostering many small firms rather than a few large ones. (This, of course, is the minimax argument which is used to defend the theory of democracy.) In small firms research and development must be individual and highly selective: the firm is forced by limited time and resources to replace the more successful (but long-term) method of 'focusing' by that of 'scanning' to attain new concepts.[4] If the firm is unable to maintain at least the average rate of improvement, it stagnates and is eventually removed. Under conditions of a high rate of obsolescence of

[4] If a series of events is presented to a subject, three main methods of developing a true hypothesis about the common elements in these events may be used: (i) trial and error, unsystematic and relatively unsuccessful; (ii) scanning, in which a narrow hypothesis formed by hunch and altered to fit at least some of the known facts when shown to be wrong. The true hypothesis may be found earlier than if the thinker uses (iii) focusing, in which the whole of the first event becomes the hypothesis. This is maintained until the first contradictory event occurs, when the common elements in the hypothesis (the previous events) and the new event become the new hypothesis. The hypothesis becomes progressively closer to the truth and is certain to succeed, but it may take longer than scanning on the basis of hunches (see Thomson, 1959: 63-87).

ideas and only limited research, firms attempt to increase their security by locating so that they can copy an innovation quickly.

A firm which is sufficiently adaptable must fulfil several requirements. It must be in close physical contact with anyone who might innovate (because it has only a limited spatial information field) in order to acquire the new methods and copy them. Since all firms are potential innovators and copiers, all firms must locate together. Firms attempt to invest the minimum of capital in the business because the failure rate is high: heavy running costs are preferred to high overhead costs. Firms must be able to hire and fire labour at short notice. The location must be adequately developed for all firms to locate there and to adapt properly. These conditions almost dictate a location in the established centre.

Behaviour patterns may change later in the history of the industry. When technical change has become less rapid, the firms and the market are more confident, and uncertainty has fallen, firms begin to internalise some of the services formerly provided by the location. Cheapness of the factors of production and accessibility to regional markets may replace speed and ease of adjustment as the dominant locational requirements of the firms. Some therefore leave the centre; the proportion of firms which do depends on the relative importance of raw materials and markets accessibility and diseconomies of scale on the one hand, and of uncertainty on the other. However, even if uncertainty does diminish, some firms may remain at the centre—to fill quick orders, to exploit the information and contacts they have gained, to serve the local market, and because the costs of obtaining information about possible new sites may offset the gains from relocating. This analysis of the location of new firms and new industries is borne out in detail in some of the studies of New York made by the Regional Plan Association: Hall (1959), Lichtenberg (1960), and Vernon (1960).

These arguments about the effects of supply uncertainties on location may be partially summarised with the aid of a simple model based on queueing theory. Suppose that there are in a city several service firms and several customer firms. The customer firms call on the service firms for a variety of functions, such as professional services, repairs, and specialised components. Starting from an initial instant of time, $t = 0$, let n be the number of demands that has occurred up to time t, and let the probability that this number of demands is n be $p_n(t)$. Assume (i) that the probability $p_n(t)$ depends only on the time interval t, that is, the number of demands is homogeneous in time; (ii) that the probability that two firms make demands upon the service firms at exactly the same point in time is infinitesimal; and (iii) that in a very small time interval Δt, the probability that a demand will be made on any firm is $\lambda \Delta t$, where λ is the average rate at which demands are made. It is easy to show that the probability distribution $p_n(t)$ derived from these assumptions is the Poisson distribution:

$$(8\text{--}11) \qquad p_n(t) = \frac{(\lambda t)^n e^{-\lambda t}}{n!}.$$

Figure 8–7: **Effects of costs of waiting on firm size**

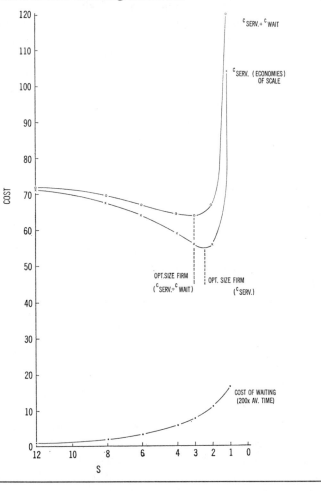

Again, we can show that the probability that two events are separated by a time interval φ, greater than a given interval θ, is

$$(8\text{–}12) \qquad \Pr(\varphi > \theta) = e^{-\lambda\theta} \, ,$$

an exponential distribution; see Feller (1957: 156-9).

Assume that the demands for service follow the Poisson distribution (8–11). When a firm demands some service from a supplier, the firm tries to find a supplier who is not occupied. If all suppliers are occupied, the firm joins a queue. When a supplier becomes free, the first customer in line is served by that supplier. There is no customer preference for suppliers. All suppliers have the same average rate of service μ, governed by the exponential distribution (8–12).

Table 8–5: **Raw material stocks,* by location**

Source of raw material†	Location of the firm			
	Sydney	Newcastle & Wollongong	Country towns	All locations
Local	12·03	10·85	8·18	11·15
Non-local	23·98	17·77	23·20	21·28
Total	14·62	14·56	17·89	

Effect of industry type	Local stock advantage‡ %
Food processing and wool products	331·2
Cement, glass, bricks and metal products	98·9
Remainder	171·6

* Values of stocks of raw materials are expressed as a percentage of each firm's total assets.

† Sources of raw material are defined as 'local' if more than 50% of materials are derived from sources located within 50 miles of the firm.

‡ The local stock advantage is measured by the value of stocks in firms with non-local materials as a percentage of stocks in firms with local materials.

Significance: The data are unweighted means for 135 firms. Significant at $p < 0.01$ are the effects of raw material location (which explains 18% of the variance in stock levels), type of industry (which explains 29% of the variance), and firms' location (explains 2% of the variance); the significant interaction between type of industry and source of raw material explains 41% of the variation in stock levels.

Let s equal the number of suppliers and $\bar{w}$ the average waiting time before a firm is served.

If we define R, the total rate of service, as

(8–13) $R = s\mu,$

then, for any given value of R, it can be shown that $\bar{w}$ falls as s increases. The lowest (cost of waiting) curve in Fig. 8–7 illustrates the shape of the relationship between $\bar{w}$ and s ($\bar{w}$ is expressed as a cost rather than as a length of time). Holding constant the total rate at which firms are supplied with their demands, the average waiting time before a firm is supplied falls as the number of supplier firms increases and as the average size of these firms decreases. A customer firm suffers less delays if there are many small firms than if there are a few large firms, even though the service capacity may be the same in both cases. In Fig. 8–7, the delay before supplies arrive is costed linearly, and this cost is added to a 'U' shaped relationship between cost of service and size of firm. This type of supply uncertainty suggests that service firms be smaller than their technical optima and that firms prefer locations with many small suppliers to locations with a few large suppliers.

Interviews with the managers of a sample of manufacturing firms in New South Wales provide some evidence with which to judge the impact of supply

Table 8–6: Stocks* of finished goods, by location

	Sales locality		
	Local†	Non-local	Total
Firm size			
Large‡	5·94	11·17	9·43
Small	11·69	17·34	13·26
Firm location			
Sydney	8·23	11·83	9·79
Newcastle and Wollongong	11·78	10·40	11·29
Country towns	12·40	16·87	14·75

* Stocks are measured as the value of the finished goods held by a firm as a percentage of its total assets.

† Markets are defined as local if more than 50% of the sales of the firm are made within 50 miles of its location.

‡ Large firms are defined as those with total assets of more than $A800,000.

Significance: Figures are unweighted means for 63 firms—sample size is reduced because many firms work to order only and so carry no stocks. Significant at $p < 0.05$ are the effects of sales locality (which explains 3% of the variance in stock levels), firms' location (which explains 6% of the variance), firm size (explains 5%), and the interactions between sales locality and firm size (5%), sales locality and industry (11%), firm location and industry (39%), and firm size and industry (6%). The main effect of type of industry is not significant.

uncertainties on the costs of production of a firm.[5] The most frequently mentioned disability of firms located in country towns was the irregular supply of goods and information to and from the firm. Table 8–5 reports the data gathered to relate raw material stocks to location.

The table demonstrates that the stocks of raw materials held by firms which are more than 50 miles from the sources of most of their raw materials are almost double the stocks held by firms which are adjacent to most materials. This effect is apparent in each of the three types of location and in most of the industry groups. Country firms with local raw materials hold lower stocks than Sydney firms which use local materials, possibly because a higher proportion of country than Sydney firms actually own their sources of local materials. The semi-metropolitan firms, in Newcastle and Wollongong, stock relatively small amounts of non-local materials, partly because these cities are well connected to the non-local sources in Sydney.

[5] The sample of firms is stratified between three types of location—Sydney (which has a population greater than 2 million), Newcastle and Wollongong (populations 250,000 and 100,000, respectively), and other country towns (populations less than 35,000)—from a population derived from trade and telephone directories. At least two firms were visited in each industry which operates in country towns, and interviews in the three large cities were arranged to duplicate this sample of industries. The managers of 228 firms, controlling 262 factories and employing 19·12% of the State industrial workforce were usefully interviewed.

Table 8–7: **Effects of variability and income on gross domestic saving***

Export variability†	Income		
	High	Low	Mean
High	20·3	14·5	16·2
Low	21·6	16·7	20·2
Mean	21·2	15·2	18·2

* Rates of gross domestic saving are expressed as a percentage of each country's gross domestic product. Income is defined as gross domestic product *per capita*, and the group of countries has been dichotomised on the basis of this variable.

† For variability of export incomes, see pp. 193-4.

Sources: (a) National income statistics: IMF (1958-60) for the years 1958-60, except for Belgium, Burma (1957-9), and Iraq (1954-6); for Indonesia, South Africa, and Thailand, income and population data from UNDESA (1958-60). (b) Variability: see Table 8–2. (c) Gross domestic saving as a percentage of gross domestic product: UNDESA (1950-9), except for Brazil, Mexico, and Panama (1950-8), Burma (1949/50-1958/59), Ghana (1955-9), Greece (1954-8), Honduras (1950-7), Israel (1952-8), and Portugal (1952-9).

Included are Australia, Austria, Belgium, Brazil, Burma, Canada, Ceylon, Chile, Colombia, Costa Rica, Denmark, Ecuador, Finland, France, Ghana, Greece, Guatemala, Honduras, Indonesia, Iraq, Israel, Italy, Japan, Mexico, Netherlands, New Zealand, Norway, Panama, Philippines, Portugal, Spain, South Africa, Sweden, Thailand, Turkey, U.A.R., United Kingdom, United States, Venezuela, West Germany.

Significance: Both main effects are significant at $p < 0.01$. Income explains 28% and variability 12% of the variation in gross domestic saving rates.

Industries vary widely in the degree to which firms near their raw materials hold lower stocks than firms which use non-local materials. The stocks of firms using non-local materials are three times those of firms with local materials in the food processing and wood products industries. These are industries in which the output of raw materials is highly variable, for physical rather than demand reasons. However, the locality of raw materials has no effect on the level of stocks held by firms in the cement, glass, brick, and metal products industries. In the remaining industries, stocks of materials in firms using non-local sources are between 55 and 83 per cent higher than in firms adjacent to their raw materials.

Data in Table 8–6 measure the impact of the location of a firm in relation to its markets upon the level of finished goods stocks of the firm. The table demonstrates that larger stocks of finished goods are held by firms which sell to non-local markets, by firms in country locations, and by small firms than by local market, metropolitan and large firms. These differences appear consistently throughout the tables of interactions, except that the locality of the market has no effect on the size of finished goods stocks held by semi-metropolitan firms. The nearness of the non-local Sydney market may account for this result.

Firms distant from their raw materials and their markets hold higher stocks than firms near their markets and materials. This conclusion indicates one way

213

in which costs created by uncertainty vary with the location of the firm. These costs may substantially affect the profitability of the firm. Stocks as a percentage of total assets are almost twice as high in firms distant from both materials and markets as in firms near both. Approximately 40 per cent of the total assets of country firms which have neither local materials nor local markets are in the form of stocks of raw materials and finished goods.

The second set of evidence about the processes whereby uncertainty affects location patterns is data on national rates of investment. Variability of export income induces variability of national income and therefore of demand. The extent to which national income varies depends on the variability of export incomes, the importance of export incomes in the national economy, and on the multiplier effect of changes in export income on national income. If the multiplier effect and the importance of export incomes are constant, more variable exports are associated with more variable national incomes. As variability increases, so does the number of changes in the profitability of investments. Therefore investors desire greater liquidity; and the accent of private investment shifts away from long-term fixed assets.

Table 8-7 contains some data on the rate of gross domestic saving as a percentage of gross national product. The rate of saving is associated with *per capita* income and with export variability: the rate of saving is high when incomes are high and when variability is low. These two factors account for 40 per cent of the differences between countries in the rate of gross domestic saving.

Integrating the Models
Each of the models introduced in this chapter has illustrated one facet of the effect of uncertainty on production decisions. Since uncertainty varies with location, part of the impact of uncertainty on location patterns has been demonstrated. This has been accomplished through the common analytical device of eliminating the effect of all other variables on location patterns and by ignoring the other models constructed here. It is now necessary to bring the models together.

The common unit of the models is a firm producing goods for a market area. The firm pays transport costs to the market, over which delivered prices are equalised. (Actually, it is sufficient that firms absorb some of the costs of transport to the market.) Then variability of prices rises as firms locate away from the minimum transport cost point. But, as variability increases, managers of plants (i) make increasingly conservative production choices, (ii) decide upon plants which are smaller in relation to the certainty optima, (iii) receive lower returns on their operations, (iv) run greater risks of bankruptcy and, consequently, (v) if location choice is available, prefer a near-central location to a peripheral site. Similarly, the discussion of uncertainty in the supply of the factors of production indicates a general tendency for uncertainty to be minimised by location at the centre of the market. A common consequence of the models is that development in off-central locations takes place more slowly than in central locations. The models are reinforcing rather than contradictory.

The integration of the models is most easily accomplished through the use of bid-rent functions (Alonso, 1966). For each land use a bid-rent function is derived, and land is assigned to the highest bidder under the appropriate market price for his goods. Alonso (1966: 52) derives the bid-rent function

(8–14) $p_f(t)$ [G_0,

which defines the price (p) bid by a firm (f) at each location (t) so that, when the quantity of land is optimised, the firm can achieve a constant level of profits (G_0). This is the bid-rent curve such that the firm is indifferent among locations.

The cost of inputs rises with distance from the market centre and, simultaneously, production decisions become more conservative, less profitable, and more risky. Hence for a firm to be indifferent among locations, the rent at these locations must vary sufficiently to offset returns differentials; in addition, the rent curve must slope steeply enough to permit profits to rise with distance from the market centre. This rate of increase of profits with distance must be sufficient to offset the increasing uncertainty, especially the rising risk of bankruptcy. That is, the firms must not achieve a constant level of profits, G_0; rather the indifference curve shows a constant level of $G_0 - G_u$ where G_u is the disutility of uncertainty. The bid price is defined so that the decreasing price of land offsets lower incomes and greater risks at the more peripheral parts of the market.

By adaptation from Alonso (1966: 42-52), it may be assumed for the firm that

(8–15) $G = V - C - R - U$,

where G is the utility of profits, V is sales, C is costs, R is land costs, and U is the disutility of uncertainty. Then

(8–16) $V = f(t)$,

where t is location, measured with respect to the centre of the market;

(8–17) $C = f(V, t, q)$,

where q is the size of site;

(8–18) $R = P(t)q$

$P(t)$ is the price of land at (t); and

(8–19) $U = f(t)$.

By profit maximising assumptions, the locational equilibrium is given by

(8–20) $0 = \dfrac{dV}{dt} - \dfrac{dC}{dV}\dfrac{dV}{dt} - \dfrac{dC}{dt} - \dfrac{dU}{dt} - q\dfrac{dP}{dt}$.

Since the model has excluded the effects of all variables other than uncertainty, the meaning of the terms in equation (8–20) may be closely defined. $\dfrac{dV}{dt}$ is the

215

Figure 8–8: **Relationship between costs, returns, profits, and location**

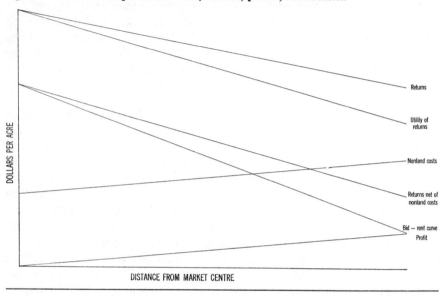

marginal revenue lost because of the reduction in firm size which accompanies the increase in uncertainty with distance; and $\dfrac{dC}{dt}$ is the marginal increase in operating costs caused by the rising price of inputs (caused, in turn, by uncertainty). The first four terms in equation (8–21) thus measure changes in the value of revenue and costs to the firm caused by uncertainty as it varies with location. Hence rental values in the region must decline from the market centre at a rate sufficient to offset the fall in the rate of profit due to uncertainty and to offset the increase in the disutility of uncertainty as distance increases. The equation becomes:

$$(8\text{–}22) \qquad 0 = G(u) - q\frac{dP}{dt},$$

where $G(u)$ is the marginal change with distance of the utility of profits caused by uncertainty.

Figure 8–8 displays the situation. Returns per acre and the utility of these returns fall as distance increases, for uncertainty rises. Nonland costs are caused to rise because of uncertainty. From these we derive for a firm the returns net of nonland costs. Since profits must exist and increase with distance from the centre (to compensate for rising uncertainty), the firm's bid-rent curve falls more steeply than the curve of returns net of nonland costs.

The diagram indicates that those firms for which uncertainty rises most rapidly with distance from the centre of the market have the steepest bid-rent curves. This uncertainty effect of distance has been related to two factors: uncertainty of sources of supply and changes in the coefficient of variation of prices at the point of production. The uncertainty in the sources of supply depends (i) for capital, on the coefficient of variation of prices and the degree of ignorance of distant places (i.e. on the cost of transmitting information), (ii) for raw materials, on the irregularities in the transport net, and (iii) for external economies, on the size of the firm and on demand changes. Thus uncertainty about inputs is largely a function of price variations, costs and irregularities of transport and communication, size of firm, and demand changes. Uncertainty caused by the coefficient of variation of received prices depends on the cost of transporting goods to the market and on the variations in prices (i.e. on changes in demand). Therefore the uncertainty facing a firm is a function of the costs of transporting goods to the market (including the costs of stocks), the extent of demand variations for the goods made by the firm, and the size of the firm. The higher the costs of transport, the greater the demand variations and the smaller the firm, the greater the rate at which uncertainty increases with distance from the centre of the market, and so the steeper the bid-rent function of the firm.

The amount of land which a firm uses and requires varies with its location. Since output per acre declines towards the periphery and labour is less immobile than land, population density falls towards the periphery, if returns to labour are similar over space. On the other hand, differences between industries in their size of site affect their location patterns. Industries in which output per acre is high (such as manufacturing) display a less elastic demand for land inputs than do industries in which large land inputs are necessary, because, *ceteris paribus*, such inputs contribute but little to variations in the total costs of firms which use little land. In any given industry, then, the size of the land input increases with distance from the market (for land is becoming relatively cheaper), while between industries, those industries that use little land are prepared to pay a higher price for that land than are industries which use more land. Land input per firm is smaller at the centre of the market than at the periphery.

The equilibrium location of the firm is derived in Fig. 8–9. The firm locates at the point at which $P(t)$, the price structure of the regional land market, is tangent with the firm's bid-rent curve. If the firm's bid-rent curve is always lower than $P(t)$, the firm cannot make normal profits: it therefore goes out of business. Figure 8–9 demonstrates that those firms characterised by steeper bid-rent curves locate nearer the market than those firms with less steep bid-rent curves. Therefore industries in which the costs of transporting the product to the market are high, in which demand variations are high and in which firms are small, locate nearer the centre of the market than those industries in which transport costs are low, demand variations slight, and in which firms are large.

Despite the fact that the analysis has introduced only one independent variable, uncertainty, a high degree of spatial specialisation is evident. By and large, uncertainty, both of supply and of demand, is an increasing function of distance from the centre of the market. A first consequence of this is that production patterns become more conservative as distance from the market rises: hence

217

Figure 8-9: **Equilibrium location for the firm**

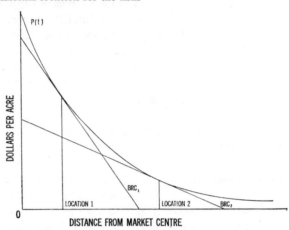

incomes per acre fall with distance from the centre. Therefore there exists a gradient of population density (if labour is mobile): densities are highest at the centre of the market and decline towards the periphery of the region. A second consequence of the pattern of uncertainty is that firms in any given industry are smaller (in terms of capital invested) on the periphery than near the market centre. If large scale yields economies, peripheral firms therefore produce at higher costs than central firms. A similar conclusion is derived from uncertainties in sources of supply. Therefore, even if the peripheral producers can survive in the regional economy, they remain at a disadvantage when compared with more central firms. A third deduction is that the optimally sized firms are more prone to bankruptcy in peripheral than in central location. The risk of failure is higher, and, to compensate for this, profit rates must rise with distance from the centre.

Uncertainty, Location, and Growth
In this section are summarised two sets of evidence relating uncertainty and location patterns. In the first, a static picture is presented of the relationship between uncertainty and location patterns in Australia; the second portion of evidence relates uncertainty to rates of national growth.

Data have been obtained for Australian industries to measure some of the factors which are associated with uncertainty. The size of factories in an industry is measured by the average number of employees per plant, weighted by the proportion of factories which are located in metropolitan areas. The variability of the output of firms is measured by the standard deviation of the percentage year-to-year changes in the value of output, and by an alternative statistic, the standard deviation of the percentage year-to-year changes in the value of output after percentage year-to-year changes in the total economy have been subtracted.

Three indices of technical change are included; they are the percentage increase in the value of production per employee, the percentage decrease in the value of salaries and wages as a percentage of the value of production, and percentage change in the average number of persons per factory, all over the period 1951 to 1961. Data for all these indices are from Commonwealth Bureau of Census and Statistics (1952-63).[6]

Industries are classified on the basis of the number of uncertainty variables in which they exhibit a value greater than the median for all industries. The seven classes thus derived are then generalised into the groups: 0-1, 2, 3, 4, 5-6 high uncertainty variables. The total employment of each town in each uncertainty class is calculated. From these data is computed an index which measures the extent to which the labour force in the town is employed in the uncertain industries. The index is the area beneath the cumulative percentage employment curve. This uncertainty index varies between the values of zero and eight, the lower end of the scale representing employment in the uncertain industries.

Table 8–8 presents the mean effects of each independent variable upon the extent to which industries in towns are uncertain. The table reveals conclusive evidence about the statistical effect of each factor in the analysis; each of the three independent variables is significant at the 0·1 per cent level and together they explain 45 per cent of the variation in the data. The effects are consistently in the direction predicted by the hypothesis. The larger a town is, the closer it is to the metropolis, and the more populous the State in which it is located, the more uncertain tends to be the employment within that town. Though there are a number of minor exceptions to these rules, the results of this analysis are generally consistent with the hypothesis.

Secondly, we examine the empirical relationship between uncertainty (or, more strictly, income variability) and rates of growth. The analysis predicts that uncertainty should be negatively associated with rates of growth of *per capita* income. The data to test this hypothesis are contained in Table 8–9.

Countries in which exports form a high proportion of the national income, in which the variability of exports is high, and which export mainly primary

---

[6] The finest areal classification of the location of industry is provided by the 1961 Census of Population. This census records the number of persons working in each industry in each town over 1000 persons. However, all the data from which the indices which specify industry types are constructed are derived from factory production statistics. Unfortunately, the two sources use different classifications of industries: in matching the two classifications, some industry codes have to be omitted because they are not obviously defined in one or other of the sources, and some industry codes have to be combined. The analyses in this report are therefore based on only 107 manufacturing industry codes and include 85% of the mainland States' factory labour force.

Linge (1965) suggested that the boundaries of some metropolitan areas are too limited. As the nearest practical approximation to Linge's suggestions, the Sydney metropolitan area is taken to include the entire County of Cumberland; Brisbane includes Ipswich; Elizabeth and Salisbury are added to Adelaide; and the Perth metropolitan area includes the Swan division. Melbourne is not regarded as underbounded.

Table 8–8: **Mean effects of town size, distance from metropolis, and state on uncertainty bearing in towns**

Town class limits (manufacturing population)	Number of towns	Town size group	Distance from metropolis ≤ 100m. N.S.W. & Vic.	Distance from metropolis ≤ 100m. S.A., W.A. & Qld	Distance from metropolis > 100m. N.S.W. & Vic.	Distance from metropolis > 100m. S.A., W.A. & Qld	Mean for town size group
> 24,640	7	A	2·21	3·65			2·83
2910–14,140	12	B	2·93	4·80		3·38	3·25
600–2280	42	C	3·60	4·28	3·96	4·25	4·02
315–550	36	D	3·83	4·34	4·09	4·60	4·23
90–275	18	E	3·76	5·11	4·38	4·66	4·43
		Mean	3·67		4·21		

Mean effect of State: 3·78 (N.S.W. & Vic.); 4·31 (S.A., W.A. & Qld).

Notes: (a) Only towns of population greater than 5000 in 1961 are included in this analysis. (b) The town classification procedure maximised the significance of an analysis of variance of a five-group classification, using the logarithm of manufacturing population as variable.

Significance: All main effects significant at $p < 0.01$. Town size explains 22%, distance explains 12%, and States explain 12% of the variation between towns in the uncertainty index.

Table 8–9: **Factors determining rates of growth of** *per capita* **income***

Exports as % of national income:

Type of export†	High Export High	High Export Low	Low Variability High	Low Variability Low	Mean effect of type of export
Manufactures	2·83	3·50	3·87	3·62	3·64
Minerals and beverages	2·50	2·17	1·62	2·17	2·13
Food	1·20	2·50	1·92	3·17	2·23
Mean effect of variability	High 2·43		Low 3·02		
Mean effect of size of export sector	2·34		3·08		

* Rates of growth of *per capita* incomes for 1951–61 are computed by compound interest formula from data in IMF (1951–61). Value of exports as a proportion of gross domestic product from data in IMF (1951–61).

† Sources of export commodities and variability of export incomes as for Table 8–2.

Included are all countries listed on p. 193, except Algeria, former Central African Federation, Cyprus, Jamaica, Morocco, and Trinidad and Tobago (for which data are lacking).

Significance: All main effects are significant at $p < 0.05$.

products, are also those countries which display low rates of growth of *per capita* income. The effect of commodities is significant at the 5 per cent level; the effects of the size of the export sector and of its variability are significant at the 1 per cent level. Size of exports explains 14 per cent, export variability explains 11 per cent, and type of commodity exported explains 14 per cent of the variance in rates of growth.

The rates of growth of exporters of manufactured goods are higher than those of countries which export primary products, as might be expected from the differing income elasticities of demand for these goods. Countries in which the export sector is large in relation to the size of the economy exhibit relatively low rates of growth, presumably because the larger the export sector, the greater the extent to which variations in the value of exports induce fluctuations in the rest of the economy, for a given multiplier effect. (This conclusion does not hold in the minerals and beverages group.) Instability of exports is associated with low growth rates, an association which is most marked among the food exporters but which is not true of the large exporters of minerals and beverages nor of the small exporters of manufactured goods.

These data are broadly compatible with the relationships predicted by the theory. Instability and growth are negatively associated, and instability is positively associated with distance from market. The combination of these propositions generates a pattern of growth (and therefore, of activity at a point in time). Most activity is concentrated in a few rapidly growing nations, which are relatively close to their markets.

9   Innovations, Learning, and Location

Both innovation and learning processes are necessary components of a theory of location under uncertainty. These processes and the associated inter-personal flows of information provide one of the main dynamics of economic development, and influence the location of that development. If people in a system are uncertain, scope exists for them to improve their performance within that system. By convention, if this improvement takes the form of new ideas, new organisations, new production processes, or new products, it is called an innovation, whereas if the improvement is derived from greater familiarity with existing techniques over a period of time, learning is said to occur. (Of course, in most actual improvements, both innovation and learning occur together.) Both processes have been analysed spatially; here they are incorporated systematically within a developing theory of location. To do this the non-spatial aspects of innovation are analysed first, and an attempt is then made to construct models of aspects of the diffusion of innovation through a spatial system. Following this, learning processes are invoked to draw long-term spatial conclusions from the innovation models.

Non-Spatial Characteristics of Innovation Diffusion
Sociologists have attained a qualitative understanding of some of the processes of diffusion and some of the factors which affect these processes. The prime concern in their research has been with relationships between (i) an innovation or a collection of innovations and (ii) an adopter, emphasising in the study not only his personal and situational traits, which include (iii) his perception of the characteristics of the innovations, but also (iv) the processes by which the innovation spreads and (v) the functions of communication media and channels in the processes (Jones, 1967). Thus the components of diffusion studies are an innovation, a source of information, an adopter, a structure for transmitting information, a culture and a time span within which the innovation diffuses (Coughenour, 1968). Most, though not all, of the work has been conducted on the diffusion of new practices among farmers, and most of it has taken place in the United States.

Figure 9–1: **Information sources used by farmers at different stages in their adoption process.**
Source: Beal and Rogers (1960: 19).

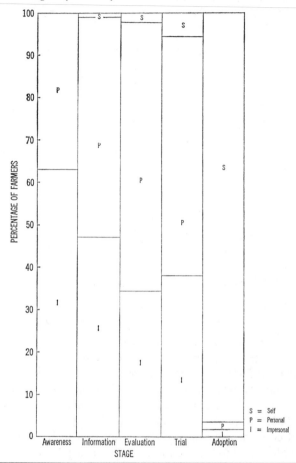

Since the results of these studies are reviewed solely in order to obtain process hypotheses to translate into spatial effects, and since the spatial model assumes a homogeneous population, the effect of the type of innovation upon the rate of its adoption (see Kivlin, 1960) is ignored. Nor do we analyse the personal characteristics of innovators (which have been examined by Chaparro, 1955, and Marsh and Coleman, 1955). Similarly, the fact that different types of community exhibit different adoption rates (Coughenour, 1964; Young and Coleman, 1959; Coughenour and Patel, 1962) is not incorporated in this study.

Typically, sociologists have visualised farmers as passing through a five-stage adoption process (Bohlen, 1968), although it is recognised that any one individual may not pass through all of the stages. The first stage is called 'awareness'; it

223

Ω

Figure 9–2: **Cumulative number of farmers at the awareness stage of 2,4-D weed spray adoption, Iowa, 1944-55.**

Source: Beal and Rogers (1960: 8).

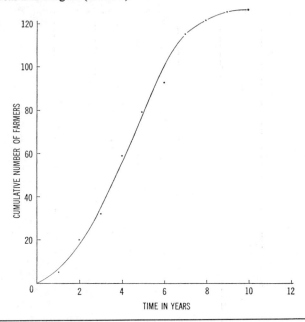

occurs when a farmer first hears of an innovation. In the second stage, the 'information' stage, the farmer gathers data about the new phenomenon and about its relationships with other portions of his farm business. The 'evaluation' stage sees the farmer assessing his data and deciding whether or not to apply the innovation on his farm. The phenomenon is actually applied on the farm in the fourth, 'trial', stage; the farmer remains in this stage until he 'adopts'—that is, until he has enough experience of the innovation to have developed habitual behaviour with respect to the phenomenon. As Beal and Rogers (1960) point out, farmers vary widely in the length of time they require to pass through these five stages: the adoption period (between awareness and adoption) for two farm practices which diffused through Iowa after World War II varied between one and ten years, with means of 1·5 and 2·1 years. In Mysore, Misra (1968: 59) found that 60 per cent of the farmers in one community only adopted an improved variety of *ragi* three or more years after they first became aware of the innovation.

Because of its spatial implications, a vital portion of diffusion research has been the identification of the communication processes, the means by which the farmers obtain the data necessary to decide to pass from one adoption stage to another. The information sources may be classified as being either personal (i.e. involving face-to-face contact with other farmers, extension officers, or commercial agents) or impersonal (based on mass communication media such as radio,

224

Figure 9–3: **Cumulative percentage of corn acreage in hybrid corn in three American States, 1934-58.**
Source: U.S. Department of Agriculture, *Agricultural Statistics*, 1961.

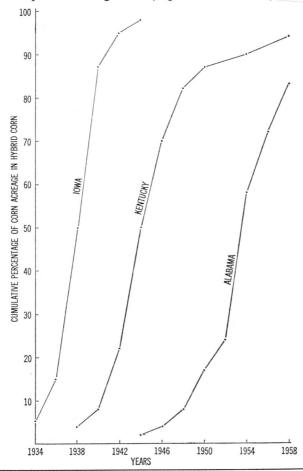

TV, newspapers and farmers' magazines). An additional, less important, source of information is the farmer's own experiments. Figure 9–1 illustrates which sources of information are important to farmers at the various stages in the adoption process. The most important sources of information that lead farmers to awareness of an innovation are impersonal sources: farmers typically first hear of an innovation through the mass media. Data sources after this, though, tend to be personal rather than impersonal, except at the adoption stage, when the most important information source is the trial of the innovation which the farmer has himself conducted. Most farmers must talk to some other people at some stage in the entire process.

A third aspect of importance is the rate at which the innovation is adopted in

225

the community as a whole. Figure 9–2, taken from Beal and Rogers's (1960) study of the diffusion of 2,4-D weed spray through an Iowa farm community, is typical of the results found in many studies. The logistic, or 'S' shaped curve of the total number of farmers who have passed a given stage is clear. And notice, too, that even in a small, relatively well-educated and prosperous community, it took eleven years before the spray was completely adopted. Figure 9–3 illustrates other data on the adoption of hybrid corn in some States of the U.S.A. Again, curves are typically 'S' shaped.

Work on the diffusion of innovations within manufacturing industry is more limited. Mansfield has analysed the diffusion of twelve innovations through the bituminous coal, iron and steel, brewing and railroad industries (1961, 1963a, 1963b). Unfortunately, problems of collecting data forced him to analyse only the larger firms in each industry; therefore the tail end of his adoption curves is probably missing. Mansfield discovered a curve of cumulative adoption which is more irregular than curves discovered in agricultural studies (possibly because he takes a smaller population) and which tends to be straight or exponential rather than 'S' shaped. The lack of the smaller firms in the industries may, if they are mostly in the tail, account for the fact that curves are not 'S' shaped. As in agricultural studies, Mansfield finds that most innovations are only slowly adopted; only in three innovations did all the major firms adopt within ten years. Unfortunately, Mansfield does not identify the communication sources used by his sample of firms. Because of the limited nature of this research and the paucity of some of the data, most of the models and equations in the remainder of the chapter are based upon the processes discovered in research on the diffusion of agricultural innovations.

Before examining spatial aspects of the diffusion process, it is necessary to relate the communication processes which have been identified to the curve of cumulative adoption by means of diffusion equations. These equations may then be used in models of spatial diffusion.

In developing a set of assumptions to describe the adoption curve, several different sets of assumptions may be made. At the very simplest level, suppose that, since adoption depends partly on being told by other farmers at least at some stage in the adoption process, the rate of adoption depends on the number of farmers who already know about the innovation. Thus in a short time period (dt), the change in the number who know (dk) is a function of the number who already know (k):

(9–1) $dk = ck\, dt$,

where c is a constant which measures the efficiency of communication. Integrating (9–1) with the assumption that $k = 1$ at $t = 0$ yields the equation

(9–2) $k = e^{ct}$.

This exponential curve increases indefinitely without bound; such a curve fits a process in which the potential for increase of k is unlimited, which is not compatible with the diffusion situation.

Figure 9–4: **Curve of equation (9–4)**

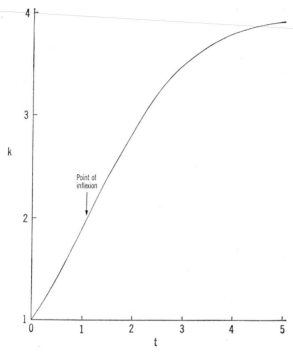

A more realistic assumption about the diffusion process is that the number who adopt the innovation (dk) in a time period (dt) depends not only on the number who already know (k), but also on the number who do not yet know ($N-k$). The justification for this assumption is that the fewer who know, the more people there remain to be convinced by those who know, and so the more likely it is that a knower meets a non-knower. The assumption implies the equation:

(9–3) $dk = ck(N-k)dt.$

The number, $k(N-k)$, is the total number of possible pairs of individuals, one of whom has adopted while the other has not yet adopted the innovation. By assuming that the change in the number of adopters depends on the total number of possible pairings, we are assuming that the population is mixing homogeneously: that is, that the probability of any one pair of individuals meeting is the same as that of any other pair meeting. There exist no cliques or subgroups in the society. The equation may be integrated to yield (if $k = 1$ at $t = 0$):

(9–4) $k = Ne^{Nct}/[N-1+e^{Nct}].$

The second derivative of equation (9–4) (i.e. the rate of acceleration of the number of knowers) is

227

Figure 9–5: **Curve of equation (9–10)**

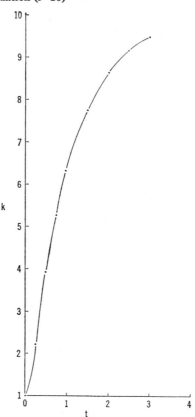

(9–5) $$\frac{d^2k}{dt^2} = c^2k(N-k)(N-2k),$$

which is positive for $k < \frac{N}{2}$, zero at $k = \frac{N}{2}$ and $k = N$, and negative for $\frac{N}{2} < k < N$. These points are reflected in the curve drawn in Fig. 9–4: the adoption process accelerates up to that point at which half the community is aware of the innovation. A comparison of Figs. 9–2 and 9–4 reveals that the 'S' shaped curve of 9–4 is quite a good approximation to the adoption curve of Fig. 9–2, though the actual point at which the adoption process ceases to accelerate is not always when 50 per cent of the population has reached that stage.

A similar equation to (9–3) is provided by Bailey (1957: 20-2). Bailey assumes a group of $(n+1)$ individuals, of whom x are susceptible to and y are infected by a disease. Bailey assumes that the spread of a simple epidemic may be approximated by

228

(9–6) $dx = -cxydt,$

where c is a constant. Adjust t so that $c = 1$.

The initial condition is that $x = n$ at $t = 0$; with this condition, (9–6) has the solution

(9–7) $x = \dfrac{n(n+1)}{n+e^{(n+1)t}}.$

Equations (9–1) and (9–3) have both assumed that all the information necessary to pass through a stage is provided by farmers who have already passed through that stage. But Fig. 9–1 shows that an important source of information, at least in the early stages in the adoption process, is the mass media. In examining the effect of mass media, we may assume that in a short period (dt), the number who are told (dk) depends on the number who do not yet know $(N-k)$:

(9–8) $dk = c(N-k)dt.$

The integral solution of this equation is

(9–9) $k = N-Ae^{-ct},$

which becomes, if $k = 0$ at $t = 0$:

(9–10) $k = N(1-e^{-ct}).$

The upward slope of this curve declines as k increases: thus equation (9–10) is represented by a curve such as that in Fig. 9–5.

While equation (9–10) is not obviously related to the adoption curve, the two equations (9–3) and (9–8) may be combined in an equation which assumes both constant source (impersonal) telling and non-constant source (personal) telling. Thus:

(9–11) $dk = [c(N-k)+c'k(N-k)]dt$

$\qquad\qquad = (c+c'k)(N-k)dt.$

The solution to this differential equation is

(9–12) $k = \dfrac{NAe^{(c+c'N)t}-c}{c'+Ae^{(c+c'N)t}},$

which becomes, if we assume that $k = 0$ at $t = 0$:

(9–13) $k = \dfrac{Nc(e^{(c+c'N)t}-1)}{Nc'+ce^{(c+c'N)t}}.$

Equation (9–13) describes the number of adopters in a system when there is a constant information source outside the system and when those who already have adopted also provide data to the non-adopters in the system. The first derivative of equation (9–13) is always positive: the number who have adopted is a monotonically increasing function of time. The second derivative (rate of acceleration),

229

Figure 9–6: **Effect of altering the parameters, c and c′, in equation (9–13) on the rate of adoption**

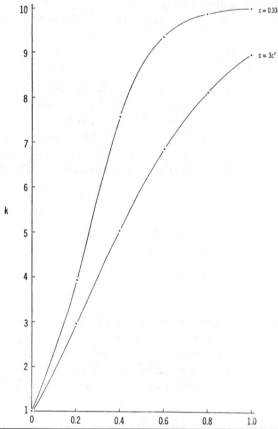

$$(9\text{–}14) \qquad \frac{d^2k}{dt^2} = (c + c'k)(N - k)(c'N - c - 2c'k),$$

is positive so long as

$$k < \frac{c'N - c}{2c'}.$$

Thus the rate of adoption increases until

$$k = \frac{c'N - c}{2c'},$$

while thereafter the rate of adoption diminishes. Figure 9–6 illustrates the effect of altering the parameters, *c* and *c′*, of equation (9–13) upon the rate at which the innovation is adopted. These parameters measure the relative importance of constant source and personal source media: as *c* and *c′* increase, so the rate of diffusion increases; as *c* increases relative to *c′*, so the importance of constant source information channels rises relative to personal telling within the system,

230

and so the diffusion process is more rapid than when c is relatively small.

All these equations represent extremely simple situations. Perhaps the easiest flaw to correct is that they all assume that the entire community eventually adopts the innovation and that the innovation once adopted is never rejected. Biologists have developed a set of models to describe the course of epidemics which recognise that once a disease has been identified in an individual, that person is taken out of contact from the rest of the community by death or isolation. Bailey (1957, 1967) describes such models. Sociologists have similarly developed models of the spread of rumours, which recognise that after a while people no longer tell others about that rumour, because of loss of interest or other factors; see Bartholomew (1967: 223-35). These models yield the important result that an epidemic will only occur if certain conditions are fulfilled: if a population of size n contains x susceptibles, y infectives, and z isolated people ($x+y+z = n$), and if in any time period (dt) the number of new infectives is $Bxydt$ and of new removals is $Cxydt$, then a small infection will cause an epidemic if N (the number of susceptibles when the epidemic begins) is greater than C/B.

But such models do not entirely apply to the diffusion of technical innovations, that is, innovations which are visible objects or methods of economic organisation. Thus there are no individuals who, after adopting the innovation, are isolated and play no further part in the diffusion process; people who have adopted play a continual role in spreading the innovation—first by telling others and then by example after they have ceased telling; and people who have rejected the innovation are not neutral, but by precept or propaganda actively affect the decisions made by the rest of the community. (Of course, the innovation may in fact be accepted by everyone before people start to reject it.) To model this general case, assume again that the population mixes homogeneously and that the innovation is adopted immediately a person becomes aware of it. A population of size N is divided into four categories of people: n adopters, m adopters who have rejected the innovation, l people who have never adopted and who have decided not to, and ($N-m-n-l$) who are uncommitted. Assume that those who have rejected the innovation or have decided not to adopt are never persuaded to change their minds. In any time period (dt), the committed rejectors ($m+l$) influence some of the uncommitted ($N-m-n-l$) to cause an increase in l of

(9–15) $dl = \gamma(m+l)(N-m-n-l)dt.$

In the same period, these ($m+l$) who have rejected the innovation persuade some of the n adopters to reject the innovation, and cause an increase in the m who have given up the innovation of

(9–16) $dm = \alpha(m+l)n \, dt.$

Thirdly, the n who have adopted persuade some of the ($N-m-n-l$) uncommitted to adopt, and lose those who have decided to reject the innovation; hence the change in n in a time period dt is:

(9–17) $dn = [\beta n(N-m-n-l) - \alpha n(m+l)]dt.$

231

Figure 9–7: **Adoption, defection, and disavowal curves for the equations (9–15), (9–16), and (9–17)**

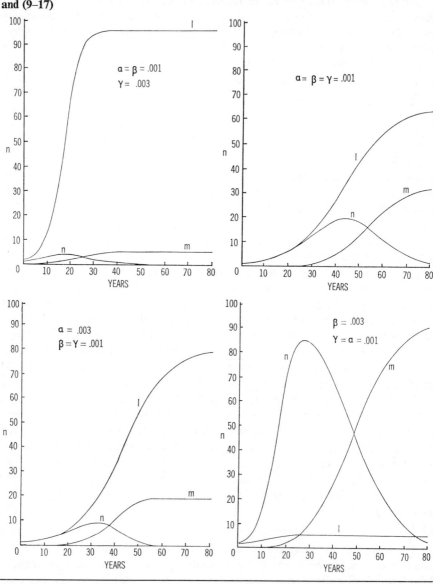

Figure 9–7 illustrates some of the curves computed from equations (9–15), (9–16), and (9–17). Each computation has assumed as initial conditions that $n = 1$ at $t = 1$, $m = 0$ at $t = 1$, and $l = 1$ at $t = 2$. Thus the defection process begins almost as soon as the adoption process. The curve of the total number of adopters at any one point in time is skewed to the right and tends eventually to

Figure 9–8: **Effects of varying the parameters of equations (9–15), (9–16), and (9–17) upon some measures of the diffusion process: upper left—total number who adopt the innovation at some time; upper right—maximum number of adopters at any one time; lower left—time at which the maximum number of adopters occurs; lower right—total time taken for the entire process.**

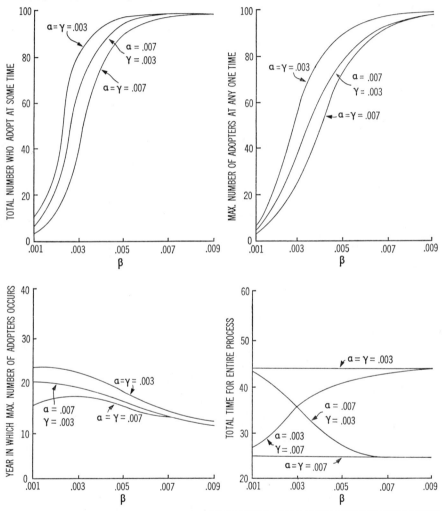

zero; as should be expected, this number, n, is larger at any moment the larger is β in relation to α and γ. Both the curve of defectors and that of those who have decided not to adopt are 'S' shaped, in form similar to that of a simple adoption process. The final number that decide not to adopt increases as α and γ increase in relation to β.

Figure 9–8 illustrates some other features of the relationship between the behaviour of the system and the values of the parameters. The curves have been drawn under the assumption that people do not start defecting until the tenth year. The relationship between the total number who adopt at some time or other and the parameter β is 'S' shaped, with α and γ having a negative effect on the total number of adopters. A similar relationship exists between the parameters and the maximum number who are in the adoption category at one time. This maximum number occurs earlier the higher are α, β, and γ, the relationship having the form of a reverse 'S'. The fourth graph illustrates the association between the time taken for all to defect or decide not to adopt (i.e. for the process to cease) and the parameters: when α is less than γ, β has a positive effect upon this length of time; β has no effect when α = γ; and the effect is negative when α < γ. A similar complex association exists between α, γ and the length of the process.

If defection does not begin until the diffusion process is complete, then the three equations may be reduced to two, for $\frac{dl}{dt}$ is always negative. The two equations are complementary, the first describing the growth of the innovation and the second, exactly similar in form, describing its decline. But apart from this simple case (which is the one normally described in studies of innovation diffusion), the relationship between the parameters and the diffusion process is not simple, and the complexity of this non-spatial model suggests that this system may not be very useful for analytic work on spatial diffusion processes.

Stochastic versions of birth-death diffusion models have also developed (see Bailey, 1957: 36-74, and Bartholomew, 1967: 204-60, for general discussions of such models). Characteristically, the continuous time models are difficult to solve, and for large populations their usefulness is limited. Hence, rather than discuss such models here, we present one probabilistic diffusion model which applies to situations where time may be thought of as discrete. Such a model might, for example, be applicable to diffusion of an innovation among farmers, who frequently can only adopt an innovation at discrete points of time: thus, a new seed can only effectively be adopted at yearly intervals, that is, just before planting. The model is related to the discrete time models of Greenwood (1935), Reed and Frost (Abbey, 1952), and Rapoport (1951), but has been adjusted to take into account the peculiarities of innovation diffusion. The simplifying assumption of homogeneous mixing is retained.

Assume that one person has adopted the innovation, and that he tells a constant number (m) of non-adopters in the first year. In the second year, these ($m+1$) knowers each tell m other people, but some of these other people may already have adopted the innovation; hence, in the second year, rather less than $m(m+1)$ people adopt. The process continues, with each adopter telling m people, some of whom already know, in each year, until all know. Such a situation may be represented by an urn model. Assume that the total number of potential innovators in the system is N, and that k know already. These k knowers each tell m people in any one generation. The total number told in a

Figure 9–9: **The effect of varying *m* and *l* upon the rate of adoption in equations (9–18) and (9–19)**

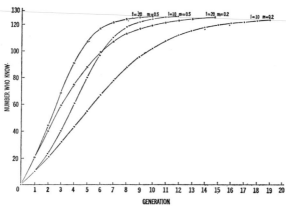

generation is thus *km*. Hence in order to find the probabilities that 1, 2, . . . , *N−k* are told for the first time in any one generation, we assume that *km* balls are drawn from an urn which contains *k* red balls (i.e. knowers) and *N−k* black balls (non-knowers). The probability that *r* are first told in one generation, given that *k* know already, is therefore:

$$(9\text{–}18) \qquad \Pr\{r;k\} = \binom{N-k}{r}\binom{k}{mk-r}\binom{N}{mk}^{-1}, (0 \leqslant r \leqslant N-k)$$
$$= 0 \qquad \qquad \text{(otherwise).}$$

Thus, given that *k* already know, the mean number told for the first time is the mean of this hypergeometric distribution, that is

$$mk(N-k)/N,$$

and the variance is

$$\frac{mk^2(N-k)}{N^2}\left\{1-\frac{mk-1}{N-1}\right\}.$$

Recursive computation of equation (9–18) yields an 'S' shape curve for the mean number told, similar in form to that of Fig. 9–4.

In order to make this stationary model more general, the influence of constant source telling from outside the system must be incorporated. Suppose that impersonal sources inform *l* persons in each generation: *l* balls are drawn from *N*, of which *k* are red (already know) and (*N−k*) are black. The probability of drawing *r* black balls is the probability that *r* people are told for the first time by a constant source in any generation:

$$(9\text{–}19) \qquad \Pr\{r_c; k\} = \binom{N-k}{r}\binom{k}{l-r}\binom{N}{r}^{-1}, (0 \leqslant r \leqslant l)$$
$$= 0 \qquad \qquad \text{(otherwise).}$$

235

Table 9–1: **Effect of time of adoption on communication media used by adopters**

Time of adoption	*l* is low		*l* is high	
	m low	*m* high	*m* low	*m* high
First 16%	9·5	17·4	0·0	0·0
17–50%	39·1	59·5	20·5	38·8
51–84%	60·0	78·0	39·6	61·5
Last 16%	72·7	87·5	52·9	72·2

Note: The figures are the percentage of adopters in each adoption category who use personal sources of information. The parameters are *l*, which affects rates of impersonal telling, and *m*, which affects the rate of personal communication.

The two equations (9–18) and (9–19) enable a curve to be fitted to an adoption time process in which both constant source (impersonal) and personal communication take place. Although more cumbersome than the differential equations, the binomial equations yield a probability distribution for the number told in any generation rather than a single number, and the parameters, *l* and *m*, indicate explicitly the types of communication within the system and their relative importance. Thus Fig. 9–9 illustrates the effect of varying *m* and *l* on the rates at which innovations are adopted. Both *l* and *m* are positively related to the slope of the curve.

Table 9–1 illustrates a prediction of the model about the effects of the time when a person adopts an innovation on the source of information he is likely to use. The trend shown in the table, whereby later adopters use personal rather than impersonal information sources, is one reported in the study of weed spray and antibiotic adoption of Beal and Rogers (1960): the laggards (last 16 per cent of adopters) are the category most dependent upon informal sources, whereas other adopters rely relatively more heavily upon impersonal sources. Beal and Rogers examine the contact of farmers with mass media, extension officers and other impersonal change agencies, and find that early adopters have more contact with these sources. By implication, the type of contact affects the major source of information used. But the model and the results in Table 9–1 indicate that the differences in media used would arise anyway, merely because people adopt at different time periods—later adopters are more likely to use personal information sources because when they become aware, personal information sources are more numerous than when early adopters become aware.

Figure 9–10 illustrates the curve fitted to the data on 2,4-D weed spray adoption of Beal and Rogers (1960). At the awareness stage the best fit curve indicates that twelve people are told each year by constant sources whereas each farmer who knows tells 0·50 persons per annum. On the other hand, the curve which best fits the trial data of Beal and Rogers suggests that ten people are told each year by constant sources while each farmer who has tried the innovation tells 0·45 people per year. The reduction in the number told by constant sources reflects the empirical observation that at later stages in the adoption process

Figure 9–10: **The fit of the probability model to data on the adoption of 2,4-D weed spray in Iowa.**
Source: Data from Beal and Rogers (1960: 8).

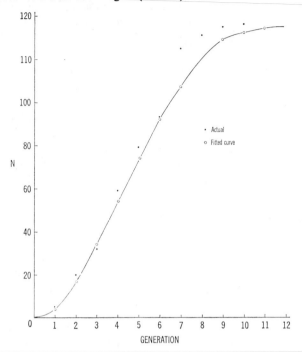

personal contact becomes more important as an information source relative to constant sources. One feature is noticeable: both the curves, which fit the data well in the early years, underestimate the rate of adoption in the last few years—there seems to be some non-stationary process at work, whereby the adoption by the last 5 per cent of farmers is encouraged by the fact that the other farmers have already adopted. As Misra (1968: 58) points out, the social pressure on a farmer to adopt an innovation increases as the proportion of adopters rises.

Spatial Diffusion of Innovations

Non-spatial diffusion studies yield several conclusions of significance to spatial diffusion research. First, the adoption process consists of several stages; adoption is not a simple function of knowledge, but requires also evaluation and trial. Secondly, much of the information necessary to support the diffusion of an innovation flows through personal contacts, though mass media are important communication sources at early stages in the adoption process and the farmer's own trial yields the evidence necessary for adoption. Thirdly, the community's adoption curve is a logistic, or 'S' shaped curve which can be reproduced by

237

deterministic and probabilistic equations the parameters of which measure the varying importance of personal and impersonal communication sources. Spatial diffusion research has relied upon these conclusions, and as in sociologists' work on innovation, so in spatial diffusion studies, the main ideas are at least fifteen years old. The pioneering work of Hagerstrand (1953) has been surpassed only technologically; Hagerstrand's methods of analysing the diffusion of an innovation have not yet been replaced.

Hagerstrand, in his analysis of the spread of agricultural innovations through an area in central Sweden, noticed that the persons who adopted an innovation in one time period tended to be located close to people who had adopted the innovation in an earlier time period. Hagerstrand suggested that this effect develops because innovations diffuse through an area by personal communication. In order to fit a model to his data, he measured the information fields of people, using as surrogates telephone traffic and migration; Brown and Moore (1969: 133-5) comment upon a variety of measures of the mean information field. Having determined that the probability of contact between people was a negative exponential function of distance—

(9–20) $F = Cd^{-n}$

where F is frequency of contact, d is distance, and C and n are constants— Hagerstrand simulated the diffusion of an innovation by Monte Carlo methods. The model assumes that one person knows the information to start, that knowledge of the innovation is absolutely associated with innovation, and that knowledge of the innovation is transmitted by private contact (the probability of this contact being governed by equation (9–20)) at constant time intervals. The corresponding non-spatial equation is (9–18), and like that equation, Hagerstrand's model yields an 'S' shaped curve of adoption. Although in 1953 Hagerstrand assumed a homogeneous plain, in a later article (Hagerstrand, 1967) he places barriers on this plain, across which only reduced communication takes place. Spatially, Hagerstrand's model yields an adoption prediction which bears close qualitative resemblance to some innovation diffusion processes for which he has data.

An analysis of State-subsidised pasture improvements helps to illustrate the fit of Hagerstrand's model to his data (see Hagerstrand, 1953: 46-70, for data on the diffusion of this innovation). The east and northeast of Hagerstrand's study region is excluded from this analysis, because, separated from the main body of the region by a north-north-east to south-south-west line of lakes and containing a higher proportion of large farms than the remainder of the region, this eastern zone evidences a diffusion pattern which is largely independent of that in the west. Figure 9–11, which maps the density of farms eligible for the subsidy, indicates the area excluded.

Figure 9–12 compares one aspect of the actual diffusion of this innovation in the study area with a trial run of Hagerstrand's model II. The origin of the innovation is taken as cell T_8d (see Fig. 9–11), which had by 1932 become the

Figure 9–11: **Distribution of farms less than 10 hectares, Ostergotland. The area NE of the dashed line has been excluded from the analysis.**
 Source: Hagerstrand (1953: 35).

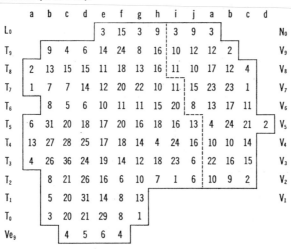

	a	b	c	d	e	f	g	h	i	j	a	b	c	d	
L_0					3	15	3	9	3	9	3				N_0
T_9		9	4	6	14	24	8	16	10	12	12	2			V_9
T_8	2	13	15	15	11	18	13	16	11	10	17	12	4		V_8
T_7	1	7	7	14	12	20	22	10	11	15	23	23	1		V_7
T_6		8	5	6	10	11	11	15	20	8	13	17	11		V_6
T_5	6	31	20	18	17	20	16	18	16	13	4	24	21	2	V_5
T_4	13	27	28	25	17	18	14	4	24	16	10	10	14		V_4
T_3	4	26	36	24	19	14	12	18	23	6	22	16	15		V_3
T_2		8	21	26	16	6	10	7	1	6	10	9	2		V_2
T_1		5	20	31	14	8	13								V_1
T_0		3	20	21	29	8	1								
Ve_9			4	5	6	4									

mode of the distribution of adopters. The total number of adopters in each year at each distance zone from this origin is calculated and expressed as a proportion of the number of eligible farms in that zone. These proportions are summed and the proportion who have adopted in each zone is expressed as a fraction of this sum. Were the plain homogeneous, these fractions would measure the number of adopters in each distance zone as a proportion of the total number of adopters. Although the graphs of the actual process do reveal some tendency for the fraction of adopters to decline as distance from the origin increases, nevertheless the function which links the adoption fraction with distance is irregular. By contrast, the graphs derived from Hagerstrand's simulation represent a much more regular process. Despite his claim that the model functions satisfactorily as a predictor of reality, this result indicates that Hagerstrand's model predicts a closer relationship between distance and adoption than exists in reality.

Misra (1968: 93-123) analysed the diffusion of agricultural co-operatives among villages in an area in the south of Mysore State. The formal model assumptions parallel those of Hagerstrand, but the model recognises imperfections in the uniform plain: Misra assumes (1968: 109-10) that the regular distance gradient of personal tellings is modified by population density (if the population is zero, no person enters a cell, and if density is less than 250 persons per square mile, the probability of a person entering the cell is one-half of the probability of a person entering a cell in which the population density is greater than 250 persons per square mile), by transport networks (inefficient transport nets in a cell reduce the probability of a person entering that cell by one-half), and natural barriers (no persons cross such barriers).

R

Figure 9–12: **Diffusion of grazing improvement subsidies within the study area: the proportion of adopters at each distance zone as a ratio of the summed proportions for all distance zones in relation to distance, and a comparison of these data with Hagerstrand's simulation of his model II.**

Source: Hagerstrand (1953: 58-62 and 254-5).

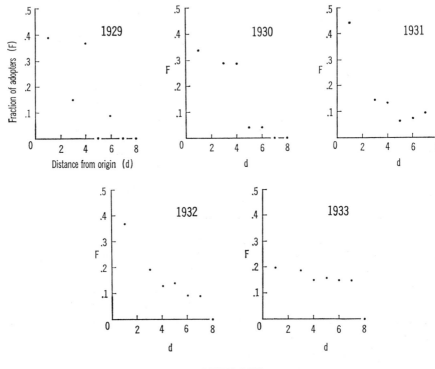

ACTUAL DATA

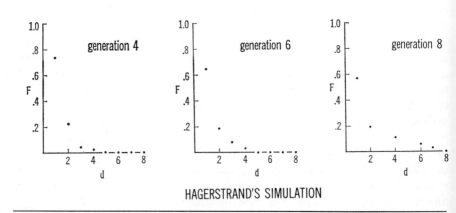

HAGERSTRAND'S SIMULATION

Misra has thus attempted to take account of spatial heterogeneity. But despite this broader framework, his data still reveal a flaw in Hagerstrand's model. An important source of information, constant source impersonal telling, has been omitted from the model, and consequently the simulations over-emphasise distance decay effects on the diffusion of the innovation. Despite the spatial regularities of interpersonal contact frequencies (Hagerstrand, 1953: 165-241; Morrill and Pitts, 1967), Cliff (1968) has shown that Hagerstrand's data do not strongly support the hypothesis that those who adopt in any stage are nearer to those who have previously adopted than are those who do not adopt in that stage. It follows that the simulations predict that adoption is more spatially concentrated than in reality it is: for example, the nine cells at the heart of the co-operative movement in southern Mysore have mean adoption levels of 1·33 in generation 2, 4·00 in g_4, and 13·11 in g_6, whereas the simulation predicts values of 3·44, 6·00, and 14·67 respectively (Misra, 1968: 104, 114). Since the total number of adopters is the same in simulation and reality, the degree of concentration of adopters is greater in the simulation than in actuality. Thus these simulation models are too simple; but they are at the same time too complex, for they are too cumbersome to use in a theoretical analysis of the effects of innovation diffusion on the location of economic activity.

Simplify, and, assuming a one dimensional process, let us examine the physicists' approach to diffusion. Consider the proportion of all adopters within the system who are located at any one point in a linear market. The rate of increase of the proportion of adopters, per unit time per unit area, across a line (normal to the direction of flow of the innovation) is

$$(9\text{--}21) \qquad -a\frac{\delta P}{\delta d} \, .$$

The region is isotropic, and a flow of ideas takes place from the origin, which tends to equalise the proportion of adopters at each point. A region of unit area in the market, between the lines d and $d+\delta d$, gains in proportion of adopters by flows at the rate (9–21). But areas beyond $d+\delta d$ gain in adopters, and so the region loses in proportion of adopters at the rate:

$$(9\text{--}22) \qquad -a\frac{\delta P}{\delta d} - \frac{\delta}{\delta d}\left(-a\frac{\delta P}{\delta d}\right)\delta d.$$

Thus the rate at which the proportion of adopters increases in the region is (9–21) less (9–22):

$$(9\text{--}23) \qquad a\frac{\delta^2 P}{\delta d^2}\delta d,$$

per unit of time. Now the rate of increase (with respect to time) of the proportion who have adopted in the region is

$$(9\text{--}24) \qquad \frac{\delta P}{\delta t}\delta d.$$

241

Hence

(9–25) $$\frac{\delta P}{\delta t} = \frac{a\delta^2 P}{\delta d^2}.$$

Equation (9–25) is Fourier's law of linear diffusion (see Mellor, 1955: 481-97). This law represents the diffusion of qualities or substances when this diffusion advances as a set of lines parallel to the origin. The equation may be generalised to more than one dimension; for two dimensions, it has the form

(9–26) $$\frac{\delta P}{\delta t} = a\frac{\delta^2 P}{\delta d^2} + a\frac{\delta^2 P}{\delta y^2},$$

where the y axis is orthogonal to the d axis.

Sneddon (1957: 274-7) shows how Fourier's law describes the conduction of heat in solids, the diffusion of a concentrated solution through an isotropic medium, the slowing down of neutrons in matter, and the diffusion of vorticity in a viscous fluid.

Particular solutions to equation (9–2) depend on the initial conditions in the system under study. Several such particular solutions have been developed and one is presented here. Suppose that at the source, $d = 0$, the level of adoption of the phenomenon is constant: that is, assume (i) that at $d = 0$, $\frac{\delta P}{\delta d} = 0$. At the end of the line, $d = H$, assume that the change in P with respect to location is very small: (ii) at $d = H$, $\frac{\delta P}{\delta d} = 0$. Assume also that in the source region, P is constant at P_o at the beginning of the diffusion process: (iii) at $t = 0$, $P = P_o$ between $d = 0$ and $d = h$. On the other hand, outside the source area no one has received the innovation: (iv) at $t = 0$, $P = 0$ between $d = h$ and $d = H$. The major theoretical problem associated with these assumptions is that they suppose that everyone in the source area adopts the innovation before it begins to spread outside the source. The conditions lead to the solution (Mellor, 1955: 486):

(9–27) $$P = \frac{P_o h}{H} + \frac{2P_o}{\pi} \sum_{n=1}^{\infty} \left[\frac{1}{n}\sin\frac{nh\pi}{H}.\cos\frac{nd\pi}{H}.\exp\left\{-\left(\frac{n\pi}{H}\right)^2 at\right\}\right].$$

(Jaeger, 1951: 364-9, presents simpler solutions, which require that the market is infinitely long.) Figure 9–13 illustrates the form which a diffusion process obeying these restrictions takes. At first, the adopters are all located in the source region, but over time they spread out over the system, and the proportion located at the source falls. The major parameter in the system is a. As a increases so the diffusion process speeds up. If a is doubled, the time taken to reach a particular distribution of adopters is halved. However, a comparison of Figs. 9–12 and 9–13 indicates that this model is little better than Hagerstrand's at predicting the diffusion of an innovation.

Figure 9–13: **Form of the diffusion process represented by equation (9–25)**

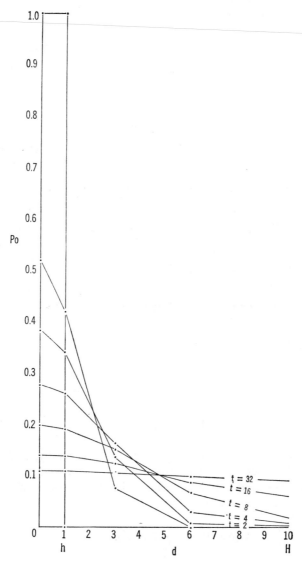

A further difficulty associated with this model is that an isotropic surface has to be assumed. In order that the diffusion equations take manageable form, both the process and the environment must be stationary in time and space. Only very simple cases of non-isotropic surfaces can be treated analytically. For example, assume a set of towns located on an otherwise empty plain. A town *A*, in which an innovation is diffusing, may spread that innovation to another town, *B*, but

243

Figure 9–14: **Some simple cases of one-dimensional non-feedback diffusion systems**

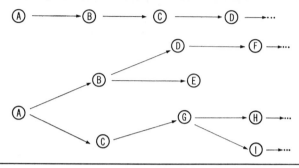

B never influences the rate of innovation in A: Fig. 9–14 illustrates some simple cases obeying this condition. For simplicity, assume no constant source telling. Then in the first town—town 1—the diffusion is influenced by no other town, and so proceeds according to equation (9–3):

$$\frac{dk_1}{dt} = ck_1(N_1 - k_1)$$

which has the solution, for $k_1 = 1$ at $t = 0$:

$$k_1 = \frac{N_1 e^{ct}}{N_1 - 1 + e^{ct}}.$$

In the second town, however, the diffusion is advanced not only by telling within the town, but also by the influence of persons in town 1:

$$(9\text{–}28) \qquad \frac{dk_2}{dt} = ck_2(N_2 - k_2) + ck_1(N_2 - k_2),$$

if distance between towns has no effect. More generally, if d_{ij} represents the retarding effect of distance on communication from town i to town j (remembering that distance need not be Euclidean), then the diffusion of the innovation in town j takes place according to

$$(9\text{–}29) \qquad \frac{dk_j}{dt} = ck_j(N_j - k_j) + \frac{ck_i}{d_{ij}}(N_j - k_j).$$

Equation (9–29) has the solution for $k_j = 0$ at $t = 0$:

$$(9\text{–}30) \qquad k_j = \frac{N_j x_j(e^{ct} - 1)}{N_j + x_j e^{ct}},$$

where $x_j = k_i/d_{ij}$, for constant k_i.

Although this unidirectional process is an extreme simplification of the diffusion phenomenon, it does yield some interesting conclusions about innovation spread. We have seen earlier that the maximum rate of diffusion of an innovation of the type represented by equation (9–3) occurs when

$$k_i = \frac{N_i}{2},$$

that is, when half the population has adopted the innovation. Equation (9–30), on the other hand, has the derivatives

(9–31) $\dfrac{dk_j}{dt} = ck_j(N_j - k_j) + cx_j(N_j - k_j)$

(9–32) $\dfrac{d^2k_j}{dt^2} = c^2(k_j + x_j)(N_j - k_j)(N_j - 2k_j - x_j),$

from which we find that in town j the maximum rate of diffusion of the innovation occurs when

$$k_j = \frac{N_j - x_j}{2}.$$

Provided that x_j is positive, this maximum rate occurs when fewer have adopted in town j than the corresponding maximum in town 1. The first town soon loses much of its initial advantage in adoption rates. This equation system, like the other deterministic diffusion equations presented in this chapter, makes a further prediction about rates of diffusion: that they are higher in towns with larger populations. That is, the size of a population and the rate at which an innovation diffuses through that population are positively related.

But an apparently more useful technique for overcoming the analytical problems posed by a non-isotropic surface has been presented by Chappell and Webber (1970). Their model also assumes that most adopters of an innovation are urban rather than rural dwellers, so that the plain may be represented by a set of towns and a set of corridors connecting those towns. Since the diffusion equation (9–25) and electrical flow equations are strictly analogous, Chappell and Webber suggest that we simulate a diffusion process by the flow of an electrical impulse through an electrical network, in which the towns are represented by capacitors and the corridors by resistors. The values of the capacitors and resistors are proportionate and inversely proportionate, respectively, to populations in towns and flows along corridors. The diffusion is simulated by feeding a pulse into selected points of radiation and is measured by monitoring the build-up of voltage at each town. The model is sufficiently general to permit not only variable flows between towns but also to analyse the effects of different types of adoption curves (self-amplification) within towns. Unlike the analytical model discussed above, it incorporates the effect of a variety of sources on one town and also permits the diffusion of the innovation back towards the origin of that innovation.

Chappell and Webber built one model of a New South Wales-like State which contained twenty-eight towns and over fifty traffic links connecting those towns.

245

Figure 9–15: **A—Some typical adoption curves used in simulating diffusion electrically; B—the spread of the simulated diffusion wave crest through New South Wales.**
Source: Chappell and Webber (1970: 31).

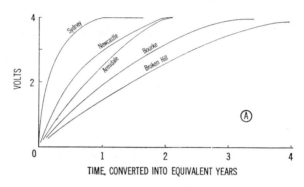

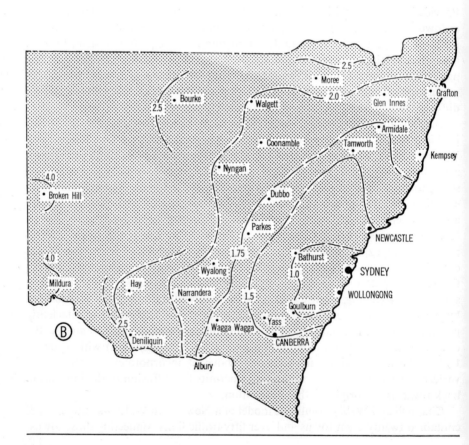

Table 9–2: **Relationship between fraction of adopters, farm density, distance from origin, and time**

Number of farms per 100 km²	Distance from origin (in km)					
	0–7·5	7·6–17·5	17·6–27·5	27·6–37·5	> 37·5	Mean
			1929			
≤ 40		0·032	0·000	0·019	0·000	0·015
41–80	0·019	0·035	0·000	0·000	0·000	0·019
81–120	0·024	0·010	0·000	0·000		0·016
> 120	0·000	0·000				0·000
Mean	0·020	0·020	0·000	0·010	0·000	
			1930			
≤ 40		0·065	0·042	0·019	0·000	0·040
41–80	0·038	0·045	0·037	0·000	0·000	0·030
81–120	0·048	0·010	0·000	0·000		0·025
> 120	0·028	0·032				0·003
Mean	0·042	0·044	0·024	0·005	0·000	
			1931			
≤ 40		0·081	0·028	0·038	0·000	0·045
41–80	0·346	0·105	0·089	0·045	0·000	0·110
81–120	0·242	0·117	0·014	0·041		0·138
> 120	0·250	0·226				0·230
Mean	0·269	0·120	0·053	0·043	0·000	
			1932			
≤ 40		0·081	0·111	0·173	0·000	0·120
41–80	0·423	0·240	0·171	0·067	0·000	0·195
81–120	0·452	0·252	0·006	0·083		0·275
> 120	0·667	0·403				0·500
Mean	0·481	0·245	0·142	0·094	0·000	
			1933			
≤ 40		0·548	0·569	0·500	0·170	0·510
41–80	0·558	0·540	0·443	0·425	0·000	0·487
81–120	0·629	0·660	0·362	0·500		0·572
> 120	0·667	0·597				0·600
Mean	0·608	0·567	0·462	0·453	0·081	

Note: Gaps in the table indicate that no cells fall into that category.
Source: Hagerstrand, 1953: 46-70 and 295-7.

Although a variety of adoption curves may be simulated, this model assumed a linear build-up of adopters in the source, Sydney, to a maximum level which was maintained through the experiment. A proportion of the adopters in Sydney diffuse out to other towns, in relation to traffic flows along the links. Figure 9–15A illustrates typical adoption curves at some of the towns, while Fig. 9–15B shows the spread of the diffusing wave crest through New South Wales. This model is much more complex than one which could be handled analytically; the method therefore permits more rapid and realistic models of diffusion.

While Hagerstrand's data do not permit a direct evaluation of these discrete space models, the data can be examined to determine whether they are consistent with the predictions. The relationship between adoption rates and population size in the discrete space model suggests that in a continuous space model population density should be positively related to rates of adoption. Each cell in Hagerstrand's study region is therefore classified according to the number of farms of less than ten hectares (i.e. the number of eligible farms) which it contains, as well as according to its distance from the origin. The fraction of adopters (number of adopters divided by the number of farms eligible to receive the subsidy) in each density and distance class is presented in Table 9–2.

Consider first the mean effects represented in Table 9–2. In each year the mean effect of distance is in the expected direction: adoption fractions decline as distance increases and increase as time passes, with only odd exceptions. The effect of farm density is more difficult to judge. In 1929, when there were only a few acceptors, farm density had no apparent effect on the rate of adoption; in 1930, adoption rates were highest where farm densities were lowest; by 1931 and 1932, however, this trend had been reversed and acceptances were directly related to farm density; but in 1933 there was an exception to the rule that adoption is greatest in areas where farm density is highest. The means thus provide some, though not strong, evidence for the notion that adoption rates are positively affected by farm densities.

The interactions between distance, density, and adoption rates are represented in the main body of the table. In the three later years (when the process may be expected to exhibit greater stability), there exist a dozen cases in which one distance zone contains cells in three or four different density classes. Of these cases, four evidence a positive association between density and adoption, one represents a negative association, and the remainder present no clear relationship. Of the nine occasions in which a density class contains cells in four or five distance classes in 1931-3, four evidence monotonic declines of adoption with distance, and three do so with only one exception. Density and distance both appear to determine adoption rates, but the associations are not at all strong.

The discrete space model makes a further prediction about the form of the diffusion process. Figure 9–16 illustrates, for three towns, the process predicted by the model. Towns more distant from the origin receive the innovation later than towns close to the origin, but the time taken for an innovation to diffuse from one town to the next falls as the distance from the origin increases. Hence

Figure 9–16: **Effect of location of towns on the rate of diffusion of innovations within them, according to equation (9–29)**

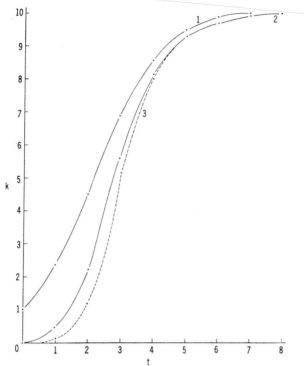

the curve relating time taken for an innovation to arrive in a place and the distance of that place from the origin should be convex up. On the other hand, once the innovation has arrived at a place, that innovation is adopted more rapidly the further the place is from the origin. Regions near the source receive the innovation earlier but adopt it more slowly than distant regions; models which do not separate reception and adoption thus confound the two effects.

Hagerstrand's data indicate that these two predictions have some validity. The lower portion of Fig. 9–17 indicates that more distant zones received the innovation later than nearer zones, but that, as the innovation spread further from the origin, it diffused more quickly: whereas the innovation spread at 4·34 km per year up to a distance of 22·5 km from the origin, the rate of diffusion from 22·5 km to 42·5 km was on average more than 120 km per annum. In the upper portion of Fig. 9–17, cells have been classified according to the year in which the innovation first appeared, and for each class is plotted the proportion of eligible farmers who have adopted as a function of time since the appearance of the first adopter. The diagram indicates clearly that cells which

249

Figure 9-17: A—The rate of adoption of innovations as a function of the time at which the innovation first arrives in a cell; B—relationship between distance from the origin and the time at which the innovation reaches a cell.

Source: Hagerstrand (1953: 46-70 and 295-7).

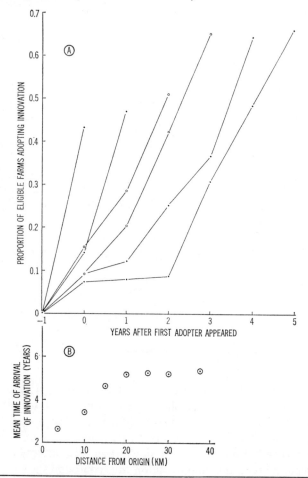

received the innovation in later years adopted it more rapidly than cells which received the innovation earlier. These relationships are predicted by the model.

Diffusion of Innovations and Location

This chapter has so far shown how equations and models may be used to predict at least some of the major aspects of the diffusion process. Although many simplifying assumptions are necessary, the equation systems do reflect features normally associated with the diffusion of innovations. This section of the chapter is concerned to draw from these studies of diffusion some conclusions of locational significance. To begin, a model of the location of innovations is proposed; then the significance of the spatial spread of innovations is analysed.

The analysis of the location of innovations is based upon a simple model which assumes that firms have knowledge about only limited areas around them. Suppose that the number of inventions produced by a group of persons is proportional to the population of that group (i.e. that each person has an equal chance of producing an invention). More specifically, let the probability of an invention in an area be

$$(9\text{--}33) \qquad p_i = k/K,$$

where k is the population of the group and K is the population of the entire system. Assume further that an innovation is an invention which results in entrepreneurial action, and that the number of innovations is a function of the number of inventions and the number of contacts which an inventor has with businessmen. The assumption that contacts with businessmen are important when people act upon inventions may be rationalised by the notion that to apply an invention to manufacture a good or to offer a service may require finance, knowledge of the techniques of manufacturing some other goods, or a general business ability, all or some of which an inventor may not command. Contacts are limited to the town in which the inventor lives: therefore, let the probability that an inventor knows a businessman useful to him be

$$(9\text{--}34) \qquad P_j = (k-1)/(K-1).$$

The probability of the innovation occurring in a place is therefore

$$(9\text{--}35) \qquad p_i p_j = k(k-1)/(K)(K-1).$$

There is a probability $(1-\sum p_i p_j)$ that the particular innovation does not occur at all in the system.

The influence of town size upon the distribution of innovations within such a system is marked. Assume for simplicity a system in which there are two towns, 1 and 2, with populations k_1 and $(K-k_1)$ respectively. Then the probability that a particular innovation occurs in town 1 is

$$(9\text{--}36) \qquad p_1 = \frac{k_1(k_1-1)}{K(K-1)},$$

and the probability that it occurs in town 2 is

$$(9\text{--}37) \qquad p_2 = \frac{(K-k_1)(K-k_1-1)}{K(K-1)}.$$

Thus the probability that the innovation occurs at all in the system is

$$(9\text{--}38) \qquad p_1 + p_2 = \frac{2k_1{}^2 - 2Kk_1 - K + K^2}{K(K-1)}.$$

Equation (9–38) has the first derivative

(9-39) $$\frac{d(p_1+p_2)}{dk_1} = \frac{4k_1-2K}{K(K-1)},$$

from which we see that the probability that the innovation occurs at all in the system is at a minimum when

(9-40) $k_1 = K/2.$

Thus the probability of an innovation occurring in a system is lowest when that system is comprised of equally sized towns, and rises as the sizes of towns become more disparate. The concentration of population is conducive to the production of innovations, if communication between inventor and business-man is necessary to transform an invention into an innovation.

Over a period of time the number of innovations in town 2 relative to the total number of innovations in the system is

(9-41) $$\frac{p_2}{p_1+p_2} = \frac{(K-k_1)(K-k_1-1)}{2k_1^2-2Kk_1-K+K^2},$$

while the population in town 2 relative to the population of the system is

(9-42) $(K-k_1)/K.$

The number of innovations per unit of population in town 2 is thus given by (9-41) and (9-42):

$$\frac{K^2-Kk_1-K}{2K_1^2-2Kk_1-K+K^2},$$

which is a decreasing function of k_1. In a town, the number of innovations per unit of population increases as the population of the town relative to the population of the system increases. Thus large towns have an advantage over small towns: relative to their population, large towns generate more innovations than small towns. This effect is marked: assume three towns, of population 10, 30, and 60 (then $K = 100$). While they contain 10, 30, and 60 per cent of the system's population, they generate 2, 19, and 79 per cent of the system's in-novations, according to equation (9-35). Large places generate more and small places generate less innovations than their populations lead one to expect.

In an efficiently operated system, information should be collected mainly from areas close to the entrepreneur. If good locations are randomly scattered through the environment, the entrepreneur is most likely to find one near his own location, because most time and energy is spent looking there. Hence, since the number of innovations occurring in a place is an increasing function of the population of that place, the number of new firms which locate in a town is also an increasing function of the size of the town. (A new firm is defined as one which incorporates an innovation.) The greater the population of a place, the faster its rate of growth of firms which incorporate an innovation.

The model of diffusion through a set of towns separated by empty spaces, represented by equation (9-29), illustrates how an innovation, once made, spreads. The differences between towns are marked at the beginning of the diffusion process, but these differences are rapidly reduced once the innovation spreads. The advantage which accrues to the first town on account of its greater adoption rate is thus short-lived, for diffusion in the second and later towns is accelerated by the spread of information from persons in the first town. In Fig. 9-18A the rate of diffusion when there are three towns is compared with diffusion rates when all people live in one town in a system. The concentrated system displays an initial advantage which is soon lost as time passes. Fig. 9-18B illustrates the effect of varying the distance between towns. The greater the d_{ij} factor which reduces inter-town communication, the greater the lag in the diffusion process in the second and third towns; but even so, the first town loses its advantage fairly quickly. An interesting facet of the model is illustrated in Fig. 9-18C. If the d_{ij} factor is small, the rate of diffusion in the second town may be sufficiently high for the adoption rate in that town to overtake the adoption rate in the first town. Finally, Fig. 9-18D compares diffusion rates in the linear organisation (the innovation passes from town 1 to town 2 and from town 2 to town 3) with diffusion rates in a hierarchy (the innovation passes from town 1 to both towns 2 and 3 at the same time). In terms of the diffusion of innovations the hierarchy is more efficient than the linear organisation, but this advantage is concentrated in the middle of the diffusion process: at the beginning and the end of the diffusion, the hierarchy is little better than the line.

Thus, in a dynamic system, in which innovations are being continually produced, a large region of concentrated population maintains advantages over less populated areas because of its relatively greater production of innovations. Even though other regions may catch up in the adoption of any one innovation, the continuous flow of innovations ensures that the region of concentrated population receives greater incomes from innovating sectors of the economy than other regions. In such a dynamic system, a spatial cross-section at any one point in time indicates that the rate of adoption of innovations is most advanced in the areas where most innovations are produced. The concentration of population and production is thus socially desirable from the point of view of maximising the rates of production and of diffusion of innovations; the concentration of population is created and maintained by the comparative advantages of that concentration which accrue from differences in the rates of innovation adoption. This advantage can be readily measured, provided that a known diffusion equation applies and that rates and the location of innovation production can be described.

But in a system which tends towards long-run static equilibrium, the innovation diffusion process models, however intrinsically interesting they may be, are not important as they stand. Eventually the innovation is diffused and in the long run firms locate at the optimum sites: the large city, favoured by the innovation production process, may not be the long-run optimum location. Diffusion models in static location theory are only of short-run significance. The following discussion introduces a model in which diffusion rates become of long-

Figure 9-18: A—comparison of rate of diffusion in one large town with the rate in three smaller, spatially separated towns; B—effects of friction of distance on adoption rates; C—diagram to show how the adoption process in the second town may overtake the process in the first town, if there is no feedback; D—comparison of diffusion rates in linear and hierarchical system of three towns.

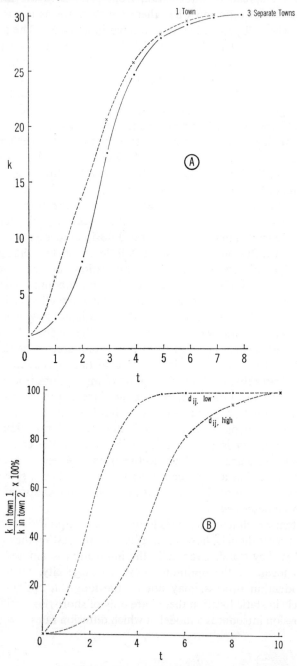

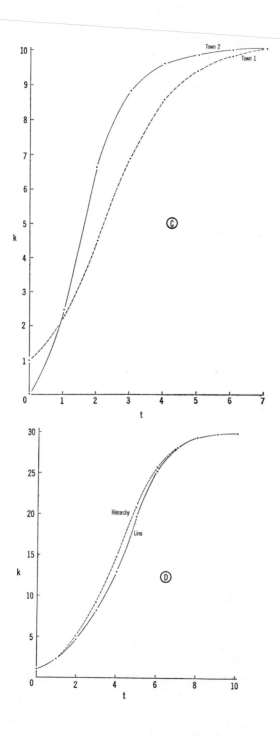

S

term significance, in which the fact that an innovation is at first spatially limited creates unstable but possibly enduring patterns of location, patterns which do not occur if the innovation is initially perfectly distributed. The model conforms essentially to the ideas of initial advantage and historical momentum. To do this the model introduces some simple notions about learning.

Learning situations are an immediate corollary of uncertainty. If entrepreneurs are ignorant, scope exists for them to learn. Entrepreneurs may change their activities in a manner which persists and recurs over a period of time and which is strengthened by repetition or practice (Thomson, 1959: 108). Learning is implied by uncertainty and is important in an analysis of location under uncertainty in two ways. Firstly the functions relating learning and time differ in two areas because of physical factors and, secondly, learning functions may differ over a homogeneous plain. In the following analysis, two simple models are constructed which illustrate the significance of learning to location theory. They are couched in terms of agricultural production but may be readily generalised to other activities.

Assume first an economic system which contains two separate types of location. A new crop is introduced into this system: it is sold on world markets at a fixed and constant price. The farmers in the system have never grown the crop before and so they must practise before attaining maximum yields. Techniques of production are fixed and constant (excepting the skills of farmers, which improve over time) and farmers within each area display identical production functions. Assume that in area A

(9–43) $Y_{t+1} - Y_t = B/t(t+1),$

and that in area B,

(9–44) $Y'_{t+1} - Y'_t = D/t(t+1).$

In equation (9–43), Y_{t+1} is the yield of farmers in year $(t+1)$, Y_t is the yield in year t, and B is a constant; similarly in equation (9–44), Y'_{t+1} and Y'_t are yields in years $(t+1)$ and t respectively, and D is a constant. The difference equation (9–43) has the solution

(9–45) $Y_t = A - B/t$

(A is an arbitrary constant), and equation (9–44) is solved by

(9–46) $Y'_t = C - D/t$

where C is an arbitrary constant. Equations (9–45) and (9–46) are hyperbolic functions, represented only in the positive quadrant of a pair of rectangular Cartesian co-ordinates (because of external criteria), having the values $(A - B)$ and $(C - D)$ respectively in year $t = 1$, and tending to the limits A and C.

Figure 9-19 contains the graphs of two such functions for possible values of A, B, C, and D. In the long run, farmers in area B, who exhibit the Y'_t learning function, produce more profitably than farmers in A. However, farmers

Figure 9–19: **Graphs of two yield learning functions**

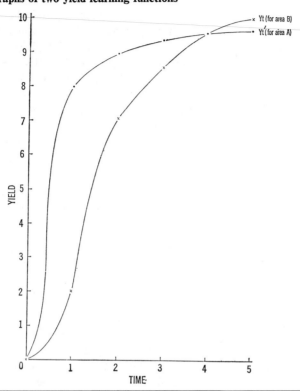

do not know the future trend of their yields and so, if the yield necessary for profits is, say, eight units, the farmers in *B* are likely to cease growing the crop, because they will have endured three consecutive losses before they obtain this yield and they will not know that the next year is to be any better. In these circumstances only the farmers in *A* grow the crop, even though their yields in the long run are lower than the yields of farmers in *B* would have been.

This model may also be used to interpret the production decisions of farmers who have migrated to a previously empty area. If all farmers exhibit the same learning functions Y_t and Y_t' for crops *A* and *B*, which are sold at fixed and equal prices, the most likely course of events is that *A* will be grown in the long run and that crop *B* will be discarded after two or three years' production: *B* is no more profitable than *A* until the fifth year of operation. The model is only useful if *B* was not grown before *A* was introduced into the area, for if *B* has been grown for three years before *A* is grown, *B* is always more profitable than *A*.

However, the model is not general, for it depends on environmental conditions. The shape of the functions Y_t and Y_t' depends on either the farmers or the environment—though environmental differences are the more likely cause of variations within a country. Although this may be useful in the realistic conditions of environmental variance, an alternative formulation generates patterns without assuming variation over the plain in physical conditions.

This second model assumes a homogeneous plain over which an innovation is diffused at a finite fixed rate. The good is produced by all farmers in region a in year 1, by all farmers in regions a and b in year 2, and so on. The farmers exhibit a yield curve such as equation (9–43). There is a linear demand curve. It is then simple to show that the returns to farmers in region a in their mth year of production are always higher than the returns to farmers in b in their mth year of production. Furthermore, the difference between the two regions in their mth year level of returns is more the greater the slope of the demand curve, the higher are yields at the limit and in the first year of production, and the larger the area over which the good is produced in each region.

However, rather than pursue such a model, which has been simplified to permit analysis, I have here simulated a more complex one with the following structure:

(i) The area planted to a crop in region i in year j is

(9–47) $s(i, j) = 0$, if $j < i$

$= c/a$, if $j = i$

$= [r(i, j) \times s(i, j-1)]/N$, if $j > i$,

subject to the condition that $s(i, j) \leqslant c$. Thus, the crop diffuses at the constant rate of one region per year; in its first year of production in a region, the crop is planted in c/a units of area (c is the maximum area available and a is a parameter); in later years, the area planted in region i is the region's return from the crop in the previous year ($r(i, j-1)$) as a proportion of costs (including normal profits), N, multiplied by the area planted in the previous year, up to a maximum acreage of c.

(ii) The yield of the crop in region i in year j is

(9–48) $y(i, j) = x-y$, if $j = i$;

$= y(i, j-1)$, if $j > i$ and $s(i, j-1) < d$;

$= \dfrac{1}{c} y(i, j-1)s(i, j-1)[x-y(i, j-1)]^2$

if $j > i$ and $s(i, j-1) \geqslant d$.

In all regions, yield in the first year of production is the same $(x-y)$; if the acreage planted in year $j-1$ is less than d, no yield improvement occurs in year j; otherwise the increase in yield depends on the previous yield and the proportion of the available acreage planted to the crop in the previous year.

(iii) The price received for a crop is

(9–49) $p = g.e^{-hv}$,

where g and h are parameters, e is the base of natural logarithms, and v is total output (the product of area and yield). This demand curve is negatively sloping and concave up; hence price and output fluctuations are dampened.

The outcome (locations, yields, returns, and areas) may be computed for various levels of the parameters, a, c, N, x, y, g, and h. Figure 9–20 presents the results for one such calculation. The available acreage in each region, $c = 10$; c/a, the area planted in the first year, is 2·5; N is the level of necessary normal returns, set at 250; x and y, the parameters of the yield curve, are set at 10 and 5 respectively; the parameters g and h determine the demand curve, which is

$$p = 100e^{-v/1000} - 25.$$

The yield curves in Fig. 9–20 are functions of both time and acreage. The six regions near the origin have yield curves which asymptotically approach 10, and these curves are soon indistinguishable from one another. Region 7 is a crucial one, which only just continues producing the good. Its yield curve is considerably below those of the first six. The last three regions have curves which level off at yields well below 10. Yields stabilise once the acreage in a region falls below 0·5.

The curves which describe the area planted to the crop in regions 1-6 are all concave up: the area planted increases more and more rapidly as time passes, up to the limit of 10. The acreage of region 7 at first falls, but after year twelve its yield increases faster than price falls and so the acreage recovers and slowly approaches the limit of 10. The three remaining regions' acreages decline continuously after first year's production. These results indicate clearly the crucial borderline role of region 7.

The third set of curves describes returns per unit area for the regions. These curves represent the results of quite complex interactions between yield increases over time, price variations, and farmers' reactions to previous years' returns. The curve for each region has a primary inverted 'U' shape, for initially yields increase faster than prices fall, whereas in later years yield rises are small in relation to price falls. But the time at which maximum returns occur in any region is not a simple function of location: the maximum return is gained as soon as year eight in regions 1–4, sixteen and nineteen in regions 5 and 6, year thirty-seven in region 7, and before year eighteen in the outermost regions. Superimposed on this primary curve are smaller cyclical fluctuations, which reflect the fact that farmers' decisions are based on the previous year's returns, so that a high price last year induces greater acreages this year, which tend to reduce this year's price. Because the demand curve is concave up, these fluctuations decrease in amplitude over time.

This computation illustrates several features of a diffusion with learning situation. Although the assumptions are simple, the behaviour of farmers is complex. The irregularities of the returns per acre curves are surprising in view of the smooth deterministic assumptions which govern behaviour. But the computation also illustrates that the innovation is confined eventually to an area near the origin of that innovation. Furthermore, as the returns curves make clear,

259

Figure 9–20: **Computations upon the model of diffusion with learning: curves of A—yields, B—areas cropped, C—returns per unit area, and D—price and output, for the regions.**

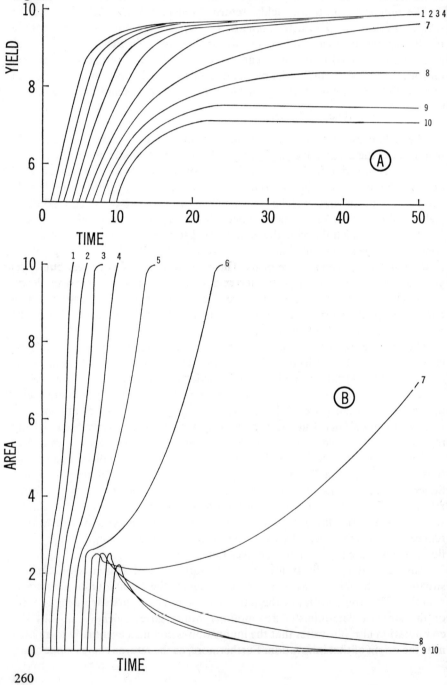

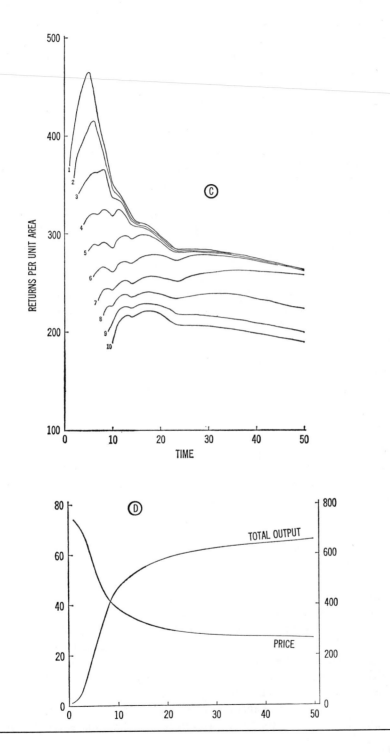

those areas which receive the innovation earliest are also those which make the greatest average profit out of it.

Thus the model indicates that if learning takes place and prices vary inversely with output, the later an innovation is adopted in an area (as compared with other areas), the less likely it is that the innovation will prove profitable in that area. This conclusion indicates that in a learning situation—that is, in an uncertain environment—the location of an innovation and the rate at which it is diffused may be of long-run significance. If an area produces an innovation it is more likely to adopt that innovation profitably than other areas. The difference in profitability over space depends on the slope of the demand curve, the volume of production, the effect of learning on yields, and the rate of diffusion of the innovation. A combination of the conclusion of the innovation production model, discussed previously, that a disproportionately large number of innovations are produced in large cities or regions, and this conclusion, that the area in which an innovation is made is most likely to adopt it profitably, indicates that the rate at which innovations are adopted profitably increases with the size of the city or region. Once the population in a system is unevenly distributed over that system, innovation production and diffusion tend to increase that degree of concentration of activity.

Conclusions

This chapter has treated more dynamic situations than those normally covered by location theory. Correspondingly, the mathematical models are complex in any case except the simplest. Even so, equations can be written and manipulated which reflect at least the coarser aspects of the diffusion of innovations in reality.

The production and diffusion of innovations is a process which increases the degree to which the economic activity in a system is concentrated. Most innovations are produced in concentrations which already exist. These regions are the first to adopt the innovations, and so receive the advantages of an early start, even though later regions adopt more rapidly than those which adopted first. Later adopters have to overcome the entrenched position of early adopters. Such a process—historical momentum or geographical inertia—is well documented in empirical location studies.

The diffusion models may be generalised to an important range of location problems, for they may be used as the basis of spatial economic growth models. Equations (9–25), for an isotropic surface, and (9–29), for a heterogeneous plain, may be used to describe the behaviour of a system of regions or nations over time as a function of their location. The effects of initial advantage may be incorporated in the equations. In such a system, k, the dependent variable, may be employed to measure not merely the adoption of innovations, but also growth related variables such as number of firms, proportion of population in secondary and tertiary activities, and so on. Incorporating an additional term to measure the multiplier effect of changes in k produces an income-location equation; similarly, the equation for the ith region may include the effects of the local resource bases. These modifications imply that the c term in equation (9–29) becomes location dependent, to measure multipliers and resource advantages. Finally, the equations must be modified to include the effect on local growth not only of the neighbouring region, but rather of all regions. Thus growth in one of a set of n spatially separated regions as a result of one impulse may be represented by the set of equations:

$$(9\text{–}50) \qquad \frac{dk_j}{dt} = \sum_{i=1}^{n} \frac{c_j k_i}{d_{ij}} (N_j - k_j),$$

for $j = 1, 2, \ldots, n$; $d_{jj} = 1$.

One final but important effect of innovation diffusion processes must be noted. The diffusion takes place gradually from an origin, and at any one point in time only a limited, bounded area around the origin has received the innovation; the last model indicates that in some cases only a limited area may receive the innovation profitably. Similarly, Morrill's (1965) results illustrate how migrating people are concentrated regionally. Areas receiving innovations sooner adopt them more profitably; areas near the origin have higher population densities than more distant regions. Consequently the diffusion, of both innovations and people, creates bounded regions of high income density around the origin. Furthermore, in more realistic probabilistic models, smaller, less sharply differentiated, bounded regions are formed within the generally settled area. For example, Hagerstrand's (1953: 268-9) maps of his model IIIb simulation in generation 57 contain four regions which are relatively bounded. Provided that diffusion processes occur, there is no need to assume a heterogeneous surface in order to suppose that the plain is comprised of bounded markets. Thus a general theory of location under uncertainty recognises two sources of bounding (probabilistic diffusion and environmental variance), and the location, size, and spacing of towns is determined with respect to both sources. Such a theory does not *have* to assume environmental variance, for bounded markets are also created by diffusion processes.

10 Uncertainty, Location, and Regional Economic Growth

Economic activity takes place in space. Though this is true, economics has been spectacularly successful even when it has used non-spatial model systems. Similarly, economic activity takes place in uncertainty; and economics has created powerful models which assume certainty. But just as some facts can only be predicted in spatial model systems, so some observations apparently demand explanation through uncertain models. This book attempts to decide what facts are predicted by model systems which are not uniquely determined, and to compare uncertain and certain models in terms of their complexity and predictive power.

The data necessary to support these decisions and comparisons are contained in the foregoing nine chapters. The introductory chapter sets up the problems which location models are required to solve, the next three chapters analyse location patterns in certain systems, and Chapters 5-9 present approaches to location systems under uncertainty.

The models which support the theoretical discussion are all formal and phrased in terms of optimal solutions. Thus the environments within which the locating individuals exist are simplistic and unrealistic; but the models thereby become powerful, in the sense of predicting intricate location patterns with some clarity. The conclusions of both the uncertainty and certainty models are firm and mathematically precise. We can readily set up systems in which the environment is similar to reality, but the conclusions which can be derived from the manipulation of these systems are so imprecise as to be practically meaningless.

An example from Pred (1967) illustrates the problem of drawing conclusions from complex systems. Pred assumes (1967: 25-30) that all individuals are assigned to a specific point in two-dimensional attribute space, the two attributes being ability to use information and the quantity and quality of information available. Most, if not all actors are supposed to act as boundedly rational satisficers. Furthermore, since locational problems vary in complexity, an actor endowed with certain level-of-information and ability-to-use characteristics can arrive at a successful solution, while in another instance the identical actor can have comparable attributes but arrive at an unsuccessful decision. Pred then discusses the factors which determine an individual's location in this two-dimensional attribute space (1967: 30-64), and proceeds to apply the matrix to the real world. One application is to a Thünen-like agricultural situation (1967: 67-81): Pred predicts (a) that some decisions are non-optimal, (b) that, because of chance, some well-endowed actors made wrong decisions and some poorly-endowed actors made good decisions, and (c) that the pattern is characterised by transition zones rather than boundary lines. The predictions are not rigorously proved. But, to say the least, these conclusions are intuitively obvious: the complexity of his model prevents more intricate and precise or less obvious predictions.

Therefore the decision-making models simplify. They assume that the location and activities of all industries or firms save one are given. Hence the problem is to locate this last, uncertain, firm or industry (other 'last' firms or industries may, of course, locate later still). This partial equilibrium approach remains valid so long as the last firm's decision does not affect the behaviour of other firms; thus, prices are assumed to be given. The more general equilibrium analysis, founded on sets of simultaneous equations, may be used to deduce the conditions for optimal location patterns. (For a recent statement of general equilibrium conditions, see Isard, 1969: 597-767.) But the general equilibrium approach cannot (at the present state of the art) yield meaningful quantitative solutions, nor can it encompass cases in which operators are uncertain (unless an infinite capacity to calculate prices and outcomes is ascribed to operators). The models in this book therefore predict decisions (and the resulting partial equilibrium patterns) rather than conditions for optimality.

Furthermore, most of the book describes theories about the way in which operators ought to behave in order to achieve given goals most efficiently. Attention has been focused on individual behaviour rather than on the phenomena which arise from mass behaviour. Only when discussing growth and diffusion do the models become predictive systems for mass behaviour. Despite this emphasis on normative models, it is maintained that these models do have some predictive power. Chapter 5 argued that some elements of individuals' behaviour patterns may be described as optimal decision taking. The later models, which assume uncertainty, suppose that individuals attempt to make decisions which are optimal from their point of view. These decisions need not be optimal for society. Our intention, then, has been to understand the impact of some processes upon location patterns rather than simply to predict actual patterns as efficiently as possible.

The predictions derived from the analysis of these uncertain systems, though precise, are therefore limited. Imprecise relations between uncertainty and location have not been analysed. Most of the models, for both certain and uncertain systems, are essentially normative, and are not necessarily efficient predictors of reality. These conditions bound the accuracy of the comparison of certain and uncertain systems. This comparison is based on the classification of patterns into point, land use, and regional systems.

Figure 10–1: **Central place patterns on a homogeneous plain.**
Source: Lösch (1959: 132).

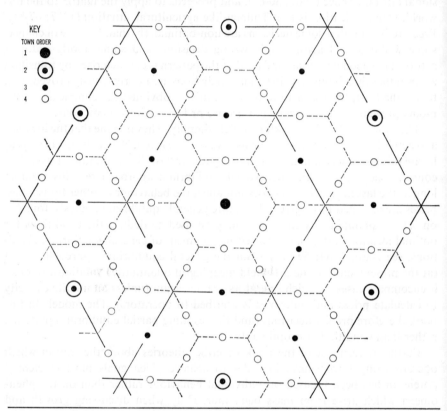

Point Location Patterns

The simplest and most elegant point location pattern under certainty is the central place pattern. This pattern develops on a homogeneous, unbounded plain under conditions of social optimality. Typical patterns are illustrated in Fig. 10–1. Although the precise relationships vary with the value of k (the ratio of the number of functions of one order to the number of functions of the next highest order), the diagram illustrates the major features of the system—hexagonal market nets and even spacing of towns of the same size.

In anisotropic conditions, a socially optimal central place system is much more difficult to construct. If the region is bounded, but production costs remain invariant over space within the region, the socially optimal solution consists of m places, located at (a_j, b_j), $j = 1, 2, \ldots, m$, so as to minimise

$$(10\text{–}1) \qquad \Phi(m) = \sum_j \int_{M_j} p \left[(x-a_j)^2 + (y-b_j)^2 \right]^{\frac{1}{2}} dx dy,$$

Figure 10–2: **Average number of sides to market areas as a function of the number of sources in a region.**

Source: Leamer (1968).

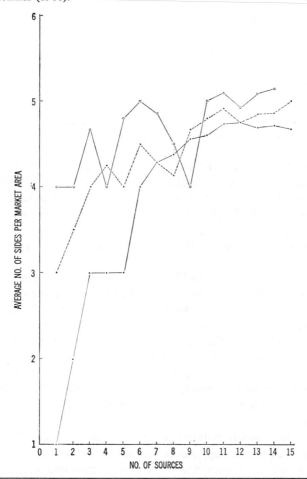

where M_j is the market area of source j, p is demand density, and x, y are the locational co-ordinates of points in the region. Cooper (1968) presents a method whereby optimal solutions to (10–1) may be obtained iteratively.

Leamer (1968) has calculated some solutions to equation (10–1) for square, triangular, and circular market regions. Figure 10–2 presents the results of some calculations made upon Leamer's diagrams. In so far as shape is adequately measured by the number of boundaries a region has, Fig. 10–2 shows that the larger the number of sources within a bounded region, the closer do the market areas of those sources approximate a hexagonal shape. But the diagram indicates that the market areas may tend to pentagons in the limit rather than to hexagons.

267

Figure 10–3: **Superimposed industry patterns in square and circular market regions, attempting to maximise the coincidence of sellers**

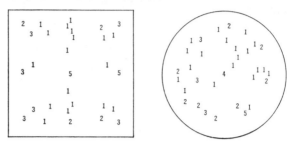

Leamer also demonstrates, however, that the total transport costs in such bounded market areas are not much greater than in a set of similarly sized hexagonal market areas, and that as the number of sources increases, so the transport cost differential between the two forms falls asymptotically to zero. A third property of this finite, one-good central place system is that as the number of sources increases, so the spacing of these sources tends to become more even.

An attempt has been made to add some of these patterns together, to gain an insight into the amount of urbanisation to be expected in such a society. The attempt is complicated by the fact that it is impossible to prove that the maximum degree of coincidence of sites has been obtained. Nevertheless, Fig. 10–3 illustrates the results of adding together the patterns predicted by Leamer for different industries in square and circular market regions. Clearly, the degree of coincidence of sellers is low: no one location contains sellers of all ranks. In the absence of agglomeration economies which can draw the sellers together, away from their individual optimum locations, the degree of dispersal of society over space is high.

It is easiest to compare patterns in certain and uncertain systems when a linear market is assumed. Suppose that a market contains ten industries, and that these ten industries comprise firms whose minimum market areas are respectively $\frac{1}{1}, \frac{1}{2}, \frac{1}{3}, \cdots, \frac{1}{10}$ of the length of the market. The location patterns for the ten industries are added together. In a certain system, the degree of coincidence of sellers is low: one site contains five, another three, and a third two sellers. In an uncertain system, the first seller in an industry locates at the centre of the market and later sellers locate at the quartiles and octiles (if marginal cost curves are equal and zero). Then one town contains nine industries, two have eight, two contain five, and two contain three industries.

A comparison of the linear market organisation in the two types of system indicates several conclusions. In the uncertain system, there exist a smaller number of small towns than in the certain system; conversely there are more

Table 10–1: **Average distance* of consumers from sellers**

Industry rank	Certain system No. of firms	Certain system Average distance	Uncertain system No. of firms	Uncertain system Average distance
10	10	0·2000	7	0·3125
9	9	0·2222	7	0·3125
8	8	0·2500	7	0·3125
7	7	0·2857	5	0·4375
6	6	0·3333	5	0·4375
5	5	0·4000	3	0·7500
4	4	0·5000	3	0·7500
3	3	0·6667	2	1·0000
2	2	1·0000	1	2·0000
1	1	2·0000	1	2·0000

* 'Average distance' is average distance of all consumers from their location to the nearest firm, in a market eight units long.

large towns in an uncertain than in a certain system. Towns more frequently contain all the industries of rank lower than the highest ranking industry in the town in uncertain than in certain systems. Whereas fifty-five firms are located in the certain market, discontinuities in the possible location choices reduce this number to forty-one in the uncertain system. The uncertain pattern is less efficient than the certain; transport costs are higher in the uncertain than in the certain system. Table 10–1 illustrates this point clearly.

In comparing these systems with reality, several points should be borne in mind. Firstly, given a system in which there exist many market areas whose sizes vary randomly and many industries, the sizes of the firms in which vary randomly, a much more continuous distribution of town sizes would be produced, by both the certain and uncertain systems, than is represented by these results. (However, the certain system would still contain more small towns and fewer large towns than the uncertain system.) Secondly, changes in the value of agglomeration to firms alter the extent to which firms locate together. And thirdly, if firms have 'U' shaped cost curves, several firms selling the same good may exist together in the same town. In uncertainty, therefore, the degree to which sellers concentrate in a few large towns increases if cost curves are 'U' shaped, for sellers other than the first in an industry may locate in the central town. As such a process increases town size, so it also increases the average distance of all consumers from sellers.

These problems make specific comparison of the predictions of the two models difficult. In any one finite market area, the uncertain model system predicts (i) that almost all sellers are located in towns, (ii) that the number of sellers in any one industry is less than the number which the market could support if those sellers were distributed evenly over the market, (iii) that the largest town is located at the centre of the market, with the next largest towns located at the quartiles (or their two-dimensional equivalents), and the third largest towns located at the outside octiles, and so on, (iv) that any town contains practically all of the industries which are of rank lower than the highest ranking industry in that town, and (v) that, if cost curves are 'U' shaped, several firms selling the same good may locate in the same town. By contrast, a finite central place model without agglomeration predicts (i) that the locations of few firms coincide, (ii) that the number of sellers is the maximum the market can sustain, (iii) that the location of the largest town is indeterminate in general, though it may be the centre in square market areas (it is off-centre in circular market areas), (iv) that towns do not contain the entire range of industries of rank lower than the highest, and (v) that two firms selling the same good never locate in the same town. A central place model with agglomeration can predict everything that the uncertainty model predicts, except the optimum town locations (which depend on the relative frequency with which different goods are purchased). A comparison of the two models, of uncertainty and central place without agglomeration, indicates (i) that those industries in which uncertainty is highest should be most concentrated in towns and (ii) that as uncertainty increases, so firms should locate nearer their market.

The discussion permits the following inferences. Both the uncertainty and the central place with agglomeration models can predict the observed features of town location within market areas, if allowance is made for site variations. The uncertainty model has the advantage that it is methodologically neater than the finite central place model, for its predictions do not rely on the catch-all of agglomeration economies. The uncertainty model predicts more relationships than the central place model, and furthermore predicts relationships which had not previously been observed. In both the finite central place model and the uncertainty model, optimum locations are not proved in any formal sense; in the one case, they depend on iterative solutions and, in the other, on use of a particular decision-making model.

Land Use Patterns

Formal land use models under certainty assume the existence of central places. People and farm production are located around these places; they sell labour and food to the towns and in return buy other goods from the towns. The transport costs inherent in this exchange of goods and services form the foundation upon which land use models are built. A simple pattern develops on an isotropic plain when firms are certain and choices are socially optimal; the pattern becomes more complicated when resource variations and agglomeration economies are examined. Under uncertainty, problems of change and of risk exist which further distort the simple patterns of the formal certainty systems.

Land use models predict the existence of zones of production around a centre of consumption. These zones depend upon the differing abilities of crops to pay for transport to the market. Because of its advantages of location, land near the

Figure 10–4: Typical von Thünen land use patterns: A—without distortion; B—with competing centre; C—with cheap transport route; and D—with variations in productivity.
Source: Haggett (1965: 170).

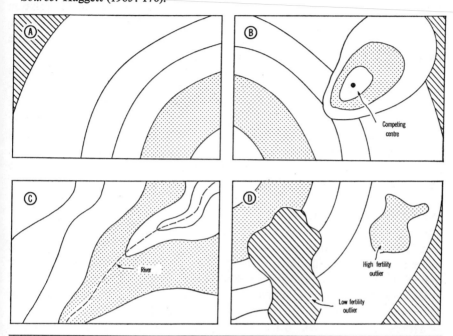

market commands higher rent than land more distant from the market; therefore, within any one land use zone, the intensity of production increases as the market is approached. At the equilibrium, no firm makes profits.

Alonso's urban land use model is essentially similar to von Thünen's one industry analysis. The model predicts that (i) the steeper the bid price curve, the nearer the centre of the city does a user of land locate, (ii) if the desire for land is strong, the poor live in central suburbs, (iii) increases in population are paralleled by increases in population density, and (iv) reductions in transport costs promote suburbanisation.

Typical von Thünen land use patterns, with and without some of the distortions due to transport and resource variations, are presented in Fig. 10–4. These diagrams illustrate clearly the main features of the simple prediction. However, in more complex societies, where agricultural production is subject to joint costs and returns, where agglomeration economies modify marketing costs and where resource variations are more complex, the simple pattern of this model disappears. Such a complex pattern appears compatible with the superficially disturbed patterns of reality which nevertheless (as Chisholm's data indicate) do present some less obvious correlations between production and location.

The uncertainty model is more complex. Since it too is founded on transport costs, it predicts the features analysed by von Thünen and Alonso. But it also predicts more. Uncertainty increases with distance from the market; therefore as distance from markets increases managers of plants (i) make increasingly conservative production choices, (ii) decide upon plants which are small in relation to the certainty optimum, (iii) run greater risks of bankruptcy, and (iv) receive higher profits upon their operations. The uncertainty land use system is more comprehensive than the equivalent certainty model.

The different models support several inferences. The uncertainty model is more general than the certainty system, for it provides a wider range of predictions, some of which are to be observed in reality. On the other hand, the uncertainty model is more complex than the von Thünen-Alonso certainty model without agglomeration. The question is whether the greater range of prediction of the uncertainty model compensates for its added complexity. Assumptions about the value of prediction and the cost of complexity are necessary to answer it.

Patterns of Regional Growth
The regional growth models are the least formally expressed of the certainty location systems—partly because they assume the complicating condition of uneven resource distributions. Correspondingly, definite predictions are more difficult to deduce from the growth models than from land use or central place models. On the other hand it is at this scale that some of the clearest effects of uncertainty on location patterns are to be discovered.

The North-Perloff-Wingo model of regional economic growth is concerned with the effect of resources upon the rate and the direction of growth. The model relies essentially upon the ideas of the multiplier effect of changes in the amount and value of goods which a region exports. The role of resources in determining the amount and the structure of exports is emphasised in this model, though it is also recognised that location and the timing of the impetus to growth (with respect to technology) are important conditioners of the growth process. Correspondingly, regional growth and variations in regional growth—in terms of both its amount and structure—are presumed to be associated primarily with inter-regional variations in the nature and value of resources. Tiebout also considers local factor costs as important determinants of regional growth.

Major modification of the model is due, however, to Hirschman and Myrdal, who emphasise the fact that growth processes are characterised by positive feedback mechanisms. The region in which growth first commences cumulates an advantage over rival regions: growth is not located merely in accordance with resources, but also in response to the location of the impetus to growth. The degree to which growth is concentrated in a few regions within a certain system depends upon the income elasticity of demand for the goods of other regions, agglomeration economies, and the effect of relative demand and wage levels for labour of varying skills upon migration differentials.

The analysis of the location and direction of growth under uncertainty depends upon two models. The static growth model is but an extension of the land use model previously discussed. However, the models of innovation diffusion may be interpreted as growth models for societies in which innovation is spatially localised but temporally continuous. The static model specifically predicts that growth is fastest where uncertainty is lowest—that is, where distances from markets are lowest—and that those industries which are most uncertain are also those industries which are most concentrated in a few regions of dense economic activity. The diffusion models, interpreted as systems for predicting the manner in which growth spreads out from localised innovations, indicate (i) 'S' shaped growth curves at any one point, (ii) particular forms to the curve which measures the degree of concentration of activity at a point as a function of time and distance of the point from the origin, and (iii) an increase in the rate at which impetuses are adopted (once received) as the number of regions which have already adopted increases.

Data have been presented which reveal how these predictions compare with reality. It is shown that, other things being equal (particularly the type of commodity exported and the importance of exports in the national economy), growth is fastest where uncertainty is lowest, and that uncertainty is lowest where distance to markets is least. The diffusion models are tested by innovation rather than growth data. These data indicate that though the specific forms of some equations of spatial diffusion are not substantiated, location and acceptance are nevertheless related and the rate of adoption of an innovation (once received) increases as distance from the innovation source increases.

The relationship between growth, uncertainty, and location on a national scale is as predicted by the static growth model. This relationship is not predicted by the certainty systems. The fact of innovation and some of its forms are compatible with the dynamic growth models. Generally, these data are compatible with the uncertainty models but not with the certainty models. The uncertainty models are more powerful, in the sense of providing a wider range of predictions, than the certainty models; but at the same time they are more complex, especially once dynamic equation systems are set up. By incorporating the necessary assumptions, the uncertainty models can predict the features of reality which are predicted by the multiplier and cumulative feedback models of growth in certainty.

Effects of Uncertainty on Location

An explanation of the pattern of location of firms and concentrations of activity relies upon three main variables: distance costs, external economies, and economies and diseconomies of scale within the firm. (Although external economies are closely related to distance costs, their separation has been found to be analytically useful.) Uncertainty affects all three of these variables. To some extent it is more useful to regard uncertainty costs as affecting these variables than as being a new variable which is taken into account in location analysis. Much of the theory of location under uncertainty can be integrated within this more general framework.

273

Uncertainty affects the scale of plants. As the coefficient of variation of received prices increases, so the optimum allocation of total capital to 'productive' investment falls. Thus even though uncertainty and firm size may not be related, variability does affect the proportion of a firm's capital which is invested in plant, as opposed to being held in reserve. But uncertainty does also limit firm size, through diminishing returns to management and through the unwillingness of capitalists to expose themselves to very large possible losses. Thus, both firm size and plant size are reduced by uncertainty. The greater the uncertainty, the greater is this reduction.

The limitation on plant size has several effects on the pattern of location in society. Firstly, uncertainty differs between industries and therefore alters the relationships of plant size more in some industries than in others. Secondly, income levels in society are reduced because plants are not operating at their technical optimum size: if income levels affect urbanisation, then the proportion of the population which lives in urban places is smaller the greater the uncertainty. Thirdly, uncertainty varies over a spatial economic system, tending to rise as distance from markets increases; therefore plant sizes and income levels (in the absence of perfect equalising mechanisms) vary over the system. And fourthly, small plants are less able to internalise services than large plants. Under uncertainty, plant size is reduced, so plants on average rely more on external services in uncertain than in certain systems. Hence plants agglomerate more in uncertainty than in certainty. The major effects of uncertainty on location through plant size are therefore to alter the relative sizes of market areas in industries, to reduce incomes (causing alterations in spending patterns), to vary plant size and income over space, and to increase the economies due to agglomerating in large towns (which contain a variety of external services).

Uncertainty also affects distance costs. The costs to society and to firms which result from distance include not merely the costs of transporting goods over space, but also some costs of uncertainty. Generally, it appears that distance costs are higher in an uncertain than in a certain economic system.

Thus price variability rises with distance from the market. From this simple model has been constructed a pattern of economic growth and population distribution. As variability increases, managers of plants make increasingly conservative production choices and receive lower returns from their operations. Similarly, if allowance is made for the type of commodity exported and income levels, the further a country is from its market, the more variable are its export prices and income, and the lower is its rate of growth of income *per capita*. The cost of distance impact of uncertainty is measured dynamically by the effect of distance on growth rates and measured statically by the reduction in production caused by the change in uncertainty which is associated with changes in price variability.

Furthermore, increases in distance from suppliers and from markets are associated with increases in the levels of stocks held by firms and with increases in the communication costs of firms. Firms are motivated to secure adequate flows of the factors of production. Uncertainties in the supply of raw materials, labour, and capital are minimised when firms locate near the sources of these inputs.

These higher distance costs have several effects on location patterns. Growth of income per head tends to be fastest near major markets; incomes per acre fall as distance from markets rises; and stock, communication, and marketing costs affect the optimum locations of firms. It appears that uncertainty causes greater increases in the costs of distance from markets than in the costs of distance from supplies. Consequently, uncertainty is positively associated with the location of activity near its markets. In high income industrial societies, this implies that uncertainty promotes concentration in a few large and central cities or regions; on the other hand, location near markets is obtained by the dispersal of urban activities in lower income, rural systems.

Equally, agglomeration economies are higher in an uncertain economy than in a relatively certain one. To the relatively static analysis of Weber may be added some further economies of location in large cities and developed regions.

The attractiveness of large cities as sites for new firms and new industries—an attractiveness which arises out of the uncertainty of these firms—is an agglomeration economy. New firms and new industries are uncertain and therefore small, and so must rely on the external services of large cities for many of their inputs. Firms prefer to locate where there are many service outlets which they may use for inputs.

Secondly, large cities and regions receive advantages over other towns and areas because of their favourable position with respect to the production and diffusion of innovations. Innovations are produced to a greater extent in large cities than small. There are two consequences. Firstly, theories about the nature of the diffusion process and data relating to actual diffusion situations reveal that innovations diffuse gradually over space: large cities and regions, by creating more innovations, maintain for themselves cost advantages over other areas. Secondly, since firms optimise data collection by gathering information about areas close rather than distant from themselves, more innovating firms locate in large cities than the mere size of those cities would lead one to expect.

Thus uncertainty increases agglomeration economies. Firms gain advantages from locating near other firms. The effect of uncertainty through agglomeration economies is to increase the degree of concentration of society into large cities, regions and nations. Both external services and innovations are provided at a higher level within population concentrations than elsewhere within the economy.

Thus uncertainty alters economies of scale, agglomeration economies, and distance costs. These alterations provide one of the primary impacts of uncertainty upon location patterns. Plants tend to be smaller in an uncertain than in a certain system: the effect of uncertainty upon the size of the market areas of firms is not generally determinate though, for, while uncertainty reduces plant size, it also reduces consumer incomes. Town spacing is thus not a determinate function of uncertainty. The proportion of a society's urban activities which is contained in a few large cities is higher in an uncertain than in a certain system

275

because plants, being smaller, use external economies more than in a certain system, and there are more external economies available. The concentration of activity within a few areas also tends to be increased by the higher distance costs in uncertainty as compared with certainty (however, this may not be true if much of the income of society depends upon rural activities).

The resulting pattern of activity is more costly in an uncertain than in a certain system. The external diseconomies of city and regional scale, especially such congestion costs as traffic costs, are higher in an uncertain system than in a system in which activity is less concentrated in a few areas. The income generated by an uncertain system is lower than the income derived from corresponding activities within a certain economy. These features occur despite the fact that entrepreneurs are trying to optimise their decisions.

A second major purpose of the discussion has been to evaluate decisions of firms which are uncertain. The theoretical analysis has suggested that uncertainty about the number and behaviour of rivals may drive firms into towns, even though their profits could be higher outside those towns. Uncertainty enhances the growth of large cities because of the need of firms to co-ordinate decisions and because of the risks of making unusual location decisions. This analysis thus indicates one reason why towns are formed, and reinforces the conclusion that uncertainty increases the concentration of activity within a few areas.

The discussion of the effect of uncertainty upon economies of scale, agglomeration economies, and distance costs suggest that new data be introduced into an analysis of location decisions and of patterns of activity. These data can be treated within existing conceptual frameworks, as has been shown above. But the theory of games is a relatively novel way of analysing the information, and the models which use its criteria are different from traditional models. The basis of this difference lies in the term 'maximum profits'. In traditional certainty analyses the use of the term is relatively simple, whereas, in an uncertain system, a firm tries to maximise profits safely, realising that opponents are behaving similarly. The firm's motives include maximum profits, but equally importantly, secure profits—for profits are only maximised in the long run if the firm remains in business. The usefulness of this concept in location theory arises because firms realise that their profits depend in part on the location of later sellers and consumers, and therefore try to secure a location which will be reasonably good no matter what other firms decide.

The models which use the game format—that is, the models of location in a linear market and of production decisions under uncertainty—have been employed to demonstrate how firms react to uncertainty. The models predict that firms make defensive decisions: long-run optimisation requires security against bankruptcy. The criterion indicates that firms aggregate together in cities to a greater extent than they would if they were certain.

From these game models arises an additional effect of uncertainty on location patterns. Whereas the adjustment of firms to the running costs caused by uncertainty may be optimal for society (given uncertainty), decisions made in accordance with the predictions of the game format models are socially sub-optimal. Even though firms may be making the best choice from their own point of view, these choices may not be the best for society. One form of loss occurs if expectations of firms are inaccurate, but this is a loss to the firm as well as to society. It is more interesting to define the occasions on which a firm's best choice is not socially optimal.

The model of location in a linear market analysed the choices of uncertain interdependent sellers, and suggested that these sellers locate at the centre of the market. While there exists only one firm in an industry, the social optimum location is the centre, but when the industry contains two or more firms, incomes in the market may be maximised when these firms separate. The socially optimum location depends on transport costs, density of demand, slope of the demand curve, and price, but unless external economies can offset the influence of these factors, incomes in the market may be higher if the sellers separate than if they congregate together. The aggregation of firms selling the same good is not necessarily non-optimal for society—this depends on external economies —but in some cases the *ex ante* maximum profit location of uncertain interdependent sellers may not be socially the best location. (If this is true, the location is not the best *ex post* site for the firm either.)

Similarly the best location before the event for firms which must agree on a common site may not be the best *ex post* location. Firms may be attracted to the largest city in a region even though some other place may offer higher profits. This notion may be linked with the more general problem of co-ordinating locational movement of external economy firms. Assume that there are several firms within an industrial complex, the profits of which depend closely on proximity to the other firms in the complex, and that relocation of the complex from point Y to point Z would be profitable (that is, the extra profits at Z would yield a market rate of return to the entire complex on the capital invested in the relocation). Society and each firm would then benefit by this movement. However, no one firm can make the move on its own, for unless all the firms relocate at the same time, the individual firms lose by the change in location. Hence the relocation of such an industrial complex requires co-ordination of decisions, in the same way that the sellers had to co-ordinate their location choices with respect to cities. The locational change will not take place unless the firms can communicate, unless they can make binding agreements, and unless they can all finance the move at the same time. The relocation of some industrial complexes is halted when some of these conditions do not hold. Social income is then less than the maximum.

The innovation models indicate another way in which uncertainty introduces location patterns which are socially less than the best. A firm which receives an innovation quickly is more likely to adopt that innovation profitably than a second firm which does not receive the innovation until later, even though, in the long run, the second firm might be able to produce more profitably. This is a model of initial advantage: historical momentum, or geographical inertia,

277

yields patterns which are non-optimal for society in the long run. Similarly, the models of location searching indicate that location patterns within a system depend in part on the origin of firms which are choosing locations. This result is socially sub-optimal.

Furthermore, firms may use the minimax criterion to make production decisions, or may use criteria which lie between the minimax criterion and the maximised expectations criterion. The resulting decisions are not the best for society. The farmers make the best choice for themselves (before the event) by using such criteria: maximum profits in the long run for the firms require that they stay in business, and so the firms may not make a bet according to the odds because a failure would bankrupt them. However, social income is maximised when all firms make the best bet according to the odds (though an allowance must be made for the costs of buying and selling businesses and of administering bankruptcies). The firm maximises long-run profits by staying in business, but it seldom matters to society which firm operates a particular plant.

So far in this chapter we have discussed the implications of entrepreneurial uncertainty for individual location choices; only when analysing growth and diffusion have mass behaviour and social patterns been considered. But one of the major methodological problems confronting location theory is the fact that individual behaviour cannot be connected with social patterns under realistic assumptions. Location theory contains process models for individual location choices and probability models for social location patterns; but there exist only weak connections between the two, connections which can only be established under the most simple assumptions about the nature of the human and physical environment within which entrepreneurs operate.

The town location model set up in Chapter 7 may be used as a first step in constructing such a link between individual decision taking and mass behaviour patterns. The environment is more complex and realistic in that model than in classical models, and this environmental complexity makes location patterns more determinate than in those classical models. In any area of given income and technology levels, the number, size, and spacing of towns in any one bounded region depends upon the size and population density of that bounded region. Thus, in the entire area, the overall pattern of town size and spacing depends upon the variations in size of the bounded regions and upon the distances separating those regions (this latter variable affects functions which serve several market regions from one outlet).

Thus there exists, in principle at least, a computable relationship between regional size and spacing and the size and spacing of towns for any area of known income and technology. The fact that this relationship can be computed for a variable environment implies that individual decisions can be linked to mass location patterns under conditions of greater realism in this model than in the classical models, where environments have to be homogeneous. Nevertheless, to establish the nature and the form of these fuller and more realistic connections between the two aspects of location theory requires that the links and models tentatively created be considerably generalised. This book represents merely the first stage in the creation of a general theory of location under uncertainty which links individual and social processes, and has done little more than identify some of the processes at work. The various models must be integrated and generalised before detailed and coherent predictions can be made about reality.

Uncertainty and Planning
The models of location developed in this book imply some conclusions about the nature and function of planning in an uncertain economy. Isard (1969) has shown how bargaining procedures may be used to solve conflicts between regions and planners, procedures which may also be used to solve conflicts between large firms. But rather than examine planning procedures, I want to describe here the implications of uncertainty for the role of planning in an 'individualistic' economy.

Planning may be defined as any activity in the market by an organisation larger than the firm. Normally, such a body is a government instrumentality, though this need not always be the case. As such, planning activities range in scale of interference from the operation of state monopolies (such as defence and nationalised industries) to the publication of data about the expected level of national income next year or about the economic state of wheat farmers in Victoria. One of the advantages gained by explicitly introducing uncertainty into locational analysis is that it permits us to identify some of the occasions upon which the operation of an individualistic market economy may be improved by interference from the planning authority. As yet there has been little direct attempt to relate planning to location theory.

Economic theory has shown that under given assumptions (which include the conditions of perfect competition), a Pareto maximum of social welfare is attained if decision taking is left solely in the hands of individuals. Planning theorists have attempted to determine the conditions under which this proposition is not true; there are several such conditions (see Jöhr and Singer, 1955: 120-8; Rosenstein-Rodan, 1963; Tinbergen, 1964: 80-101; Seth, 1967: 10-12, 33-7; and Tinbergen, 1967: 32-7, for further discussion of these conditions). Firstly, if the future is not known with certainty, the conditions for Pareto optimality are not fulfilled. Secondly, if some production is subject to external economies or diseconomies, an individual decision taker need not make decisions which maximise social welfare. If, thirdly, production levels are affected by experience, then temporary interference may be useful: this is the infant industry argument. Fourthly, if individual decisions are not independent but rather depend on other decisions, then individual errors may cumulate rather than counterbalance each other: the business cycle seems to exemplify this argument. And fifthly, if production is subject to decreasing marginal costs throughout its range, competition forces prices to the level of marginal costs, which is below average costs: production is consequently continuously at a loss or is monopolised.

I want now to attempt to identify occasions upon which specific types of interference may promote social welfare. Most of these cases lie in the first

279

category—of sub-optimality due to the unknown future—but the third case (experience as a determinant of production levels) also arises. The implications of external economies for planning have received some attention already (see, for example, the work on traffic congestion and costs of public utilities in Australian cities by Neutze, 1965), but they are of little relevance to the models constructed in this book. The fourth and fifth conditions are generally important in an economic system, but they do not specifically apply to any one model developed here.

It is assumed that the aim of planning is to maximise income. Thus, interference is potentially useful whenever production and location decisions yield less than the optimum which occurs under uncertainty. The costs of planning are not considered explicitly. Such costs may be greater than the returns, in which case planning is not profitable.

The models developed in this book have considered uncertainty as due to three sources: about the behaviour of rivals (the problem of firms' locations), about the state of the environment (production decision problems), and about techniques of production (discussed in terms of diffusion and learning). Each of these sources is associated with particular planning behaviour.

The models in Chapter 9 indicated that social inefficiencies arise as a consequence of finite rates of innovation diffusion and of learning. These inefficiencies are due, firstly, to the fact that entrepreneurs do not adopt innovations quickly and, secondly, to the fact that learning processes may imply sub-optimal locational equilibria. The first circumstance implies that welfare would be increased if the planning authority promoted the rate of diffusion of innovations by mass media advertising and by paying individual entrepreneurs to advocate the innovation to others. The amount of this promotion should be fixed to maximise the difference between the gain in the value of production due to more rapid diffusion (over and above values of production under 'natural' rates of diffusion) and the cost of promotion. In the second case, a subsidy might be paid to producers until they attain yields close to the asymptote of the learning curve; thus the market is given an opportunity to evaluate producers and locations after producers' yields have reached approximately their limiting value rather than while some producers are still learning. It is worthwhile introducing such a subsidy if its cost is less than the difference between the value of the location pattern with subsidy and the value without the subsidy. The size of the subsidy can be determined so as to maximise the difference between its cost and the increase in social welfare occasioned by that subsidy.

Chapter 8 analysed cases in which uncertainty is due to the unknown future state of nature. Such uncertainty causes firms to hold reserves and stocks and creates pressures for those firms to make conservative production decisions. The planning authority can provide some of the information necessary to reduce this uncertainty—for example, it can publish estimates of the probable future state of the economy. But the accuracy of much knowledge about the future remains low: the planning authority is hardly able to provide reliable information about the future prices of a given good, consumer behaviour, or the state of the physical environment. Thus, some production and location decisions at least must be taken in the face of uncertainty and be less valuable to society than decisions taken in certainty. Although the cause of the income loss cannot be overcome, there exists, at least in principle, one cure for the problem. For a given region it is possible to compute the socially optimal production decision of a firm and to compute the probability distribution of yearly returns. Given these data, firms can be insured against returns less than a given value, the premium being fixed so as to make the scheme just balance for that region over a long period of time. The scheme is valuable to society if administrative costs are less than the increase in production caused by socially optimal decision taking; producers participate if the premium is less than their increase in profit.

The models in Chapters 6 and 7 assume that uncertainty is due to the behaviour of rivals; the decisions made are specifically location decisions. In these cases, conservative decision taking causes place size to be larger than the certainty optimum. Assume that for a given planning horizon the optimum pattern can be defined. Then, within towns, this optimum can be attained by land use planning, that is, by allocating (in advance) particular sites for particular activities and by refusing to permit such activities to locate outside these sites. For decisions about locations between towns or regions, firms should be paid the full value of any external economies they yield and taxed the value of the diseconomies they cause.

It has been assumed so far that the planning authority can define optima for the future. Much of the cost of planning is due to attempts to make these definitions. Even after data have been gathered, predictions may be wrong. In particular, experience in administering subsidies indicates that it is difficult to recognise long-term changes when short-term variations are superimposed upon them; and it is always impossible to anticipate and plan for the unexpected. In many cases it may be that the cost of defining long-run optima may be greater than the losses caused by socially sub-optimal decisions. But even if this is not so, many of the planning decisions may have to be taken in the face of uncertainty. Then those decisions should be made in the manner outlined in Chapter 5.

The assumption of uncertainty in a location model can therefore contribute several results. Firstly, economies of scale in plants are reduced, external economies are increased, and distance costs (especially to the market) rise. These results normally increase the degree of concentration of economic activity within the system. Secondly, uncertainty assumptions may be used to demonstrate the existence of towns and to provide specific predictions about the locations of these towns in bounded market areas. Thirdly, uncertainty provides some reasons why location patterns may not be the best for society. The empirical estimates which have been quoted are crude, but they indicate that uncertainty and its surrogates may account for between 5 and 25 per cent of the locational variance in societies, depending on the surrogate and the scale of the system.

Although the models employed and the measurements made are simple, the impact of uncertainty on location is clearly predictable and measurable. In addition, the assumption of uncertainty affects the methodology of location analysis. To a small degree, the assumption helps to bridge the gap between individualistic decision models and social location patterns, and it enables us theoretically to identify the potentially useful roles of a planning authority in determining the location pattern of an economic system. These results are sufficiently encouraging to indicate that an integrated mathematical statement of the general theory of location under uncertainty should be made.

References

ABBEY, H. (1952) 'An examination of the Reed-Frost theory of epidemics', *Human Biology*, **24**: 201-33.

ACKLEY, G. (1942) 'Spatial competition in a discontinuous market', *Quarterly Journal of Economics*, **56**: 212-30.

AJO, R. (1965) 'On the structure of population density in London's field', *Acta Geographica*, **18**: 1-17.

ALCHIAN, A. A. (1950) 'Uncertainty, evolution and economic theory', *Journal of Political Economy*, **58**: 211-21.

ALLEN, G. R. (1959) *Agricultural Marketing Policies*, Oxford.

ALONSO, W. (1966) *Location and Land Use: Toward a General Theory of Land Rent*, Honolulu.

ANDERSON, T. R. and EGELAND, J. A. (1961) 'Spatial aspects of social area analysis', *American Sociological Review*, **26**: 392-8.

ANDREWS, R. B. (1953a) 'Mechanics of the urban economic base: historical development of the base concept', *Land Economics*, **29**: 161-7.

— (1953b) 'Mechanics of the urban economic base: the problem of terminology', *Land Economics*, **29**: 263-8.

— (1953c) 'Mechanics of the urban economic base: a classification of base types', *Land Economics*, **29**: 343-9.

— (1954a) 'Mechanics of the urban economic base: the problem of base measurement', *Land Economics*, **30**: 52-60.

— (1954b) 'Mechanics of the urban economic base: general problems of base identification', *Land Economics*, **30**: 164-72.

— (1954c) 'Mechanics of the urban economic base: special problems of base identification', *Land Economics*, **30**: 260-9.

— (1955) 'Mechanics of the urban economic base: the concept of base ratios', *Land Economics*, **31**: 47-53.

ANSCOMBE, F. J. (1950) 'Sampling theory of the negative binomial and logarithmic series distributions', *Biometrika*, **37**: 358-82.

ARROW, K. J. (1951) 'Alternative approaches to the theory of choice in risk-taking situations', *Econometrica*, **19**: 404-37.

ARROW, K. J. (1959) 'Functions of a theory of behavior under uncertainty', *Metroeconomica*, **11**: 12-20.

ATKINSON, J. W. (1957) 'Motivational determinants of risk-taking behaviour', *Psychological Review*, **64**: 359-72.

BAER, W. (1964) 'Regional inequality and economic growth in Brazil', *Economic Development and Cultural Change*, **12**: 268-85.

BAILEY, N. T. J. (1957) *The Mathematical Theory of Epidemics*, London.

— (1967) *The Mathematical Approach to Biology and Medicine*, London.

BALDWIN, R. E. (1956) 'Patterns of development in newly settled regions', *Manchester School of Economic and Social Studies*, **24**: 161-79.

BARTHOLOMEW, D. J. (1967) *Stochastic Models for Social Processes*, London.

BEAL, G. M. and ROGERS, E. M. (1960) 'The adoption of two farm practices in a central Iowa community', *Iowa State University, Agricultural and Home Economics Experimental Station, Special Report*, **26**.

BEAVER, S. H. and KOSINSKI, L. (eds.) (1964) *Problems of Applied Geography*, **2**, Warsaw.

BECKERMAN, W. (1956) 'Distance and the pattern of intra-European trade', *Review of Economics and Statistics*, **38**: 31-40.

BEER, S. (1959) *Cybernetics and Management*, London.

BENSUSAN-BUTT, D. M. (1960) *On Economic Growth: an Essay in Pure Theory*, Oxford.

BERKOVITZ, L. D. and DRESHER, M. (1960) 'Allocation of two types of aircraft in tactical air war: a game-theoretic analysis', *Operations Research*, **8**: 694-706.

BERNOULLI, D. (1738) 'Specimen theoriae novae de mensura sortis', *Commentarii academiae scientiarum imperiales Petropolitanae*, **5**: 175-92.

BERRY B. J. L. (1963) *Commercial Structure and Commercial Blight*, Chicago.

— (1966) *Essays on Commodity Flows and the Spatial Structure of the Indian Economy*, Chicago.

— (1967) *Geography of Market Centres and Retail Distribution*, Englewood Cliffs.

— and GARRISON, W. L. (1958a) 'The functional bases of the central place hierarchy', *Economic Geography*, **34**: 145-54.

— (1958b) 'Recent developments of central place theory', *Regional Science Association, Papers and Proceedings*, **4**: 107-20.

BIRD, J. (1968) *Seaport Gateways of Australia*, London.

BLACKWELL, D. and GIRSHICK, M. A. (1954) *The Theory of Games and Statistical Decisions*, New York.

BLUMENFELD, H. (1955) 'The economic base of the metropolis', *Journal of the American Institute of Planners*, **21**: 114-32.

BOGUE, D. J. (1950) *The Structure of the Metropolitan Community: A Study of Dominance and Subdominance*, Ann Arbor.

BOHLEN, J. M. (1968) 'Research needed on adoption models', *North Central Regional Research Bulletin*, **186**: 15-21.

BORCH, K. H. (1968) *The Economics of Uncertainty*, Princeton.

BORCH, K. H. and MOSSIN, J. (eds.) (1968) *Risk and Uncertainty*, London.

BORTS, G. H. (1960) 'Equalisation of returns and regional economic growth', *American Economic Review*, **50**: 319-47.

— and STEIN, J. L. (1964) *Economic Growth in a Free Market*, New York.

BRADBURN, H. M. and BERLEW, D. E. (1961) 'Need for achievement and English industrial growth', *Economic Development and Cultural Change*, **10**: 8-20.

BRAITHWAITE, R. B. (1955) *Theory of Games as a Tool for the Moral Philosopher*, Cambridge.

BROOKFIELD, H. C. (1969) 'On the environment as perceived', *Progress in Geography*, **1**: 51-80.

BROSS, I. D. J. (1953) *Design for Decision*, New York.

BROWN, G. W. (1960) 'Computation in decision making', in Machol, R. E. (ed.), *Information and Decision Processes*, New York, pp. 1-14.

BROWN, L. A. and MOORE, E. G. (1969) 'Diffusion Research in Geography: A Perspective', *Progress in Geography*, **1**: 121-57.

BRUNHES, J. (1925) *La Géographie Humaine*, Paris.

BUREAU OF AGRICULTURAL ECONOMICS (1961) *The Canning Fruit-Growing Industry: An Economic Survey*, Canberra.

BURGESS, E. W. (1925) 'The growth of the city : an introduction to a research project', in Park, R. E., Burgess, E. W., and McKenzie, R. D. (eds.), *The City*, Chicago, 1967, pp. 47-62.

BURTON, I. and KATES, R. W. (1964) 'The floodplain and the seashore', *Geographical Review*, **54**: 366-85.

CAESER, A. A. L. (1964) 'Planning and the geography of Great Britain', *Advancement of Science*, **21**: 230-40.

CARNAP, R. (1950) *Logical Foundations of Probability*, Chicago.

CARTER, C. F. (1954) 'A revised theory of expectations', in Carter, C. F., Meredith, G. P., and Shackle, G. L. S. (eds.), *Uncertainty and Business Decisions*, Liverpool, pp. 48-57.

CARTER, C. F., MEREDITH, G. P., and SHACKLE, G. L. S. (eds.) (1954) *Uncertainty and Business Decisions*, Liverpool.

CASETTI, E. (1969) 'Alternate urban population density models: an analytical comparison of their validity range', *Studies in Regional Science*, **1**: 105-16.

CHAMBERLIN, E. H. (1950) *The Theory of Monopolistic Competition*, Cambridge, Mass.

CHAMBERS, E. J. and GORDON, D. F. (1966) 'Primary products and economic growth: an empirical measurement', *Journal of Political Economy*, **74**: 315-32.

CHAPARRO, A. (1955) Role Expectation and Adoption of New Farm Practices, Ph.D. thesis, Philadelphia.

CHAPPELL, J. M. A. and WEBBER, M. J. (1970) 'Electric simulation of spatial diffusion processes', *Regional Studies*, **4**: 25-39.

CHERNOFF, H. (1959) 'Motivation for an approach to the sequential design of experiments', in Machol, R. E. (ed.), *Information and Decision Processes*, New York, pp. 15-26.

CHERNOFF, H. and MOSES, L. E. (1950) *Elementary Decision Theory*, New York.

CHERRY, C. (1961) *On Human Communication*, New York.

CHISHOLM, M. D. I. (1962) *Rural Settlement and Land Use*, London.

CHORLEY, R. J. and HAGGETT, P. (eds.) (1967) *Models in Geography*, London.

CHRISTALLER, W. (1966) *Central Places in Southern Germany*, Englewood Cliffs. Translated by C. W. Baskin from *Die Zentralen Orte in Süddeutschland*, Jena, 1933.

CLARK, C. (1951) 'Urban population densities', *Journal of the Royal Statistical Society*, Series A, **114**: 490-6.

— (1967) *Population Growth and Land Use*, London.

CLARK, P. J. (1956) 'Grouping in spatial distributions', *Science*, **123**: 373-4.

CLIFF, A. D. (1968) 'The neighbourhood effect in the diffusion of innovations', *Institute of British Geographers, Transactions*, **43**: 75-84.

COMMONWEALTH BUREAU OF CENSUS AND STATISTICS (1961) 'Population: local government areas and urban centres—New South Wales', *Census of the Commonwealth of Australia, 30th June 1961, Field count statement*, No. 6, Canberra.

— (1952-63) *Secondary Industries, Part 1: Factory and Building Operations*, Canberra.

COOPER, L. (1963) 'Location-allocation problems', *Operations Research*, **11**: 331-43.

— (1968) 'An extension of the generalized Weber problem', *Journal of Regional Science*, **8**: 181-97.

CORTÉS, J. B. (1961) 'The achievement motive in the Spanish economy between the thirteenth and eighteenth centuries', *Economic Development and Cultural Change*, **9**: 144-63.

COUGHENOUR, C. M. (1964) 'The rate of technological diffusion among locality groups', *American Journal of Sociology*, **69**: 325-39.

— (1968) 'Some general problems in diffusion from the perspective of theory of social action', *North Central Regional Research Bulletin*, **186**: 5-14.

— and PATEL, N. B. (1962) 'Trends in the use of recommended farm practices and information in twelve Kentucky neighborhoods', *University of Kentucky, Agricultural Experiment Station, Lexington, Progress Report*, **111**.

COWLING, K. and PERKINS, R. J. (1963) 'Producer behaviour in the choice of sugar beet varieties: comparisons of game theoretic solutions with actual selections', *Bulletin of the Oxford University Institute of Economics and Statistics*, **25**: 109-18.

COX, K. R. and GOLLEDGE, R. G. (eds.) (1969) *Behavioral Problems in Geography: A Symposium*, Evanston, Illinois.

CURRY, L. (1964) 'The random spatial economy: an exploration in settlement theory', *Annals of the Association of American Geographers*, **54**: 138-46.

— (1967) 'Central places in the random spatial economy', *Journal of Regional Science*, **7**: 217-38.

DACEY, M. F. (1960a) 'Analysis of central place and point patterns by a nearest neighbor method', *Proceedings, International Geographical Union Symposium on Urban Geography*, 55-75.

— (1960b) 'The spacing of river towns', *Annals of the Association of American Geographers*, **50**: 59-61.

— (1964a) 'Two-dimensional point patterns: a review and an interpretation', *Regional Science Association, Papers*, **13**: 41-55.

— (1964b) 'Modified Poisson probability law for point pattern more regular than random', *Annals of the Association of American Geographers*, **54**: 559-65.

— (1965) 'The geometry of central place theory', *Geografiska Annaler*, **B 47**: 111-24.

— (1966a) 'A probability model for central place locations', *Annals of the Association of American Geographers*, **56**: 550-68.

— (1966b) 'A compound probability law for a pattern more dispersed than random and with areal inhomogeneity', *Economic Geography*, **42**: 172-9.

— (1968) 'An empirical study of the areal distribution of houses in Puerto Rico', *Institute of British Geographers, Transactions*, **45**: 51-69.

DALY, M. T. (1967) 'Land value determinants: Newcastle, New South Wales', *Australian Geographical Studies*, **5**: 30-9.

DANSKIN, J. M. (1962a) 'A theory of reconnaissance: I', *Operations Research*, **10**: 285-99.

— (1962b) 'A game-theory model of convoy routing', *Operations Research*, **10**: 774-85.

DAVIS, L. (1966) 'The capital markets and industrial concentration: The U.S. and U.K., a comparative study', *The Economic History Review*, 2nd Series, **19**: 255-72.

DEAN, A., AURBACH, H. A., and MARSH, P. C. (1958) 'Some factors related to rationality in decision making among farm operators', *Rural Sociology*, **23**: 121-35.

DEUTSCH, M. (1958) 'Trust and Suspicion', *Journal of Conflict Resolution*, **2**: 265-79.

DEVLETOGLOU, N. E. (1965) 'A dissenting view of duopoly and spatial competition', *Economica*, **32**: 140-60.

DRYDEN, M. M. (1964) 'Capital budgeting: treatment of uncertainty and investment criteria', *Scottish Journal of Political Economy*, **11**: 235-59.

DUNCAN, O. D. (1959) 'Service industries and the urban hierarchy', *Regional Science Association, Papers and Proceedings*, **5**: 105-20.

— SCOTT, W. R., LIEBERSON, S., DUNCAN, B., and WINSBOROUGH, H. L. (1960) *Metropolis and Region*, Baltimore.

DUNN, E. S. (1954) *The Location of Agricultural Production*, Gainesville, Florida.

ECONOMIC COMMISSION FOR EUROPE (1955) *Economic Survey of Europe in 1954*, Geneva.

EDWARDS, W. (1954) 'The theory of decision making', *Psychological Bulletin*, **51**: 380-417.

U

EDWARDS, W. (1955) 'The prediction of decisions among bets', *Journal of Experimental Psychology*, **50**: 201-14.

ENKE, S. (1951) 'Equilibrium among spatially separated markets: solution by electric analogue', *Econometrica*, **19**: 40-7.

ENNEN, E. (1956) 'Les différents types de formation des villes européennes', *Le Moyen Age*, **11**, series 4: 397-411.

ESTALL, R. C. and BUCHANAN, R. O. (1961) *Industrial Activity and Economic Geography*, London.

EVANS, P. A. (1953) 'Experimental evidence concerning contagious distributions in ecology', *Biometrika*, **40**: 186-211.

EZEKIEL, M. (1938): 'The cobweb theorem', *Quarterly Journal of Economics*, **52**: 255-80.

FAGAN, R. H. (1969) 'Australian metalliferous mineral industries: a framework for locational analysis', Department of Human Geography Seminar Paper, Canberra.

FELLER, W. (1957) *An Introduction to Probability Theory and Its Applications*, vol. 1, New York.

FLOOD, M. M. (1960) 'Sequential decisioning', in Machol, R. E. (ed.), *Information and Decision Processes*, New York, pp. 34-52.

FRIEDMANN, J. R. P. (1955) *The Spatial Structure of Economic Development in the Tennessee Valley*, Chicago.

— (1961) 'Cities in social transformation', *Comparative Studies in Society and History*, **4**: 86-103.

FRIEDRICH, C. J. (1929) *Alfred Weber's Theory of the Location of Industry*, Chicago.

FUNCK, R. (1966) 'Comments on Isard and Smith', *Peace Research Society, Papers*, **4**: 99-104.

GARRISON, W. L. and MARBLE, D. F. (eds.) (1967) *Quantitative Geography, I: Economic and Cultural Topics*, Evanston, Illinois.

GASSON, R. (1966) 'The influence of urbanisation on farm ownership and practice', *Studies in Rural Land Use*, **7**.

— (1967) 'Some economic characteristics of part-time farming in Britain', *Journal of Agricultural Economics*, **18**: 111-20.

GEORGE, K. D. (1966) 'Productivity in distribution', *University of Cambridge, Department of Applied Economics, Occasional Paper*, **8**.

GETIS, A. (1963) 'The determination of the location of retail activities with the use of a map transformation', *Economic Geography*, **39**: 14-22.

GOLDMAN, S. (1953) *Information Theory*, London.

GOLLEDGE, R. G. (1960) 'Sydney's metropolitan fringe: a case study in urban-rural relations', *Australian Geographer*, **7**: 243-55.

GOULD, P. R. (1963) 'Man against his environment: a game theoretic framework', *Annals of Association of American Geographers*, **53**: 290-7.

— (1966) 'On mental maps', Michigan Inter-University Community of Mathematical Geographers, Discussion Paper, **9**.

GOULD, P. R. and WHITE, R. (1968) 'The mental maps of British school leavers', *Regional Studies*, **2**: 161-82.

GRAYSON, C. J. (1960) *Decisions under Uncertainty: Drilling Decisions by Oil and Gas Operators*, Boston.

GREENHUT, M. L. (1956) *Plant Location in Theory and Practise: The Economics of Space*, Chapel Hill.

— (1957) 'Games, capitalism and general location theory', *Manchester School of Economic and Social Studies*, **25**: 61-88.

— (1963) *Microeconomics and the Space Economy*, Chicago.

— and COLBERG, M. R. (1962) *Factors in the Location of Florida Industry*, Tallahassee.

GREENWOOD, M. (1935) *Epidemics and Crowd Diseases*, London.

GROTEWALD, A. (1959) 'Von Thünen in retrospect', *Economic Geography*, **35**: 346-55.

GUNAWARDENA, K. A. (1964) Service Centres in Southern Ceylon. Ph.D. thesis, Cambridge.

HAGERSTRAND, T. (1953) *Innovation Diffusion as a Spatial Process*, Chicago, 1967; translated by A. Pred, from *Innovationsförloppet ur Korologisk synpunkt*, Lund.

— (1967) 'On Monte Carlo simulation of diffusion', in Garrison, W. L. and Marble, D. F. (eds.), *Quantitative Geography, I: Economic and Cultural Topics*, Evanston, Illinois, pp. 1-32.

HAGGETT, P. (1965) *Location Analysis in Human Geography*, London.

HAIG, R. M. (1926) 'Toward an understanding of the metropolis', *Quarterly Journal of Economics*, **40**: 179-208, 402-34.

HALL, M. (ed.) (1959) *Made in New York*, Cambridge, Mass.

HALL, P. (ed.) (1966) *Von Thünen's Isolated State*, trans. C. M. Wartenburg, Oxford.

HAMILTON, F. E. I. (1967) 'Models of industrial location', in Chorley, R. J. and Haggett, P. (eds.), *Models in Geography*, London, pp. 361-424.

HART, A. G. (1941) *Anticipations, Uncertainty and Dynamic Planning*, Chicago.

HARTSHORNE, R. (1926) 'The economic geography of plant location', *Annals of Real Estate Practice*, **6**: 40-76.

HARVEY, D. W. (1963) 'Locational change in the Kentish hop industry and the analysis of land use patterns', *Institute of British Geographers, Transactions*, **33**: 123-44.

— (1966a) 'Geographical processes and the analysis of point patterns: testing models of diffusion by quadrant sampling', *Institute of British Geographers, Transactions*, **40**: 81-95.

— (1966b) 'Theoretical concepts and the analysis of agricultural land-use patterns in geography', *Annals of the Association of American Geographers*, **56**: 361-74.

— (1968a) 'Some methodological problems in the use of Neyman type A and

289

negative binomial probability distributions for the analysis of spatial point patterns', *Institute of British Geographers, Transactions*, **44**: 85-95.

— (1968b) 'Pattern, process and the scale problem in geographic research', *Institute of British Geographers, Transactions*, **45**: 71-8.

HATHAWAY, D. E. (1960) 'Migration from agriculture: the historical record and its meaning', *American Economic Review*, **50**: 379-91.

HEADY, E. O. (1960) *The Economics of Agricultural Production and Resource Use*, Englewood Cliffs.

HENDERSON, J. M. (1959) 'The utilization of agricultural land: a theoretical and empirical inquiry', *Review of Economics and Statistics*, **41**: 242-59.

HERBERT, J. D. and STEVENS, B. H. (1960) 'A model for the distribution of residential activity in urban areas', *Journal of Regional Science*, **2**: 21-36.

HICKS, J. R. (1948) *Value and Capital*, Oxford.

HIDORE, J. J. (1963) 'The relationship between cash-grain farming and landforms', *Economic Geography*, **39**: 84-9.

HIRSCHMAN, A. O. (1958) *The Strategy of Economic Development*, New Haven.

HOBBS, D. J., BEAL, G. M., and BOHLEN, J. M. (1964) 'The relation of farm operator values and attitudes to their economic performance', *Iowa State University, Department of Economics and Sociology, Rural Sociology Report*, **33**.

HOFFER, C. R. and STANGLAND, D. (1958) 'Farmers' attitudes and values in relation to adoption of approved practices in corn growing', *Rural Sociology*, **23**: 112-19.

HOOTON, F. G. (1950) 'Risk and the cobweb theorem', *Economic Journal*, **60**: 69-80.

HOOVER, E. M. (1937) *Location Theory and the Shoe and Leather Industries*, Cambridge, Mass.

— (1948) *The Location of Economic Activity*, New York.

HOSELITZ, B. F. (1953) 'The role of cities in the economic growth of underdeveloped countries', *Journal of Political Economy*, **61**: 195-208.

— (1955) 'Generative and parasitic cities', *Economic Development and Cultural Change*, **3**: 278-94.

— and MOORE, W. E. (eds.) (1963) *Industrialisation and Society*, Paris.

HOTELLING, H. (1929) 'Stability in competition', *Economic Journal*, **39**: 41-57.

HOUSE, J. W. (1953) 'Medium sized towns in the urban pattern of two industrial societies: England and Wales—U.S.A.', *Planning Outlook*, **3**: 52-79.

HOYT, H. (1939) *The Structure and Growth of Residential Neighbourhoods in American Cities*, Washington.

— (1966) 'Growth and structure of twenty-one great world cities', *Land Economics*, **42**: 53-64.

HURD, R. M. (1903) *Principles of City Land Values*, New York.

HUTCHINSON, W. M. (1958) *World-wide Marine Distance Tables*, London.

INTERNATIONAL MONETARY FUND (1951-61) *International Financial Statistics*, Washington.

INTERNATIONAL URBAN RESEARCH (1959) *The World's Metropolitan Areas*, Berkeley.

IRWIN, F. W. and SMITH, W. A. S. (1957) 'Value, cost and information as determiners of decision', *Journal of Experimental Psychology*, **54**: 229-32.

ISARD, W. (1956) *Location and Space-Economy*, Cambridge, Mass.   H D 5 8

— (1960) *Methods of Regional Analysis*, Cambridge, Mass.   4 D 5 9

— (1967) 'Game theory, location theory and industrial agglomeration', *Regional Science Association, Papers and Proceedings*, **18**: 1-11.

— (1969) *General Theory: Social, Political, Economic and Regional*, Cambridge, Mass.

— and DACEY, M. F. (1962) 'On the projection of individual behaviour in regional analysis', *Journal of Regional Science*, **4**: 1-34.

— and PECK, M. J. (1954) 'Location theory and international and interregional trade theory', *Quarterly Journal of Economics*, **68**: 97-114.

— and REINER, T. A. (1962) 'Aspects of decision-making theory and regional science', *Regional Science Association, Papers and Proceedings*, **9**: 25-34.

— and SCHOOLER, E. W. (1959) 'Industrial complex analysis, agglomeration economies and regional development', *Journal of Regional Science*, **1**: 19-33.

— SCHOOLER, E. W. and VIETORISZ, T. (1959) *Industrial Complex Analysis and Regional Development*, New York.

— and SMITH, T. E. (1966) 'A practical application of game theoretical approaches to arms reduction', *Peace Research Society, Papers*, **4**: 85-98.

— and VIETORISZ, T. (1955) 'Industrial complex analysis and regional development, with particular reference to Puerto Rico', *Regional Science Association, Papers and Proceedings*, **1**: U1-U17.

JAEGER, J. C. (1951) *An Introduction to Applied Mathematics*, Oxford.

JEFFRESS, L. A. (ed.) (1951) *Cerebral Mechanisms in Behavior*, New York.

JERVIS, F. R. (1957) 'Private company finance in the post-war period', *Manchester School of Economic and Social Studies*, **25**: 190-211.

JEWKES, J. (1930) 'The localisation of the cotton industry', *Economic History* (supplement to *Economic Journal*, **40**): 91-106.

JOHNSTON, R. (1965) 'Sales in Australian central business areas: 1956-57—1961-62', *Australian Geographer*, **9**: 380-1.

JÖHR, W. A. and SINGER, H. W. (1955) *The Role of the Economist as Official Adviser*, trans. J. Degras and S. Frowein, London.

JONES, G. E. (1967) 'The adoption and diffusion of agricultural practices', *World Agricultural Economics and Rural Sociology Abstracts*, **9**: 1-34.

KALDOR, N. (1934) 'The equilibrium of the firm', *Economic Journal*, **44**: 60-76.

KALECKI, M. (1939) *Essays in the Theory of Economic Fluctuations*, London.

KATES, R. W. (1962) *Hazard and Choice Perception in Flood Plain Management*, Chicago.

KEYNES, J. M. (1921) *A Treatise on Probability*, London.

KING, L. J. (1961a) 'The functional role of small towns in Canterbury', *Third New Zealand Geographical Conference, Proceedings:* 139-49.

— (1961b) 'A multivariate analysis of the spacing of urban settlements in the

United States', *Annals of the Association of American Geographers*, **51**: 222-33.

— (1962) 'A quantitative expression of the pattern of urban settlement in selected areas of the United States', *Tijdschrift voor Economische en Sociale Geografie*, **53**: 1-7.

KIVLIN, J. E. (1960) Characteristics of Farm Practices Associated with Rate of Adoption, Ph.D. thesis, Philadelphia.

KLEMME, R. T. (1959) 'Regional analysis as a business tool', *Regional Science Association, Papers and Proceedings*, **5**, 71-7.

KNIGHT, F. H. (1921) *Risk, Uncertainty and Profit*, Boston and New York.

KOLMOGOROV, A. N. (1950) *Foundations of the Theory of Probability* (a translation of 'Grundbegriffe der Wahrscheinlichkeitrechnung', *Ergebnisse der Mathematik und Ihre Grenzgebiete*, **2**, 1933), New York.

KOSTROWICKI, J. (1964) 'The influence of industrialisation and urbanisation on land use and agriculture in Poland', in Beaver, S. H. and Kosinski, L. (eds.), *Problems of Applied Geography*, **2**, Warsaw, pp. 175-92.

KUHN, H. W. and KUENNE, R. E. (1962) 'An efficient algorithm for the numerical solution of the generalized Weber problem in spatial economics', *Journal of Regional Science*, **4**: 21-33.

LANGHAM, M. R. (1963) 'Game theory applied to a policy problem of rice farmers', *Journal of Farm Economics*, **45**: 151-62.

LAUNHARDT, W. (1885) *Mathematische Begründung der Volkswirtschaftslehre*, Leipzig.

LEAMER, E. E. (1968) 'Locational equilibria', *Journal of Regional Science*, **8**: 229-42.

LEFEBER, L. (1964) 'Regional allocation of resources in India', in Rosenstein-Rodan, P. N. (ed.), *Pricing and Fiscal Policies*, London, pp. 18-29.

LERNER, A. P. and SINGER, H. W. (1937) 'Some notes on duopoly and spatial competition', *Journal of Political Economy*, **45**: 145-86.

LICHTENBERG, R. M. (1960) *One-Tenth of a Nation*, Cambridge, Mass.

LIEBERMAN, B. (1960) 'Human behavior in a strictly determined 3×3 matrix game', *Behavioral Science*, **5**: 317-22.

LINGE, G. J. R. (1965) *The Delimitation of Urban Boundaries for Statistical Purposes*, Canberra.

LÖSCH, A. (1938) 'The nature of economic regions', *Southern Economic Journal*, **5**: 71-8.

— (1959) *The Economics of Location*, translated by Stolper, W. F. and Woglom, W. H., from the second revised edition of 1943, New Haven.

LOTKA, A. J. (1925) *Elements of Physical Biology*, Baltimore.

LOWENTHAL, D. (ed.) (1967) *Environmental Perception and Behavior*, Chicago.

LUCE, R. D. and RAIFFA, H. (1957) *Games and Decisions*, New York.

LUTTRELL, W. F. (1962) *Factory Location and Industrial Movement*, London.

MACHOL, R. E. (ed.) (1960) *Information and Decision Processes*, New York.

MACKINTOSH, W. A. (1923) 'Economic factors in Canadian history', *Canadian Historical Review*, **4**: 12-25.

MCLAUGHLIN, G. E. and ROBOCK, S. (1949) *Why Industry Moves South*, Washington.

MCLELLAND, D. C. (1963) 'The achievement motive in economic growth', in Hoselitz, B. F. and Moore, W. E. (eds.), *Industrialisation and Society*, Paris, pp. 74-96.

MALMGREN, H. B. (1958) 'What conclusions are to be drawn from empirical cost data?', *Journal of Industrial Economics*, **7**: 136-44.

MANSFIELD, E. (1961) 'Technical change and the rate of imitation', *Econometrica*, **29**: 741-66.

— (1963a) 'The speed of response of firms to new techniques', *Quarterly Journal of Economics*, **77**: 290-311.

— (1963b) 'Intrafirm rates of diffusion of an innovation', *Review of Economics and Statistics*, **45**: 348-59.

MARCH, J. G. and SIMON, H. A. (1958) *Organizations*, New York.

MARGOLIS, J. (1958) 'The analysis of the firm: rationalism, conventionalism and behaviourism', *The Journal of Business*, **31**: 187-99.

MARSCHAK, J. (1954) 'Towards an economic theory of organization and information', in Thrall, R. M., Coombs, C. H., and Davis, R. L. (eds.), *Decision Processes*, New York, pp. 187-220.

MARSH, C. P. and COLEMAN, A. L. (1955) 'The relation of farmer characteristics to the adoption of recommended farm practices', *Rural Sociology*, **20**: 289-96.

MARTIN, J. E. (1966) *Greater London: An Industrial Geography*, London.

MEAD, W. R. (1953) *Farming in Finland*, London.

MEDVEDKOV, Y. V. (1966) 'The concept of entropy in settlement pattern analysis', *Regional Science Association, Papers and Proceedings*, **18**: 165-8.

MELLOR, J. W. (1955) *Higher Mathematics for Students of Chemistry and Physics*, New York.

METZLER, L. A. (1950) 'A multiple-region theory of income and trade', *Econometrica*, **18**: 329-54.

MILL, J. S. (1848) *Principles of Political Economy*, Boston.

MISES, R. von (1941) 'On the foundations of probability and statistics', *Annals of Mathematical Statistics*, **12**: 191-205.

MISRA, R. P. (1968) *Diffusion of Agricultural Innovations*, Mysore.

MOGLEWER, S. (1962) 'A game theory model for agricultural crop selection', *Econometrica*, **30**: 253-66.

MONKHOUSE, F. J. (1960) *The English Lake District*, Sheffield.

MORRILL, R. L. (1960) 'Simulation of central place patterns over time', *Proceedings, International Geographical Union Symposium on Urban Geography*, 109-20.

— (1963) 'The development of spatial distributions of towns in Sweden: an historical-predictive approach', *Annals of the Association of American Geographers*, **53**: 1-14.

— (1965) *Migration and the Spread and Growth of Urban Settlement*, Lund.

MORRILL, R. L. (1967) 'The movement of persons and the transportation problem', in Garrison, W. L. and Marble, D. F. (eds.), *Quantitative Geography, I: Economic and Cultural Topics*, Evanston, Illinois, pp. 84-94.
— and PITTS, F. R. (1967) 'Marriage, migration and the mean information field: a study in uniqueness and generality', *Annals of the Association of American Geographers*, **57**: 401-22.
MOSES, L. N. (1958) 'Location and the theory of production', *Quarterly Journal of Economics*, **72**: 259-72.

MUELLER, E., WILKEN, A., and WOOD, M. (1961) *Location Decisions and Industrial Mobility in Michigan, 1961*, Ann Arbor.
MUMFORD, L. (1961) *The City in History*, London.
MUTH, R. F. (1961) 'The spatial structure of the housing market', *Regional Science Association, Papers and Proceedings*, **7**: 207-20.
MYRDAL, G. (1957) *Economic Theory and Underdeveloped Regions*, London.
NASH, J. F. (1950) 'The bargaining problem', *Econometrica*, **18**: 155-62.
— (1953) 'Two-person cooperative games', *Econometrica*, **21**: 128-40.
NEUMANN, J. von (1951) 'The general and logical theory of automata', in Jeffress, L. A. (ed.), *Cerebral Mechanisms in Behavior*, New York, pp. 1-41.
— (1956) 'Probabilistic logics and the synthesis of reliable organisms from unreliable components', in Shannon, C. E. and McCarthy, J. (eds.), *Automata Studies*, Princeton, pp. 43-98.
— and MORGENSTERN, O. (1944) *Theory of Games and Economic Behavior*, Princeton.
NEUTZE, G. M. (1960) A Theoretical and Empirical Evaluation of the Economics of Location, with Special Reference to New Zealand, D.Phil. thesis, Oxford.
— (1962) 'Depressed agricultural areas and location economics', *Australian Journal of Agricultural Economics*, **6**: 41-9.
— (1965) *Economic Policy and the Size of Cities*, Canberra.
— (1967) 'Major determinant of location patterns', *Land Economics*, **43**: 227-32.
NEYMAN, J. (1939) 'A new class of "contagious" distributions, applicable in entomology and bacteriology', *Annals of Mathematical Statistics*, **10**: 35-57.
— and PEARSON, E. S. (1933) 'The testing of statistical hypothesis in relation to probabilities *a priori*', *Proceedings of the Cambridge Philosophical Society*, **29**: 492-510.
NICHOLLS, W. H. (1956) 'The effects of industrial development on Tennessee Valley agriculture, 1900-1950', *Journal of Farm Economics*, **38**: 1636-49.
— (1960) 'Industrial-urban development and agricultural adjustments, Tennessee Valley and Piedmont, 1939-54', *Journal of Political Economy*, **68**: 135-49.
— (1961) 'Industrialization, factor markets and agricultural development', *Journal of Political Economy*, **69**: 319-40.
NICHOLSON, I. (1965) *The X in Mexico: Growth within Tradition*, London.

NORTH, D. C. (1955) 'Location theory and regional economic growth', *Journal of Political Economy*, **63**: 243-58.

— (1961) *The Economic Growth of the United States 1790-1860*, Englewood Cliffs.

O'CONNOR, A. M. (1963) 'Regional contrasts in economic development in Uganda', *East African Geographical Review*, **1**: 33-43.

O'CONNOR, D. J. (1954) 'Uncertainty as a philosophical problem', in Carter, C. F., Meredith, G. P., and Shackle, G. L. S. (eds.), *Uncertainty and Business Decisions*, Liverpool, pp. 11-18.

OKUN, B. (1967) 'Interstate population migration and state income inequality: a simultaneous equation approach', *Economic Development and Cultural Change*, **16**: 297-313.

— and RICHARDSON, R. W. (1961) 'Regional income inequality and internal population migration', *Economic Development and Cultural Change*, **9**: 128-43.

PALANDER, T. (1935) *Beiträge zur Standortstheorie*, Stockholm.

PARK, R. E., BURGESS, E. W., and MCKENZIE, R. D. (eds.) (1967) *The City*, Chicago.

PERLOFF, H. S. and DODDS, V. W. (1963) 'How a region grows: area development in the U.S. economy', *Committee for Economic Development, Supplementary Paper*, **17**.

— DUNN, E. S., LAMPARD, E. E., and MUTH, R. F. (1961) *Regions, Resources and Economic Growth*, Baltimore.

— and WINGO, L. (1961) 'Natural resource endowment and economic growth', in Spengler, J. J. (ed.), *Natural Resources and Economic Growth*, Washington, pp. 191-212.

PFOUTS, R. W. (1957) 'An empirical testing of the economic base theory', *Journal of the American Institute of Planners*, **23**: 64-9.

— and CURTIS, E. T. (1958) 'Limitations of the economic base analysis', *Social Forces*, **36**: 303-10.

PIRATH, C. (1934) *Die Grundlagen der Verkehrswirtschaft*, Berlin.

PIRENNE, H. (1936) *Economic and Social History of Medieval Europe*, London.

PREBISCH, R. (1950) *The Economic Development of Latin America and its Principal Problems*, New York.

— (1959) 'Commercial policy in the underdeveloped countries', *American Economic Review*, **49**: 251-73.

PRED, A. (1965) 'Industrialization, initial advantage, and American metropolitan growth', *Geographical Review*, **55**: 158-85.

— (1966) *The Spatial Dynamics of U.S. Urban-Industrial Growth, 1800-1914: Interpretive and Theoretical Essays*, Cambridge, Mass.

— (1967) *Behavior and Location: Foundations for a Geographic and Dynamic Location Theory*, Lund.

PRESTON, M. G. and BARATTA, P. (1948) 'An experimental study of the auction value of an uncertain outcome', *American Journal of Psychology*, **61**: 183-93.

PROBST, A. E. (1963) *Razmeshchenie Sotsialisticheskoi promyschlennost*, Moscow;

v

translated and abridged by J. Crosfield and Sons Ltd as *The Location of Communist Industry*, Warrington, originally published 1962.

RAGHEB, I. (1966) 'Patterns of urban growth in the Middle East', *United Nations Bureau of Technical Assistance Operations and Bureau of Social Affairs and Government of U.S.A., Working Paper*, **8**.

RAPOPORT, A. (1951) 'Nets with distance bias', *Bulletin of Mathematical Biophysics*, **13**: 107-17.

— and CHAMMAH, A. M. (1965) *Prisoner's Dilemma*, Ann Arbor.

ROBOCK, S. H. (1963) *Brazil's Developing Northeast*, Washington.

ROGERS, A. (1965) 'A stochastic analysis of the spatial clustering of retail establishments', *Journal of the American Statistical Association*, **60**: 1094-103.

ROSENSTEIN-RODAN, P. N. (1943) 'Problems of industrialisation of eastern and south-eastern Europe', *Economic Journal*, **53**: 202-11.

— (1963) 'Planning within the nation', *Annals of Collective Economy*, **34**: 193-207.

— (ed.) (1964) *Pricing and Fiscal Policies*, London.

ROTHSCHILD, K. W. (1947) 'Price theory and oligopoly', *Economic Journal*, **57**: 299-320.

SAARINEN, T. F. (1966) *Perception of Drought Hazard on the Great Plains*, Chicago.

SAMUELSON, P. A. (1952) 'Spatial price equilibrium and linear programming', *American Economic Review*, **42**: 283-303.

SAVAGE, L. J. (1954) *The Foundations of Statistics*, New York.

— (1962) *The Foundations of Statistical Inference, A Discussion*, London.

SCHELLING, T. C. (1960) *The Strategy of Conflict*, Cambridge, Mass.

SCHULTZ, T. W. (1953) *The Economic Organization of Agriculture*, New York.

SCHWARTZMAN, D. (1963) 'Uncertainty and the size of the firm', *Economica*, **30**: 287-96.

SCOTT, P. (1964) 'The hierarchy of central places in Tasmania', *The Australian Geographer*, **9**: 134-47.

SETH, M. L. (1967) *Theory and Practice of Economic Planning*, New Delhi.

SHACKLE, G. L. S. (1949) *Expectation in Economics*, Cambridge.

— (1953) 'Comment', *Yorkshire Bulletin of Economic and Social Research*, **5**: 64-6.

— (1955) *Uncertainty in Economics*, Cambridge.

SHANNON, C. E. and MCCARTHY, J. (eds.) (1956) *Automata Studies*, Princeton.

SHERRATT, G. G. (1960) 'A model for general urban growth', *Management Sciences: Models and Techniques*, **2**: 147-59.

SHEVKY, E. and WILLIAMS, M. (1949) *The Social Areas of Los Angeles: Analysis and Typology*, Berkeley.

SHUBIK, M. (1959) *Strategy and Market Structure*, New York.

SIEGEL, S. (1957) 'Level of aspiration and decision making', *Psychological Review*, **64**: 253-62.

SIEGEL, S. and FOURAKER, L. E. (1960) *Bargaining and Group Decision Making*, New York.

SIMON, H. A. (1957) *Models of Man*, New York.

SINCLAIR, R. (1967) 'Von Thünen and urban sprawl', *Annals of the Association of American Geographers*, **57**: 72-87.

SINGER, H. W. (1936) 'The "Courbe des Populations"—a parallel to Pareto's law', *Economic Journal*, **46**: 254-63.

SIROYEZHIN, I. M. (1968) 'Risk and uncertainty in the management of Soviet firms', in Borch, K. and Mossin, J. (eds.), *Risk and Uncertainty*, London, pp. 359-63.

SKELLAM, J. G. (1952) 'Studies in statistical ecology: I, spatial pattern', *Biometrika*, **39**: 346-62.

SMAILES, A. E. (1961) *North England*, London.

SMITH, A. (1759) *The Theory of Moral Sentiments*, London.

SMITH, W. (1953) *An Economic Geography of Great Britain*, London.

— (1955) 'The location of industry', *Institute of British Geographers, Transactions*, **21**: 1-18.

SMITHIES, A. (1941) 'Optimum location in spatial competition', *Journal of Political Economy*, **49**: 423-39.

SMOLENSKY, E., BECKER, S., and MOLOTCH, M. (1968) 'The prisoner's dilemma and ghetto expansion', *Land Economics*, **44**: 419-30.

SNEDDON, I. N. (1957) *Elements of Partial Differential Equations*, New York.

SONNENFELD, J. (1967) 'Environmental perception and adaptation level in the Arctic', in Lowenthal, D. (ed.), *Environmental Perception and Behavior*, Chicago, pp. 42-59.

SPENGLER, J. J. (ed.) (1961) *Natural Resources and Economic Growth*, Washington.

STAFFORD, H. A. (1963) 'The functional bases of small towns', *Economic Geography*, **39**: 165-75.

STEA, D. (1969) 'The measurement of mental maps: an experimental model for studying conceptual spaces', in Cox, K. R. and Golledge, R. G. (eds.), *Behavioral Problems in Geography: A Symposium*, Evanston, Illinois, pp. 228-53.

STEINDL, J. (1945) 'Capitalist enterprise and risk', *Oxford Economic Papers*, **7**: 21-45.

STEVENS, B. H. (1959) 'An interregional linear programming model', *Journal of Regional Science*, **1**: 60-98.

— (1961) 'An application of game theory to a problem in location strategy', *Regional Science Association, Papers and Proceedings*, **7**: 143-57.

— (1968) 'Location theory and programming models: The Von Thünen case', *Regional Science Association, Papers and Proceedings*, **21**: 19-34.

— and BRACKETT, C. A. (1967) *Industrial Location; a Review and Annotated Bibliography of Theoretical, Empirical and Case Studies*, Philadelphia.

STEWART, C. T. (1958) 'The size and spacing of cities', *Geographical Review*, **48**: 222-45.

SUMMERS, G. W. (1962) *Financing and Initial Operations of New Firms*, Englewood Cliffs.

THOMAS, E. N. (1960) 'The stability of distance-population-size relationships for Iowa towns from 1900 to 1950', *Proceedings, International Geographical Union Symposium on Urban Geography*, 13-24.

THOMAS, M. (1949) 'A generalisation of Poisson's binomial limit for use in ecology', *Biometrika*, **36**: 18-25.

THOMPSON, H. R. (1956) 'Distribution of distance to nth neighbour in a population of randomly distributed individuals', *Ecology*, **37**: 391-4.

THOMPSON, W. R. (1965) *A Preface to Urban Economics*, Baltimore.

THOMSON, R. (1959) *The Psychology of Thinking*, London.

THRALL, R. M., COOMBS, C. H., and DAVIS, R. L. (eds.) (1954) *Decision Processes*, New York.

TIEBOUT, C. M. (1956) 'The urban economic base reconsidered', *Land Economics*, **32**: 95-9.

— (1957) 'Location theory, empirical evidence and economic evolution', *Regional Science Association, Papers and Proceedings*, **3**: 74-86.

TINBERGEN, J. (1964) *Central Planning*, New Haven.

— (1967) *Economic Policy: Principles and Design*, Amsterdam.

TISDELL, C. (1963) 'Uncertainty and Pareto optimality', *Economic Record*, **39**: 405-12.

TOBLER, W. (1963) 'Geographic area and map projection', *Geographical Review*, **53**: 59-78.

TURING, A. M. (1937) 'On computable numbers with an application to the Entscheidungsproblem', *London Mathematical Society, Proceedings*, **42**: 230.

ULLMAN, E. L. (1958) 'Regional development and the geography of concentration', *Regional Science Association, Papers and Proceedings*, **4**: 179-98.

UNITED NATIONS DEPARTMENT OF ECONOMIC AFFAIRS (1949) *International Capital Movements During the Inter-War Period*, New York.

UNITED NATIONS DEPARTMENT OF ECONOMIC AND SOCIAL AFFAIRS (1951-63) *Yearbook of International Trade Statistics*, New York.

— (1963) *A Study of Industrial Growth*, New York.

— (1965) *Statistical Yearbook*, New York.

UNITED STATES DEPARTMENT OF AGRICULTURE (1918) 'Influence of a city on farming', *United States Department of Agriculture, Bulletin* **678**.

— (1961) *Agricultural Statistics*, Washington.

VANCE, J. E. (1960) 'Emerging patterns of commercial structure in American cities', *Proceedings, International Geographical Union Symposium on Urban Geography*, 485-518.

VERNON, R. (1960) *Metropolis 1985*, Cambridge, Mass.

VINING, R. (1955) 'A description of certain spatial aspects of an economic system', *Economic Development and Cultural Change*, **3**: 147-95.

WALD, A. (1939) 'Contributions to the theory of statistical estimation and hypothesis testing', *Annals of Mathematical Statistics*, **10**: 299-326.

— (1950) *Statistical Decision Functions*, New York.

WEBBER, M. J. (1967) Uncertainty, Location and Regional Economic Growth, Ph.D. thesis, Canberra.

— (1969) 'Sub-optimal behaviour and the concept of maximum profits in location theory', *Australian Geographical Studies*, **7**: 1-8.

— (1971) 'Empirical verifiability of classical central place theory', *Geographical Analysis*, **3**: 15-28.

WEIMER, A. M. and HOYT, H. (1939) *Principles of Urban Real Estate*, New York.

WENSLEY, A. J. and FLORENCE, P. S. (1940) 'Recent industrial concentration, especially in the Midlands', *Review of Economic Studies*, **7**: 139-58.

WHITE, G. F. (ed.) (1961) *Papers on Flood Problems*, Chicago.

WILLIAMS, J. D. (1954) *The Compleat Strategyst*, New York.

WILLIAMSON, J. G. (1965) 'Regional inequality and the process of national development: a description of the patterns', *Economic Development and Cultural Change*, **13**: supplement.

WINGO, L. (1961) *Transportation and Urban Land*, Washington.

WOLPERT, J. (1964) 'The decision process in spatial context', *Annals of the Association of American Geographers*, **54**: 537-58.

YEATES, M. H. (1965) 'Some factors affecting the spatial distribution of Chicago land values 1910-1960', *Economic Geography*, **41**: 57-70.

YOUNG, A. (1928) 'Increasing returns and economic progress', *Economic Journal*, **38**: 527-42.

YOUNG, J. N. and COLEMAN, A. L. (1959) 'Neighborhood norms and the adoption of farm practices', *Rural Sociology*, **24**: 372-80.

ZIMMERMANN, E. W. (1933) *World Resources and Industries*, New York.

ZIPF, G. K. (1949) *Human Behavior and the Principle of Least Effort*, Cambridge, Mass.

Index

Abbey, H., *234*
Abnormal profits, *23;* and competition, *25, 27;* and equilibrium, *28*
Accessibility, and rent, *60;* and town growth, *74, 80; see also* Distance; Transport costs
Ackley, G., *163*
Admissible acts, *100, 122-3*
Adoption, *see* Innovation
Agglomeration, *2, 11, 14-15, 20, 22, 25-6, 115;* and agriculture, *56, 67-8, 271;* and innovation, *250-3, 275;* and probability models, *41, 42-3;* and regional growth, *81-2, 83, 87, 133, 272;* and site conditions, *162;* and town formation, *35-6, 47, 121, 143, 165, 268-9;* and town growth, *23, 39;* distorting central places, *28;* factors of, *35, 38;* in uncertainty, *91, 131-4, 160-3, 165, 274-5;* measurement of, *39-40;* problem of, *20-1, 27, 121; see also* Concentration; External economies
Aggregation: in theory, *7, 40, 49;* methodological problems of, *7-8, 278-9, 282*
Agricultural land use, *8, 49-60;* and growth theory, *83-4;* and labour orientation, *20;* contrast of certainty and uncertainty, *270-2;* in uncertainty, *117, 195-204, 214-18;* imperfections in, *107-8;* games, *134-5; see also* Urban land use
Agricultural product cycles, *135-6*
Ajo, R., *64*
Alchian, A. A., *8*
Allen, G. R., *135, 283*
Alonso, W., *60-4, 65, 68, 215, 271-2, 283*
Ambition, *see* Psychological factors
Analogue methods: for innovation diffusion, *245-6, 248;* for inter-regional equilibrium, *58;* for oligopoly, *119;* for location polygon, *13; see also* Simulation
Anderson, T. R., *66*
Andrews, R. B., *73, 78*
Anscombe, F. J., *43*
Anticipations: and planning, *149;* and urban land values, *56*

301